Rhetoric, Comedy, and the Violence of Language in Aristophanes' *Clouds*

Rhetoric, Comedy, and the Violence of Language in Aristophanes' *Clouds*

DAPHNE ELIZABETH O'REGAN

New York   Oxford
OXFORD UNIVERSITY PRESS
1992

Oxford University Press

Oxford   New York   Toronto
Delhi   Bombay   Calcutta   Madras   Karachi
Kuala Lumpur   Singapore   Hong Kong   Tokyo
Nairobi   Dar es Salaam   Cape Town
Melbourne   Auckland   Madrid

and associated companies in
Berlin   Ibadan

Copyright © 1992 by Daphne Elizabeth O'Regan

Published by Oxford University Press, Inc.,
200 Madison Avenue, New York, New York 10016

Oxford is a registered trademark of Oxford University Press

Library of Congress Cataloging-in-Publication Data
O'Regan, Daphne Elizabeth.
Rhetoric, comedy, and the violence of language in
Aristophanes' Cloud / by Daphne Elizabeth O'Regan.
p.   cm.   Includes bibliographical references (p.   ) and index.
ISBN 0-19-507017-8
1. Aristophanes.   Clouds.   2. Aristophanes—Technique.
3. Violence in literature.   4. Rhetoric, Ancient.   5. Comedy. I. Title.
PA3875.N8074   1992   882′.01—dc20   91-29030

1 3 5 7 9 8 6 4 2

Printed in the United States of America
on acid-free paper

ACKNOWLEDGMENTS

In reflecting on my debts in the writing of this book, I think first of those who have taught me: Harry Berger, Kevin Clinton, Mary-Kay Gamel, Judith Ginsburg, Erich Gruen, W. Ralph Johnson, John Lynch, Gary Miles. I thank them for their instruction and their example. For careful and penetrating criticism of the manuscript I thank Bruce Heiden, Thomas Hubbard, and the anonymous readers for Oxford University Press; their comments were extremely helpful. For patient reassurance I thank my editors at Oxford. But my most profound gratitude—for help too extensive to be detailed here—is owed to Phillip Mitsis and Pietro Pucci. Without their encouragement, their suggestions, and their doubts, this book and I would be vastly impoverished. To them I owe much of the pleasure in my long association with the *Clouds*. And, finally, I wish to acknowledge my family and my friends for the joy they have given me, for their support, their time, and for their love.

CONTENTS

Rhetoric, Comedy, and the
Violence of Language in
Aristophanes' *Clouds*

Introduction

It is well known that fifth-century Attic comedy was a profoundly public art.[1] Like other expenses mandated by the city in its own interests, it was paid for through taxation (as were, for example, warships),[2] while it was produced and acted by citizens as part of their civic responsibilities or privileges.[3] The resulting plays were staged in comic competitions that were but one part of much larger festivals; for our *Clouds,* this was the City (or Great) Dionysia, a celebration whose events and ceremonies were dedicated to expressing (and reinforcing) Athenian ideology, while at the same time displaying the democratic city's power and prestige.[4] The participants in this festival and the audience for comedy were the Athenian citizens. Gathered in the theater in "civic assembly,"[5] they were the same group, seated in similar order, as that which elsewhere voted the political and legal decisions of the city.[6] Thus political (and judicial) rhetoric and theatrical discourse would have influenced each other reciprocally, the audience for each conditioned by its experience of the other. Likewise, the tasks of a comedian were, in one sense, those of any other speaker: he had to further his own (and the public) good by winning over his listeners, who, in judging his *logos,* or speech,[7] to be best, would render him victorious over his rivals.[8]

Thus the audience, context, and requirements of the comic contest paralleled other public, political institutions in which speech played a decisive role in the democracy, while the spectators reproduced their civic duties in performing their theatrical ones.[9] Comedy itself, moreover, could legitimately be expected to address subjects as topical, difficult, and profound as any raised in assembly, court, or even tragedy (yet another form of speech before the same audience),[10] but in the comic mode. For its spectators brought to each individual comedy all that they had learned not only outside the theater but inside it as well. They came to the comic competition prepared to enjoy further productions in a recognized and conventional genre. The comic play was set apart by distinctive costumes, character types, staging, meters, and time of performance. Generic norms shaped its form and established its creative tools: the use of farce and wit, stereotypical characters and situations, slapstick, wild dancing, obscenity, insult, puns, and sophisticated allusions to mock a wide variety of political, social, and theatrical butts.

Given the premium Athenian democracy placed on language ideologically, practically, and festively, it should come as no surprise that the *Clouds* itself is a play obsessed with *logos:* its teachers, its speakers, and its listeners. But the *Clouds'* interest is more topical than this summary indicates, for its subject is sophistic rhetoric, and in particular such rhetoric's claim to a power as irresistible as physical force. This overriding concern structures the whole and determines the parts of the play. It begins with an ordinary man's search for new, more effective speech; portrays his education (or lack thereof) at the hands of an abstracted, sophistic Socrates; recounts (in the parabasis) the failures of Aristophanes' own sophisticated comedy, the verbal first *Clouds;* stages (in the agon) the inevitable victory of sophistic rhetorical techniques; farcically confronts this victorious *logos* with real violence (in the repudiation scenes and a second agon); and ends with the destruction of the socratic school, Socrates, his students, and their rhetoric. While speech and its power are rarely absent from the aristophanic comedies we possess, this focus seems particular to the *Clouds*. Other plays may present the word as a tool of the power-hungry or weigh the merits of various types of speech, dramatic and otherwise; the *Clouds'* comic analysis goes further. Every element of the play works together[11] to pair contemporary rhetorical theory with the generically comic "natural" man. The result is highly damaging to the power of the word. For as comic man proves immune to speech, responsive only to the promptings of the body, so the "invincible" force of rhetoric is revealed as derived not from verbal technique but from an appeal to the appetites freed from all civic or moral constraints. The consequences are fatal. Deprived of the allies which had guaranteed its priority, the distinctively human achievement of *logos* is left helplessly exposed to *bia,* the corporal force man shares with animals.[12] Not surprisingly, it is this physical violence which turns out to be the preferred "persuasive" strategy of ordinary men.

However, despite its centrality to both plot and thematic development, the *Clouds'* treatment of *logos* has not claimed much attention. Several factors have contributed to this. The first is the scholarly focus on Socrates. The controversy about whether or not the *Clouds* portrays the "historically accurate" Socrates has generated a vast literature; this study will not add to it.[13] My principal concern is not tracing the connections, or lack thereof, among the *Clouds*, Plato, and Xenophon but rather observing the comic logic of our play. For the fascination of Socrates has frequently obscured the importance of what he has to offer—his cosmological speculation and his violently powerful speech.[14] Yet those studies which do not revolve around Socrates are often motivated by beliefs about the nature of comedy and its relationship to its audience. These interpretative lines, which rightly direct attention to the *Clouds'* participation in the comic genre and use of comic devices, all too often rescue the play from the role of philosophical source by limiting its reach. Comedy emerges as playing to its audience in a relatively straightforward way. As fantasy it represents the satisfying world the audience would like but can never achieve. As political tool it affirms a particular orientation—democratic, moderate, or conservative/aristocratic. As humor it stimulates the series of disconnected belly laughs that signals success.[15] Instead of complexity, ambiguity, and challenge, comedy is marked by satisfaction of private desires and conventional requirements: for laughter that vents personal and class aggression, for play that obscures the complex realities that bedevil political and social life, or for the fun of vicarious sex and violence.

All these approaches capture central elements of the *Clouds*. However, to adopt one at the expense of the others slights the *Clouds'* comic subtlety and the challenging problems it raises.[16] Insofar as the question of *logos* takes us to the heart of a whole complex of issues being elaborated by the leading intellects of the day, discussed by the man on the street, and debated by the citizens in the assembly, the *Clouds* is clearly both topical and philosophical. To ignore the intellectual, rhetorical, and political background to Aristophanes' jokes is to misunderstand them and to overlook his participation in the intellectual ferment of the times. But, at the same time, jokes are the point; the *Clouds* is a series of jokes long and short, vulgar and sophisticated. The political, social, and philosophical issues associated with *logos* are confronted with the resources of comedy, and this fact not only determines the form and content of the *Clouds*—from individual lines, to scenes, to the play as a whole—but shapes its meaning. The *Clouds* is revealed as a work of impressive thematic unity[17] which, integrating imagery, puns, obscenities, and jokes of all kinds, structures its examination of *logos* as a series of hilarious clashes between comedy and philosophy, between the (comically defined) "comic" and "philosophic" man, and, most reductively, between mind and phallus, thought and sausage.

The results are a foregone conclusion, but this does not mean that the contest is resolved in comedy's favor. In confronting the difficulties of speech among men and in the city, Aristophanes does not exempt comic *logos*. Our second *Clouds* is the product of a failure of *logos:* it is the extensively revised version of a play which placed last in the comic contest of the City Dionysia in 424/23 B.C.[18] The reason for this disaster is simple, at least according to the *Clouds* (and the *Wasps*): Athenian stupidity. Imagining his audience to be smart and sophisticated, Aristophanes had discarded many of the obscene and violent aspects of conventional comedy in favor of purely verbal wit. The failure of this earlier attempt, the inadequacy of *logos* alone to win over the audience and carry the poet to victory, is written deep into our own play's humor, structure, and even its "message." For the human nature which jeopardizes speech onstage, motivates Strepsiades' actions, and ensures Socrates' downfall does not differ substantially from that in the stands. There a crude and foolish audience has already demonstrated its indifference to speech, disdaining Aristophanes' novel *logos* to bestow victory on his rivals' vulgar and violent farce.

Thus the *Clouds'* thematic content intersects with its historical situation[19] to transform its relationship with the norms of fifth-century dramatic production and comic genre. The result is a comedy unique among those we have and one that comments upon its own uniqueness, struggling to define how it can and should be enjoyed. For the accumulated public, political, social, and theatrical experience brought by Aristophanes' fellow citizens to all comedy, including this new *Clouds*, is what, along with their own natures, has already led them to a gross error in judgment. The *Clouds'* "original" audience (that of the first version) and its reactions exist only to be rejected: an example of democratic decision making gone awry, a paradigm of how not to watch the current installment of the play. The incorporation of these mistakes into the comic "argument" of our new play obliges its "new" audience to watch itself along with the drama, and privileges—indeed, compels—novel responses. Our vision is doubled as our inevitable pleasure in the conventionally comic is problematized. The clash of mind and body which might have seemed limited to the stage, and to a generic confrontation between philosophy and comedy, is instead reproduced inside the comic, and even in the spectators themselves, as this previously resistant audience is (re)educated through its experience of the second *Clouds*. The perhaps daunting interpretative task this seems to impose may be simplified by the circumstances of the second *Clouds*. We do not know if our *Clouds* was ever performed.[20] Thus for our play, the compelling immediacy and rush of dramatic presentation, the necessity of unhesitating appeal to the vast mass of the spectators—whatever their backgrounds, prejudices, and experiences—may have been augmented from the beginning by a sense of leisure often lacking in the pressure of civic discourse and democratic decision.[21] Our own reactions, as well as every movement of plot and language, can not only be experienced but also examined for how they came to be and what they mean.[22]

Thus it is no surprise that our *Clouds* has been called the "first comedy of ideas," "self-aware," "pessimistic."[23] Certainly it suggests ideas which in another mode would be profoundly serious, even frightening. Our laughter cannot hide and even expresses the forces which work upon and constantly erode *logos*, comedy, philosophy, and the civic world. Yet, as the *Clouds* itself proudly shows us, our joy in this comedy and our engagement with it are also grounds for hope. For such attentive pleasure rescues what the *Clouds'* own drama has put in jeopardy—the love of *logos*, of comedy, and of all that goes with it. Thus our joy accomplishes for Aristophanes now the traditional goal that eluded him with his first play. In acknowledging the virtues of our second *Clouds*, we vindicate the claims of its predecessor, and of aristophanic verbal comedy in general. Finally Aristophanes emerges victorious, twice the best of comedians.

The complex dynamic just outlined is traced in the second and subsequent chapters scene by scene and even line by line. Chapter 1 provides the necessary background. The linear form has been chosen for several reasons. I hope it will facilitate analysis on multiple levels, convey the extent to which the *Clouds'* themes are interdependent and mutually evolving, preserve the progress and "surprise" vital to the play's dramatic and rhetorical success, and, finally, link the reader to the spectators' experiences as they encountered and learned to appreciate our second *Clouds*. However, despite the linear form, what follows is not a commentary. I intend neither to reconstruct the general social/political/theatrical background of the *Clouds* nor to rectify aristophanic "error." While this may appear to implicate me in simply (re)tracing Aristophanes' prejudices and presuppositions, I hope it will also allow me to recover some unnoticed elements of the *Clouds'* project and delineate some aspects of its logic and critical intent.

Such an exclusive focus may seem rather narrow; in fact, it reproduces the limits our comedy imposes on its own explicit subjects. The *Clouds* is a play that contrasts with its predecessors. In our drama, unlike the *Acharnians*, the Peloponnesian War is prominent neither narratively nor thematically. Its early mention in the prologue serves merely to relegate the war to the background, where it remains a minor irritant, far less urgent than rhetorical salvation from familial and economic disaster. Likewise, unlike the *Knights*, the preeminent role of speech in the achievement of political (and legal) power is of little concern, at least to the characters. Strepsiades explicitly disavows political ambition; Pheidippides' interests and intentions, once he subdues his father (and mother), are left unclear. However, democracy, its citizens, its values, its institutions, and its political practices are inevitable derivatives of the discussion of *logos,* human nature, education, and the *Clouds'* other themes. Multiplying references and the traditionally close alignment of a positive view of *logos* with Athenian democratic ideology and practice enlarge the play's resonance, particularly as its thematic direction becomes increasingly pessimistic. The *Clouds'* profound political/social implications are clear; the comedy itself comments obliquely on them, even as it continues to press its own, more fundamental, concerns. These implications have been elaborated by studies whose primary orientation is political and social and which link the *Clouds* to precise historical events, specific agendas, and such topical and troublesome issues as the role of the aristocratic youth in the city and the abuse of philosophical training to achieve, maintain, or justify oligarchic rule.[24] Such studies are important and their insights will be discussed frequently. However, by limiting themselves to these aspects of the play, they fail to capture the full dimensions of the *Clouds'* project. For if the *Clouds* is a "political" work, it locates its contribution to the democratic city in its profound and comic examination of *logos* and the human relationship to the word.[25]

Finally, a word of explanation about the texts and translations in the following chapters. For the text of the *Clouds* I have used Dover's edition; places where I have differed from that edition are noted. For the scholia I have used Koster; for the comic fragments, Kassel and Austin; for Gorgias' *Encomium of Helen* and the sophists in general, Diels and Kranz; for Plutarch, the Teubner edition; and for Xenophon's *Memorabilia,* the text of Jaerisch. Otherwise I have generally followed the *Oxford Classical Texts.* To make the argument as accessible as possible, I have translated all Greek used in the body of the text. In most cases the English is given with the Greek; for some shorter passages the Greek is relegated to the notes. In general, I have tried to avoid Greek words in the argument, but I have used a few really central terms (such as *logos* or *eros*), throughout. In cases where discussion centers on particular Greek terms, I have often retained the transliterated Greek; such transliterated terms always follow their English equivalents in the translations before appearing in the body of the text. Finally, in all cases the English translations are to be considered guides to the Greek. I have aimed more at consistency—using the same word(s) for the same things—and comprehensive reproduction of meaning(s) and connotations than at beauty. Thus I have attempted, where possible, to remain close to the word order of the Greek; when several meanings of a single word are in play, I have given what seem to me to be the significant possibilities, separated by slashes. Where this has conflicted with translation into elegant or even standard English, clarity in rendering what is present in the Greek has always taken precedence.

1

The Changing Role of *Logos:* Background

While the *Clouds'* focus on *logos,* human communication, and the power of rhetoric might seem odd to a modern audience, such a choice would hardly have surprised contemporary Athenians—late fifth-century Athens was experiencing a period of political and speculative turmoil centering in many respects on speech.[1] This chapter outlines some of the major features of this controversy as they can be reconstructed from the limited sources which have survived. Its purpose is to help situate *logos* in the practical and conceptual framework of the time, and thus aid in the recovery of the full resonance of Aristophanes' comedy. The orientation is one which will facilitate analysis in subsequent chapters, where frequent reference will be made to the issues and the images to be discussed here.

Athenian political and social institutions are generally agreed to have fostered what Goldhill calls an "extraordinary prevalence of the spoken word."[2] Kennedy puts aptly a truth that must have been vivid to many Athenians: "In a democratic state, words could change history. They performed the functions of gold, of divine intervention, of massed armies of men. Surely the word was a remarkable thing."[3] Words were also increasingly the medium of political power. The last quarter of the fifth century witnessed the emergence of a new style of politics, which, based on a democratic right to speak afforded all citizens equally *(isegoria),* permitted the rise of a new kind of leader, one who appealed directly to the *demos,* speaking before, and persuading, the sovereign people.[4]

The premium this placed on speech and skill at speaking was mirrored in changing political terminology. *Rhetor,* or speaker, the increasingly frequent term for politician, was "expressive and exact. The politicians of this period were naturally thought of as *rhetores* for they led by their eloquence."[5] The ascendency of Pericles, widely believed to be owed, among other things, to a tongue sharpened by close association with sophists,[6] had forced upon public attention the importance of the ability to speak and the power that such ability bestowed. The death of Pericles and the subsequent rise of Cleon focused the issue even more clearly. Pericles had been preeminent not only in rhetoric, but in family, intelligence, and character;[7] those who succeeded him did not share his gifts. To his opponents, Cleon seemed equally lacking in personal, social, and political qualifications: integrity, noble birth, military skill, and political insight.[8] These deficiencies made it clear that Cleon—"the master of a new technology of political power,"[9]—in fact, possessed an influence derived in large part from his tongue.[10] He, and the primarily young men who followed his example, were following a new route to preeminence. Skipping the arduous generalship, the performance of military exploits, and a long political apprenticeship, these men avoided the risks of holding office, while enjoying the benefits of power,[11] masking their self-interest with a rhetoric of devotion to the interests of city or *demos* which catapulted them to leadership in the assembly and the courts.[12] Whatever the real reasons for their success—administrative ability, response to public need, representation of the disenfranchised[13]—and however it should be interpreted, to many at the time the grounds for their power seemed obvious and dangerous: Athens was a city drunk on language; *logos* and appreciation of *logos* had replaced the traditional martial deeds *(erga)* which had supported and defended the city in its glorious past.[14] But such distaste could not hide the fact of power, whatever its origin. While some in the traditional political class retreated to private life, convinced that "politics had become a calling in which only the most vulgar can succeed," and scorning the new rhetoric and politics as simply a new necessity of pandering to the mob,[15] the aspiring learned a different lesson. Plutarch records the revelation of the youthful Alcibiades: birth, wealth, courage, influential friends and relations were trivial; for influence with the many, nothing counted more than *logos*.[16] Others like Hyperbolus, Cleophon, Phaiax, and Antiphon were learning the same thing.

There was no lack of models or teachers. Periclean Athens had attracted the most notable intellectuals of the day—Protagoras, Zeno, Anaxagoras, and others[17]—while Gorgias' rhetorical display in 427 stunned a city already dedicated to the word. Their additions, theoretical and stylistic, to the new art of speaking fascinated and influenced important contemporary speakers and poets, not only the older Thucydides and Pericles, but also the younger Critias, Alcibiades, and Agathon, men in the intellectual (and political) vanguard.[18] Athens had in residence, or as visitors, a regular crowd of sophists and exponents of rhetoric, Prodicus, Hippias, Euthydemus and his brother Dionysodorus, Thrasymachus, and Antiphon are among those still known. If these were not enough or were not available, a large number of books could be consulted. In the *Phaedrus,* Plato lists a number of technical works to which a speaker could turn;[19] the fragmentary remains of sophistic writings testify to many more. While the identity of those who did, or did not, frequent the sophists may remain in doubt,[20] there is little disagreement about the pervasiveness of rhetoric, discussion, and argument or their importance in the social, cultural, political, and legal life of the city. The aspiring speaker had only to go to the assembly or the courts, to semiprivate demonstrations or disputations in the streets and the gymnasia, to hear the latest in the style and art of persuasion.[21]

Increasing prominence of speech and rhetorical technique and theory was matched by increasing controversy about the nature of *logos* and the significance of its use. The year after the death of Pericles (428) saw the beginnings of Cleon's ascendency and the Mitylenean debate. Thucydides' presentation makes this a forum for a new negative analysis of the power of *logos* and its speakers that invites his readers to meditate upon how far Athens had already fallen from the ideal articulated in Pericles' funeral oration. There, Pericles made faith in and commitment to speech and discussion one of the distinguishing features of his idealized Athens.[22] Thucydides' Cleon represents the new perversion of this ideal. Described as the most violent of the citizens, and by far the most persuasive to the *demos*,[23] Cleon is dedicated to *logos* only insofar as it helps him maintain his position. His continuous rhetorical thundering reflects no respect for others, no belief in discussion, and no commitment to the tongue rather than the hand, in short, no understanding of the special role of *logos* in human relationships or in the maintenance of the *polis*. His views reflect this, for to support his previously enacted decree, Cleon attacks the prized Athenian debate as a sham, singling out in particular the new sophistic rhetoric. Its speakers, delighted with their own cleverness, use and abuse the power of words for not public but private ends. Its listeners have similar motives: pleasure in judging rhetorical skill and appearing fashionably familiar with the latest techniques. As all try to maximize personal benefit, the city is lost. The best city is not one where everyone speaks, but where the laws rule in silence. *Logos* itself is undermining the democratic *polis*.[24]

Thucydides' dramatic presentation—beginning with a coordination of speech and violence and ending with a threat to democratic ideals which underlines the paradox of Cleon's attack on the very speech which is his tool—is shaped by his hostility to Cleon and by the necessities of his narrative.[25] Yet it also mirrors a contemporary debate, and in contemporary terms. Since the coordination of language and violence will also be central to the *Clouds,* we will begin here, for from this entry point we can trace some of the more commonly perceived implications of the theory and practice of the powerful new (sophistic) speech.

The imagery of words as projectiles and debate as wrestling was not something new with the sophists—we can find instances from Homer on[26]—but they seem to have appropriated this metaphor, revised it, and endowed the imagery of martial language with programmatic significance. The trend may have begun with Protagoras' famous *Overthrowing Arguments,* or *Kataballontes (logoi),* a book whose title alone, a wrestling metaphor,[27] is enough to suggest the novelty of the conception. The focus here is not on the attitudes of the speakers or climate of debate but on the competition and interaction of the arguments and speeches themselves. Words alone determine victory or defeat. These implications were driven home by another of Protagoras' works, *About Wrestling,* or *Peri Pales,* which showed how an accomplished, and thus definitionally sophistic, speaker could refute *(anteipein)* practioners of the art of wrestling or the other arts.[28] Punning title and subject again reflect a sophistic agenda, for the titular art of wrestling advertised perfectly the revolutionary significance of the new competitive art supreme, the art of speaking.

Such imagery, traced here in outline, rapidly became so associated with sophists as to become a popular shorthand—positive or negative—for their rhetoric and its effects.[29] An anecdote in Plutarch about Pericles illustrates this with a witty and revealing joke about protagorean "overthrowing" *(kataballein).* Asked by the Spartan king who was the better wrestler, Pericles or himself, Thucydides (who was Pericles' political rival) responded:

ὅταν, εἶπεν, ἐγὼ καταβάλω παλαίων, ἐκεῖνος ἀντιλέγων ὡς οὐ πέπτωκε,
νικᾷ καὶ μεταπείθει τοὺς ὁρῶντας.

(Plu. Per. 8)

Whenever, he said, I overthrow *(kataballein)* him wrestling, he refuting *(antilegein)* that he has fallen, wins and persuades the onlookers.

In the public struggle for civic control,[30] Pericles' weapon is sophistic *logos*,
marked as such through the use of the programmatic, sophistic art of refutation
(antilegein). With this he reverses the outcome of the physical wrestling match,
undoing his overthrow at the hands of Thucydides with his tongue by persuading
the spectators of what is not true. The charge of verbal deception is standard, yet,
ethics aside, the point is clear. The physical art of wrestling, and incidentally the
aristocratic ideal of physical and martial excellence that went with it, are outmoded and bested. The implications of this transformation are consistent with
those of a similar image given the platonic Gorgias. Explaining how the responsibilities of the teacher of rhetoric should be construed, Gorgias first claims that
before a multitude the power of a rhetor is so great as to easily surpass that of
any expert; he continues about the persuasive art of rhetoric:[31]

ἡ μὲν οὖν δύναμις τοσαύτη ἐστὶν καὶ τοιαύτη τῆς τέχνης· δεῖ μέντοι, ὦ
Σώκρατες, τῇ ῥητορικῇ χρῆσθαι ὥσπερ τῇ ἄλλῃ πάσῃ ἀγωνίᾳ. καὶ γὰρ
τῇ ἄλλῃ ἀγωνίᾳ οὐ τούτου ἕνεκα δεῖ πρὸς ἅπαντας χρῆσθαι ἀνθρώπους,
ὅτι ἔμαθεν πυκτεύειν τε καὶ παγκρατιάζειν καὶ ἐν ὅπλοις μάχεσθαι, ὥστε
κρείττων εἶναι καὶ φίλων καὶ ἐχθρῶν, οὐ τούτου ἕνεκα τοὺς φίλους δεῖ
τύπτειν οὐδὲ κεντεῖν τε καὶ ἀποκτεινύναι. οὐδέ γε μὰ Δία ἐάν τις εἰς
παλαίστραν φοιτήσας εὖ ἔχων τὸ σῶμα καὶ πυκτικὸς γενόμενος, ἔπειτα
τὸν πατέρα τύπτῃ καὶ τὴν μητέρα ἢ ἄλλον τινὰ τῶν οἰκείων ἢ τῶν φίλων,
οὐ τούτου ἕνεκα δεῖ τοὺς παιδοτρίβας καὶ τοὺς ἐν τοῖς ὅπλοις διδάσκοντας
μάχεσθαι μισεῖν τε καὶ ἐκβάλλειν ἐκ τῶν πόλεων.

(Pl. Grg. 456c6ff.)

The power then is such and so great of this art [of rhetoric]; yet it is necessary,
O Socrates, to use the rhetorical art just as every other competitive (gymnastic)
exercise. For it is not necessary to use the rest of the competitive exercises on
everyone just because we have learned to box or to wrestle or to fight in armor,
so as to be stronger *(kreitton)* than friends and enemies, nor, for this reason, is
it necessary to strike friends, nor to goad them *(kentein)*, and to kill them.
Nor indeed, by Zeus, if anyone frequenting the wrestling school *(palaistra)*,
being fit in body and skilled in boxing, then should strike his father and mother
or any other of his kinsmen or friends, not for this reason is it necessary to hate
the trainers and those who teach fighting in arms and to banish them from the
cities.

Leaving aside the antisocial possibilities of a rhetorical skill that can be analogized
to the beating of parents (these issues will be taken up by the *Clouds*), the threat
to the old values is clear. The ability to help friends and harm enemies, the definitive aristocratic virtue, is now a function of the knowledge of rhetoric, for skill
at speaking now makes one stronger *(kreitton)* in the only contest that counts, the

verbal agon.[32] Likewise this contest has usurped values formerly displayed in battle or other heroic exploits.[33] Skill and daring are now the prerogative of the orator, the sophistic athlete and hero.

> καὶ τὸ ἀγώνισμα ἡμῶν κατὰ τὸν Λεοντῖνον Γοργίαν διττῶν [δὲ] ἀρετῶν
> δεῖται, τόλμης καὶ σοφίας· τόλμης μὲν τὸ κίνδυνον ὑπομεῖναι, σοφίας δὲ
> τὸ πλίγμα(?) γνῶναι. ὁ γάρ τοι λόγος καθάπερ τὸ κήρυγμα τὸ Ὀλυμπί-
> ασι καλεῖ μὲν τὸν βουλόμενον, στεφανοῖ δὲ τὸν δυνάμενον.
>
> (DK 82 B 8)

And our contest, according to Gorgias of Leontini, has need of a double excellence *(aretai),* of daring and of wisdom *(sophia).* Of daring to bear the risk, but of wisdom to know the moves. For the *logos,* let me tell you, just as the proclamation at the Olympics, calls the one who is willing, but crowns the one who is able.

Traditional excellences or virtues *(aretai)* serve a new kind of contest. Gorgias' delayed introduction of *"logos,"* following on citation of wrestling[34] and entering in the context of the athletic games, jolts us with the bold programmatic novelty of its claims. The complementary arenas of the old Iliadic ideal—to the best in deeds of war (defined as the ability to act) and in council (defined as the ability to speak)—collapse.[35] The new heroic deeds are to be worked with the tongue.[36] Thus, in *Philoctetes,* a play in which the power and meaning of language are central, we find Odysseus, the proto-sophist,[37] advising Neoptolemos, son of Achilles:

> ἐσθλοῦ πατρὸς παῖ, καὐτὸς ὢν νέος ποτὲ
> γλῶσσαν μὲν ἀργόν, χεῖρα δ᾽ εἶχον ἐργάτιν·
> νῦν δ᾽ εἰς ἔλεγχον ἐξιὼν ὁρῶ βροτοῖς
> τὴν γλῶσσαν, οὐχὶ τἄργα, πάνθ᾽ ἡγουμένην.
> (S. *Ph.* 96–99)

O son of a noble father, I myself, being young once,
had an idle tongue, but a hand which did deeds;
but now going forth to the test, I see for men
the tongue, not the deeds, leading everything.

Put to the sophistic test, in the real, postheroic world, the tongue is to replace the hand; the word, the sword; powerful speaking, physical might.[38] However, such preference does not imply allegiance to the traditional civilized ideal that eschews force as improper between members of the same community, and, correspondingly, values persuasion as correct and appropriate. Rather, the reverse is true. The grounds for Odysseus' choice of verbal as opposed to physical force is strictly logistical—it is more likely to work.[39]

This coordination of *logos* with *bia,* of speech with physical violence, finds its theoretical exposition in the *Encomium of Helen,* where Gorgias' praise of *logos* (and exoneration of Helen) promotes a fundamental change in our perception of speech—and in the process makes several assertions about men, speech, and reality that are key to the *Clouds*. The process begins with the first words of the argument:

> ἢ γὰρ τύχης βουλήμασι καὶ θεῶν βουλεύμασι καὶ ἀνάγκης ψηφίσμασιν
> ἔπραξεν ἃ ἔπραξεν, ἢ βίαι ἁρπασθεῖσα, ἢ λόγοις πεισθεῖσα, ⟨ἢ ἔρωτι
> ἁλοῦσα⟩.
>
> (*Encomium* 6 [DK 82 B 11.6])

For either by the purposes of chance and the resolutions of the gods and the decrees of necessity *(anagke)* she did what she did, or snatched by force *(bia)*, or persuaded by words *(logos)*, ⟨or seized by love *(eros)*⟩.

Although it may appear that being snatched away by force is qualitatively different from being persuaded by words, the *Encomium* asserts the opposite: superhuman agency (chance, gods, necessity) and kidnapping parallel persuasion effectively and morally. Indeed, the former act as foils; listed separately, they work together to reveal the true dimensions of persuasive *logos*.[40] Like the divine, the power of the word is irresistible;[41] like force, it is compulsive. The conventional opposition between violence and speech breaks down as Gorgias concludes: if Helen acted as she did because she was persuaded, it was as if she were stolen by force *(bia)*, for persuasion *(peitho)*, although it does not have the form of necessity *(anagke)*, has the same power *(dunamis)*.[42] This claim, which makes persuasion synonymous with language[43]—suppressing the erotic persuasion *(peitho)*[44] traditionally agent of Helen's seduction[45]—clears Helen absolutely of blame. Volition is no longer an issue,[46] for *logos'* ability to make incredible and unclear things appear to the eyes of opinion *(doxa)*[47] is so great as to render those who hear it helpless. The natural condition of the human soul—its necessary reliance upon unstable opinion alone[48]—renders us unconditionally at the mercy of every skillful speaker, our souls as powerless to resist his words as our bodies are to resist drugs.[49] What we know of poetry (that it can arouse the listener's emotions independent of personal circumstance) and of spells (that they can bewitch the soul) is true of *logos* in general: it operates through deception, or *apate*,[50] independent of truth or motivation and unchecked by any constraining reference to the real or perceptible.[51] In this environment, where the wrestlings of *logos* buffet and dominate the human soul,[52] a *logos* written with skill will please and persuade a crowd sooner than one which is true.[53] Given this power, *logos* can easily be seen to merit Gorgias' description of it as a great master,[54] a power Euripides' Hecuba negatively describes when she calls persuasion *(peitho)* a tyrant among men, alone worth the trouble to learn.[55]

The persuasion of such *logos* achieves the goals of violence, personal autonomy and power over others, but with greater success. As Protarchus remarks in the *Philebus*,[56]

> Ἤκουον μὲν ἔγωγε, ὦ Σώκρατες, ἑκάστοτε Γοργίου πολλάκις ὡς ἡ τοῦ
> πείθειν πολὺ διαφέροι πασῶν τεχνῶν—πάντα γὰρ ὑφ' αὑτῇ δοῦλα δι'
> ἑκόντων ἀλλ' οὐ διὰ βίας ποιοῖτο, καὶ μακρῷ ἀρίστη πασῶν εἴη τῶν τεχνῶν
>
> (Pl. *Phlb.* 58a6)

I, indeed, O Socrates, used to hear Gorgias each time often [say] that [the art] of persuasion differs much from the other arts—for it makes all things slaves *(doula)* to itself willingly, but not through force *(bia)*, and is by far the best of all the arts

The surprising mention of slaves *(doula)* here undermines the complacency of those who normally approve the products of speech and once again significantly blurs the contrast between it and physical violence. To stress the unfettered power of *logos* and speaker, it degrades the listeners as helplessly passive and transforms a traditionally central and positive characteristic of persuasion—its mutuality—into further proof of the word's unique power. Willing slaves are better slaves. Xenophon glosses this pragmatically in the *Memorabilia*. Defending Socrates from the charge of fostering violence in the young, he asserts that intelligent and capable speakers are the least violent, for they know

ὅτι τῇ μὲν βίᾳ πρόσεισιν ἔχθραι καὶ κίνδυνοι, διὰ δὲ τοῦ πείθειν ἀκινδύνως τε καὶ μετὰ φιλίας ταὐτὰ γίγνεται. οἱ μὲρ γὰρ βιασθέντες ὡς ἀφαιρεθέντες μισοῦσιν, οἱ δὲ πεισθέντες ὡς κεχαρισμένοι φιλοῦσιν. . . . ἀλλὰ μὴν καὶ συμμάχων ὁ μὲν βιάζεσθαι τολμῶν δέοιτ' ἂν οὐκ ὀλίγων, ὁ δὲ πείθειν δυνάμενος οὐδενός· καὶ γὰρ μόνος ἡγοῖτ' ἂν δύνασθαι πείθειν. καὶ φονεύειν δὲ τοῖς τοιούτοις ἥκιστα συμβαίνει· τίς γὰρ ἀποκτεῖναί τινα βούλοιτ' ἂν μᾶλλον ἢ ζῶντι πειθομένῳ χρῆσθαι;

(X. *Mem.* 1.2.10–11)

that enmities and dangers attend force *(bia)*, while through persuasion safely and with friendship the same things come to pass. Those forced, as if having been deprived, hate, but those persuaded, as if having been done a favor, feel affection. . . . But indeed, the one daring to use force would have need of allies not a few, but the man able to persuade of no one; for even alone he would consider himself able to persuade. And to commit murder is for such men least expedient; for who would wish to kill someone rather than to use him living and persuaded?

The argument is transparently based on the popular rhetorical grounds of probability.[57] Even if it be disbelieved, its form is revealing: the changed status of *logos,* its effective equivalence to violence, and the totally amoral, selfish grounds for its use have become commonplace.

The political and social implications of such a *logos* are clear. Such power drains the listeners' consent of significance, making the word more insidious and, in some ways, more terrible than the "tyranny" of the dagger to which Socrates mockingly compares it in the *Gorgias*.[58] Inside the polis, citizens now suffer the same fate as those without a city: they are potential slaves, individually and collectively exposed to a new kind of violence. The old understanding of the social compact based on the suppression of *bia* within the social unit and its replacement by *logos* is corroded. The democratic ideology, which promoted allegiance to the word taken as the contrary to force, is distorted. The equal right to speech *(isegoria)*, which expressed the equality of citizens in a democracy, becomes an instrument of "tyranny." For *logos,* the leader of souls *(psychagogos)*, unbalances private and public relationships; its command over the individual soul writ large translates into political muscle.[59] The tongue replaces the armed band as the most effective means to absolute power. It becomes, as Plato makes his Gorgias say, the "greatest good and the cause, at once, of freedom for these men and of rule over others for each in his own city . . . moreover, through the same power [of rhetoric] you will hold the doctor as slave and the trainer as slave; the businessman will appear to make money for another and not himself, for you, the one able to speak and persuade the multitude."[60] The consequences are obvious: paralleling public fears of an increasingly powerful *logos* monopolized as a personal tool will be an erosion of its privileged moral and civic status; such a *logos* can command no more respect than the weapons of force to which it is (metaphorically) assimilated.

But withdrawal from commitment to speech, paradoxically caused by an excessive estimate of its power, would, of course, be fatal. Just as *peitho* makes willing slaves, it must begin with willing victims; basic to persuasion is the agreement to listen and to be persuaded if the right *logos* can be found. The citation from Gorgias quoted above polemically acknowledges this by turning it to *logos'* advantage, but the notion of willingness also circumscribes the power of the word. Speech must provide a reason to listen and to continue listening. Gorgias found that reason in a familiar poetic tradition: skillful sophistic *logos* commands the souls of its listeners because it, like poetry, provokes pleasure or *terpsis*.[61] Anticipating this, the audience enters into a state of "psychic complicity" with the speaker, and is ready, perhaps even anxious, to be enslaved by the word and experience the emotions it arouses.[62] The dangers of inserting *logos* into the continuum of the desires, which could make it just one of many (for example, for power, for money, for sex), are masked by the completely aesthetic and verbal nature assigned such pleasure. The techniques of rhetoric and the formal aspects of composition—poetic meters, elaborate figures, careful choice of words—suffice to stun the hearers and impress their souls.[63]

The notion of psychic complicity provoked by the pleasures of skillful speech has several advantages: it explains the possibility of persuasion and its results, justifies rhetoric as an art[64] that can be taught and learned independently of what is to be said, and revives the normal understanding that persuasion proceeds with the compliance of the listener. However, it also has serious flaws which were enthusiastically exploited by critics of the sophists. Departing from the implied pact between speaker and listener which must precede the act of speech logically and chronologically, they attacked both the form and genesis of this preverbal agreement.

Plutarch's story and the eulogy of verbal skill Plato gives Gorgias demonstrate one approach. Reworking the martial imagery designed to advertise the force of *logos,* they conceded its enormous civic power but pointed to a curious side step in its strategy. *Logos* wrestles not with the adversary, or victim, of the speaker but with an already pliant audience. It is the onlookers, the assembly or the jury, who through their democratic and leveling presence—their collective strength— transform the unmediated violence of a real fight (where force is applied to the unwilling and the loser has no right of appeal) into a sophistic wrestling match of tongues. It is they who experience the force of the word and translate this into forceful action, establishing the victory of Pericles, enslaving the doctor, trainer, and businessman. The *terpsis,* or pleasure, of speech functions so well because it is forced into open confrontation with neither violence nor other interests and emotions (for example, the desire of the businessman to keep his money). Thus, as we saw above in Cleon's censure, the Athenians willingly embrace the pleasures of the word while displacing, or not noticing, the cost.

This criticism, while discounting the power of *logos* to work its will directly, nevertheless grants it considerable seductive power; another view was less kind. What may seem self-evident when discussing poetry, drama, the demonstrations of rhetoric given by Gorgias, or even, on occasion, judicial oratory[65]—that the pleasure of listening alone is sufficient to attract and win over an audience—is less clear in those civic arenas which treat the expedient.[66] Confronted with the power of orators in the city, this second view located their power not in the verbal delights of art and technique, but in flattery, promises, bribes, threats, and other covert or open appeals to appetites far less reputable than that for skillful speech.[67] The compact between speaker and listener becomes an agreement of mutual gratification only apparently based on the giving and receiving of *logos.* The imagery of martial *logos* reverses itself, and the apparently masterful *logos* and its speakers become slaves forced to take the forms dictated by the desires of those whom they seem to dominate.[68]

These critical views were reflected on the stage. Thus in the *Hippolytus* (also of 428 B.C.) we can find *logos* portrayed as seductive and destructive.[69] As Phaedra remarks after the nurse's explicitly sophistic speech justifying adultery,

$$\tau o\hat{v}\tau' \ \check{\varepsilon}\sigma\theta' \ \mathring{o} \ \theta\nu\eta\tau\hat{\omega}\nu \ \varepsilon\mathring{\mathring{v}} \ \pi\acute{o}\lambda\varepsilon\iota\varsigma \ o\mathring{\iota}\kappa o\nu\mu\acute{\varepsilon}\nu\alpha\varsigma$$
$$\delta\acute{o}\mu o\nu\varsigma \ \tau' \ \mathring{\alpha}\pi\acute{o}\lambda\lambda\nu\sigma', \ o\mathring{\iota} \ \kappa\alpha\lambda o\grave{\iota} \ \lambda\acute{\iota}\alpha\nu \ \lambda\acute{o}\gamma o\iota\cdot$$

(Eur. *Hipp*. 486–87)

This it is which destroys well-governed cities
and houses of men, overly attractive words *(logoi)*

The ambiguously overly attractive *logoi* are those skillful and deceptive words which pander to the pleasure of the hearer (and the speaker); privately, and also publicly, they mean ruin. Comedy echoed this in its own key. This period saw many attacks direct and in passing on demagogues, sophists, and the new culture of technically skillful *logos: Banqueters* in 427 (see 205 PCG), *Acharnians* 425, *Knights* 424, *Konnos* 423, *Kolakes* 421, *Marikas* 421, *Hyperbolus* 420, to mention only a few.[70] To many what such men do cannot really be dignified with the honorable name of speech, for it simultaneously flouts civic and conventional structures while failing to provide the traditional and historic benefits of speaking. Rather what is produced is something new, hostile to the city and its laws. As Eupolis complains about a fashionable contemporary speaker: "He is best at babbling *(lalein),* most unable to speak *(legein)* ($\lambda\alpha\lambda\varepsilon\hat{\iota}\nu$ $\check{\alpha}\rho\iota\sigma\tau o\varsigma$, $\mathring{\alpha}\delta\nu\nu\alpha\tau\acute{\omega}\tau\alpha\tau o\varsigma$ $\lambda\acute{\varepsilon}\gamma\varepsilon\iota\nu$ 116 PCG)."[71] The distinction is telling. This new speech for all its power is better known to those who disparage it as empty babbling.

The problem of the civic use of rhetorical skill was, then, current and actively discussed at the time of the *Clouds*. However, the perceived change in the role of *logos* was more unsettling than the discussion above can suggest. For conflict between *logos* and the city, justice, and law undermined traditional distinctions and relationships that were fundamental to the self-definition and the idealized and ideological history of the democratic *polis*. The latter half of the fifth century in particular knew "scientific" analyses of human history that viewed it not as a fall from an original blessed state, but as an emergence from an existence which man shared with other animals,[72] living in isolation, dwelling in caves, eating raw food (including, cannibalistically, each other), mating indiscriminately and incestuously, and indulging in endless and mutual violence.[73] In short,[74]

> ἦν χρόνος ὅτ' ἦν ἄτακτος ἀνθρώπων βίος
> καὶ θηριώδης ἰσχύος θ' ὑπηρέτης
> (DK 88 B 25.1–2)

There was a time when disordered was men's life
and bestial and servant of might

In the escape from this chaotic and bestial condition, speech (and intelligence) were given essential and well-recognized roles. Theseus' famous praise of the human condition in Euripides' *Supplices* is typical:[75]

> αἰνῶ δ' ὃς ἡμῖν βίοτον ἐκ πεφυρμένου
> καὶ θηριώδους θεῶν διεσταθμήσατο,
> πρῶτον μὲν ἐνθεὶς σύνεσιν, εἶτα δ' ἄγγελον
> γλῶσσαν λόγων δούς, ὥστε γιγνώσκειν ὄπα
> (Eur. *Supp.* 201–4)

I praise who of the gods separated our life from
a confused and savage state,
first of all having instilled intelligence, then having given
tongue, messenger of words *(logos)*, so as to know voice

But while language was inserted as decisive at various steps in the evolution of civilized life and linked to a variety of advances, social, political, and technological, these were but variants of its fundamental responsibility: to make the *polis* possible through the gift of communication and to symbolize the necessary and beneficial cooperation that is its basis.[76] For as the xenophonic Socrates puts it, the gods gave man expression:

> δι' ἧς πάντων τῶν ἀγαθῶν μεταδίδομέν τε ἀλλήλοις διδάσκοντες καὶ
> κοινωνοῦμεν καὶ νόμους τιθέμεθα καὶ πολιτευόμεθα
> (X. *Mem.* 4.3.12)

through which we give a share of all good things to one another, teaching, and
form a community and establish laws and administer the city

His words illustrate a general trend.[77] In the conceptual scheme that links *logos* to justice and its other partners, the persuasion of *logos* and the agreement to use words instead of blows is key to the pact among citizens that founds community and to the laws and the practice of justice that preserve it.[78] Thus while in Hesiod justice *(dike)* seems the most common contrary of violence,[79] now *logos* and persuasion begin to intrude[80] as the mechanisms by which the laws can be established, justice accomplished, and violence averted.[81] Lysias' later praise of Athens as the most democratic and civilized of states illustrates a characteristically "strong parallelism between the oppositions *nomos* [law] / absence-of-*nomos* and *peitho* [persuasion] / *bia* [force],"[82] characteristically, again, augmented by the introduction of a specific role for *logos,* the agent of persuasion and of social intercourse generally. Thus describing the foundation of the democracy, Lysias asserts that the Athenians established the rule of law:

> ἡγησάμενοι θηρίων μὲν ἔργον εἶναι ὑπ' ἀλλήλων βίᾳ κρατεῖσθαι, ἀνθρώποις δὲ προσήκειν νόμῳ μὲν ὁρίσαι τὸ δίκαιον, λόγῳ δὲ πεῖσαι, ἔργῳ δὲ τούτοις ὑπηρετεῖν, ὑπὸ νόμου μὲν βασιλευομένους, ὑπὸ λόγου δὲ διδασκομένους.

(Lys. 2.19)

> having considered it to be the work of beasts to be ruled by each other through force *(bia)*, but to be appropriate for men, through law *(nomos)*, on the one hand, to determine the just, through speech *(logos)*, on the other, to persuade, and in action to serve these, by law *(nomos)* being ruled, but by *logos* being taught.

But if speech is uniquely human[83] (and democratic and Athenian), violence, or *bia,* is animal. Violence is animal because corporal force is something man shares (to a greater or lesser degree) with the other animals. *Logos* he does not.[84] However, to characterize man through speech is not, or not simply, to make a scientific or historical observation (although it was given physiological and historical bases),[85] nor to designate violence as irrational or ineffective in a human setting, nor even to sever *logos* and *bia* completely: violence can maintain a particular *logos,* and violent acts derive from a linguistic context of plans, hopes, desires, or fears. Nevertheless there is a fundamental difference between speech and violence in the social setting that is addressed by the prescriptive[86] and prophetic terms of its associated oppositions, man/animal, civilized/savage. For, in a certain sense, to abandon *logos* for *bia* is to act the animal and to invite or compel one's neighbors to do the same, mutually rendering justice, the laws, and speech irrelevant.[87] The repression of such private violence is key to the continued existence of the *polis* because, unless controlled, it can rip the social, and even familial, unit apart, returning man to the mute chaos of natural life.[88] This is given "historical" expression in the platonic Protagoras' story of early man.[89] According to this account, early men, living alone and scattered, were at the mercy of the violence and superior physical strength of other animals, "for they did not yet have the political art, of which the military art is a part."[90] They could not save themselves by coming together in cities, for again being without the art of politics they injured each other unjustly, and so dispersed once more (Pl. *Prt.* 322b8). The political art became possible only after the introduction of *aidos* (respect or shame) and justice relegated violence to its proper sphere outside the city, where it can be safely addressed to those who do not inhabit one's own civic space. *Dike,* implicitly the laws (which emerge in Pl. *Prt.* 326d5), *aidos,* and *logos,* the manipulation of which is the essence of Protagoras' political art,[91] form a complex of mutually dependent elements each one of which is necessary, but alone not sufficient, for individual security and civilized, civic life.

But the city, and especially the democratic city,[92] assumed a further role. As in Pericles' vision, speech and city, *logos* and *polis,* were mutually supportive. For if the city, founded at least in part on the gifts of *logos,* was necessary for physical survival, it was also the only arena for speech. Only there could man realize the potential of his unique possession, which, as Aristotle summarizes, renders him able, unlike other beasts, to indicate the useful and harmful, and therefore the just and unjust. And these moral perceptions, continues Aristotle, are the hallmark of the human, the community of which establishes household and city. Thus the ability to speak is fundamental to the city, the "natural" habitat of human beings, for "the one who is unable to take part in community or does not need to on account of self-sufficiency, being no part of the *polis,* is like beast or god."[93] Buxton's table of opposites corresponding to the opposition persuasion/ violence, that is, *peitho/bia* (which we could also identify with speech/violence or speech/lack of speech) illustrates well the interdependent elements of this optimistic view that included man's command of *logos* as fundamental to his achievement of polis and rule of law.[94]

peitho	*bia*
civilized	uncivilized
inside *polis*	outside *polis*
nomos	absence of *nomos*
dike	absence of *dike*
mankind	animals
Greeks	barbarians

These basic antitheses defined the place of civilized man and the actions and values that would maintain it. To transgress one was to endanger all, for what was left behind was never very far away. The *polis* stood posed in stark contrast to the natural life that surrounded it and even inhabited it: to the chaos, injustice, and brutality of the world ignorant of justice and law, where persuasion and *logos* were disregarded, undervalued, or impossible. This was the world of slave and enslaver, non-Greek, primitive man, child, animal,[95] and of unrestrained human nature, for without civic restraints, man would quickly revert to savagery.[96] The revolution at Corcyra showed that along with social partnership, an early casualty would be *logos* itself.[97]

But this traditional danger had been joined by a new one. Not just the abandonment of *logos,* but its use, too, now seemed to threaten the organizing polarities and habits of thought and action that had supported the ideology of the democratic *polis*—and even the human position. Nor was it only a matter of lies or trickery for personal ends.[98] Rather, in spite of the democratic views of sophists like Protagoras and the association of the advanced intelligentsia with Pericles, by the time of the *Clouds,* the democratic idealization of speech seems to have given way to an increasing perception of an oxymoronically antisocial *logos,* associated above all with the sophists and their rhetoric. Sophistic speculation theorized such a *logos,* and those who shared or learned their intellectual orientation, their cosmology, and their rhetorical techniques reaped its benefits.[99] Spoken by self-avowed natural men, this speech was no longer a communal good, but a private tool; not opposed to *bia,* but identified with it; not in harmony with justice and the laws, but destructive of them; able to command an automatic obedience more appropriate for slaves or animals than free citizens.

It is this negative perspective that the *Clouds* explores, and, as even our brief survey can suggest, the issues were, and are, explosive. *Logos,* rhetoric, power, the functioning of language in communal life, the nature of man, the virtues and vices of philosophers and their theories, the meaning of violence and its relationship to persuasion are not subjects of interest only in fifth-century Athens nor ones treated only, or even primarily, by Aristophanes. In general, I believe Aristophanes' vision has a recognizable and substantial, if comically indirect, correspondence to the contemporary situation—the nature of this correspondence and the shape it takes will be discussed in the chapters that follow. But to appreciate the full dimensions of his elliptical, hyperbolic treatment, Aristophanes' play must be read within the contemporary debate just outlined. Only thus can we isolate the characteristic patterns, comic and philosophic, and the *logoi*—speech, reasoning, imagery, terminology—that shape the *Clouds'* dramatic, thematic, and verbal content. But the *Clouds* filters these issues through the comic medium of one ordinary man, his privileged son, and their interaction with Socrates, two (sophistic) *logoi,* an ambiguous, reflective comic/philosophic/rhetorical chorus of clouds, and the audience, vulgar and wise, that watches the spectacle. The following chapters will take up their story.

2

Setting the Scene: Lines 1–132

From the first moments of the *Clouds,* the audience is oriented in a comic world quite different from those of the *Acharnians* and *Knights*. As the Peloponnesian War is dismissed and civic problems ignored,[1] Strepsiades' opening complaint and his subsequent interaction with his son, Pheidippides, present us with a new kind of issue, language, its power, and the grounds for this power. Strepsiades is in trouble because he cannot speak effectively, while those who can, work their will on him and others. The examples of the matchmaker and Strepsiades' wife lead into the introduction of the sophists,[2] men who theorize a new heaven and a new earth and have devised a supremely powerful *logos,* mastery of which will rescue Strepsiades from his misfortunes. Comic convention,[3] as well as Strepsiades' assertions, prepare us to believe this. Language must possess the overwhelming influence that makes it the ultimate weapon in the struggle for survival. At the same time, however, that we are presented with this picture we are introduced to a comic dynamic that undermines it. From the beginning, the comic festival provides the arena where the weapons of comedy—pun, nonsense, incongruity, obscenity—can suggest, at first only indirectly, that there is something amiss with what we are learning about this sophistic *logos* and those who wield its power.[4]

The *Clouds* opens with a monologue. All alone Strepsiades laments his fate.[5] No one will listen to him, and this is precisely the problem. Because his words command no force, he is beset with debts not of his making and he is unable to persuade his son to curtail his expensive ways. Moreover, this past ineffectiveness has now landed Strepsiades in further trouble: his irate creditors are about to take him to court. Once there, his inability to speak will surely cause the loss of his sureties. When Strepsiades tries again the same tactics that have already failed, ordering Pheidippides to reform, their exchange illustrates his powerlessness. Pheidippides is oblivious; the pleasures of horse racing and the immediate joys of sleep far outweigh his father's words.

When Strepsiades turns from his present problems to dwell on their origins, we learn more: Strepsiades is not only afflicted with ineffective speech himself, but he is beset by others who are excessively persuasive. This is responsible for his marriage, source of all his troubles. Agonized and furious, Strepsiades groans,

εἴθ᾽ ὤφελ᾽ ἡ προμνήστρι᾽ ἀπολέσθαι κακῶς
ἥτις με γῆμ᾽ ἐπῆρε τὴν σὴν μητέρα.

(41b–42)

Would that the matchmaker had perished wretchedly
the one who aroused/transported *(epairein)* me to
marry your [Pheidippides'] mother.

The paratragic tone of these lines underscores Strepsiades' plight and his presentation of himself as hapless victim.[6] Motivated by self-interest, the matchmaker detached Strepsiades from his previous rural existence, where he enjoyed golden age abundance. Describing the charms of Strepsiades' future wife, she aroused him to wed a woman of the city and, punningly in the same verb, transported him to this wordy world,[7] where he lives in torment. Her tool was language,[8] something the simple Strepsiades was helpless to resist. The punning verb *epairein*—which can mean "aroused/excited" and also "transported," in both senses of the English term—seems to capture all these aspects of the matchmaker's action. Its metaphorical and rhetorical senses here overlap those in the famous passage of the *Birds* where Peisthetairos, the consummate sophistic rhetor, explains to the informer that it is by *logos* that men are winged, their minds transported, their way of life transformed.[9]

πάντες τοῖς λόγοις / ἀναπτεροῦνται.

(*Birds* 1438–39)

all are winged by words.

ὑπὸ γὰρ λόγων ὁ νοῦς τε μετεωρίζεται
ἐπαίρεταί τ᾽ ἄνθρωπος.

(*Birds* 1447–49)

for by words both the mind is elevated
and man transported *(epairein)*.

The joke in the *Birds* plays off the rhetorical sense of *epairein*—the ability of *logos* to "transport," "carry away," or "arouse" its listeners[10]—against the literal one: the informer wants wings; he is offered words. *Clouds* 42 reverses this process. In our passage, *epairein* not only describes the effect of the matchmaker's words, literal and metaphoric, but ties her action to a major theme of the play: the powers of sophistic speech and the basis for these powers.[11] This was a context in which the matchmaker would feel at home. The ambiguity of her role and the prominence of language in her activities had already implicated the figure of the matchmaker in a negative interpretation of the power of language and made her a usefully pejorative image for speakers of the new sophistic rhetoric. The nurse in the *Hippolytus,* a sophistic figure whose words resemble enchanting spells and charms or a drug *(epoidai* Eur. *Hipp.* 478, *philtra* 509, *pharmakon* 479),[12] is called a matchmaker after her attempt to win Hippolytus for Phaedra (Eur. *Hipp.* 589). Likewise, in Xenophon's *Memorabilia* 2.6.36 Socrates declines to exaggerate the virtues of Critobulus by citing Aspasia: that good matchmakers report the good things with truth, but those who lie end up hated by the deceived (ἐξαπατηθέντας).[13] The matchmaker was an appropriate symbol of the power of skillful language and its ability to deceive because the seclusion of Greek women made it impossible for a man to see or know marriageable girls himself. Instead he had to rely on the words of a matchmaker, who described (and sold) the attractions of a girl to her prospective husband.[14] Thus Strepsiades' necessary dependence upon and helplessness before the matchmaker's words is emblematic of man's (and particularly Athenian man's) dependence upon and necessary susceptibility to *logos* in general. Strepsiades himself could be considered an example of that inevitable human ignorance described by Gorgias, that inability to see the real thing, which makes men easy prey for persuasive discourse.[15] This being the case, we can agree with Strepsiades that like his more famous fellow victim, Helen (who herself experienced social and physical dislocation on account of the power of the word), he cannot be held responsible for his predicament. Strepsiades has been seduced.[16]

But this is a joke! Gorgias' view has been called tragic,[17] but Strepsiades is a comic character. His lugubrious paratragic tone does not mean that we are confronted with tragedy. Our laughter assumes that serious mention of Gorgias here is ridiculous and sophistic theory irrelevant. The discrepancy between Strepsiades' comic situation and the dimensions assigned it by his language, and potentially uncoverable by philosophic speculation, is underscored by another meaning of *epairein*. In *Lysistrata* 937, the context clearly shows that in vulgar, everyday language this same verb can mean "get it up," get/have an erection.[18] The comic meaning confronts the philosophic/sophistic one and exposes another origin for Strepsiades' problem. As Nussbaum comments, the entire opening scene portrays Strepsiades as a man "essentially motivated by self-interest, probably of a hedonistic kind."[19] It is noticeable that the litany of rural blessings lacked one critical element, sex.[20] The matchmaker could remedy this; her words were so potent because they spoke directly to Strepsiades' *eros*[21] and manipulated his desires.[22] Through her *logos* Strepsiades could glimpse the figure of the niece of Megacles—seductively rich, upper-class, and female.[23] Thus the matchmaker's agent is not so much the charm of *logos,* but what it can promise.[24] Her persuasion recalls the power of an older Peitho, the goddess Persuasion, traditionally attendant upon Aphrodite, responsible for arousing erotic desire and securing its fulfillment with the full panoply of seduction.[25] Her success reminds us that all persuasion *(peitho)* should be considered an integrated whole: "a continuum within which divine and secular, erotic and non-erotic came together."[26]

The increasing preeminence of rhetoric had obscured this older *peitho* and all it implied, for contemporary persuasion was something very different: a function of technical manipulation of the word.[27] But the suppression of the erotic side of persuasion involved in making language its unique agent fosters a dangerous imbalance in the understanding of human motivation. The comic perspective on the matchmaker's success comments upon this ironically and obscenely. By recalling the traditional connection of persuasion with desire—a connection obviously compatible in its ruder forms with (comic) human nature[28]—a joke that first seemed to confirm the power of *logos* over men theoretically detached from physical reality ends up simultaneously suggesting the opposite. Far from dominating or creating this preverbal world, *logos* is powerful insofar as it is connected to satisfaction of its drives. Nor should we imagine these limited to carnal lusts alone. The seductive attributes of the niece of Megacles are comically broad; greed or need of all kinds—for food, sex, power, class—are the "erotic" stimulants that found successful persuasion.

The briefly evoked interaction of the matchmaker and Strepsiades will turn out to encapsulate many of the issues central to the *Clouds* and to illustrate the dynamic with which they shall be treated. Its charm is their reduction to the bare minimum, shorn of the distracting presence of the sophists, Socrates, his students, his teachings, the *logoi,* and the whole rhetorical/philosophical superstructure. Seen from one perspective, our passage appears to raise the issue of the power of language and the limits of human knowledge, confirming that words alone have the ability to transform man's life. The comic meaning of *epairein* and our pleasure in it, however, deny this. From this perspective, such philosophical elaboration is completely beside the point, a smoke screen obscuring the brutally simple basis of real persuasion. The clash of views, the intimate confrontation of comic and philosophic, will drive the play from the choice of words and imagery to the construction of jokes and scenes. Sophistic assumptions are posited only to be undercut, instantly and hilariously. But, however various the forms of confrontation, certain questions persist: What is the nature of man? What world does he inhabit? and What does this mean for language and its power?

Strepsiades' characterization as old-fashioned and ignorant and the double-edged "eulogy" of *logos* suggested so far continue in his story of his family life.[29] For while Strepsiades attributes all his disasters to his wife's persuasive powers and his own verbal impotence, the possibility is shadowed that he misunderstands his difficulties. The comedy continues, ever so faintly perhaps, to problematize the very power of *logos* that it is ostensibly, through Strepsiades, suggesting.

As Strepsiades describes his wife, she briefly emerges as the very image of *peitho,* both old and new, whose seat was traditionally the lips and mouth.[30] The niece of Megacles had all the equipment necessary for persuasion or seduction: a body annointed with perfume and a tongue skillful in sweet sexy kisses and sweet sexy discourse.[31] As is to be expected, Strepsiades is helpless before this potent combination. He is unable to stand up to his wife's words or her sexuality. To defend himself against her excessive physical and social demands, Strepsiades can only hold up his cloak, the *himation,* and punningly complain of his wife's sexual and financial extravagance, ὦ γύναι, λίαν σπαθᾷς "O woman, you weave/spend/make love too much" (55).[32] The cloak, or *himation,* which here makes it debut, is the physical symbol of the social covering that makes the private natural man into the civic social one. It is Strepsiades' self-respect in bed and the public sign of his status as head of the household and Athenian. It is precisely these aspects of Strepsiades that his wife's verbal and erotic *peitho* is unravelling.[33]

With the birth of a son, the persuasive power of Strepsiades' wife became even more disastrous. From the beginning, both parents felt that the name given their child would have decisive effect. At issue was not only the child's class affiliation and way of life, but even his character. A name including "(h)ippos,"

or "horse," as Strepsiades' wife wished, would associate the boy with the political, urban upper classes. Strepsiades' proposal, to name him after his paternal
grandfather, would tie the child to the thrifty self-sufficient world of the country.[34]
In his concern about the name given his child, Strepsiades shows a characteristically great respect for, and a characteristically concrete and old-fashioned understanding of, the power of words. For while the choice of Strepsiades' wife reflects
what is appropriate socially, Strepsiades seems motivated by the belief that proper
names influence or reveal something of their holders.[35] Time, however, has revealed the quaint naiveté of this assumption. For although the first fight ended in
compromise—the child would be named Pheidippides, a name incorporating parts
of both parents' suggestions—Strepsiades' apparent, if partial, victory was illusory. Pheidippides' conduct was completely unaffected by his name. This should
not be altogether surprising. Not only does standard comic practice frequently
make the son the contrary of the father and his wishes (as, for example, in the
Wasps), but Strepsiades' beliefs were at odds with contemporary theory. The latest theories located the power of speech not in its connection, predictive or coercive, to some concrete and extra-linguistic reality, but in the opposite, a detachment and resulting arbitrariness—most apparent in proper names but true of all
logos—that make words tools whose precise applications and power depend on
the skill of the speaker. Given this, it was, perhaps, inevitable that Strepsiades'
wife should prevail in the rhetorical contest of Pheidippides' upbringing.

As their child grew, the mother sought to reinforce the implications of the
upper class "(h)ippos" part of his name; the father, those of the rural "pheid,"
or "thrifty." Like the later debate of the *logoi,* this "education" took the form
of two speeches proposing contrasting lives: here, urban aristocrat and parsimonious farmer.[36] As Strepsiades gives us to understand, Pheidippides' choice of the
life proposed by his mother and consequently his environment, behavior, and even
nature were functions solely of her superior verbal skill. Strepsiades suffered from
the same old problem: his *logos* had no force.

ἀλλ' οὐκ ἐπείθετο τοῖς ἐμοῖς οὐδὲν λόγοις

(73)

but he [Pheidippides] was not persuaded by my words at all

The story of Pheidippides' education seems to fit the preoccupation with language characteristic of Strepsiades and perhaps to contrast his traditional understanding with a different model. However, we may wonder if this identification
of the problem is really correct. Confronted with a choice between a hard rural
life and an easy urban one, it is not surprising that Pheidippides preferred his
mother's vision. (Indeed, Strepsiades himself had already been persuaded to leave
the countryside and the life he is so nostalgic about in retrospect.) Further, Pheidippides' mother had topological advantages. She spoke holding her son on her
lap and caressing him—as she stroked him physically, so her words fondled his
self-esteem, offering him a life of luxury, prominence, and political power like
that of his uncle Megacles.[37] From this angle, Pheidippides' choice is unremarkable; nor does much skill in persuasion seem required to account for it. Instead,

Strepsiades' story once again hints at an alternative or a dangerous supplement to the power of speech that, in some sense, reattaches it to "reality," even if we abandon the notion of predictive force.[38]

But Strepsiades is oblivious to these undercurrents; his trust in *logos* is unshaken. It is in this context that he discovers his way out (75). Characteristically, even before we know what it is, its viability again seems to depend on language. Once more Strepsiades must try to persuade Pheidippides. The difficulty of his task and the probability he will fail are conveyed by the verb in line 77: *anapethein* is "used especially of persuading someone contrary to his inclinations or his existing standards or opinions."[39] Lines 87–90 repeat the notion of persuasion *(peithein)* four times. To effect this persuasion, Strepsiades adopts the time-honored strategy of appeal to filial piety. Possibly reversing his mask, to demonstrate more clearly the "art" of his approach, Strepsiades ponders how to induce Pheidippides to tell him that he loves him (82), so that he will obey him (87).[40] The point, when we finally learn it, is hardly surprising: more, and more successfully persuasive, *logos*. Pheidippides is to apprentice himself to the sophists so that he can perfect a new variety of speech. This and only this will save his father and allow him to escape his creditors in court.

Strepsiades' subsequent introduction of the sophists to his son is also, of course, Aristophanes' to the audience.[41]

> ψυχῶν σοφῶν τοῦτ᾽ ἐστὶ φροντιστήριον.
> ἐνταῦθ᾽ ἐνοικοῦσ᾽ ἄνδρες οἳ τὸν οὐρανὸν
> λέγοντες ἀναπείθουσιν ὡς ἔστιν πνιγεύς,
> κἄστιν περὶ ἡμᾶς οὗτος, ἡμεῖς δ᾽ ἄνθρακες.
> οὗτοι διδάσκουσ᾽, ἀργύριον ἤν τις διδῷ,
> λέγοντα νικᾶν καὶ δίκαια κἄδικα.
>
> (94–99)

Of wise souls *(psychai)* this is the Thinkery *(phrontisterion)*.
Here dwell men who speaking about the heavens
persuade *(anapeithein)* that it is an oven cover,
and this is around us; we, then, [are] coals *(anthrakes)*.
These men teach, if someone gives them silver,
how to prevail saying both just *(dikaia)* and unjust *(akika)* things.

The passage merits careful attention, for it outlines much of what we shall learn about sophists and their teachings and establishes the primary orientation of the comedy toward these central figures. At issue is not, or not primarily, the sophists' persons, idiosyncrasies, immorality (although all these certainly feature on occasion), but, in a larger sense, their theories and practices.

The "intellectual" orientation begins immediately. From the first words we realize that we are up against something new. The opening line,

> ψυχῶν σοφῶν τοῦτ᾽ ἐστὶ φροντιστήριον.
> (94)

Of wise souls *(psychai)* this is the Thinkery *(phrontisterion)*.

could not have failed to startle. *Phrontisterion,* or Thinkery, is a comic coinage introduced in this play;[42] the notion that such a place could be the earthly residence of wise or skillful souls[43] is hard to understand and left unexplained. It seems as if the residents must be half dead, since what is left of them is that which remains after death, separated from the body.[44] Bodies are, or seem to be, irrelevant and even forgotten.[45]

The next few lines widen the focus, and things begin to get a bit clearer.

> ἐταῦθ' ἐνοικοῦσ' ἄνδρες οἳ τὸν οὐρανὸν
> λέγοντες ἀναπείθουσιν ὡς ἔστιν πνιγεύς,
> κἄστιν περὶ ἡμᾶς οὗτος, ἡμεῖς δ' ἄνθρακες.
>
> (95–97)

Here dwell men who speaking about the heavens
persuade *(anapeithein)* that it is an oven cover,
and this is around us; we, then, [are] coals *(anthrakes).*

The men who live in this weird place have beliefs that, while highly parodic, readily identify them as comic members of the new intelligentsia, for they are physicists and concern themselves with explaining the natural world. Speculation (and disputation) about the heavens was a trademark activity of philosophers and intellectuals of all sorts.[46] To uneasy and irritated contemporaries, Plutarch records, such irreverent, agnostic, if not atheistic, speculation seemed to reduce the divine to irrelevance:[47]

> οὐ γὰρ ἠνείχοντο τοὺς φυσικοὺς καὶ μετεωρολέσχας τότε καλουμένους,
> ὡς εἰς αἰτίας ἀλόγους καὶ δυνάμεις ἀπρονοήτους καὶ κατηναγκασμένα
> πάθη διατρίβοντας τὸ θεῖον
>
> (Plu. *Nicias* 23)

They did not tolerate the physicists and stargazers as they were then called, as dissolving the divine into unreasoning causes, unpremeditated forces, and necessary properties.

Although the men to whom Strepsiades proposes to entrust his son are not yet identified, certain key features of their teachings—scepticism, novelty, abstraction—are already clear.

Their discourse, however, is not only innovative and controversial but rigorous and persuasive. Like the astronomers, whom Gorgias cited as models of persuasive speech,[48] these thinkers, too, can persuade people to believe in the strange new world that they propose. This is impressive testimony to their skill. Once again we see *anapeithein* (96), this time, however, successful. Its repetition here, echoing that of line 77, testifies that Strepsiades has happened upon the right remedy for his problems—these men have exactly the power he lacks. Further, their theories are coherent. As the structure of line 97, with the connectives καί . . . δέ, indicates, the wise souls' view of man is a logical corollary to their understanding of the sky. This is the first example of a logic that will become familiar as the play progresses: men reflect the world they inhabit. As the heavens, the traditional abode of the gods, are drained of theistic significance, retaining only physical existence as an oven, so men become coals, prey to the forces and governed by the laws natural to their environment.[49]

This may be logically satisfying, but there are a couple of troubling points that are pregnant for the future. First is the apparent contradiction between the wise souls' account of themselves and that which they propose for mankind as a whole. The wise souls themselves dwell in a Thinkery and identify themselves not as bodies in a natural world, but the reverse, thought and reasoning, as is appropriate for their peculiar, man-made abode. The fact that they have deduced everything we have just learned appears to bear out their claim, but the conclusions seem to deny this is possible. If men are really *anthrakes,* ''coals,'' or even primarily physical entities, it is not clear what legitimate role remains for their souls *(psychai)* or even why they should be particularly interested in thinking.

The conclusion that men are *anthrakes* is the more disturbing because although it may seem the final element in an argument that renders it appropriate and even necessary, its form is irrepressibly comic. What makes men coals, or *anthropoi anthrakes,* is a pun, placed at the end of the line for maximum visibility and punch. The generic fun of comedy—the same pun had been used in the *Acharnians*—and the speculation of philosophy have arrived at the same conclusions.[50] However this comic duplication of, or dimension to, the theories of the wise souls is something intended neither by them nor Strepsiades. They are not joking.[51] Rather, the pun marks the intrusion of Aristophanes and draws attention to his comic art.[52] What we have is a familiar line of inquiry mocked in a familiar way. The recall of the *Acharnians,* coupled with the reuse of mockery familiar from Cratinus—the scholia note he had already mocked Hippon using similar terms in an earlier play—alert the audience to the fact that the figures Strepsiades is introducing will be subjected to a criticism in some sense generic.[53] The dynamic of the passage with the matchmaker is repeated, and its implications begin to come clear. If comic logic can arrive at the same results as philosophical speculation, perhaps comedy is the proper vehicle to elaborate the implications of such theorizing and illuminate the meaning of a world and men taken in purely physical terms: responsive only to their material qualities and requirements, expressive only of natural and corporal ''laws'' and necessities. Moving comically to capitalize on the discrepancy noted above in the wise souls' account of themselves and everybody else, our play will suggest that such a world may be congenial not to wise souls devoted to things of the mind, but instead to men whose natural existence, as bodies, is best glossed by the laws of bodily desire.[54]

But the intrusive pun suggests additional lessons. Not only does it draw our attention to the fact that we watch comedy, but it begins to bring into focus the nature of this comedy, and the way it will relate to its originals (the sophists) and its audience. For this pun, in a certain sense, tests the spectators of the *Clouds.* We are not required to detect it to find the passage funny. The fun of humiliating the pompous *sophoi* (wise), a condescending laugh at the idea that men are coals, and the concommitant reduction of sophistic views to a comforting and familiar silliness could be satisfaction enough. But when we note the pun, the passage becomes more demanding. The *Clouds* marks itself as more than buffoonery and traditional abuse and begins to teach us how to ''read'' its comic art. The pun operates by detaching us from our everyday understanding and plunging us for a

moment into a world where language means too much, as it substitutes or aug-
ments expected signifieds through play with signifiers.[55] Our laughter registers our
surprise, but also our pleasure, for success in freeing ourselves from the meaning
which context, story, familiarity at first seemed to require, enables us to synthe-
size a new more comprehensive sense that speaks to us allusively through the play
of *logos*. This is also the strategy of the *Clouds*. Our play will not oppose a
"straight," "theoretical" discourse to the sophistic one, but as the pun here deforms and redoubles the sense,[56] so the *Clouds* will employ the resources of *logos*
and of comedy—systematic mockery, distortion, allusion, generic play, and a joking bending of the rules—to graft a comic "double," an unwanted commentary,
on its already parodic rendering of what the sophists propose. Thus, as in this
emblematic pun, the comedy of the *Clouds* consistently points to something more,
a significant excess in a story that could seem in itself complete. Careful attention
will reveal that what seem our comedy's very comic excrescences are the places
where Aristophanes indicates another dimension of his work.[57]

In taking up the perspective this pun suggests, the audience follows the lessons
of the *Clouds* to become that ideal audience, the one attentive to the play of *logos*,
the parabasis will define as worthy of Aristophanes' art. However, this makes yet
another doubling. For the passage which invited us to laugh at the sophists and
their theories, characterized the *Clouds'* polemic against them, and taught us how
to read it, finally also draws us into an unacknowledged brotherhood with its
targets. For the pun and sophistic rhetoric which is its butt exploit (and enjoy) the
same ambiguity and freedom of language.[58] Ideal spectator and sophist, comedy
and rhetoric, are linked through common delight in the independent creations of
logos.

The final lines of Strepsiades' description return us to the plot.[59]

οὗτοι διδάσκουσ᾽, ἀργύριον ἤν τις διδῷ,
λέγοντα νικᾶν καὶ δίκαια κἄδικα.
(98–99)

These men teach, if someone gives them silver,
how to prevail saying both just *(dikaia)* and unjust *(adika)* things.

Although description of their theories may have tempted us to dismiss them as
stargazers preoccupied with remote and trivial speculation, the sophists' *logos* is
of extraordinary practical value. But it is not divorced from what has gone before.
The wording insists on a connection that is more than sequential or exemplary
between cosmological speculation and rhetorical skill. An amoral world, ruled by
natural forces and laws, where the sky has been emptied of gods and meaning and
value are determined by the exercise of autonomous human reason and debated
by the independent human voices, is the necessary context for the art of the sophistic rhetor to whom *dikaia* and *adika,* just and unjust things, are interchange-
able.[60] Strepsiades' own instruction will vividly demonstrate the importance of
cosmology in the acquisition of sophistic speech.

By the end of Strepsiades' introduction, the audience has learned much about the program and comic affiliations of what I will call Aristophanes' sophists (although that term has not been used), and an equally large amount about how his comedy will approach them and their teachings. The *Clouds'* sophists are parodies, partaking in the traditional humor occasioned by pretentious intellectuals with advanced and iconoclastic views. But at the same time the comic distortion will not be random, nor will we have simply the pleasures of familiar abuse. Rather, the *Clouds* will use the conventionally comic to construct a critique whose complexity denies a simple response. The sophists seem simultaneously silly and yet dangerous, in possession of a power whose implications they may not fully understand, believers in the mind who theorize the body, distant from ordinary citizens while teaching them. And finally, the paradox remains that those who appreciate our comedy will also be best able to appreciate the targets of its mockery.

However, one central point remains obscure. For while the characteristics and generic nature of the inhabitants of the Thinkery are now clear, neither the audience nor Pheidippides knows the crucial thing: What particular characters (or individuals) will be slotted into this generic type? What are the names of these men? To whom, precisely, does Strepsiades refer? The answer in line 101—a strange collocation of mental processes and aristocratic terminology which makes a strong social/political claim for these philosopher/rhetoricians—jolts Pheidippides, and then presumably the audience, into awareness.[61] These sophists, for the purposes of our comedy at least, are to be identified with those pale and shoeless braggarts, among whom are Socrates and Chairephon (102–4). For Pheidippides the suggestion that he frequent such men is shocking; the idea that lines 94–99 could describe Socrates and his fellows apparently is not. Whether or not the audience would, or should, share these reactions has been hotly debated.[62] No answer to this dilemma will be proposed here. Rather as our comedy has commenced, its Socrates and his associates will be treated now as representative, now as particular, but always first and foremost, as aristophanic and parodic.

This parodic, aristophanic Socrates possesses an equally parodic product, the object of Strepsiades' desires.

> εἶναι παρ' αὐτοῖς φασιν ἄμφω τὼ λόγω,
> τὸν κρείττον', ὅστις ἐστί, καὶ τὸν ἥττονα.
> τούτοιν τὸν ἕτερον τοῖν λόγοιν, τὸν ἥττονα,
> νικᾶν λέγοντά φασι τἀδικώτερα.
>
> (112–15)

There are with them, they say, two *logoi,*
the stronger *(kreitton),* whatever that is, and the weaker *(hetton).*
Of these two *logoi,* one, the weaker *(hetton),*
they say to prevail saying the more unjust things.

As few have failed to notice, these *logoi,* here assigned to Socrates, in fact recall Protagoras'[63] famous claim:

> τὸν ἥττω λόγον κρείττω ποιεῖν
> (DK 80 B 6b)

to make the weaker *(hetton)* logos the stronger *(kreitton)*

The shock of recognition here, the fascination of the original, and the multiple distortions it undergoes in Strepsiades' account have prompted much study; several things are of interest to us. The first is the absolutely amoral, purely rhetorical connotations of stronger and weaker, *kreitton* and *hetton,* in the protagorean formula.[64] *Hetton,* or weaker, means prima facie less convincing; *kreitton,* stronger, more convincing; or, from another perspective, the *hetton* will be the unconventional minority view; the *kreitton,* the conventional majority one. The transformation of the *hetton logos* into the *kreitton*—that is, of the weaker argument into the stronger one—is also a process to be understood amorally. The *hetton logos* becomes *kreitton* when rhetorical skill persuades its listeners that this is the case, in other words, that this *logos* is correct.[65] Thus the value-free world of the sophists is not transgressed by the protagorean formula. Rather, it concentrates our attention on the impact of rhetorical skill in a world where the strength or weakness of any particular *logos* is a function of the skill of its speaker, the same *logos* becoming now *hetton* now *kreitton* in an endless fluctuation.[66]

From his first words, Strepsiades distorts all these aspects of the protagorean claim. Line 112, with its dual forms, stresses the existence of two independent *logoi,* stable in position, unchanging in content.[67] Instead of a unified *logos* which can be used to express accounts *(logoi)* whose relative positions change depending upon the skill with which they are articulated,[68] we are confronted with the oddity of a *hetton,* or weaker, *logos* which even in the moment of its triumph remains identifiably *hetton.* Conversely, we must assume, the *kreitton,* or stronger, even in defeat, cannot be called the *hetton.* The paradox thus created seems to be resolved by another of Strepsiades' innovations: he assigns the *logoi,* in particular the *hetton,* a fixed content, unjust things (115), and a moral value: it is itself unjust (116).[69]

Strepsiades thus decisively identifies the *hetton logos* with only one of the options of the sophistic rhetor mentioned in line 99: to prevail saying unjust things. This restriction highlights its power, and thus that of rhetoric, in a way that the less unexpected triumph of the *kreitton,* saying just things, would not.[70] Given an inherently weaker case, unsupported by extralinguistic sanctions or the audience's beliefs, the *hetton logos* can, and need, rely on nothing but skillful *logos* to win its inevitable victory.[71] However, even these (slanderous) innovations do not solve the problem. For precisely the *hetton*'s victory should reverse the views of its hearers, revealing what seemed to be unjust to be just, and vice versa, a process culminating in the rehabilitation of the *hetton logos* itself.[72] At that moment, the *kreitton logos* should stand convicted of injustice and weakness. Why it continues to merit its name and its association with the just, or even how it can be called a *logos* at all, given that the *hetton* has assumed the power of *logos* for itself, remains a mystery which Strepsiades' own confusion in line 113 underlines. He is not quite sure what the *kreitton* is or how it works.[73] But in any case it is irrelevant. To solve his father's problems, Pheidippides need learn only the unjust *hetton.*

ἢν οὖν μάθῃς μοι τὸν ἄδικον τοῦτον λόγον,
ἃ νῦν ὀφείλω διὰ σέ, τούτων τῶν χρεῶν
οὐκ ἂν ἀποδοίην οὐδ' ἂν ὀβολὸν οὐδενί.
(116–18)

> If, then, you learn for me this unjust *logos,*
> what now I owe on account of you, of these debts
> I would not repay not an obol, to no one.

Strepsiades' strange assumption that one can learn one of the *logoi* without the other[74] definitively separates the *hetton* and *kreitton logoi* and binds the *hetton* to the sophists. The project he gives the *hetton* is carefully chosen to justify its designation as unjust and to represent its dangerously antisocial nature. For this *hetton logos* is the precise converse of a traditional definition of justice: "to say true things and to return whatever someone should take" (ἀληθῆ τε λέγειν καὶ ἃ ἂν λάβῃ τις ἀποδιδόναι Pl. *R.* 331d1).[75] In thus promising to free man from the necessity of being just, our aristophanic *hetton logos* uncouples the traditional pairs *logos*/justice *(dike)* and *logos*/law *(nomos).* In so doing, it threatens to dismantle the structure of conventional civic life and return man to a prepolitical existence of savage isolation.[76] The question not addressed is the consequent status of language itself.

But Strepsiades' own rhetorical skills are inadequate to secure this world he desires. His appeals to familial affection, or *philia,* in 79 (the endearing diminutive), 81, 82, 86, 106, 110, are useless, but at least secure him a hearing. Threats to sever the familial relationship, however, are genuinely counterproductive: Pheidippides refuses to listen any longer and departs (121–25). Such a complete breakdown of communication warns us not to underestimate the necessity of *philia,* even in the moment of its inadequacy. Although it may seem feeble when weighed against the triumph of the matchmaker's appeal to *eros* or the promises of the sophists' rhetorical techniques, *philia* has a central role to play in making communication, and thus persuasion, possible at all.

It is in this context—of verbal failure of all sorts—that Strepsiades decides to enter the Thinkery himself.[77] The language with which he expresses his resolve is suggestive of what is to come:

> ἀλλ' οὐδ' ἐγὼ μέντοι πεσών γε κείσομαι,
> ἀλλ' εὐξάμενος τοῖσιν θεοῖς διδάξομαι
> αὐτὸς βαδίζων εἰς τὸ φροντιστήριον.
>
> (126–28)

> But I, indeed, although thrown, will not stay down,
> but after praying to the gods I will learn,
> myself going into the Thinkery.

The image of line 126 is commonly identified as taken from wrestling.[78] It equates the preceding argument to a fight or wrestling match and initiates the study of the relationship between language and violence that will be central to the rest of the play. In going to the Thinkery, Strepsiades seeks instruction that will make him more availing in future battles of this kind. The sophists are advertised masters of this art; through them is acquired the all-important weapon in the urban jungle Strepsiades now inhabits, the skillful word.

This first scene has begun our introduction to the problem and comic solution which will motivate the plot, to its characters—an ordinary man, his fashionable, aristocratic son, and some comic "sophists"—and to the nature of the particular comedy we watch. The following scene (and the next chapter) will develop further the suggestions of the beginning, but before continuing, it seems worth pausing for a moment to note the limits of the fiction that is being laid out—a fiction constructed of elements whose conjunction is comic and thematic, not historical and realistic. For the prologue and opening scene have also eliminated possible subjects and closed off certain lines of development.[79] Most conspicuously absent is the Peloponnesian War. Dismissed in lines 5ff., it is pushed to the background, pictured as responsible not for any aspect of Strepsiades' hellish situation nor for any of his actions, now or later, but for the minor inconvenience of snoring slaves, whose slumber, along with Pheidippides', is the foil to Strepsiades' wakeful misery. Indeed, the war's only negative impact on Strepsiades, and positive contribution to the themes of the play, is its liberating effect upon these natural utterances, the snores. Before slaves could not snore because they could be punished. Now the possibility of desertion has liberated their vocal cords, and Strepsiades' last verbal power is being eroded, because, we must assume, he can no longer back up his commands with convincing violence.[80] Thus, what was the motive for the *Acharnians* (and later for *Peace*) is a minor inconvenience for Strepsiades (and insignificant for the *Clouds*), providing only a thematic grace note. Likewise, the legal and political conditions of Athens do not enter into Strepsiades' calculations.[81] Our *Clouds,* for all that *logos* is to play a central role, does not repeat the orientation of the *Knights* or its transparently political allusions. For even as he enters the domain of the sophists, men whose students were primarily not only wealthy but members of that elite whose words manipulated and constructed the speculative, literary, ideological, social, legal, and political currencies of Athens,[82] Strepsiades' ambitions are represented as mundane. His comic goal is not reworking the world, controlling the state, or even preeminence in the courts, but simply avoiding his debts.[83]

Thus the *Clouds* presents us with a situation, and a character, resolutely ordinary, careful in its narrative avoidance of the fantastic or "incredible,"[84] located in the private life of a well-off, if debt-ridden, aging Athenian.[85] Yet there remains something decidedly odd in Strepsiades' decision to seek instruction at the Thinkery; at the very least, the logical student should have been his son. The comedy motivates Strepsiades' action "realistically" yet does not obscure the unlikeliness of this encounter.[86] Strepsiades' last speech in this scene, replete with allusions unintended by the character, reminds us that we are to witness an unusual (comic) experiment the results of which may prove highly enlightening: the willing intrusion of an ordinary "stupid" (129) man—not a successful speaker, but a perennial (and suggestible) member of the audience—into the speculative environment of violent *logos* and those who control it. It is in this sense that the *Clouds* has a larger and even "political" reach. For it promises to tell us something about the relationship of citizen to *logos,* a relationship that founds democratic theory and practice.

3

Meeting the Wise Souls and Their Gods: Lines 133–313

Strepsiades', and the audience's, introduction to the wise souls and their gods elaborates the themes of his initial description. As we listen to the exemplary tales of the student, see the interior of the Thinkery, meet the master, and finally hear the voices of the clouds, Socrates is assimilated ever more closely to the type ''comic philosopher'': ludicrously otherworldly, preoccupied with ridiculous and trivial speculation, inhabitant of a world of theory. Reciprocally, Strepsiades is confirmed as the representative of the practical comic man. The reverse of the ascetic sophists, he is embedded in the fleshy reality of the body. His contempt and bewilderment, emotions he shares with his fellow Athenians in the audience, dismiss as silly everything that does not obviously and at once contribute to the satisfaction of desire. The development of these types occupies the foreground throughout Strepsiades' introduction and instruction. However, the clashes and jokes which form its substance have additional lessons. For as with the original introduction of the sophists, these scenes teach us how to ''read'' Aristophanes' comedy and assess its orientation. This is intellectual comedy. To react appropriately, our views must not match those of the buffoonish Strepsiades, nor should we imagine that Aristophanes' mockery parallels in content or in form that of his character(s). Finally the sophists' pursuits are revealed as not merely a laughing matter. The presuppositions of sophistic analysis and the terms in which it is conducted make it potentially revolutionary. The sequence that begins with the fart of the gnat could end by depriving not just god but, in a sense, man, too, of speech.

The first words we hear from the inhabitants of the Thinkery show their reversal of ordinary categories. Strepsiades is entering a place where thought is paramount, ideas have replaced offspring,[1] and mysteries (143) are derived from observation of the natural world and practice of a measuring art that will reveal its true dimensions. This study is remote from the ordinary cares of men and from the pains and pleasures of the body. When Chairephon is bitten by a flea, in the Thinkery the reaction is not physical but mental: Socrates wonders how far it can jump. The measurements required to answer this question eliminate anthropocentric distortion and seek an explanation strictly relevant to the phenomenon in question. The jump of a flea will be measured in flea feet.

The methodology illustrated by the analysis of the jump of the flea will have far-reaching consequences: most importantly, the independence accorded the natural world is balanced by a reduction of its meaning in human terms. These implications begin to be visible when Chairephon, in turn, asks Socrates a question, this time about the song of a gnat. Schmid identifies the entire passage as one in a series of jokes about natural science pertinent to Socrates' early interest in physics, this one turning on Archelaos' explanation of *phone*—that is, articulate sound, voice, or speech.[2] Clearly such an explanation would be of more than casual interest to men teaching about rhetoric and the role of speech in human affairs. The actual theory itself, that "the genesis of *phone* is the striking of the air,"[3] will be central to the conception of the *Clouds*. Through comic manipulation, the production of speech and voice will be assimilated to Anaxagoras' explanation of thunder, "thunders are the striking together of clouds,"[4] and both will be analogized to another kind of sound, farts. Through an obscene parody of sophistic concern with coherence, extent, and rigorous application of natural models, Aristophanes will prove that the insignificant, obviously natural whine of the gnat, the thunder of the clouds, the patron saints of rhetoric, and ultimately the human voice as well, all sound for the same reason. All are simply flatulence. The story of the gnat is an omen of things to come.

The initial question about the gnat is simple—"whether it sings through its mouth or its bottom" (κατὰ τὸ στόμ' ᾄδειν ἢ κατὰ τοὐρροπύγιον 158)—but things quickly progress beyond just a query about orifices. Socrates' response changes our understanding of the origin, the cause, and hence the meaning of the gnat's voice.

> ἔφασκεν εἶναι τοὔντερον τῆς ἐμπίδος
> στενόν, διὰ λεπτοῦ δ' ὄντος αὐτοῦ τὴν πνοὴν
> βίᾳ βαδίζειν εὐθὺ τοὐρροπυγίου·
> ἔπειτα κοῖλον πρὸς στενῷ προσκείμενον
> τὸν πρωκτὸν ἠχεῖν ὑπὸ βίας τοῦ πνεύματος.
>
> (160–64)

He asserted that the intestine of the gnat is
narrow *(stenos)*, and right through it being narrow/thin/subtle *(leptos)*, the breath
proceeds by force straight through the bottom;
then the hollow cavity adjacent to the narrow one,
the ass, sounds under the violence of the blast.

Line 164 is comic reduction and mockery of a subject already trivial.[5] The puniness of the subject is enlarged to include the silliness of the topic and of such intellectual pursuits in general by the recurrent use of *stenos,* or narrow, and *leptos,* or (re)fine(d), both code words (positive or negative) associated with things intellectual.[6] The joking oscillation in their sense from "subtle" (the appropriate meaning in theoretical contexts) to "small" plays off size against importance to ridicule such sophistic concerns. When Strepsiades goes on to voice his approbation, however, exclaiming that those who can see through (discern) a gnat's ass should have no trouble in court (167ff.), the impact is double. While his ignorance and enthusiastic misunderstanding are laughable, so too is the absurd element of truth in his statement. That such speculation is connected to big-time legal power is not so far off: a certain *leptotes* (153), meagerness or subtlety, ties them together. In a contradictory gesture, the student's story and Strepsiades' reaction assert both the potency and the tenuousness of such rhetoric and such endeavors.

The joke, however, is more complex. For not just topic, but method is being satirized, and in the process a line of imagery and of comic criticism is established that will be central to the rest of Strepsiades' education and the picture of rhetoric it will present. For Socrates not only reveals the gnat's song to be propelled out its ass, but also deprives the gnat itself of any significant agency in the production of this sound. While Chairephon asked about the gnat, Socrates responds with the proximate causes of the sound itself: breath, blast, ass, which themselves respond to impersonal force ($\beta\iota\alpha$), the all-important driver and expression of nature's law. What we hear is the unintended, but natural and necessary, result of the forced passage of air through adjoining narrow and hollow spaces. Like a fart, such a sound can be assumed to be an undesired and unanticipated product of the guts, as surprising to the gnat, at any particular moment, as everyone else. What is produced can no longer be considered song but simply unintelligible noise.[7]

The peculiar fate of the song of the gnat is prompted by more than the "comic preoccupation with excretion,"[8] for the terms of this brief story enlarge its application. The word used to describe the sound made by the gnat, *aidein*, or sing (158), ties it, at least initially, to poetry, traditionally a type of speech of great power, and, as we saw in chapter 1, cited by Gorgias as the prototype of all potent skillful speech. Thus a threat to poetry undermines the foundation upon which language's claim to power is erected. But *aidein* may have also tied the gnat more directly to the practice of rhetoric. For "sing" and "sing the same thing" were used by Aristophanes and others to mean "speak in vain," particularly in a legal context, and in *Birds* 39ff. this double meaning compares the Athenians to cicadas.[9] Such usage, along with the connection of the gnat's song to speech, suggests that our gnat may be a comically reduced stand-in for a more seriously poetic and rhetorical insect, the musical *tettix*, or cicada, which presides as well over Plato's very different dialogue about rhetoric, the *Phaedrus*.[10] Recognition of the cicada's shadowed presence clarifies the threat to traditional speech, and traditional understanding of speech, posed by Socrates' analysis and the (parodic) transformation worked on the song of the gnat.[11] The sophists promise to change our understanding of not only the "how," or mechanics, of the production of sound and speech, but coincidentally of the "why," or meaning, of such production as well. To put it comically, in the hands of the sophists *phone* and even *logos* itself will become like farts, irresponsible and nonvolitional, the result of causes within the speaker but in an important sense beyond his control. Such utterances are best understood not by interpretation of content but by observation of the compelling natural forces which caused them.[12] They are, in fact, just another kind of comic excretion.

The fate of the gnat reveals that those who believe it to sing are guilty of credulous anthropomorphizing. The natural world must be observed with strict respect for its independence and explained in terms of its inherent forces. But, as we learn in the story of the lizard (169–73), for all his attachment to this world, Socrates neither really inhabits it nor is aware of its dangers. Rather, his natural world is abstract, a set of laws, forces, pathways, and so forth, comfortable for those who live in a Thinkery. When he ventures outside and seeks to observe this world—here the tracks and revolutions of the distant moon (171ff.)—Socrates is ludicrously unfortunate: he is shat upon by a lizard on the roof.[13] This is a fate shared by Thales and Anaxagoras among others. Socrates is the familiar and ridiculous figure of the philosopher who is so foolishly attached to "higher" things that he forgets his necessary residence on earth among those who live "lower" realities. The shit of the lizard is his appropriate "downfall," the standard comic revenge of the "real," physical world for his neglect and indifference. In its incongruous change of planes, mental, physical, and contextual, it emphatically recalls him to the human position upon the ground[14] and prophesies that the natural world, postulated by the philosopher in theory but not understood in fact, will intervene to obstruct his view of higher things and cheat him of his discoveries. The fart that Socrates was so happy to assign to the gnat will come back to haunt him in the shit of the lizard.

Strepsiades' malicious amusement at this story (174) testifies to the pleasure afforded by the misfortunes of the "wise" and underlines the standard comic element in Socrates' plight. The fact that he and the audience would laugh in tandem links Strepsiades' own reaction to the Thinkery and its studies to the reaction of his fellow Athenians in the theater. Comedy and the comic man portrayed by and participating in this laughter do not forgive the philosopher his devotion to exalted "trivialities" and his irritating claim to our respect for this attitude.[15] The resentment thus aroused[16] vents itself in laughter when these figures are exposed as charlatans and vitally ignorant.[17] Their humiliation vindicates our mundane knowledge, while their inquiry is presented as silly and obscene. Further, this process suppresses Socrates' novelty and diminishes his threat. Comfortable patterns of inconsequence, the repetition of familiar comic devices reassure us, for in becoming a "Thales" (180), that stereotypical comic intellectual,[18] Socrates becomes simply a copy, one in a chain of similar figures. But such traditional comedy can only mask uneasiness and ambiguity, since in marginalizing the philosopher and philosophic speculation, it brings them to center stage and marks a continuing perception of difference. Laughter, which testifies to the discomfort this provokes, at once acknowledges (or creates) the philosopher's special status and denies it, just as pleasure in his humiliation requires a suspicion of his superiority, delight in the reduction of his studies bespeaks a sense of their potency.

Having introduced this comic philosopher, the *Clouds* now levels at him another familiar charge: all this offensive philosophizing is really only a pretense; philosophers are human like the rest of us. In their reactions to the story of the cloak (filched from the wrestling school *[palaistra]* under the cover of a geometry lesson and subsequently sold to buy food [175–79]), the student and Strepsiades, another potential student, covertly agree that high-minded philosophical studies mask, or are themselves, a spectacularly devious and successful means for the manipulation of others.[19] The theft of the cloak demonstrates the practical promise already evident in Strepsiades' description of the two *logoi:* enhanced ability to satisfy one's own needs, justly or unjustly.[20] The scholia on line 96 record that

Eupolis makes a fundamentally similar but more bitter accusation: "Socrates having taken up in turn the [verbal] display, singing Stesichorus to the lyre, stole the wine pourer."[21] Under the guise of participation and contribution, the philosopher transgresses the language and rules that sustain the common and conventional culture. The Socrates of Eupolis' play was a parasite who abused men's respect for a moment devoted to traditional speech in order to steal its prop, the wine pourer. Our Socrates, however, is more insidious; he does not confine his theft to material goods, but makes away with the very culture itself, or at least with his audience's ability and desire to participate in it. The cloak has already appeared as Strepsiades' social covering, threadbare from his social dislocation and consequent "hardships." He will lose it, or rather abandon it as the necessary price of his salvation, when he finally enters the Thinkery. This process is previewed here. In the company of Socrates, the discussion of abstract truths provides the opportunity to snatch away the old society and its rules which covered men like a cloak, enforcing certain actions, prohibiting others.[22] In the heart of the old *palaistra,* a school dedicated to the outmoded martial sports and the obsolete virtue of a well-tuned body,[23] Socrates uses the implements of the old culture to teach a new skill, verbal wrestling. The sophists are the trainers in this art, which promises profit and impunity.[24] Further, it works in secret, distracting its audience with "higher" things as it snatches away the very substance of their common social life. Right now, however, the threatening aspects of this story go unnoticed. Instead, the successful theft renews Socrates' attraction and rekindles Strepsiades' enthusiasm. In a phrase (183) that "is meant to remind us of urgent physical needs,"[25] he demands to enter the Thinkery and start studying immediately.

Strepsiades' response combines with the student's final anecdote to ensure that the audience will grasp the motive for Strepsiades' sudden interest in knowledge. Our hero is propelled not by zeal for abstract truths or love of learning but by a strictly self-interested utilitarian goal: saving his own skin. If this is corruption, then he is essentially corrupt long before he encounters Socrates. The following scene, his introduction to the Thinkery proper, confirms his motives and demonstrates their corrosive effect on the understanding, and potentially the practice, of philosophy. In the process, as Strepsiades confronts first the students and then Socrates himself, the comedy continues to flesh out the body/mind contrast already suggested; at the same time, however, the humor begins to cut both ways. Whereas before Strepsiades seemed primarily a vehicle for mockery of the philosophers, now he himself is mocked. As the comedy turns against its rustic tool, the audience is put in a delicate position, for Strepsiades' increasingly stupid and concrete responses must begin to alienate the spectators from him, and thus, indirectly, impugn the comic approach he seems to embody and to enjoy.

Our introduction to the students at once confirms their relationship with their master—like him they are preoccupied with things beyond, above, or below this world (186–94)—and comically insists on the corporality they prefer to forget. The appropriately pale and emaciated students enact with their bodies what should be concerns of the mind—bending over to study the earth, while their asses practice astronomy. Meanwhile Strepsiades' "straight" response to this, his assumption that they are searching for onions (188–90), mirrors in miniature his instrumental approach to the Thinkery's studies and his concrete and bodily orientation. As such, he typifies a response familiar to the audience. His fixation on money, food, and sex, his reduction of the abstract to the concrete, his standard jokes are the staples of comedy, or at least a certain type of comedy,[26] and mark Strepsiades as the comic "man on the street," representative of the views, motives, and desires postulated as characteristic of the common man who inhabits (and watches) comedy.[27]

The next few lines begin to develop what this means.

> Στ: τί δῆθ' ὁ πρωκτὸς εἰς τὸν οὐρανὸν βλέπει;
> Μα: αὐτὸς καθ' αὑτὸν ἀστρονομεῖν διδάσκεται.
>   ἀλλ' εἴσιθ', ἵνα μὴ 'κεῖνος ὑμῖν ἐπιτύχῃ.
> Στ: μήπω γε μήπω γ', ἀλλ' ἐπιμεινάντων, ἵνα
>   αὐτοῖσι κοινώσω τι πραγμάτιον ἐμόν.
>   (193–97)

> STREP: Why then do their [the students'] assholes (*proktos*)
>   look into the heavens?
> STUDENT: They are learning astronomy by themselves.
>   But [you students] go inside, so the master won't meet you.
> STREP: Not yet, not yet, but let them stay so
>   I will impart my little affair/penis (*pragmation*) to them.

This is the humor of the man who views philosophers and speculation through the folkloric prism of the iconic and generic Thales. His initial obscene question emphatically exposes the students in their philosophical posture as contemptibly human in the grossest physical way. His joke/threat that he will rape/discuss with them extrapolates from what has gone before and plays on the standard comic use of *pragma* for penis.[28] The pointed double meaning, which in forcing together two such incompatible planes in a single word repeats in miniature the mind/body or abstract/concrete dichotomy developed in these scenes, calls on a comic *logos* which apparently reflects everyday vernacular usage to attack not just students but studies and the whole philosophical orientation. Even if Strepsiades' joke is as yet playful, the very possibility of such a play on words is ominous. The future of the students in a world of Strepsiadeses does not look bright. And this is the world of the audience, at least for the moment.[29] Our laughter at the wit of the pun cannot be cleanly separated from the comical, generic, vulgar aggression it releases. Such laughter compromises the spectators as Strepsiades' accomplices[30] and suggests that this kind of comedy taps what it represents, a hostility founded on incomprehension. Coupled with a limited and driving self-interest, this becomes a combination of which Strepsiades is only a parodic and extreme expression.

Strepsiades' joke, thus, stages a vulgar comedy hostile to the prospect of philosophy and exemplifies its approach—physically vulgar, crudely personal, and intellectually limited. The next scene, his entry into the Thinkery, discredits both him and this comedy. Already labeled crude and boorish, Strepsiades' mystification in the face of the ordinary, capped by his failure to understand a simple map (206ff.), makes it clear that he is the new comic victim: "intellectually mocked for his failure to grasp conceptual notions or symbolic logic."[31] Our laughter at his mistakes now renders our earlier laughter with him at the students' expense embarrassing and suspect. There is a certain reluctance to identify with one so clearly stupid and so obviously the target of ridicule. Conversely our sympathy is engaged for those who must suffer such a fool. Green suggests the proper response: the mockery of Strepsiades "should make us look more carefully at his attitude to the φροντιστήριον [Thinkery] and its educational dialectic."[32] Strepsiades and his reactions become, in one sense, a warning. To allow him to represent us or to take him as univocal with Aristophanes, thus making of the *Clouds* simply one long figurative buggering of philosophy and philosophers, culminating in their playful destruction, would be insulting to all concerned. Thus at the conclusion of this scene, our laughter may have changed a little.[33] For as we reject Strepsiades and move beyond the comedy of generic shit and violence that he enacts and enjoys, we do not abandon it. Rather, this type of comedy is to be put to new uses, incorporated with its conventions into a more comprehensive humor that uses it, mocks it, and examines the laughter it provokes.

Strepsiades' meeting with Socrates both continues their constrasting characterizations and inaugurates a new type of comedy (or perhaps resumes the comedy of the first two stories of the student). The new game begins with Socrates' first words, for the hilarious novelty of his strange entrance, which critics have likened to that of a paratragic *deus ex machina*,[34] predicts his distance from ordinary men and ordinary modes of thought. A true resident of the Thinkery, Socrates is elevated in word and deed. As he himself explains in lines 227–34, he has ascended to a drying rack[35] to improve his mind and facilitate understanding of *ta meteora,* or celestial phenomena. For, as he explains, he hopes on high to become pure thought *(noema)*, mingling with its sister element, the air, free of the pull of the body and its juices, avoiding the universal law that the earth draws moisture to itself, as happens even in watercress (227–34).

Staging and speech mark this Socrates immediately as the brilliant parodic extrapolation of the approach to intellectuals we have seen thus far in the play. Like his students, Socrates suffers the hilarious indignity of being forced to enact his mental gymnastics bodily, while at the same time this elevation plays on generic conventions to label him abstracted philosopher, intellectual boaster, and hubristic atheist.[36] His explanation of this position may, at first, be impressive, or incomprehensible,[37] enough to command a stunned silence, even if it appears to reduce the definitive human activity of thinking to a mechanical process governed by laws operative across the natural continuum. But the concluding watercress (234) seems to ensure the comic, nonsensical flavor, releasing our pent up (confused?) laughter. As the level of discourse changes in a disconcerting way, theory intrudes into daily life, problematizing our understanding of ordinary things while seeming to trivialize the problems of philosophy. And if we are still wondering what is going on, we share this problem with Strepsiades, whose foolish rejoinder—"the thought draws the moisture into the watercress" (236)—mindlessly repeats and concretizes a few words of the mysterious utterance he has just heard.[38]

However, while line 236 is clearly a joke, it is not clear at whose expense. First of all, we laugh at Strepsiades; he is once again the bumpkin, incapable of abstract reasoning. But Strepsiades' silly errors may seem to uncover a larger one in Socrates, and one which irritates by its pretension to superior knowledge. Both speech and rejoinder (which does, in fact, jumble the categories that the aristophanic Socrates had kept separate) seem equally products of *logos* alone, used without regard to sense and reference. Our laughter, which dismisses Strepsiades and Socrates in the same breath, denying the difference between them, enjoys the intuitive rightness of this perception and admits the relief of evading the problem posed by Socrates. Yet while the humorous identification of buffoon and philosopher once again takes symbolic revenge for the embarrassing complexities of philosophic discourse, it also seems to put Strepsiades and the audience in similar positions. Both fail the puzzle of Socrates' words.

For Socrates' introduction is not purely nonsensical—it has a certain comically "philosophical" coherence and rigor. Even if we agree with the judgment of Socrates implicit in Strepsiades' response, his nonsense should not blind us to the comic "accuracy" of Socrates' reasoning. For the hilarious speech given Socrates, which has long been recognized as parodying Diogenes of Apollonia, for whom the vital intelligent principle was air, mercilessly mocks the jargon and assumptions of such speculation—it does not actually transgress the basic theories. Unlike his character, Aristophanes is not just repeating a few words gleaned at random from a discourse he neither cares about nor understands. Ambrosino (1985) has demonstrated, point by point, the comic congruence between our Socrates and his model. Even the ridiculous watercress makes (comic) philosophical sense; it features in intellectual discussion as an example of a plant gluttonous for liquid.[39] The scene thus stages the type of comedy promised by the punning introduction of the sophists and illustrates its strategy: Aristophanes' brilliant parody departs from the claims and practices of the sophists themselves, ferreting out their most hilarious and troublesome consequences. What we see and hear is not the nonsense of unwitting repetition that deforms through ignorance, but a *logos* with a certain grammar, that obeys certain rules. Thus this scene, our introduction to Socrates, gives us our first taste of that comic procedure identified here by Ambrosino, one which "consists in taking something or someone mercilessly at his word, and in fixing him to the extreme, exaggerated consequences of his point of view."[40] Or to put it in another way, Aristophanes' art transforms and comments upon its original by taking it at its word, but comically speaking.

But Socrates' words have still another function. Although not "rhetorical" per se, they are the first words of a sophistic speaker heard in the play and convey attitudes and assumptions that are key to the *Clouds'* portrait. This is a man who aspires to be a wise soul resident in a Thinkery, not body on our common earth, or even citizen.[41] Before, in the story of the lizard, we saw the conventional comic interpretation and reaction; now we learn the philosophical reasoning behind this elevated posture. The normal human position and all that it implies perpetuate our ignorance, distorting and suppressing the play of the mind. Such an attitude marks Socrates as strikingly distant from the concerns of ordinary comic man. The language he is assigned continues this characterization, for it shows Socrates to be more than willing to reuse and abuse the old *logos,* just as he has discarded the traditional values it expressed.[42] But while Socrates may appear blasphemous and hubristic to Strepsiades and the audience, the "colloquial prosody" in his opening line[43] jokingly contrasts this popular reaction with Socrates' own blasé attitude. For Socrates is simply reporting the facts as he sees them. He has gone aloft because his studies have indicated this as the best way of observing and operating in a theoretical, amoral, and atheistic universe of laws and forces. This rejection of the body in favor of the mind, otherworldliness, and freedom of speech and conception will be central to the *Clouds'* Socrates, his impact on Strepsiades, and vice versa.[44]

Strepsiades, however, neither understands what the elevated Socrates is doing, nor does he care. Unable to perceive the relationship between this babble and his all too earthly problems, he attempts to call Socrates back down to more mundane concerns.[45] What Strepsiades wants is the *logos* that pays nothing back, and he swears by the gods he will pay whatever is required (244–46). As Strauss observes, given what Strepsiades wishes to learn, his promise to pay can hardly carry much weight; this is something Socrates should consider.[46] Likewise, the implications of this *logos'* name are worth the attention of the spectators as well. For by identifying the *hetton logos* in these terms, the comedy begins its characterization as reflective. It is Strepsiades himself who wishes to pay nothing back; his words here recall lines 114ff. We (and Strepsiades, too) should begin to suspect that this *logos* will not repay study.

In any case, instruction commences immediately. Socrates begins at the beginning; his hours aloft have enabled him to state definitively:

> . . . πρῶτον γὰρ θεοὶ
> ἡμῖν νόμισμ᾽ οὐκ ἔστι.
> (247–48)

> . . . for, first of all, gods
> have no currency *(nomisma)* with us.

Ignoring Strepsiades' mystification and bumbling attempts to understand,[47] he continues impatiently:

> βούλει τὰ θεῖα πράγματ᾽ εἰδέναι σαφῶς
> ἅττ᾽ ἐστὶν ὀρθῶς; . . .
> καὶ συγγενέσθαι ταῖς Νεφέλαισιν εἰς λόγους,
> ταῖς ἡμετέραισι δαίμοσιν;
>
> (250–53)

> Do you want to see/know divine affairs clearly
> what they are correctly? . . .
> and to have intercourse *(suggenesthai)* with the clouds,
> our goddesses *(daimones)* in propositions *(eis logous)*?

The clouds' introduction at this point is no accident. As we have seen from the beginning, freedom from the restraints imposed by a moral theistic universe is central to the practice of the *hetton logos*.[48] The gods must go. Nor is Socrates removing one set of gods only to substitute another. There is no contradiction between his atheism and his subsequent introduction of the clouds.[49] Rather, as suggested by *eis logous* here and the later use of *epideixis,* or rhetorical display, in line 269,[50] the clouds are introduced as arguments. Strepsiades will meet them in conversation; they are goddesses *(daimones)* because of their power as propositions.[51] Using the clouds, Socrates can expose the reality of "divine affairs," namely that they are not divine at all. But the clouds themselves are not immune to this process. The sequence of arguments initiated by their entrance will end by stripping them of their independence and implicitly their divinity as well.

But if Socrates hoped to raise Strepsiades to his own theoretical, verbal level, he is disappointed. Aroused by the verb *suggenesthai,* which can mean both conversational and sexual "intercourse," Strepsiades agrees eagerly (253).[52] The misunderstanding typifies his orientation toward the entire philosophical endeavor. Strepsiades is, and will remain, comically ruled by the body, not so much rejecting things of the mind as not even thinking of them. The beauties of discourse will never seduce him like even the thought of the female form can. All this is lost on Socrates, however. Unaware of Strepsiades' desires and unsurprised by what he takes to be enthusiasm for things intellectual and linguistic, he summons the clouds into the argument with an impressive prayer.[53] The clouds are invoked, given divine parentage, and invested with epithets that simultaneously suggest their roles as natural phenomena and as usurpers of the gods.[54] The honorifics "revered goddesses," "mistresses," "highly honored" (σεμναὶ θεαὶ 265, δέσποιναι 266, πολυτίμητοι 269) confirm their rivalry with the Olympians; description as "those who send thunder and lightning" (βροντησικέραυνοι 265) betrays the form it will take.[55] Zeus is the traditional keeper of thunder and lightning. These are his weapons, indicating and sustaining his supreme power. With these he expresses his will and punishes those who flout divine rules. When the clouds are identified as the origin of thunder and lightning, their role in things to come is clear—they will make the celestial presence of Zeus redundant. Understanding the clouds is the first step to the oven world which is the natural home of sophistic rhetoric.

In response to Socrates' summons, the audience finally hears the voice of the comic chorus, and Strepsiades, the voice of the sophistic "deities," who will conduct him to the *adikos logos.* These are the punningly fluent clouds, whose very first word, *aenaoi* 275, proclaims them simultaneously natural phenomena and rhetorical *logos,* "ever-flowing" and "glib."[56] The nature of what follows has occasioned much controversy. The tragic/lyric elements of the clouds' ode— elevated, even homeric language, tragic clichés in 285 and possibly 290, retention of lyric alpha, dactylic meter, and extensive responsion[57]—have prompted some critics to interpret the chorus' entering ode, or parodos, as an essentially humorous creation, which begins the work of establishing the clouds' mocking, rhetorical character.[58] Others take it more seriously.[59] The assessment of tone is important, for the nature of the clouds' first utterance is seen as definitive for their role throughout. Those who find the chorus unsmiling here tend to favor a similar interpretation of the end of the play as well: the chorus, endowed at the moment of its entrance with a noncomic status which implicitly condemns the blasphemy of Socrates, assumes an equally "straight" and "tragic" role with his downfall. Extrapolating from such a reading of the chorus, this interpretive line often concludes that Strepsiades was correct in burning the Thinkery and that the play's final scene, beginning with the clouds' speech (1454ff.), stages the aristophanic "message" about the proper solution to the sophistic/socratic problem.[60] As Köhnken points out, this assessment of the parodos ignores its highly comic context: the parodic prayer of Socrates, the comic reactions of Strepsiades before and during the ode in 267ff. and 293ff., the parody of dithyramb that follows in lines 335–38, as well as the comic meter in the last lines of each stanza.[61] This context makes the exalted tone and formal structure seem not so much serious as surprisingly, and even ludicrously, incongruous.[62]

The truth may be somewhere in the middle, for while the ode may be read as legitimate homage to Athens, and savored as such, its context and the comic history of its language also compel the audience to keep a skeptical distance. For the clouds' ode is consistent with what we shall learn to be their nature. It reflects both the manner of their invocation and the desires and expectations of those who see them and whom they see—Socrates, Strepsiades, and the assembled Athenians.[63] For just as the clouds' rainy yet divine nature corresponds to their introduction and matches Strepsiades' fears of getting wet, so their words both echo Socrates' prayer[64] and anticipate, in the strophe, the comically debunked, pretentious language Strepsiades cites as inspired (and possibly spoken) by clouds (335ff.).[65]

The reuse, or anticipation, of clichéd language in the strophe provides an important clue to the possible tone of the parodos as a whole: perhaps what is to seem ridiculous in Strepsiades' mouth is at least suspect in the clouds'. Thus one critic has found the strophe to be "a string of predictable epithets [which] enforces an overpowering sense of genre," and as the clouds move from heaven to earth, it seems likely that the antistrophe matches clichéd poetry with clichéd praise of Attica. There "lyrical elevation is at its most extreme, cliché is pervasive and inflation seems more evident than ever."[66] Silk attributes this to Aristophanes' failures as a lyric poet; parody may be an equally likely explanation.[67] For if the strophe is taken as mirroring and mocking Strepsiades' literary tastes and expectations, the antistrophe reaches in its reflective mockery beyond the dramatic audience to the theatrical one, the Athenian crowd. In this context, the antistrophe's standard phrasing—*liparos* is a "stock epithet,"[68] 299–301 contain conventional phrasing, Cecrops is widely used in contemporary political rhetoric,[69] the praise of the Athenian piety is common, as is noting the number of her festivals—becomes more than simple, if generic, *laudes Atticae*. It recalls the language dismissed as seductive and misleading in the parabasis of the *Acharnians*. There the poet was praised for hindering the audience's foolish pleasure in flattery (ἥδεσθαι θωπευομένους *Ach.* 635) which made them ripe for rhetorical deception (ἐξαπατᾶσθαι *Ach.* 634; see 636) by foreign/unusual speeches (ξενικοῖσι λόγοις *Ach.* 634, often taken as a reference to Gorgias). For the Athenians' susceptibility was such that the simplest clichés, intoning "violet crowned" (ἰοστέφανος *Ach.*

637) or "gleaming" (λιπαρός *Ach.* 639 = our own *liparos* above) won them over completely. Memory of that rebuke should temper our pleasure here. Rather than being creatures strayed from tragedy, it is possible that with their first words the clouds speak a language appropriate for verbal deities summoned by a sophist, mouthing rhetorical (and religious) commonplaces which are translated into a bewitching spell only by the delight of the hearer. The last lines, however, break through the dramatic/rhetorical enchantment. The allusion in comic meter to the comic chorus' provocations merges chorus and clouds to remind the audience of the larger purpose of these *logoi.* What we see is mockery not just of Socrates and Strepsiades, but, through them and their reactions, of the assembled Athenians too. Much better to let Strepsiades enact the complex interaction of *logos* and desire on stage than to reproduce this process in the stands.

But what may seem comic mockery to the audience is terrifying reality to Strepsiades. His reaction is fearful and, of course, physical. While at first, during Socrates' prayer, he only fears getting wet (267–68), after the thunderous opening strophe his situation becomes more complicated.

> καὶ σέβομαί γ', ὦ πολυτίμητοι, καὶ βούλομαι ἀνταποπαρδεῖν
> πρὸς τὰς βροντάς· οὕτως αὐτὰς τετραμαίνω καὶ πεφόβημαι.
> κεἰ θέμις ἐστίν, νυνί γ' ἤδη, κεἰ μὴ θέμις ἐστί, χεσείω.
>
> $\qquad\qquad\qquad\qquad\qquad\qquad\qquad\qquad\qquad$ (293–95)

And I do feel awe, indeed, O highly honored ones, and I want
  to fart back *(antapopardein)*
to the thunders; I am trembling so at them and am so afraid.
And if it is right *(themis)*, now, in fact, and even if it is
  not right, I am going to shit *(khezein)*.

The clouds' voices have awakened in Strepsiades a religious awe, but one whose constraints are vitally limited. For although this awe implicates him in a moral and religious world—he wonders if his actions are *themis,* or right—its result is to exile him from that world. He's going to fart, and right *(themis)* or not, he has to shit.[70] Strepsiades puts his need strongly; both his situation and its expression, *khezein,* the word he uses for "shit," are popular, farcically vulgar, and practically confined to Old Comedy.[71] Such an end to a line which began by weighing the requirements of *themis* is jarringly funny, emphasizing the highly comic situation that, while derived from Strepsiades' awe, surely cannot be *themis* by any standards. As Fisher notes, "The audience would laugh with the sudden release of tension after the pseudo-serious poetry of the chorus. Aristophanes releases it suddenly but predictably—the audience now knows what sort of interruption to expect from Strepsiades."[72]

The audience knows not only what to expect from Strepsiades, but from comedy; Strepsiades' reaction is, in fact, standard. Shitting is the normal comic reaction to fear, and the entire subject of shit is the hallmark of comedy, always able to raise a laugh, used by every comic writer including Aristophanes.[73] Its effect, through a kind of comic synecdoche, is to reveal an embarrassing (but universal) subjection to the body and its drives.[74] Thus Strepsiades' appropriate religous awe and consequent regard for *themis* paradoxically contrast with his equally appropriate comic reaction to the fear this awe engenders. And once again the messy results leave no doubt of the priority of the body and its necessities. We are left to draw the inevitable comic inference: that in a competition, the corporal exigencies will outweigh all "higher" considerations, of decorum, of morality, and of reverence.[75] Like Socrates, but for different reasons, the comic Strepsiades is, in the last analysis, beyond (or below) the reach of religious strictures, even before his instruction begins. But the audience, too, is not exempt from this comic appraisal. For our laughter here, and its subject, recall Strepsiades' pleasure at the story of the shit of the lizard.[76] There audience and character laughed in tandem; here Strepsiades is the butt. Yet our laughter creates a contradictory movement, for while it distances us from him, at the same time such similar taste in jokes must affiliate spectators and character to prove the comic point. For pleasure in such things is itself typically comic, at once the source and justification of comedy and confirmation of its perspective.[77]

This complex relationship between the audience, Strepsiades, and the kind of comedy he enjoys and embodies is developed further in Socrates' rebuke.

> οὐ μὴ σκώψει μηδὲ ποήσεις ἅπερ οἱ τρυγοδαίμονες οὗτοι,
> ἀλλ᾽ εὐφήμει· μέγα γάρ τι θεῶν κινεῖται σμῆνος ἀοιδαῖς.
>
> (296–97)

Don't joke nor do what those wretched comedians *(trugodaimones)* do,
but be reverently quiet; for some great swarm of goddesses is moving
to the song.

Because jokes about shitting are "the purest kind of obscene comedy"[78] in their ludicrously complete stripping away of civilized veneer, they can come to typify one aspect of the generically comic and often form the text of jokes about genre—about the writing of comedy and about the comic vision. The first fifteen lines of the *Frogs* are the best known example, but the same dynamic is at work here. *Trugodaimones* are comedians; the expression plays on the pun *trugoidia* that comedy uses to describe itself and differentiate its earthy genre from the exalted *tragoidia* of the tragic play.[79] Since line 50 we have known that Strepsiades smells of *trux*, the raw wine comedy parodically puts at the beginning of its mocking song. In talking about shit, he acts like a comic playwright, not because he wishes to mock,[80] nor because his voice is to be taken as identical with Aristophanes', but because his actions and reactions effect the raw and unrestrained revelation of physical imperatives which is characteristic of comic practice. In his rebuke, Socrates at once acknowledges this nature of comedy and brings to center stage the polemic between it and philosophy. Strepsiades and comedians are chastised for reminding us of the body when what is called for is something quite different—holy silence and the reverential contemplation of higher things, particularly the achievements of the philosophic intellect. The crack in the dramatic illusion implicit here in line 296 (a crack that will turn into a full-scale rupture in a few lines) recalls this larger perspective. It suggests what, in a few moments, our play will insist on: that while Strepsiades may be our comic stand-in, the audience can be something more. We are invited to participate in the comedy not just as further examples of human dependence on the body and indifference verging on hostility to things of the mind, but as spectators for whom the *Clouds'* characters, plot, and humor, vulgar and otherwise, are points of departure for reflection, to be read inside the rules of the genre and the polemic the comic Socrates has just named.

4

Martial Speech, Fluid Shapes,
Thunderous Sounds: Lines 314–509

From the moment Socrates ennumerates the gifts of the clouds, we realize that our *Clouds* will consider rhetoric in its strongest and most polemical sense: as invincible verbal violence. As we saw in chapter 1, this angle on sophistic speech was not an invention of Aristophanes. Rather, the genius of his conception lies in its topicality; no member of his audience could have failed to hear in his outrageous comedy the voice, however distorted, of his models.[1] We are to witness something "entirely" sophistic, but first, intervening between Strepsiades' introduction to this martial art and his preliminary instruction is the appearance of the cloud chorus. The previous scenes started the development of an instructive and ambivalent relationship between Strepsiades and the audience. The entrance of the clouds continues this. Multiple ruptures of dramatic illusion recall the spectators to their special status as collected Athenians at the comic festival. Extensive play with the relationship of comedy to the reality which it confronts reminds them that they witness not "real life" but comic plot, in which they should attend to not one voice but their harmony. Thus as we watch Strepsiades learn his first sophistic lesson—there are no gods—our wider perspective and the comic convention that compares demagogic rhetoric to thunder and farting lets us in on the joke: as thunder *(bronte)* becomes fart *(porde)*, voice and speech *(phone)* will not be far behind. A rapacious stomach, or *gaster,* drives speakers to fart out what may appear to the naive to be their thunderous words. As Aristophanes' imagery begins to affiliate his comedy with the bleakest assessment of the "pleasure of speech" and its true basis, a comic commentary on Socrates' views starts to take shape. Far from beings of airy speculation—as Socrates in his elevated posture seems to assume—sophistic rhetors and students are, in fact, kin to comic man, motivated not by the rarified requirements of mind and intelligence, *nous* and *gnome,* but by hungers of the body. Ultimately, the sophistic hero, like his comic counterpart and the other animals as well, is defined and driven not by *sophia,* or wisdom, but by his belly.

The suggestion of violent language we noted in Strepsiades' final words in the prologue is confirmed by Socrates' identification of the clouds. When Strepsiades hesitantly guesses that they must be heroines,[2] Socrates impatiently responds:

49

ἥκιστ', ἀλλ' οὐράνιαι Νεφέλαι, μεγάλαι θεαὶ ἀνδράσιν ἀργοῖς,
αἵπερ γνώμην καὶ διάλεξιν καὶ νοῦν ἡμῖν παρέχουσιν
καὶ τερατείαν καὶ περίλεξιν καὶ κροῦσιν καὶ κατάληψιν.

(316–18)

Not at all, but heavenly clouds, great goddesses to idle men
the very ones who bestow intelligence *(gnome)* and discourse and mind on us
and [the ability] to talk marvels, circumlocute, strike *(krousis)* and capture *(katalepsis).*

These heavenly clouds (whose cosmic role will be discussed below) share Socrates' elevation and confer the mental qualities vital to sophistic speculation. But this is not all. The list which begins with "intelligence" *(gnome)* ends with "strike" and "capture" *(krousis* and *katalepsis),* terms marked by the suffix *-sis* and their meaning as the tactics of a verbal brawl.[3] Dover translates *krouein,* the verbal form of *krousis,* as to " 'strike' an audience with a telling point or an opponent with an argument which discomfits him."[4] *Katalepsis* echoes this; Starkie translates it "perhaps 'seizing' in the sense of capturing the mind by means of rhetoric."[5] Another possible meaning is "capturing" or "occupying" the advantageous positions in an argument.[6]

The speculative/martial flavor of Socrates' description of the clouds is comically exaggerated and transformed in Strepsiades' reply:

ταῦτ' ἄρ' ἀκούσασ' αὐτῶν τὸ φθέγμ' ἡ ψυχή μου πεπότηται
καὶ λεπτολογεῖν ἤδη ζητεῖ καὶ περὶ καπνοῦ στενολεσχεῖν
καὶ γνωμιδίῳ γνώμην νύξασ' ἑτέρῳ λόγῳ ἀντιλογῆσαι·

(319–21)

That's why having heard their voice, my soul is aflutter
and already desires to argue subtly/trivially *(leptologein)* and to quibble
    narrowly *(stenoleskhein)* about smoke *(kapnos)*
and having struck *(nuttein)* thought with thoughtlet, to refute *(antilogein)* another *logos;*

These lines begin a complex characterization of the *logos* that is the object of Strepsiades' quest. First of all it is clearly philosophical. The clouds' voices have swept Strepsiades away in a familiar transport: his soul is elevated and winged; he experiences a (parodic) desire to reason and speak subtly about esoteric (and trivial) matters.[7] Thus the comedy again, but more explicitly, proposes the winging quality of *logos* famous in *Birds* 1440ff. and discussed in chapter 2.[8] But there is more here than simple parody of elevated intellectual pretensions. Rather, constrasting comic perspectives are built into the language of the passage and shadow the philosophical ideal from the beginning. Winging and wings can allude to *phalloi* and erections.[9] This sexual overtone to Strepsiades' excitement (which recalls his arousal by the matchmaker and hopes for the cloudy goddesses) stresses by comic synecdoche his complicity in the *logos* that seduces him. Far from detaching him from his earthly concerns, Strepsiades' "verbal" elevation is part and parcel of his solution to them. Further the instrumental *logos* his aroused soul desires is mocked not just as trivial, but as curiously reminiscent of the song/fart of the gnat. Both are characterized by *leptos* and *stenos,* and even if the context may initially suggest a "physical" sense there but a "mental" one here, such a dichotomy cannot stand in the latter part of this scene. There we will learn that human voice and gnat's noise do, in fact, sound for reasons that comically converge: each in its own way is a product of the gut.

The remainder of Strepsiades' introduction to the clouds will flesh out these suggestions; the last line of our current passage confirms instead another aspect of the sophistic rhetoric. Line 321 is a parody of Homer, one of two such images in the extant plays of Aristophanes, both in the *Clouds*.[10] The homeric allusion, the metaphoric equation of sophistic refutation *(antilogein)*[11] to striking in battle *(nuttein)*, and the sophistic and martial terminology all send clear signals. What Socrates promises and Strepsiades hopes to learn is sophistic rhetoric at its most controversial: the violently effective language which is the perfect weapon for speakers who are heroes, able to subdue all comers.[12] And while Socrates may imagine lofty disputation, Strepsiades has quite other hopes; such a *logos* is to be the force that will make him more availing in the verbal battles here on earth. Lines 320–21 at once portray this discourse as frivolous and marvel at its potency, for we are left with little doubt that if Strepsiades can learn what Socrates has to teach, his little notions (321) will prevail over much more weighty arguments.[13]

As is appropriate for patrons of rhetoric and deities of *logos,* the clouds' *phthegma* alone, their unaided voice or language, has sufficed to provoke all this. After all, as Gorgias points out, one of the amazing things about *logos* is that it performs its wonderous works invisibly.[14] As an argument, it is intellectual knowledge of the existence of the clouds, not their physical presence, that is important. Seeing them with the eyes is, or should be, irrelevant. But it is hardly likely that the clouds or the chorus will be allowed to remain invisible much longer. Not only does the literally minded Strepsiades want to see them, but after their strange absence during the parodos, the audience does too. In lines 322–27 Aristophanes plays with both these expectations and desires, confirming two very different aspects of the clouds—as goddesses and clouds for Strepsiades and as chorus for the audience.

The entrance of the chorus is marked by numerous ruptures of dramatic illusion[15] that ensure that the cloud chorus can neither submerge their identity as chorus in their dramatic persona as clouds nor shed their theatrical context. The game begins immediately. When Socrates instructs Strepsiades to look at the clouds on Mount Parnes (323ff.), Strepsiades' inability to see them is mysterious, the audience's is not—Parnes can be seen from almost everywhere in Attica, except the theater; there the Acropolis obscures the view.[16] The experience of the audience is thus only functionally equivalent to that of Strepsiades. We are sitting in the theater; he is at some unspecified place in Attica. We await the entrance of a comic chorus presented by Aristophanes, which will take the form of clouds; Strepsiades expects the entrance of cloud-goddesses invoked for him by Socrates. Our experience of the beings that are about to enter cannot and should not reproduce the characters'; nor as we pass together through the experience of "philosophy" and "rhetoric," should our perception duplicate Strepsiades'. The following lines trumpet this necessary doubleness of the audience's experience,[17] and add yet a third layer to the cloud chorus' identity. For while Strepsiades can only really see the clouds after they are fully on stage, implicated in Socrates' argument and the world of the plot, the audience has already had another look at them. Line 325 alludes to the fact that the moment in which the clouds become visible is, perforce, the moment when the members of the chorus line up to enter the theater.[18] Lines 326ff. proclaim this theatrical necessity; they announce the clouds' arrival not from heaven but through the *eisodos,* the same entrance to the theater used earlier by the audience.[19] Seeing them there, we realize not only that they are a comic chorus taking up the role of clouds, but that individual Athenian citizens, like the spectators, make up this theatrical unit.[20] This suggests another perspective on the clouds' role as goddesses of speech. For if it is the clouds as deities, arguments, subjects, and metaphors that inspire the newfangled *logos* of trendy intellectuals, it is as representatives of the Athenian public[21] that they provide the rewards that nourish the practitioners of the verbal arts with the types of delicacies catalogued by Strepsiades in line 339.

The famous explanation of the clouds' female shape continues to play with the ambiguities of their introduction. What Strepsiades and the audience both want to know is why these so-called clouds look like women, with noses.[22] Normally, as the bewildered Strepsiades points out, clouds resemble wool. In response, Socrates, through questioning, leads Strepsiades to admit that "wild" clouds often take shapes. Socrates then enlightens his pupil; in fact:

Σω. γίγνονται πάνθ' ὅτι βούλονται· κᾆτ' ἢν μὲν ἴδωσι κομήτην
ἄγριόν τινα τῶν λασίων τούτων, οἱόνπερ τὸν Ξενοφάντου,
σκώπτουσαι τὴν μανίαν αὐτοῦ κενταύροις ἤκασαν αὐτάς.
Στ. τί γὰρ ἢν ἅρπαγα τῶν δημοσίων κατίδωσι Σίμωνα, τί δρῶσιν;
Σω. ἀποφαίνουσαι τὴν φύσιν αὐτοῦ λύκοι ἐξαίφνης ἐγένοντο.

(348–52)

> soc: They [the clouds] become everything that they wish; and if they
>   see a long-haired
>   brute/pederast some one of these hairy men, such as the son
>   of Xenophantos,
>   mocking *(skoptousai)* his mania they make themselves like centaurs.
> strep: What if they see the robber of the public monies, Simon, what do they do?
> soc: Showing forth his nature *(physis),* they suddenly become wolves.

This mocking reflection of those the clouds behold can, perhaps, be connected with their "natural" habits; however, within the logic of the play, Socrates' explanation is a little hard to understand. While most of the clouds' shapes reveal man's nature to be best understood in animal terms, thus repositioning him in the natural world, it is not easy to imagine the centaur as other than fabulous and metaphoric, nor to overlook a certain judgmental quality of the clouds' mockery that seems inappropriate in the sophistic universe.[23] When Socrates explains that the clouds look like women because they have seen the effeminate Cleisthenes (355), we are able to make sense of this only if, like Strepsiades, we share, or are at least familiar with, the common view that Cleisthenes is culpably feminine himself.

The multiple ambiguities of Socrates' description of the clouds have led to an equally large number of interpretations. Fundamental seems to be Strauss' observation that in taking various shapes to be seen here on earth, the clouds are "goddesses of imitation and therefore the natural teachers of all imitative or likeness-making arts, and hence in particular of the art of speaking."[24] Thus we can detect precepts of the art of speaking behind the clouds' fluidity and the way they choose their forms. Their changing and reflective nature mimics the chameleon-like freedom from fixed content of the reactive *hetton,* or weaker, *logos,* who as the prefix *anti* suggests, mirrors in stance and arguments the views of its opponent, but from a changed perspective.[25] Success in this endeavor, and in all speaking, requires a *logos* flexible enough to respond appropriately to the arguments and also the souls of its interlocutors, applying the celebrated principle of *kairos*—that is, speaking according to the moment or opportunity.[26] And *kairos* may well determine the clouds' shape now. Only after learning that they appear female to mock Cleisthenes does Strepsiades address them directly as goddesses for the first time (358ff.).

But the clouds have an even closer affiliation with speech. For our clouds are known only through *logos* and are inaccessible outside it; to appear in the comedy they must shake off their natural form (of clouds 288) and enter looking like something else, namely women. But these female shapes are not themselves what is to be communicated. We are not supposed to think of women when we see the clouds, but of Cleisthenes, and not just of Cleisthenes, but of his conduct, and not only of his conduct, but of an evaluation of it: that he is effeminate. Thus, as Ambrosino has pointed out, the clouds' shapes function not literally but as part of a code whose elements have no "natural" or "necessary" connection (or resemblance) to what is to be communicated. Their forms are as arbitrary as *logos,* and thus must be "translated" for those unfamiliar with the system:[27] a service Socrates performs here for Strepsiades, and for us.[28] These aspects of the clouds' communication lead Ambrosino to conclude that the clouds represent the possibility of the production of signs in general and, in particular, of language.[29]

Ambrosino draws many powerful conclusions from this insight; however, in assigning the clouds a fixed role and significance, even if an extremely flexible one, she fails to account for the many different ways the chorus can function within the play—and in particular, fails to consider their comic dimension at all. But this is something our *Clouds* insists upon. For the charm of this passage is its open flirtation with the clouds' existence as chorus, assigning to them both comedy's subject matter and Aristophanes' creative technique.[30] If the clouds are to represent language, it must be, above all, comic language, and aristophanic comic language at that. For it is comedy whose special subject is the mockery (*skoptein* 350) of mania, here briefly that of the standard targets Cleonymos and Cleisthenes,[31] at greater length the other projects—finding peace, judging lawsuits, learning to speak sophistically—that motivate its plots. These manias, which are not insanities but passions resembling erotic desire in their crazy intensity (as the context of 348ff. shows),[32] are rooted in man's nature, whose individual and collective outline they reveal. But reveal aristophanically, for the clouds mirror or mock these manias indirectly, assuming one shape, that of a wolf, to mock something further, Simon's lust for public money (351–52). Their strategy, thus, is

Aristophanes' own, for the essence of his art is metaphor and allusion, the humorous (re)vision of the manias of Athens and Athenians into mocking emblematic spectacle.[33]

Thus grafted onto the mockery of Simon and his fellow victims are the issues not so much of *logos* in general, but of comic *logos* and how it functions. And Socrates' lesson to Strepsiades is Aristophanes' to us about how to interpret the comic shapes of our clouds/*Clouds*. But to understand it, it is necessary to distinguish the levels of their "discourse" a little more precisely. Our clouds/*Clouds* communicate doubly, literally and metaphorically or allusively. And it is this second level of meaning, created through and layered on top of the first, that connects the story to the larger social/political world. For as Socrates tells Strepsiades, and indirectly and metaphorically the audience as well, the literal forms of the *Clouds*— the dramatic shapes assumed by chorus and actors—do not exhaust what is to be communicated,[34] nor in a sense even express it—they are only signs. Instead, the full sense of the clouds/*Clouds* emerges through an act of interpretation based on knowledge of language and genre—the metaphoric system in use generally and that specific to comedy—and guided by a creative decision about the overall shape of our play and of its parts. To a certain extent, it is this "system" we are trying to reconstruct here, so that we may more accurately follow the hint of the comedy itself, cooperating with the poet in the creation and recognition of clouds/*Clouds* whose fullest meaning will be at once derived from and superimposed on the theatrical reality we see.[35]

But if the comic *logos* which shapes the clouds/*Clouds* works mimetically and metaphorically to mock what it sees, then the obvious question remains, What is the significance of a chorus of clouds who look like women? The answer will influence our reading of not only this passage but the entire play, as we try to assess the clouds' role in the deception of Strepsiades and the downfall of Socrates.

Most obviously, the chorus' female shape, which reflected Strepsiades' prejudices, also mirrors his hopes for intercourse with sexy goddesses (252ff.) and recalls his related first mistake (marrying an inappropriate wife) which a similar desire foisted upon him through that persuasive matchmaker who (like the clouds) "elevated" him with her speech. Further, the clouds' divinity seems to echo Strepsiades' faith in *logos*' omnipotence, but their reflective nature and cloudy, yet female, form may also hint how his comic project will turn out—not like Strepsiades hopes or the audience, conditioned by genre, may expect. Perhaps Strepsiades has been seduced again—this time by a "mad" lust for a *logos* to demolish his creditors—and will be driven by his desire into ruin.[36] For "women" fashioned from clouds traditionally mocked excessive desires through their paradoxical fulfillment, allowing men to enact their own punishment by pursuing the nebulous shapes their mania has divined. Ixion was one victim of such a cloudy goddess.[37]

The clouds must also, of course, reflect the aristophanic Socrates and the *logos* he provides.[38] We have seen how their opening song echoes his invocation. So now their airy cloudiness mocks his position as trendy intellectual and reflects his arrogant assumption that he can look down on men and escape connection to their mundane earth.[39] Their rhetorical entry and deployment as arguments suggest a comic rendering of that philosophical mode of personification which Socrates often used to advance his concluding points.[40] But their female form and persuasive powers, which evoke the goddess Peitho, suggest a very different mode of action for these seductive *logoi*. For while their cloudy natures must reflect that inevitable *apate*, or deception, which gorgianic theory made basic to all (persuasive) speech among men trapped in reliance on opinion,[41] their assumed, insubstantial (and deceptive) femininity also matches the eager *eros* of Strepsiades' first response much more closely than the *epideixis*, the intellectual engagement, proposed by Socrates. Further, this female form has sinister connotations. Women had long been associated with the difficult ambiguity and ambivalent nature of *logos*, which can serve equally well to lie or to tell the truth and provides no sure mark to distinguish one from the other.[42] Thus the clouds that can only look like women become redoubled figures of *apate*—the glorious foundation of skillful persuasion, or its principal defect.[43] Aristophanes' mockery suggests that the sophistic *logos* they represent mistakes the grounds for its success; that the delusion that lies at its heart may be of a very different kind, and have very different consequences, than the theory postulates. Perhaps, like its spokeswomen here, it too is insubstantial and cannot deliver what it seems to promise.

Finally, the perceptive spectator might realize that the audience too is not exempt. For where else would the clouds have just seen Cleisthenes and what else do the *Clouds*/clouds confront but the assembled Athenians? All of Aristophanes' comedies, and perhaps all Athenian comedy, must finally reflect the theater and the city around the stage. As Reckford observes, in this "distorting mirror" Athenians could see themselves, "through carefully staged deceptions, could see how Athenian politics, the 'real' and everyday business of Athens, had become a farce."[44] And just what kind of farce and with what kind of consequences for the comedy we watch, the parabasis and following will make only too clear. For Reckford's insight is particularly true of the *Clouds*, whose obscene, vulgar, and violent shape is a mocking revelation not just of the characters' manias, but of the spectators'.[45]

With the clouds' entrance and identification, our introduction to the comic characters is complete, as is our introduction to the *Clouds*' comedy and its (postulated) audience. Thus when Strepsiades, won over by the chorus' comic confirmation of his morality and pleasurable humiliation of others, finally greets the clouds in terms suitable to their "divine" stature, his words initiate the next part of the drama. We are to watch Strepsiades undertake the sophists' rhetorical curriculum, beginning with what has been consistently presented as its prerequisite: atheism.[46] The demonstration begins with rain; the clouds' role is obvious;[47] the reasoning is familiar. In these intellectual explanations, only mechanical causes will be cited, and, as with the gnat, they will exhaust the significance of the phenomenon in question. From rain, the move to thunder is natural, and fatal to the Olympian system. To deprive Zeus of thunder is to make him mute. However, unlike rain, this terrifying speech is not simply transferred to the clouds. True, they produce thunder, but not volitionally. The repeated passives in 375ff. stress the clouds' purely instrumental role, while simultaneously rendering the sound produced accidental. As Socrates gives his "scientific" explanation,[48] their downward slide from awesome to ridiculous starts immediately:

ὅταν ἐμπλησθῶσ᾽ ὕδατος πολλοῦ κἀναγκασθῶσι φέρεσθαι
κατακριμνάμεναι πλήρεις ὄμβρου δι᾽ ἀνάγκην, εἶτα βαρεῖαι
εἰς ἀλλήλας ἐμπίπτουσαι ῥήγνυνται καὶ παταγοῦσιν.

(376–78)

Whenever they are filled with much water and are forced along,
hanging down, full of rain, by compulsion *(anagke)* then, heavy
bumping into each other, they burst forth *(rhegnunai)* and they make noise *(patagein)*.

The clouds' bursting forth with voice that Socrates originally seemed to promise (357), that significant thunder which communicates the gods' will—or their own—now stands revealed as simply making noise *(patagein)*.[49] The next step, Socrates' analogy to the rumbling of Strepsiades' stomach overfull of soup at the Panathenaic festival (386–87), parodies the socratic use of lowly examples to begin a crucial comic reinterpretation of, or addition to, the sophistic lesson. For the familiar excremental joke[50] that climaxes and ends the sequence reverses the perspective to clinch at once the "theoretical" and the comic point. From Strepsiades' own contribution, a generically hilarious and illustrative story of diarrhea[51] and explosive gas, we learn the inevitable: thunder is really no different from a gigantic fart.

χὤσπερ βροντὴ τὸ ζωμίδιον παταγεῖ καὶ δεινὰ κέκραγεν,
ἀτρέμας πρῶτον, παππὰξ παππάξ, κἄπειτ᾽ ἐπάγει παπαπαππάξ·
χὤταν χέζω, κομιδῇ βροντᾷ, παπαπαππάξ, ὥσπερ ἐκεῖναι.

(389–91)

Just like thunder the little soup rumbles and shouts terribly/cleverly,
gently at first, pappax pappax, and then it steps up the pace papapappax;
and when I shit, really it thunders, papapappax, just as these.

Strepsiades' subsequent and punning comic discovery—this is why the names *bronte* (thunder) and *porde* (fart) are similar[52]—parallels the scientific one. We have learned about the clouds what we already know of the gnat, that to credit the sounds they make with meaning is simply silly.

The point of the lesson from the sophists' perspective has been clear from their introduction. As was parodically implied with the oven world which housed the sophistic speaker, residence in the mute, natural world liberates the voice of man.[53] Again, we can find an illustration in Pericles. Plutarch records that central to Pericles' cultivation of rhetoric was his lack of fear of the divine, acquired by studying with Anaxagoras, notorious nonbeliever in conventional religion, who stated that the sun was a hot rock and explained thunder as the result of clouds striking together.[54] What we have just learned and Socrates' follow-up lesson about lightning—that it, too, is the accidental result of *anagke,* having nothing at all to do with men[55] (404ff.)—obviously parody this process. Here, as later, Pericles, the consummate rhetor, hovers parodically behind Strepsiades, the stupid student. But this time, demystification of the heavens does not nurture the divine oratory of a Pericles. Rather, for Strepsiades, freedom from fear of the gods means oaths are nothing to worry about. In the world of our comedy, the consequence of the seemingly disinterested, but alarmingly potent, sophistic speculation about the cosmos turns out to be the shoddy, self-seeking lies of the perjurer. In the final analysis, complete freedom to speak is nothing more than perfect freedom to deceive.[56]

Strepsiades finds this lesson most pleasant. It is a relief to have his fear of divine punishment assuaged, especially since he had decided on perjury anyway, even before entering the Thinkery.[57] Entering into the spirit of things, it is he who provides the example for this second lesson: lightning is like the spitting/diarrhea of an overheated sausage (*gastera* 409) whose juice/shit struck him in the eye as he cooked.[58] Once again the example extends the significance of the explanation. For it is not simply that the hurling of lightning against perjurers is replaced by an accidental spitting. Strepsiades' misadventure with the sausage graphically illustrates what will be decisive in this new world: technical skill and attention. These will be the only criteria for judgment of actions and sole determinant of their success. Strepsiades was hit by the lightning of the sausage because he was careless (ἀμελήσας 409). His lack of attention brought its own "punishment," one empty of any moral value. The application of this principle is obvious.

The disappearance of the gods liberates the human voice to speak as it can and will, and frees man to measure his intellect against the problems of the cosmos. But can a lesson that reduces thunder to farts and lightning to the spitting of a sausage really be so optimistic? The form taken by Aristophanes' parodic presentation, the comic degradation suffered by Socrates and his theories, not only parallels their probable fate in the real world, where they are put to uses never intended, but shows why this is inevitably the case. Ironically, sophistic liberation leads to a more profound enslavement of speech, this time to the appetites.

As usual, this insight is doubly motivated, both philosophically and comically. On the one hand, the congruence between man and his natural environment, central to sophistic theorizing since the beginning of the play, is central again. Repetition of key words like *patagein* (πατάγειν), to sound, and its cognates (378, 382, 384, 389) underlines the coherence of the sophistic view: the same rules are applicable throughout the natural world, to a variety of natural events.[59] Likewise, Socrates' offer, "I will teach you from yourself" (ἀπὸ σαυτοῦ 'γώ σε διδάξω 385) does more than merely lead into a joke about his propensity for lowly examples, it also refers to the Delphic motto "know yourself."[60] However, like his earlier citation of Pindar, Socrates' use of the motto transforms it. Instead of conveying its traditional warning to avoid hubris and acknowledge human limits, the motto here asserts a human integration into the cosmos so complete that the human body can become a perfect paradigm for nature's laws: know your stomach and you will know the mechanisms of heaven.[61] In such a context, only the small-minded would find anything incongruous in making a fart the model for the thunder of the heavenly clouds.

Comedy agrees but from a different perspective: what is true of the patron deities is equally true of the client practitioners. Common idiom and comic convention have long asserted that thunderous sophistic rhetoric, the lightning of the demagogues, is really a fart, a blast of hot, smelly air—their words, shit.[62] The metaphoric equations hinted at since line 293, rhetoric = thunder and rhetoric = fart/shit, were pervasive on the comic stage. Plutarch records that contemporary comedians called Pericles "the Olympian" especially to mark and satirize the impact of his stormy speech, saying that:[63]

> βροντᾶν μὲν αὐτὸν καὶ ἀστράπτειν ὅτε δημηγοροίη,
> δεινὸν δὲ κεραυνὸν ἐν γλώσσῃ φέρειν
>
> (Plu. *Per.* 8.4)

he thunders and lightnings whenever he addresses the *demos*,
and carries a terrible/clever thunderbolt in his tongue

Aristophanes testifies to this in Dicaiopolis' explanation of the origin of the Peloponnesian War:

> ἐντεῦθεν ὀργῇ Περικλέης οὐλύμπιος
> ἤστραπτ', ἐβρόντα, ξυνεκύκα τὴν Ἑλλάδα
>
> (*Ach* 530–31)

Then in anger Pericles the Olympian
lightninged, thundered, confounded Greece

However, this metaphor was not confined to Pericles. The *Wasps* applies it to popular juries (*Wasps* 620ff.) and demagogues in a way that confirms it as commonplace, akin to our "thundering on." Thus in Bdelycleon's recital of contemporary rhetorical clichés, rhetors who trick the people with meaningless popular slogans are portrayed as blackmailing the allies, threatening: "you will give the tribute, or having thundered, I will overturn your city" (*Wasps* 671).[64] And, of course, Cleon was a primary exponent of this violent, ranting, and, sadly, effective talk. Thus the Sausage Seller finds him thundering away to the Boule about that demagogic stock in trade, conspiracy:

> ὁ δ' ἄρ' ἔνδον ἐλασίβροντ' ἀναρρηγνὺς ἔπη
> τερατευόμενος ἤρειδε κατὰ τῶν ἱππέων,
> κρημνοὺς †ἐρείδων† καὶ ξυνωμότας λέγων
> πιθανώταθ'·
>
> (*Knights* 626–29)

But he then, within, bursting forth/farting (*anarregnus*),
talking monsters, hurled thunder-striking words against the knights,
hurling crags and saying conspirators
most persuasively;

The images of storm and thunder mock rhetoric through exaggeration, evoking homeric imagery of the relentless rush of arms. Another common image, that of farting forth a stream of shitty filth, was more directly abusive. In the passage quoted, Cleon acts the part of the sophistic warrior, but one who farts out his thundering words *(anarregnus)*.[65] This may be no great surprise. Description of the corrupt and bombastic language of such degraded imposters as flatulence is central to the *Knights* and its violently negative picture of contemporary rhetoric. Cleon's ass and his mouth are one and the same. When slave D (or Demosthenes) bids the Sausage Seller examine Cleon's tongue, what gapes wide turns out to be his *proktos,* or asshole (*Knights* 375ff.).[66] Cleon's rival, however, is no better. The speech that the Sausage Seller, in his turn, belts out to the Boule—perhaps through his own asshole (*Knights* 640)—is in keeping with the favorable omen that encouraged him, the fart of a homosexual (*Knights* 639), for the verb used, *anakrazein* (*Knights* 642), as Henderson observes, plays on the meaning "break wind"[67] with a compound of the same verb we have just seen in connection with Strepsiades' stomach (389). A passing jab, moreover, reveals that this metaphor was not limited to the *Knights,* or Aristophanes. The babbling rhetorical asshole was also one solution to Eubulos' ingenious riddle.[68]

> ἔστι λαλῶν ἄγλωσσος, ὁμώνυμος ἄρρενι θῆλυς,
> οἰκείων ἀνέμων ταμίας, δασύς, ἄλλοτε λεῖος,
> ἀξύνετα ξυνετοῖσι λέγων, νόμον ἐκ νόμου ἕλκων·
> ἐν δ' ἐστὶν καὶ πολλὰ καὶ ἂν τρώσηι τις ἄτρωτος.
>
> (Eubulos 106.1–4 PCG)

it is babbling *(lalein),* tongueless, the female named the same as the male
dispenser of its own winds, hairy, elsewhere smooth
speaking senseless things to the sensible, dragging tune from tune
it is one and many, and if anyone should pierce it, unwounded.

The play on *lalein,* a word used particularly of intellectual babble, on one and many, and on correct names shows that the target here was the new intellectuals, effeminate homosexuals whose speech is windy farting.[69] And, in fact, the first answer that comes to mind for the comic interlocutor is the demagogue Callistratus.[70]

This background allows us to catch the full resonance of the parodic lesson which comically and metaphorically transforms thunder into farting, while simultaneously speaking of Strepsiades' exemplary fart as speech.[71] An audience attentive to the larger dimension the *Clouds* has proposed for its comedy would catch on easily: farting and rhetoric are once again equivalent, but with something added. The fate of the gnat, Strepsiades' desire to "communicate" something to the students' asses, his initial and suitably sophistic desire to fart back (in refutation) to the thunderous song of the sophistic goddesses[72] and now the explanation of the clouds' voice fall into place and extend the significance of Socrates' lesson. This is not simply an insulting insistence that sophistic rhetoric is so stupid, degraded, and degrading as to resemble farting, although this alone would be pleasant revenge on those who use and abuse the power such speech can bestow. Rather the absurd sophistic lesson has been structured to accommodate a complementary comic one. For as natural utterance supreme, expressive of human dependence on the body and bodily subjection to natural rules, the farts of a comic man aptly (and parodically) models the utterance of the human animal who is the sophistic speaker.[73] Generic comic "facts" and our play's sophistic theories merge as natural man thunders or farts out what is required by his need. Strepsiades' greed and his consequent tremendous fart at the Panatheneia are emblematic for his engagement in the whole sophistic enterprise.[74] Fear drove him to act sophistically when he farted back to the clouds (293ff.). In line 437 we learn that a similar necessity *(anagke)* "presses" *(piezein)* him to try and shit forth the sophistic *logos*.[75] Such speech, like a fart (or thunder), is best construed as a by-product. To understand it, content is irrelevant, it denotes only the mechanisms and forces of appetite and need.[76] Belief that additional communicative value is present or possible is a delusion, an example of the same fallacy that produced the "song" of the gnat and the "divine voice" of the clouds.[77]

However, one mystery remains, whose solution will again enlarge the issues and increase the resonance of our play. Granted that the rhetorical blast is produced under pressure of need, how can it work on an audience also made up of bodies? The processes of digestion, food, and cooking so liberally invoked in the lessons just past suggest an answer: *gaster,* in the sense of both "sausage" and "stomach."

In introducing the *gaster,* Aristophanes is not only following a logical lead of the image of farting and rehearsing a standard comic preoccupation with food, but capitalizing on a long-standing connection of the stomach with the practice of skillful speech. When Plato's Socrates, in his crusade against rhetoric, bluntly asked whether rhetoric was truly the supreme art or merely sister to cookery,[78] he was invoking a controversy first hinted at in *Odyssey* 14.122ff. There Eumaeus observed to Odysseus that human speech is shaped by need; to win what they lack, men substitute what will please for what is true.[79] In this struggle between the true and the expedient, the *gaster* functions as symbol of the appetites,[80] dictating what shall be said and what shall be heard.[81] The skillful sophist was a "speechcook" (λογομάγειρος), a name recorded for Antiphon.[82] The comparison acknowledges the pleasures of language and the skill of its purveyors, yet condemns both speaker and audience; both sides are motivated by *gaster* and desire. Sophistic rhetoric meets its speaker's needs, while seeming to serve those of the listeners, tickling their palates with tasty but transitory goods dished up for ulterior motives and consumed with a foolish pleasure that guarantees success. Thus the exasperated Bdelycleon, responding to his father's question about the real destination of the enormous Athenian revenues, says they go:

> ἐς τούτους τοὺς ʽοὐχὶ προδώσω τὸν Ἀθηναίων κολοσυρτόν,
> ἀλλὰ μαχοῦμαι περὶ τοῦ πλήθους ἀεί.ʼ σὺ γὰρ ὦ πάτερ αὐτοὺς
> ἄρχειν αἱρεῖ σαυτοῦ τούτοις τοῖς ῥηματίοις περιπεφθείς.
>
> *(Wasps* 666–68)

> to those, the 'I will not betray the Athenian rabble,
> but will fight for the mass always.' For you, O father,
> you elect them to rule you, cooked round/cajoled by these phraselets.

The scholia comment that what Bdelycleon means is "deceived, flattered, wheedled,"[83] and this common equation between food and persuasive rhetoric, mentioned here in passing, informs the entire *Knights*.[84] The orator supreme in the *Knights* is the Sausage Seller, by nature of his trade uniquely competent to control the state as public demagogue. To succeed, slave D (Demosthenes) tells him, he must only:

> . . . ταῦθ᾽ ἅπερ ποιεῖς ποίει·
> τάραττε καὶ χόρδευ᾽ ὁμοῦ τὰ πράγματα
> ἅπαντα, καὶ τὸν δῆμον ἀεὶ προσποιοῦ
> ὑπογλυκαίνων ῥηματίοις μαγειρικοῖς.
> *(Knights* 213–16)

> . . . Do those very things which you [normally] do;
> stir up and make sausage, both, of things/public affairs,
> all of them, and the *demos* always win over
> sweetening [it] up with cookery phraselets.

Given this road to success,[85] the Sausage Seller can afford to be confident: he is equally able as speaker and saucemaker.[86] He was correct in his belief that these were parallel skills: the rhetorical conflict is finally resolved in his favor when he proves himself the better provider for Demos and his *gaster* (*Knights* 1207ff.). Such speech is indistinguishable from food, and its production and consumption are governed by rules of the stomach.[87] This is the comic perspective on the heroic art that Strepsiades seeks, and the transformation comedy works on the *terpsis,* the pleasure (of speech), which Gorgias made the basis of its power.[88] The threat inherent in inserting *logos* into the continuum of desires is made good and more. But this transformation also significantly broadens the application of this famous, and controversial, notion. The imagery of farting, of food, and of cooking—our comically revised *terpsis*—not only explains (and denigrates) those who listen but those who speak as well. Strepsiades hopes to cook up a lawsuit as he cooked up a sausage. He will act driven by the same greed and perhaps with as little skill or success.

The conventional evaluation of *gaster* indicates how much is at stake. For just as, traditionally, possession of *logos* associates man with the divine and distinguishes him from beasts, so the stomach and its necessities reintegrate him into the animal world.[89] It limits desire to a simple physical hedonism[90]—whose elements include not only food but, by cultural synecdoche, sleep, sex, luxury[91]—and compels satisfaction of its needs at any cost, including violence.[92] *Gaster* thus takes its place as contrary to *logos* (and its associated partners, justice *[dike],* law *[nomos],* and so forth), and the *gaster/logos* opposition becomes another representation of the poles of human existence, opposite borders of the human on the famous continuum animal-man-god, or savage-civilized-divine.[93] This being the case, the effort of civilization to remove human existence as far as possible from the bestial could be phrased as a move from *gaster* to *logos,* from stomach to speech. Thus Plato in *Timaeus* 72e3ff. attempts to resolve the competition between *gaster* and *logos*/philosophy by asserting polemically that the very physiological organization of the human body mediates against excessive eating or desire for food lest: "on account of gluttony *(gastrimargia)* the whole race end up un-philosophic and unmusical, heedless of the most divine of the things we have."[94] Likewise, the xenophonic Socrates defends himself against the charge of depriving his students by asking: "do you suppose anything to be more worthy than not to be enslaved to the stomach *(gaster)* nor to sleep and sex, or to consider other things sweeter than these?"[95] Not surprisingly, the sweeter pleasures are those of the philosophical conversation, and, in a decisive rejection of corporal goods, Socrates concludes: "but I believe that to need nothing is divine, and as little as possible nearest the divine."[96] To train the *gaster* and dominate it is fully human, and even divine; to indulge it is to experience disgraceful slavery[97] to what Pucci calls the beast within.[98]

These are the conventional terms of the *gaster/logos* antithesis—represented in extreme and parodic outline by the ascetic philosopher Socrates, devoted to *logos,* and the aristocratic *kreitton logos,* devoted to *sophrosyne,* or moderation and self-control.[99] But our comedy proposes such figures only to confront them with oth-ers—Strepsiades, Pheidippides, and *hetton logos*—who reveal how partial and naive is such an understanding of human nature and of *logos,* at least in contem-porary Athens, among ordinary men. It is not just that in any competition between mind and body, the body is (almost) sure to win, with obvious consequences for the relative status of *gaster* and *logos,* nor that the force of language does not derive from its aesthetic charm, nor even that the pressures of the *gaster* distort our speech. Rather, the *Clouds'* negative assessment of *logos* ends with the col-lapse of the *gaster/logos* opposition altogether. Speech stands revealed not as something competitive with, or complementary to, the stomach, but as its product, best understood through analogy with intestinal rumblings. While this could result in a positive reevaluation of the *gaster,* our comedy concentrates on the opposite (traditional) threat: to submerge man completely, and without possibility of es-cape, in the animal world, dominated by physical appetites, responsive alone to the laws of force and necessity—*bia* and *anagke.*[100] That such a conclusion could be drawn from the celebration of a religious festival makes it the more ironic. For sacrifice, which should mark the difference between man and animal,[101] becomes instead the forum for the blasphemous discovery made likewise by the Cyclops in Euripides' play: the *gaster* is the mightiest god; for the wise, eating and drinking are Zeus.[102]

This image of "communication," born of a conflation of philosophical and comic, mocks philosophical speculation and the optimistic understanding of man and rhetoric. As Socrates and Strepsiades are overwhelmed by enthusiasm and ascend via imagery of the stomach to the realm of the mind,[103] the primary ob-scenities and graphic descriptions stress student's (and implicitly teacher's) nec-essary corporality. The piling up of vulgarities, which become more and more excessive and finally run away with the argument altogether in lines 390–91, is incongruous and extremely funny. Here as in lines 293ff. the body finally takes over (this time in word, the last time in deed) in a comic counterpoint to the intellectual endeavors. The apparently familiar messages—subject and speakers are as unworthy of thought as we normally assume flatulence and gluttony to be; philosophers and their students are really just bodies like ourselves—may be gratifying, but the primary obscenities in the passage also stimulate an independent pleasure. Such terms are directly linked to the joys of the audience's own bodily experience and afford pleasurable release from the constraints of civilized adult life, recalling our former free delight.[104] The laughter thus provoked may obscure for one wild moment the august issues of the sophists and their rhetoric, but this "distraction" from the comic "argument" is, in another way, a staging of it. In our pleasure, theatrical experience and theoretical implication merge in mockery from which the audience's reaction, too, is not exempt.

The rest of this scene underlines the gross discrepancy between the assumptions of the clouds and Socrates and the gastric, comic reality that confronts them in the person of Strepsiades. The humor thus subtly prepares for the parabasis, where for the first time we will encounter the themes of failure and disappointment, deriving from the very contrast developed here. The ludicrous mismatch of perceptions begins with the clouds' first words. For when the chorus breaks their long silence it is to commend this greedy, inept cook for his eagerness for wisdom, *sophia* (412ff.). The clouds apparently think that Strepsiades wants to become a wise soul,[105] and to this philosophical figure of their imaginations they promise both happiness *(eudaimonia)* and skill in speaking—if only he is intelligent, mindful, enduring, and indifferent to bodily things (412ff.). They end their injunctions:[106]

> οἴνου τ' ἀπέχει καὶ γυμνασίων καὶ τῶν ἄλλων ἀνοήτων
> καὶ βέλτιστον τοῦτο νομίζεις, ὅπερ εἰκὸς δεξιὸν ἄνδρα,
> νικᾶν πράττων καὶ βουλεύων καὶ τῇ γλώττῃ πολεμίζων.
>
> (417–19)

and keep away from wine and exercises/gymnasia and the other mindless things
and believe this to be best, which is reasonable for a clever man,
to prevail acting and deliberating and warring *(polemizon)* with the tongue.

The scholia comment on the artfully delayed and epic *polemizon,* "not warring with the tongue itself, but with the tongue just as using a weapon—for this is the weapon of the rhetor—and battling down the opponents with this."[107] Once again a joking invocation of programmatic sophistic imagery resolves philosophical wisdom, or *sophia,* into martial rhetoric,[108] and while the idea of the soldier of the tongue may seem adequate motivation for the hardihood required by the clouds,[109] the philosophical *logos/gaster* opposition plays in the background. Not just polemical imagery, but philosophical "necessity" motivates the prohibition of wine, exercise or gymnasia, and sex—for the irrational pleasures of Aphrodite are those to which the chorus euphemistically refers (417).[110] For the Thinkery, mastery of *logos* is contingent upon cultivation of the mind and both must be preceded by renunciation of the body. Thus when Strepsiades readily assures the clouds that he has what it takes—his devious soul, restless intellect, and thrifty, hardy, stomach make him a natural pupil of speech; he wants only to be appropriately and rhetorically beat into shape[111]—the audience may have its doubts. From the beginning Strepsiades has been presented as focused on food and money, now the the comedy creates the suspicion that he is approaching the problem of the *gaster* as one of economics. Responding to his own desires, he intends to be a model, that is, inexpensive, pupil not an ascetic philosopher.[112]

The dialogue at the end of the scene exploits the potential contradictions implied thus far. Strepsiades' request, that the clouds make

$$\tau\hat{\omega}\nu\ \text{'}E\lambda\lambda\dot{\eta}\nu\omega\nu\ \epsilon\hat{i}\nu\alpha\acute{i}\ \mu\epsilon\ \lambda\acute{\epsilon}\gamma\epsilon\iota\nu\ \dot{\epsilon}\kappa\alpha\tau\grave{o}\nu\ \sigma\tau\alpha\delta\acute{i}o\iota\sigma\iota\nu\ \check{a}\rho\iota\sigma\tau\sigma\nu$$
(430)

of the Greeks, me to be the best in speaking, by one hundred *stadia*

subtly plays off the historically positive view of a beneficial *logos* against the *Clouds'* pessimistic perspective. As commentators have noted, the imagery recalls Eupolis' famous description of Pericles:[113]

> (A.) κράτιστος οὗτος ἐγένετ' ἀνθρώπων λέγειν·
> ὁπότε παρέλθοι ⟨δ'⟩ ὥσπερ ἀγαθοὶ δρομῆς,
> ἐκ δέκα ποδῶν ᾕρει λέγων τοὺς ῥήτορας.
> (B.) ταχὺν λέγεις γε. (A.) πρὸς δέ ⟨γ'⟩ αὐτοῦ τῶι τάχει
> πειθώ τις ἐπεκάθιζεν ἐπὶ τοῖς χείλεσιν,
> οὕτως ἐκήλει καὶ μόνος τῶν ῥητόρων
> τὸ κέντρον ἐγκατέλειπε τοῖς ἀκροωμένοις
> (Eupolis 102 PCG)

> (A.) This one was the strongest/best of men in speaking *(legein)*;
> whenever he came forward just as those good at the race,
> speaking, he beat the rhetors by ten feet.
> (B.) You mean quick indeed. (A.) But in addition to his quickness
> a certain persuasion *(peitho)* sat upon his lips,
> thus he bewitched and alone of the rhetors
> used to leave a goad *(kentron)* in the listeners

This is the promise of gorgianic rhetoric—to create a speech capable of striking and altering the souls of its hearers through the force of verbal art alone. Such persuasion is irresistible and the product of a genuine *sophia* operating for the public good. While Pericles' words operate on his audience like a goad on horses, driving them at speed over a course already determined, Eupolis' text seems to commend this skill.[114] It recalls an aristocratic and skillful charioteer who guides his horses safely to victory; the analogy with the city is clear.[115] In Strepsiades' mouth, however, this image is devastatingly mocked. The great political power and civic benefits of the magical art of rhetoric are buried by the sleaziness of our hero's ambitions.[116] To the clouds' promise of complete power in the assembly 432), he responds with horror:

> μή μοι γε λέγειν γνώμας μεγάλας· οὐ γὰρ τούτων ἐπιθυμῶ,
> ἀλλ' ὅσ' ἐμαυτῷ στρεψοδικῆσαι καὶ τοὺς χρήστας διολισθεῖν.
> (433–34)

> Don't talk to me, at least, about great proposals; for I do not desire these,
> but it is enough for me to twist the case and give my creditors the slip.

The shadow of Pericles and mention of the tremendous civic power of *logos* and skilled rhetoricians have suggested unmistakably the enormous political and social implications of our drama's subject. Strepsiades' response represses this line of development, at least explicitly. Strepsiades is to be neither abstracted philosopher nor sophistic hero. His shallow desires comment negatively on the grandiose promises of the clouds and of rhetoric, suggesting that the exalted martial battle of the assembly (and the law courts 468ff.) differs only apparently from the petty wrestlings[117] he imagines. In his loving recitation of his future reputation—a "catalogue of abusive terms used against a man who is a tricky opponent in lawsuits," cheat, liar, opportunist, goad, twister, and so forth (444ff.)[118]—the implied contrast with the encomium of Pericles is as stark as the length of Strepsiades' song is hilarious.[119] This is the pinnacle of his aspirations and his most accomplished and witty verbal moment, a display of virtuosity probably delivered in one breath as a choker or pnigos.[120] The shape of the comedy comments mockingly on the nature and manias of the ordinary men it confronts and their likely interaction with *logos,* but the clouds are oblivious. True to their programmatic, sophistic delusions, they respond to Strepsiades' song and his revealingly inappropriate final offer to be made into sausage for the thinkers (455), with a (mock) encomium suitable for a hero of sophistic battle: a ludicrously elevated fulmination in dactylo-epitrites about virile spirit and epic, heavening-reaching glory (λῆμα 457, κλέος οὐρανόμηκες 460).[121]

The final lines switch the focus back to Socrates and *sophia* but maintain and develop the joke. When the clouds request that Strepsiades' *nous* and *gnome,* or mind and thought (477), be tested, Socrates begins promptly, bidding his student:

ἄγε δή, κάτειπέ μοι σὺ τὸν σαυτοῦ τρόπον,
ἵν' αὐτὸν εἰδὼς ὅστις ἐστὶ μηχανὰς
ἤδη 'πὶ τούτοις πρὸς σὲ καινὰς προσφέρω.
(478–80)

Come now, tell me your character,
so that knowing this, whatever it is, novel *(kainai)* contrivances/seige weapons *(mechanai),* straightway, on this basis, I may bring to bear on you.

The metaphor follows from that of the sophistic warrior but adds another dimension. Teaching Strepsiades will be like taking a city, battering down its walls.[122] The prize inside will be Strepsiades' true and liberated self. These novel sophistic lessons are well begun, for what else are the walls of civic life but the laws, conventions, and social sanctions, principal among them the divine rules?[123] Socrates' tuition will destroy these in miniature in the individual—a process given concrete expression by the requirement that Strepsiades enter the Thinkery without his cloak (497ff.)—and finally in the city at large. Thus man will individually and collectively be returned to a state of nature, where, free of received opinions and social conditioning,[124] he can realize his potential and uncover the basic human drive: an appetite for *sophia* coupled with a passion for the intellectual products of *logos.*[125] Thus calling on rhetorical terminology,[126] Socrates' final requirement is: Strepsiades must show enough mental agility to snatch up every bit of wisdom presented to him.

> ἄγε νυν ὅπως, ὅταν τι προβάλωμαι σοφὸν
> περὶ τῶν μετεώρων, εὐθέως ὑφαρπάσει.
>
> (489–90)
>
> Come now, whenever I toss out something wise
> about things on high, immediately snap it up/interrupt.

The reply—"What indeed? Dog-like, shall I eat wisdom?" (τί δαί; κυνηδὸν τὴν σοφίαν σιτήσομαι; 491)—is discouraging, predictable, and in harmony with the sight of Strepsiades' comic phallus as he removes his cloak.[127] As the preceding jokes have made abundantly clear, Strepsiades is not after wisdom, nor has he embraced the duality that would require him to renounce *gaster* for *logos*. Socrates had asked if it was in Strepsiades' nature *(physis)* to speak (486). Strepsiades' joke and its characteristic form, his inability to understand metaphor,[128] comment negatively on this possibility, for both are motivated by his inability to free himself (or *logos*) from the binding reality of the physical world. As such they exemplify and express the pessimistic comic view of what is under the cloak: something essentially gastric, wedded to the concrete and instrumental, more akin to dogs than the cerebral beings Socrates imagines. A dog would be very unlikely to snatch up wisdom unless it were an edible tidbit; it may be that natural man will have the same predisposition.

Although not perceiving the dangerous gap between the human nature he postulates and that which confronts him, nor realizing the implications of this for *logos,* Socrates is furious at the old man's stupidity. Perhaps Strepsiades needs a good beating (493).[129] However, the potential for real violence is quickly past, for, as Strepsiades sees it, there is no contradiction between his bent for the physical and speech; he trusts the violence of language in the everyday world of litigious Athens. Asked what he would do if he were assaulted, Strepsiades' suitably sophistic answer—take witnesses and begin a court battle (494ff.)—wins him initiation into the mysteries of the Thinkery.[130]

5

Aristophanes' Failures—The Parabasis: Lines 510–626

In spite of theoretical misgivings and dissonances, at the moment of Strepsiades' disappearance into the Thinkery, things look good, and the chorus' subsequent praise (510–17) encourages us further. Perhaps the awkward combination of comic man and philosopher may work out well, at least for our hero. Such expectations are reinforced both by the rules of comedy (where the hero normally procures complete satisfaction, often through unorthodox, not to say immoral, means)[1] and by the spectacles of the *Knights* and the *Acharnians*. These plays, as well as the *Birds,* portray skillful speech, however comically interpreted, as central to individual power and impunity in Athens.[2] We may not like it, it may not seem particularly edifying, but we confidently await Strepsiades' success, anticipating that such doubts as the comedy has already raised will remain a thought-provoking shadow, rather than a barrier, to the expected progress of the plot.

The intrusion of the parabasis at this crucial moment gives the first concrete hint that such is not to be. The failures recounted in its various parts—of "Aristophanes" and his sophisticated first *Clouds,* of the comic clouds/chorus, and of the moon—are jarring and contrast strongly with the expectations built up by the first part of the play.[3] Most obviously, Strepsiades' future is threatened. The audience that failed to appreciate the novel creations and verbal power of the first *Clouds* does not differ significantly from that which will judge political oratory and judicial pleading, the object of the sophists' teachings. The failure of such a "sophistic" play is worrying for the future of the sophistic speakers in ours. But there is more at stake than the power of rhetoric. For following the story of the first *Clouds* is a startling new accusation of neglect made by the clouds/chorus itself. Speaking in terms that leave no doubt about the reference to the thunderous comic omens of the *Knights,* the clouds paradoxically charge that this wildly popular play was a failure too—although winning first prize, it had no noticeable effect on its hearers. Apparently even "successful" speech is disturbingly impotent when it comes to action in the real world. And supposedly divine or natural regulatory phenomena do not fare much better. The parabasis ends with the picture of the irrelevance of the phases of the moon to Athenian legal and religious "rites" alike.

The parabasis as a whole thus refracts the drama's thematic preoccupations through a new lens, using the vicissitudes of comic *logos* to paint an increasingly grim picture of the status of *logos* in the city. But as usual for our comedy, it also reaches beyond these thematic concerns to instruct (or manipulate) the audience of this particular *logos,* our second *Clouds.* For in the parabasis proper, the explicit recall of the first *Clouds'* failure and the catalog of its unappreciated virtues suggest that without this internal, yet intertextual, perspective the second is incomplete.[4] The ''vulgar'' second *Clouds* must be considered not something new, but rather something different from the first—a play whose fullest meaning emerges only through reflection on this difference and its causes.[5] And one thing our comedy is not is a palinode, penitently making good the ''deficiencies'' of the first. Nor, if Aristophanes could be said to have been a ''trendy intellectual'' with the earlier play, does he become conservative *kreitton logos* with the later. Instead the parabasis proper both opens a gap between poet and his parodic creations, establishing him and his comic *logos* as a synthesis of their disparate virtues, and seeks to create the proper audience for these aristophanic inventions. For the parabatic story of the first *Clouds* and its inappreciative audience rhetorically prompts for a different, better response from us now: this time around we can, and should, avoid the role of vulgar dullards who discard *logos* for the pleasures of (vicarious) sex and violence proferred by Aristophanes' rivals. Thus the parabasis provides the *Clouds'* final lesson on how to understand its comedy, which from the beginning has made the comic and our reaction to it decisive terms in its ''argument.'' We can understand what we see only by watching our second, revised comedy and ourselves, its second audience, from the complex, intertextual perspective inescapable in the knowledge of first audience and first play.

The linkage of parabasis to drama is previewed in the chorus' first song, the kommation (510–17), whose unusual combination of anapaestic (510–11) and lyric rhythms (512–17)[6] at once links it to the lyric passages of the previous scene (457ff.) and looks forward to the parabasis proper. Likewise, the clouds' emphasis on Strepsiades' manly courage (*andreia* 511) and wisdom (*sophia* 517) as he tints[7] his nature with younger/newer/revolutionary affairs (*neotera pragmata* 515–16) perpetuates the humorous misconceptions we have just witnessed. While this may seem to be positive, it is, in fact, ominous. For as the mixed meters hint, the mistaken optimism of the kommation about the nature of its subject at once recalls the treatment of these problems in the previous scene and anticipates their variation in the parabasis. Aristophanes' and the chorus' own comic failures will derive from a similar mistaken optimism about the nature of (Athenian) men and their relationship to *logos* and *sophia.*

The parabasis proper, lines 518–62, begins with the chorus assuming a new role, that of the comic playwright, a fictional Aristophanes himself.[8] First person is used, and, as usual, the chorus advances the claims of the poet and his comedy,[9] but this time, surprisingly, the subject is not our current play, but another— the first *Clouds.* This, we are told, was a superior linguistic and imaginative product; it deserved to win and to earn for its creator a reputation as wise *(sophos).* But these conventional *laudes* have an ironic twist. As we already know, and as the poet hastens to remind us, this superior product lost; apparently its overwhelming merit was much less compelling than the poet wished and assumed.[10] It is this unique double vision—the play of the first *Clouds* against the second and the spectators' reactions against the poet's expectations—that gives this new parabasis its point. Using the popular comic technique of abuse of the audience, Aristophanes brilliantly transforms his earlier humiliation into further grounds for his superiority. He lost because he was too good. He had thought his audience wise *(sophoi)* themselves, and for this reason had given them first taste of his most novel and most skillful comedy (525ff.), the chaste and moderate *(sophron* 537) first *Clouds*,[11] which, eschewing a whole list of standard comic standbys—the dangling phallus, beating, cries, torches, sexy dances (537–44)—entered the comic contest relying on itself and its words alone.[12] Contrary to Aristophanes' hopes, however, the audience disappointed him; they preferred instead the conventional fare of his vulgar rivals (524).

The catalog of the first *Clouds*', and thus Aristophanes', virtues, culminating in his claim of complete reliance on *logos,* not only points up the shortcomings of his rivals but performs an additional less orthodox function. Substance, phrasing, and vocabulary alike work to link the comedian and his comedy to the picture of the sophists and their rhetoric developed in our play. Like the sophists, particularly their most outspoken exponent, the *hetton logos,* Aristophanes relies on language alone for his victory (537ff. = 893), boasts of novel ideas (καιναί ιδέαι) as his stock in trade (546ff. = 896; cf. 1399), speaks of his language as violent and his comedies as participants in a battle (520ff. and 549ff. = 942ff.),[13] and finally disdains those who fail to realize how very superior is his new type of speech. All this is underscored by his emphasis on his own *sophia* (520) and conspicuous use of the verb *sophizethai* (547), "to be clever or subtle," with its echo of *sophistes,* or "sophist," to describe his activity on the stage.[14]

That the parabasis proper suggests a relationship between Aristophanes and the sophists is not a new observation; however, its import has been generally misunderstood. Most critics have failed to see the thematic significance of this deliberate linkage of a fictional comic "Aristophanes" with the equally fictional comic "Socrates" and "sophists," and have instead treated the parabasis as evidence of ambivalence on the part of the historical Aristophanes himself—he admired the rhetoric, but deplored the social views of the sophists.[15] While this may be true, such an interpretation slights the creative genius of the parabasis and underestimates the dramatic and thematic significance of the story it tells. Given what the first half of the *Clouds* has led us to believe about the power of new, clever, technically skilled, and violent speech, Aristophanes' advertised reliance on just this type of language makes the failure of his comedy extremely thought-provoking. Contrary to what we expect, the linguistic brilliance of the first *Clouds* did not render this comedy victorious. Rather it remained unworthily and surprisingly weaker (ἡττηθείς οὐκ ἄξιος ὤν 525), a *hetton logos* unable to fulfill this *logos'* promise, even though seeming to command its art: the rhetorical techniques guaranteed to transform *hetton* into *kreitton logos*. In the case of Aristophanes, at least, the proclaimed force of such speech has failed to operate. Confronted by this failure we are driven to ask: How could the power that is to rescue Strepsiades and that makes the sophistic warrior invincible be so ineffective in the comic agon?

The previous scenes suggest an answer that the parabasis makes only too clear:

Aristophanes had mistaken his listeners. For the prize collection of boobs, now revealed as not wise *(sophoi)* at all, that makes up the comic audience, language, however forceful, sexy, and witty, is no substitute for the real thing: the mindless spectacle of physical violence, erotic dances, and familiar timeworn jokes—all the elements of comedy that the first *Clouds* had abjured.[16] This comedy's defeat reveals once again that the gorgianic pleasure *(terpsis)* of the word, which located the basis of persuasion in aesthetic fulfillment, is no match for the competition. The spectators' spiritual kinship with Strepsiades extends to include both his indifference to wisdom (and its verbal products) and his vulgar fondness for the humor of sex, defecation, and violence.[17] This mismatch between their natures and that of the first *Clouds*—whose optimistic commitment to novelty and *logos* rather than the familiar and corporal betrays a (mis)understanding of human nature shared by Socrates—spelled defeat for that temperate *(sophron)* comedy of words. On the comic stage, at least, the fabled Athenian infatuation with the word is a lie. Rather, the audience of the first *Clouds,* and by extension Athenians and men generally, are indifferent to language per se. Skillful speech is unimportant; impoverished wit can readily be covered up by appeals to the appetites, the slapstick stuff of the belly laugh; real violence cannot be surpassed for entertainment. The compact forged between successful playwright and audience is based not on verbal art or aesthetics but on quite other types of gratification.

Upon this characterization of the comic audience and their tastes developed in the story of the first *Clouds,* Aristophanes builds his criticism of the sophists.[18] For this audience, which was demonstrably incapable of appreciating the novel ideas *(kainai ideai)* of "Aristophanes," is the same audience which relishes the *hetton logos,* is called by him *sophoi* (899), apparently in earnest, and is the acknowledged condition of his success (891). The lessons of the parabasis must be extended to the agon of the *logoi* (889–1114), another innovation of the second *Clouds.* Structural similarity (the parabasis proper closely resembles epirrhema and pnigos of the agon), agonistic context and content (like the *logoi,* Aristophanes and his competitors are engaged in a contest to be judged by others), and explicit equation (both open by addressing the same group, the audience in the theater)[19] emphatically repeat that the collected Athenians who decided the comic contest are also the audience for the debate of the *logoi,* and in fact, the ultimate arbitrators of all successful *logoi* in Athens. The conclusion is unavoidable: Aristophanes' misfortunes and the parabasis' bleak view of real Athenian tastes prove that the *hetton logos* and the sophists, whose extreme mouthpiece he is, mistake the grounds of their success. For these "wise" are ignorant of even the bankrupt love of speech which is satisfied at the expense of others. The *kreitton logos'* charge of fostering addiction to discourse is untrue, never endorsed, or even mentioned, by the *hetton.* Rather, in the *hetton*'s world, language is desirable solely as a tool for private gratification, and this *logos* himself, in spite of his name and claims (893, 1038), owes his victory not to skill or the pleasures of verbal *terpsis* but, like the vulgar playwrights, to promised ability to satisfy desires quite independent of speech. He wins the agon not because the audience is *sophoi,* that is "wise" in the sense intended in the parabasis, "appreciative of *logos,*" but precisely because they are not. His success with the masses is due not to words, but to the reverse, a lack of *sophrosyne*, or moderation and self-control, shared by speaker and listener alike (1060).

As a result, the opponent of the *hetton logos*—the *kreitton logos*, which despises the newfangled talk—and the opponent of the vulgar playwrights—the innovative and verbal first *Clouds*—share a tellingly similar fate. Failing, each in its own way, to cater to the appetites of the mob of Athenians, they are rejected, exposed as weaker than their competitors ($\dot{\eta}\tau\tau\eta\theta\epsilon\grave{\iota}\varsigma$ 525 = $\dot{\eta}\tau\tau\dot{\eta}\mu\epsilon\theta$' 1102). But while in the agon the defeat of the *kreitton logos* seems to bolster *logos,* in the parabasis the failure of Aristophanes' *sophron* first comedy suggests how dangerous jettisoning *sophrosyne* can be. For *sophrosyne,* that self-control of the appetites which Aristophanes endorses and his rivals spurn, is precisely the virtue that guarantees speech a hearing and must be considered basic to its power.[20] In its absence, *logos* is abandoned to compete without reinforcements, and without success, against the pleasures and requirements of the body. The weakness of language implied in its dependence on *sophrosyne* to secure a hearing can be concealed as long as the urgings of the appetites and those of speech coincide. The dangers when they do not are documented by Aristophanes' earlier experiences in the comic contest. Thus the unanticipated failure of the first *Clouds* to become the stronger *logos* again exposes fatal contradictions in the speculative sophistic wedding of a powerful *logos* and (postulated) natural man. As man becomes increasingly identified with animal and *gaster* becomes increasingly dominant, the status of *logos* cannot help but deteriorate.

But while the common fate of Aristophanes' first *Clouds* and the *kreitton logos* highlights the character of the comic audience that rejects them both, this does not mean these two are allies. Rather, the parabasis also begins the work of emancipating Aristophanes and his comedy from the *kreitton logos* as well. We are not to watch a play bolstering conventional, conservative views. For, as with the sophists, the multiple and real similarities between the *kreitton logos* and the fictional Aristophanes—both espouse *sophrosyne* (962, 1006, cf. 1027) and are defeated by *logoi* which reject this virtue (1060), both are concerned with a beautiful and decorous appearance, both mock the effete and those who scorn the city, both are concerned about their reputation among their fellow citizens—mask a fundamental difference between them. And as before it has to do with *logos*.

The first *Clouds* is a comic and intellectual work, whose *sophrosyne,* decorum, and chaste beauty are products of a devotion to *logos* and commitment to innovation. Not only are appeals to the visible and physical discarded in favor of the verbal, but the traditional is rejected in favor of the new, and in all cases the power of speech is thought sufficient to stand alone. In the credo of the first *Clouds* to reuse a joke, however time-honored and effective, is as "vicious" as dragging on an old woman dancing the sexy *kordax* (555). Both belittle the centrality and independence of the word and deny the worth of wise and witty originality. In contrast, the *sophrosyne* of the *kreitton logos* is a parodic and petrified virtue which condemns everything of value in the first *Clouds.* This very different brand of *sophrosyne* is recognizable through its silence (963), its rejection of innovative language (966ff.), its cultivation of the body instead of the tongue (986ff., 1012ff.), the inability of its proponents (including the *kreitton logos* himself) to speak, their hatred of mockery (992), their preference for the fist instead of the word, and their ready willingness to enforce the speech desired.[21]

The clash between these very different versions of *sophrosyne* is underlined by the parabasis' significant anticipations and reversals of the lines in the agon which characterize the *kreitton logos'* attitude toward poetry. The first *Clouds'* glory was that its novel wit needed no buttresses. The reverse is true for those schooled by the *kreitton logos;* they had to repeat exactly what their fathers already recited. A ludicrously outmoded poetic status quo (paralleling the social and sexual one) was maintained at all costs; anyone who played the "buffoon" by following "modern"[22] trends was "crushed, severely beaten for obscuring *(aphanizon)* the Muses" (ἐπετρίβετο τυπτόμενος πολλὰς ὡς τὰς Μούσας ἀφανίζων 972). Thus while the parabasis censures Aristophanes' vulgar rivals for staging violent beatings to conceal *(aphanizon* 542) inadequate, repetitious language, the *kreitton logos* takes the opposite stance: he proposes to beat anyone who innovates as offending against the Muses. And along with poetic novelty must go not only aristophanic comedy, but indeed all comedy. For decorum and good reputation demand the outlawing of joking (992) and laughter (983) as well.

This repressive, nonverbal formulation of *sophrosyne* is as foreign to the first *Clouds* as Aristophanes' comedy is remote from the *hetton logos'* rejection of that virtue. Conversely, practitioners of the *kreitton logos' sophrosyne* are as unlikely to appreciate the sophistic and *sophron* first *Clouds* as the mob which follows the *hetton logos.* Just as the fictional Aristophanes' association with the *hetton logos*—his claim to rely totally on the power of original and rhetorically apt words—ends up exposing the shallowness of the sophistic claim to do so, so his association with the *kreitton logos* ultimately functions to expose the deficiencies of this *logos'* "traditional" view of *sophrosyne* and the place it assigns speech. Ridiculing both sides, the poet attempts to carve out a middle ground where virtues claimed by both can be cultivated,[23] where decorous beauty and hilarious novelty are not mutually exclusive, where individual freedom does not obscure the needs and role of the city, where *logos* is emancipated from physical desire and repressive violence, where one could have a legitimate reputation for wise and innovative language, and where aristophanic comedy could flourish.[24]

To ensure the glorious future of this type of comedy is the task of our new *Clouds.* We have already seen how the opening scenes began "teaching" the spectators, bringing them to appreciate the kind of "intellectual" comedy they confronted. The parabasis continues this (re)creation of the *Clouds'* ideal audience, while confronting a terrible risk of this process and of the production of novel intellectual comedy in general: the danger that the comic audience will fragment. For the story of the first *Clouds'* defeat exposes what Reckford describes as "a possibly unbridgeable gulf . . . between the clever people in the audience, the *sophoi* and *dexioi* [clever] who appreciate his [Aristophanes'] wit, and the philistine others."[25] A major project of the second *Clouds* is to avoid this.[26] For as the wording and progress of the parabasis proper make clear, the *Clouds'* "lessons" and its wit, even if complex and intellectual, are aimed not at the few but at the Athenian masses who throng the theater.[27] Thus while the parabasis begins with an exclusive movement—dismissing the entire audience as witless fools, in favor of a select group of the wise and clever[28]—its final "three lines of persuasive rhetoric"[29] reverse this narrowing process and switch the terms of the contrast:[30]

> ὅστις οὖν τούτοισι γελᾷ, τοῖς ἐμοῖς μὴ χαιρέτω.
> ἢν δ' ἐμοὶ καὶ τοῖσιν ἐμοῖς ευφραίνησθ' εὑρήμασιν,
> εἰς τὰς ὥρας τὰς ἑτέρας εὖ φρονεῖν δοκήσετε.
>
> (560–62)

Anybody who laughs at these, let him not enjoy mine.
But if in me and my inventions (*euremata*) you all [plural] rejoice,
in other times you [plural] will seem to think well.

Already prompted by the terms of the contrast at the beginning of the parabasis to identify with those superior beings who can appreciate aristophanic comedy;[31] at the end, we suddenly find that they are actually a majority.[32] We are goaded to make the effort necessary for membership in this new sophisticated majority by a rhetorical foil, an indefinite but vulgar "anybody" who has been left behind in the educational process and now hardly identifiable, laughs his inadequate laughter alone. By abandoning him in his exposed and debunked position and joining, instead, the appreciative, intelligent many embodied in the plural "you," we confirm our merit and the poet's, retroactively conferring upon him his traditional goal—victory in the comic contest. In reward, we are seductively promised similar benefits: in preferring Aristophanes, we permanently mark not only his intelligence but our own.

Thus the parabasis proper, in its attempt to prompt appreciation of the excellence of the poet and his products, really does follow the conventional program for this part of the play, while its rhetorical strategy—to play on the desire to seem intellectually in the know instead of stupidly ordinary—is one commonly adopted to win acceptance of novel notions. Yet this strategy and what it suggests—the existence of an audience appreciative of (aristophanic) verbal invention—clash strongly with everything we have seen so far: the dramatic picture of the relationship between man and *logos,* reelaborated by the parabatic story of the first *Clouds.* In thus running counter to the comedy's thematic pessimism, a pessimism it has reinforced, the parabasis frames our play's negative assessment of the power of speech with a complementary optimism, this too rooted "offstage" in the "extra-dramatic," but this time positive, reaction of the audience. Thus the parabasis proposes a way of avoiding the role of vulgar fools that we seemed to have been assigned, or assigned ourselves.[33] Yet simple repudiation of the vulgarity of the first *Clouds'* spectators does not completely erase the audience's former actions. The uncomfortable knowledge remains that what the spectators reject now they found natural before.

But there is another problem: success in weaning the spectators of the second *Clouds* from their inadequate reactions and desires means this newly chastened audience, primed to appreciate verbal wit, must watch instead a work whose vulgarity and violence patently violate these standards. For as numerous commentators, beginning with the scholia, have observed, our second *Clouds* incorporates

every trick, comic resource, and vice spurned by the first.[34] As the drama progresses—and even here in the parabasis[35]—we repeatedly witness the care with
which our play employs precisely those comic devices it lists as rejected by its
clever and *sophron* original. We have already seen Strepsiades' phallus used to
mock intellectual endeavor; the beating of old men (the creditors) to make up for
inadequate speech and the final torching of the Thinkery, with the cries of the
students, lie in the future. The parabasis leaves no doubt about the reason for their
inclusion: to render Aristophanes' "formerly unsuccessful play more appealing to
the coarse humorous tastes of his mass-audience and judges."[36] Once again our
Clouds is reflective; the form of this revised version mirrors back what the experience of the first *Clouds* proved to be the nature of its audience. But this leaves
reformed spectators in an awkward position. For if taken as a serious, final evaluation, the parabasis must problematize pleasure in our play by reducing it to the
sum of its self-defined vulgar theatricality. Watching, or reading, this degrading
and degraded effort seems to compel the spectators to reproduce the experience,
if not the desire or the pleasure, of that "anybody" who is indifferent to novelty
and wit; enjoying it confirms their membership among fools such as those who
failed the test of the verbal first *Clouds*. The only difference is that now, for this
comedy, the audience's formerly mistaken expectations and desires would be appropriate, if newly distasteful; the only consolation, the knowledge that the poet
shares our distaste. Given the absence of compulsion, the audience of the second
Clouds might at this point better serve themselves and Aristophanes by refusing
such degradation, abandoning our current play, and taking up instead its superior
and sophisticated original.[37]

Such an aboutface and such a "wise" choice would be as foolish as the choice
of the Aristophanes who entered the first *Clouds* in the comic contest expecting to
win. The wise, or newly wise, who throw aside the second *Clouds* ignore the
lessons in the fate of the first and make the "philosophical" mistake of believing
themselves suddenly transformed and translated to a world of *logos* rather than
gaster. As the failure of the first *Clouds* and the drama of the second show us,
such ignorance of the play of *gaster* in human life is misguided and even dangerous, fostering an incomprehension of the motivations of speakers and listeners
that can lead from misunderstanding to rejection and violence. Instead, the parabasis offers another way out of our dilemma, one that allows us to integrate its
self-criticism and intertextual perspective with the type of comedy the *Clouds* has
proposed itself from the beginning: a comedy whose very comic elements are
terms in its "argument."[38] For the explicit parabatic exposure of the problems of
audience and comedy functions not only thematically and persuasively but also
instructively, continuing the *Clouds'* lessons on how to interpret its comedy with
a final one that will shape our response to the entire play, what has come before
and what will follow. To be among those who can genuinely appreciate Aristophanes' novel art in the second *Clouds* requires that we supplement what we
see, never regarding what are now exposed as the added, excessive, and vulgar
forms of comedy—the numerous obscene antics, violence, and repeated failures
of *logos* portrayed on stage—as simply self-sufficient and self-contained moments
or episodes in the chain of the plot. Such a one-dimensional understanding would

miss the point of the intertextual perspective the parabasis provides. For the very presence of such elements now must allude to their absence before, and the effects of that absence.[39] After the parabasis, we know that to "see" these debased re-visions fully requires us to question their significance for the vulgar comic world visible on stage since line 42,[40] for the role and power of speech, and for human nature as represented by Strepsiades, his son, the *logoi,* and, not least, ourselves.

Such a perspective can begin to salvage the primacy of *logos* and to rehabili-tate our play by the standards it attributes to what it has named its superior origi-nal. For this re-vision allows (or helps to construct) another dimension to its hu-mor in which the coarse and vulgar actions of the second *Clouds* can become, in addition, suggestive thematic gestures, whose full meaning emerges only when we realize that they at once bespeak, and communicate within, our comedy's internal, yet intertextual, exchange. Thus the experience of the "ideal" spectators in a sense reverses the movement of the drama itself. In remaking body into *logos* and elevating concrete actions and events into signifying elements in a "higher" construct,[41] they revive, at least in part, the power of *logos* that the parabasis condemned, while their refined preference for such verbal pleasure rehabilitates the *logos/gaster* antithesis that had seemed swamped on- and offstage.[42] Further, their experience again suggests the affinity between the "wise" of all persuasions. For as we saw above, those who rise to the challenge of aristophanic comedy display an intelligence also valued in the Thinkery, exercising it on verbal comic inventions which cannot be neatly separated from sophistic novelties of a similar sort.[43] Thus the parabasis, which is embedded in the drama of a world hostile or indifferent to the word, and which at first seems to confirm this picture, ends up proposing to produce an audience wise to the pleasures of speech and susceptible to its particular power.[44]

But just as the wisdom of our second *Clouds* cannot simply duplicate the verbal cleverness of the first, the wise it produces can not be the same as those who should have appreciated that earlier play. Our play, in fact, has been rendered wiser by the experience of its predecessor, and proposes to share its wisdom with us through its very revision, its concession to, or acknowledgement of, the pres-sures and also pleasures of the body and the appetites. Thus its comedy assigns the evolving ideal spectators still another task: the rehabilitation also of the vulgar comic pleasures. For if such humor can "speak" in the larger context provided by the parabasis, the glee it evokes has an important role as well. We are not required to stifle our laughter at the second *Clouds'* "vicious" gestures, attempt-ing the philosophical posture it mocks as ludicrously unbalanced and incomplete, but only experience such pleasure doubly, appreciating it, at least afterward, as a term written into our comedy, and one which is immensely significant. For as we watch the second *Clouds,* our responses to it, mingling familiar vulgar delight with newer more "sophisticated" pleasure, reproduce the clash of body and mind, corporal desires and *logos,* portrayed on stage. The active awareness of this fos-tered by the parabasis makes sure we recognize both our own participation in, or likeness to, that which is the object of our mirth and, as well, the conditions of our inevitable tenure in this human world, which must be the stage of our speak-ing and our listening. The result is a collective and individual recognition of the interplay of *gaster* and *logos,* its implications for democratic Athens and for the comic stage, and our own role in these processes, both civic and theatrical.

The ode which follows the parabasis (563–74) eases the audience back into the dramatic world of the comedy. It begins with the chorus assuming the conventional posture and point of view for this part of the parabasis, when, in the first person of the comic chorus, they celebrate their own part in the comic festival and call the gods to the dance.[45] But this religious flavor, the elevated lyric dactyls in the central part of the ode, the poetic vocabulary, and the "elaborate allusive reference common in epic and serious lyric,"[46] do not mean that the ode should be interpreted "straight" as rebuking the atheism of Socrates or somehow indicative of the "real" stance of the clouds.[47] Instead the ode functions in a variety of ways, all within its comic context, to be not cultic hymn, but introduction to the next part of the parabasis and its themes. Thus, the chorus sings neither exclusively as comic chorus nor as clouds, but as a mix of the two[48] with suitably mingled divinities: the traditional Zeus, ruler on high of the gods, and Poseidon, as well as the "intellectual" Aether and the sun, both "seen from a perspective appropriate to clouds, as cosmic forces."[49] The meters reinforce this mixture, for it is the comic Aether who is evoked in lyric dactyls, which echo the equally elevated and comic parodos where he was first mentioned.[50] Such connections and contrasts ensure that we do not cease to regard this "elevated" ode as comic, tied to both its dramatic and formal contexts.

The ode's blending of the "roles" clouds and chorus paves the way for the epirrhema (575–94) where this dual aspect, meteorological and comic, allows a further development of the themes of the previous section. Once more the audience is faulted. Speaking as clouds, in language that recalls the parabasis proper,[51] the chorus rebukes them again and for similar reasons (575ff.). Despite all the clouds can do, traditional omens of thunder and rain (580), their advice goes unheeded, and they, the principal benefactors of the city, are unrecognized.[52] Clearly the clouds, qua clouds, suffer the same fate as "Aristophanes."[53] Not only do their rebukes reiterate his, but as Hubbard points out, these clouds are emblematic of the unappreciated first *Clouds,* while their complaints are aired in a passage apparently retained from that play[54] and loaded with redoubled significance.

But the parabasis and epirrhema are even more tightly linked. The chorus here speaks not only as clouds/*Clouds,* but as representatives of comic chorus and comedy in general. Their benefits are those of the poet: the giving of civic advice, most recently to reject the tanner Paphlagon (the comic Cleon of the *Knights*) as general (581–82).[55] The thunder and lightning which the audience witnessed and neglected were not only meteorological but comic, the rhetoric of the *Knights,* which we have just been reminded (549) smote Cleon again and again.[56] Thus the chorus describes their "speech" in terms which recall the cleverness and novelty of that previous drama,[57] while drawing attention to the operation of comic *logos* itself in a way that once again allies comedy with its target. Line 583—"and we spoke terribly/cleverly *(deina),* and thunder burst out through lightning" (κἀ-ποοῦμεν δεινά βροντὴ δ' ἐρράγη δι' ἀστραπῆς)—begins by playing with the expression *deina legein,* to speak skillfully or cleverly, the same joke we already saw in connection with Strepsiades' sophistic stomach disorders. It ends with a quotation from Sophocles[58] that multiplies the theatrical resonances of the clouds' words through a "booming" paratragedy which at once exemplifies and alludes to the devices of both verbal comedy and skillful speech in general. Yet, as usual, this comic *logos* is confirmed by comic "reality." Continuing the fusion of the clouds' meteorological and comic identities, Aristophanes "borrows" real events to bolster his claims. Lines 584–86 assert that the sun and the moon agreed with the clouds/chorus; by refusing to shine, they too rejected what is now identified as "Cleon."[59] The epirrhema's final joke clinches the reference to the *Knights* and fuses the poet's advice there with the chorus' here. Using the verb *didaskein* (590), with its double meaning "to teach/explain" and "to produce a drama,"[60] the clouds/chorus recall a famous image from the *Knights,* Cleon as rapacious gull, to repeat its "message": clap the thievish demagogue in the stocks, recover his loot, and restore the ancient ways.[61]

This recall of the *Knights* and reiteration of its advice and imagery—all couched in a passage that seems to derive, at least in part, from the first *Clouds*—adds another dimension to the problems of audience and language addressed in the parabasis proper. For of course such advice is hilariously futile—Cleon is dead. Its futility throws a ludicrous and disturbing light on the proverbial divine guardianship of Athens which this advice should "exemplify," but more than that, the current futility of the chorus' advice only echoes their more puzzling allegation: that the *Knights* itself was a failure, like the first *Clouds* it went unappreciated and ignored by the Athenian citizens. In fact, the *Knights* was a wild success, at least in terms of the comic contest that was the subject of the parabasis. Not only did it win first prize, but as we have just been reminded (553ff.), it was so popular that Aristophanes' competitors felt compelled to copy it. Yet this victory in the comic agon turns out to have been vitally limited. After listening and applauding, the audience went on to do as it wished anyway: elect Cleon general (587). Perhaps this should not be surprising given what we have learned about thunder and lightning in the preceding part of the play—that they are meaningless, unrelated to, and without impact on events on earth—nor when we remember the grounds of success in the *Knights* itself—successful appeal to the mass *gaster*. But, in any case, the "failures" of the clouds/chorus chronicled here reveal the goals of the parabatic "Aristophanes" and his dreams for his *Clouds* as silly and insufficient: among the mass of Athenians, the thunder of (skillful) speech, even when apparently appreciated, does not count for much. Thus our play ironically reuses a passage from the failed first *Clouds* to suggest another subtle, but equally distressing, kind of verbal failure. As the story of the *Knights* shows, simply listening to, and even acknowledging, the *logos* of others may be inadequate to prompt the action promoted by a speaker, however well received.[62]

Yet this pessimistic view seems contradicted by its illustration. Surely, Cleon's election as general, however deplored by the chorus/clouds, owed a great deal to his command of *logos*. Likewise, Paphlagon in the *Knights* is shown relying on a stormy rhetorical *logos* not very different from the (comic) thunder and lightning the clouds/chorus claimed to have deployed against him (583).[63] How can we account for Cleon's successful speech? History may provide a multitude of answers, many of them positive. The *Knights* and the *Clouds* impose a negative interpretation which uses Cleon's very success to extend again the significance of the parabasis, moving beyond the failure of the first *Clouds* and its implications for the sophists and "sophisticated" comedy to a broader picture of *logos* in the city. For the story of the *Knights'* impotence here reproduces the movement of that comedy's plot. In its offstage "failure" we see Paphlagon's and for similar reasons: both were outdone by the targets of their rhetoric. Just as Paphlagon loses because he cannot satisfy the appetites of Demos (he failed to provide enough tasty treats) and because, paradoxically, he relies too much on *logos* (witness, for example, the inadequacy of his rhetoric compared to the Sausage Seller's appeal to the Council's stomachs),[64] so the wildly vulgar aristophanic comedy loses its contest with Cleon (if not with the other comedies) for similar reasons: it can offer no concrete advantages. Thus the failure of the successful *Knights* to influence Athenian political decisions proves once more, at least in the context of our play(s), the dominance of the appetites: the subordination of *logos* to *gaster*. The second half of our *Clouds* will make dramatically clear the pertinence of this observation for sophistic rhetoric.

The parabasis ends with more joking about rhetoric, prepared for by the antode (595–606) which, like the ode, reworks the identities of the chorus with a different emphasis, this time bringing us back to the world of Athenian religious practice. For the antode's cultic form[65] and content, which identify "the chorus firmly as Athenian singers"[66] traditionally invoking the traditional gods, clashes strongly with what we shall see next: the antepirrhema's (607–26) witty combination of the substance of Strepsiades' lesson about the lack of relationship between human and celestial with the clouds' complaint in the epirrhema that their omens were ignored. In a speech that "reads almost as though the chorus are presenting a legal case in defence of the Moon and against the people of Athens,"[67] the clouds charge that the Athenians repay the moon for saving them money—the only benefit they really appreciate—with neglect. The calendar and the lunar cycle are out of sync, and the worst thing is that no one cares.[68] The Athenians persist in their favorite pastimes, eating and litigation, completely heedless of supposedly regulatory natural/divine phenomena. Concern that Socrates' teachings smack of atheism and undermine public morality is mere posturing. In fact, the Athenians are indifferent to the requirements of religion, as well as to the absence of any external sanction for their social forms. When physics and social reality are out of step, it is evidently quite hilarious to think that it is social reality that should accommodate itself. Like the rest of the parabasis, the implications of this are devastating, both for the traditional view—which requires harmony between human and divine—and for the new reasoning—which relies on a paradigmatic, if mechanical, nature. It is apparent that the human world, and human beings, can and will carry on quite independent of both these urgent *logoi*.

Thus the parabasis is a unified whole whose various parts reflect and replay against a larger backdrop issues raised by the interaction of the generic intellectual Socrates and the common bumbler Strepsiades. Continuing to perform their comic function, our clouds and *Clouds* mock the manias of those they confront and reveal their natures—here, since we are temporarily outside the world of the drama, the comic audience itself, the assembled citizens of contemporary (comic) Athens.[69] At its end, we are prepared to witness the rest of the comedy with a more questioning and skeptical eye, scrutinizing not just what we see on stage but even ourselves and our reactions as contributors to an increasingly strong thematic undertow that seems to pull inexorably in the direction of verbal impotence in any confrontation between *logos* and the desires. Yet the parabasis' presumption that, this time around, the audience may appreciate aristophanic invention and approach the second *Clouds'* comedy from the new perspective it provides suggests that the vulgar drama and its negative implications are not the whole story. Our own reflection on the *Clouds* tempers, at least in part, its bleak assessment. Thus the broader comedy of our *Clouds* nourishes a more comprehensive wisdom than its purely verbal original or its vulgar rivals. In a characteristic movement, it rejects all sides, encouraging us to emulate none of the parodic extremes and figures it presents and mocks. Instead, wise poet and wise spectators must attempt a synthesis of such reduced reactions and incomplete conceptions.

6

Strepsiades' Failures: Lines 627–888

The scene between the parabasis and the agon picks up the story where we left it before the parabasis. Strepsiades finally begins the standard sophistic curriculum: instruction in language (627–92), practice in thinking and the definition of problems (693–734), and, finally, application of these skills to situations from real life (735–90).[1] These are to be his last moments in the Thinkery, for he will, of course, fail. Further, his failure will take its characteristic form and one predicted by events in the parabasis. For the "variety of jokes"[2] which makes up Strepsiades' and Socrates' dialogue have a common point. Not only do they continue to portray the disjunction between philosopher and ordinary man, but this scene with its now familiar dynamic, in which the jokes which climax each sophistic lesson turn that lesson on its head, is itself the climax to the entire episode of the instruction of Strepsiades. Strepsiades' crude humor, the futility of his efforts to be sophistic, his inability to be abstract, to understand the metaphoric nature of *logos,* or to leave behind social or physical reality, hammer home the comic point of the first part of the play. With the agon will begin something new.

The scene begins on the note of Strepsiades' failure. Socrates exits the Thinkery abusing his pupil, but still hopeful, inviting him into the light (632). If we suppose this light to represent the intellectual world of the mind, Strepsiades rapidly proves the impossibility of this goal. Wishing only to learn the "very unjust speech" (*adikotatos logos* 657) he believes will save him, he is indifferent to language per se and insensible to the meter and rhythm (638ff.) which gorgianic theory makes the foundation of its *terpsis* and hence its power. Stymied, Socrates finally turns to the study of correct usage, or *orthoepeia.* As line 658 suggests, this is the sine qua non of the verbal power Strepsiades seeks. For while poetic devices may make persuasive *logos* irresistibly sweet, correct diction (and grammar) are central to sophistic wrestling and debate.[3] That 627–92 parody this widespread sophistic concern has long been noted by the commentators. And although precise reconstruction of Aristophanes' sophistic models is impossible, it is clear that interest in gender and the reform of common speech was particularly associated with Protagoras.[4] Thus, when in lines 662ff. Socrates instructs Strepsiades to differentiate between male and female chickens by using *alektor,* rooster, and *alektruaina,* hen, and changes the ending of the word for (wooden) vessel, or *kardopos,* to -*e,* or *kardope,* to reflect its feminine gender, we know we are within the realm of rhetoric. This is the type of expertise expected of one who would make the weaker *logos* the stronger. Ordinary speech is to be made consistent

80

through a one-to-one correspondence with the structure of the reality it might be supposed to represent and the correction of gender and forms on abstract, morphological grounds.[5] Such a corrected language should enable the speaker to make points unambiguously, invoke nature precisely, and quibble effectively with his opponent by playing with the significance of terms.[6]

Up to this point, the lesson proceeds smoothly, although the audience might wonder about the superior effectiveness of such a corrected *logos*. The parabasis has suggested that neither *logos* alone nor supposedly normative natural phenomena actually carry much weight with the Athenian public. Demonstration of a divergence between social usage and natural norm does not automatically trigger either correction or rejection of the social "error," and it is far from clear that things would be different with speech. But Strepsiades, at any rate, is enthusiastic, at least until the discussion turns to proper names.

The issue arises with a joke about Cleonymos. Socrates had used this name to demonstrate masculine endings during discussion of the really "feminine" *kardopos*. Strepsiades reverses this when he jokes that, properly speaking, the name of Cleonymos, the notorious coward, who must be female, should end in -*e* like the new *kardope* (680). The comic Socrates, however, seems to take this seriously. Disturbed by his pupil's apparent misunderstanding, he immediately begins a lesson on male and female names (681ff.) which, however, leaves Strepsiades thoroughly baffled. Wedded to the concrete, this ordinary, social man is unable to grasp that at issue are not real persons or things, but words.[7] The resulting witty, generic mockery of Cleonymos (673) and Ameinias (691), playing on a ludicrous "confusion" about the correct gender of these so-called men, mocks these standard scapegoats and Strepsiades' stupidity only in passing. For Strepsiades and the humor he provides and enjoys are again tools of the comedy, the means, not the mouthpieces, of a larger aristophanic mockery. The real target here is the goal of a self-sufficient language, obedient to an abstract set of rules and an abstract "natural" world, indifferent to the actual—in this case, social—world constituted by what "we all" (693), comedy and its audience, already know.[8] It is not only the idea that a vessel has a gender in the same way as a woman that is ludicrous, but the idea that "true" gender is always determined by observation of the natural world, when "we all know" the reverse. The mockery of comedy suggests that the "real" nature of Cleonymos and Ameinias is most accurately captured not scientifically or philosophically but comically and "metaphorically," defined not by their anatomy but by their behavior, just as earlier this same Cleonymos was exposed by the clouds as a deer. Correctly named, these men are not masculine but feminine. Strepsiades' joke confronts a speculative interest in language with its concrete, everyday use to convey judgments and meanings derived neither from nature nor from theory but from social practice and personal involvement. It is in this latter world, where the comic *logos* is at home, that the "unjust speech" Strepsiades seeks will also have to work, manipulating the social reality and the code that expresses it.

But the lesson has a further point, for Strepsiades' inability to understand the abstract is matched by his continuing interest in the concrete.[9] Translation into the school has not altered him nor changed his overriding concerns. The gap between

Socrates' philosphical presuppositions and the nature of his pupil remains.[10] As Strepsiades relates meter to measures (of food 639ff.), attempts to figure out how instruction about rhythm will help him with the ordinary problems of breadwinning (648), and then reduces its rhetorical pleasures to a crude joke about sex (652ff.), he remains a man of the *gaster:* his behavior, as Socrates comments, stupid and characteristic of a man from the rude country (654). Strepsiades' interpretation of everything he hears, and his questions about everything he learns, drag language and thought down, from speculative to practical, from metaphoric to literal, from an end to a means. As Nussbaum comments, the "key question is always *ti kerdano;,* 'what shall I gain?' (257; cf. 1064, 1115, 1202); the key psychological principle is egoistic hedonism."[11] But, in spite of all this, contact with the crude Strepsiades has not enlightened Socrates—he still sees neither the disjunction between the universe he thinks about and the social world he shares with other men nor the danger this world poses to his arguments and even his existence.

All of these motifs come to a head, or rather do precisely the opposite, in the instruction in reasoning of lines 694ff. Once again we see Socrates gamely start over. Get into that flea-ridden bed and "reason out something of your own affairs *(pragmata)*" (ἐκφρόντισόν τι τῶν σεαυτοῦ πραγμάτων 695), he orders. Terminology and practice are typically socratic.[12] Newly stripped of his cloak and of his conventional beliefs, Strepsiades is to cover himself up and cogitate for himself about his own affairs. This advice is expanded with more standard philosophical vocabulary and injunctions not to sleep that recall the hardihood required of Strepsiades before he was allowed to enter the school (415ff.).[13]

> φρόντιζε δὴ καὶ διάθρει
>   πάντα τρόπον τε σαυτὸν
> στρόβει πυκνώσας. ταχὺς δ', ὅταν εἰς ἄπορον
>   πέσῃς, ἐπ' ἄλλο πήδα
> νόημα φρενός· ὕπνος δ' ἀπέ-
>   στω γλυκύθυμος ὀμμάτων.
>
>   (700–706)

Think, now, and examine closely
    and in all directions
whirl, having concentrated yourself. and quickly, whenever into bafflement
    you fall, jump to another
idea of mind; and let sleep,
    sweet-hearted, stay away from your eyes.

The exalted tone of the song,[14] however, is quite at odds with what Strepsiades is experiencing. For Strepsiades enacts these metaphorical injunctions bodily—twisting and jumping to evade the fleas.[15] His subsequent paratragic lament (709–15) makes even more hilariously obvious this difference between the philosophical interpretation of Strepsiades' experience and its comic reality.[16] The song begins with an epic sweep—Strepsiades' adversities endanger his ribs (πλευρὰς 711) and life/soul (ψυχὴν 712). This is appropriate for Strepsiades' new pursuits; perhaps he is finally participating, or going to participate, in sophistic heroic endeavor. The context, however, and the ensuing progress of his sufferings show how fatuous is this idea, for the fleas are not only assaulting Strepsiades' soul and his ribs but pulling off his balls and burrowing up his ass. The "downward" progression, coupled with the mounting anguish, is ironically comic.[17] Strepsiades is being buggered by these philosophical fleas; his plight has not really changed since he entered the Thinkery dragging the flea-ridden cot, or exited complaining about the infestation (634). Nothing he has learned has been sufficient to distract him. When his comical pain is reproved, the response is more paratragedy—Strepsiades is like Hecuba, deprived of everything dear: his goods and his skin, his soul and his shoes. This (para)tragic experience has suggested to some that there is real tragedy to be detected here: Strepsiades is suffering in a doomed attempt to be what he is not, a philosopher. Thus Nussbaum sees this episode as a dramatic metaphor for socratic elenchos. "The paralyzing effect of the *elenchos,* compared in the *Meno* to the numbing effect of a stingray, finds its comic expression in the *Clouds* in the scene in which Strepsiades, enjoined to look into himself and find a solution to his *aporia,* feels himself being bitten by bedbugs that drink his life's blood and torture his genitals. . . . Talking to Socrates undoubtedly *was* like being bitten and drained."[18]

This is the reverse of the effect intended. The paratragedy of Strepsiades' outbursts ensures that we view the scene not in the tragic context of struggle, confrontation with human limits, and bitter acknowledgement of the precariousness of man's existence, but as mockery of such a profound and philosophical interpretation of humanity. In the context of comedy, the quotation of tragedy mocks the assumptions of the "higher" genre. The clash of genre does not temporarily transport the audience to another world, but, as they laugh, anchors it more firmly in the current one. Form parallels and reinforces theme. This, however, is not to deny Strepsiades' seriousness. Strepsiades himself is unaware that he could be paratragic or metaphorical. Rather, for the moment his bodily pains have eclipsed even his financial worries. Although we first saw him being bitten not by the expected bugs but by thoughts of his creditors, now we see the opposite. He is unable to think about his upcoming lawsuits for even a minute. The fleas are just too pressing. This unedifying spectacle is precisely the issue, for the essence of the scene is that it is not metaphor. Attempts to interpret it metaphorically put us in the same position as the clouds, who not only intone pointlessly profound advice, couched in philosophical images, but apparently take Strepsiades' antics as attempts to follow their instructions. The last thing that Strepsiades is doing is trying to think. The scene represents what it presents, the priority of the body. The belief that the mental could replace or duplicate the physical, the tragic, the comic, or the metaphoric, the actual, is simply ridiculous.

A final climactic joke sums this up for the rest of the play. Prompted to look for a *nous aposteretikos* (728), that is, a "fraudulent thought," one for defaulting on his debt, Strepsiades, pondering the need for such a *gnome aposteretris* (730), falls silent. The contrast between what he is bidden to search for and what he actually seeks is significant. The changed endings, from the abstract and trendy *-ikos* to the concretely feminine *-tris,*[19] which "reminds us of αὐλητρίς and ὀρχηστρίς,"[20] or flute girl and dancing girl, instance again Strepsiades' characteristic move from philosophical and theoretical to concrete. The comic fruit of this change is not long in coming, and is decisive. When Socrates suspects his pupil has fallen asleep, an indignant denial (732) leads him to hope for the best— perhaps Strepsiades has fallen into that abstracted daze characteristic of thinkers. "Do you have something?" (ἔχεις τι; 733), asks Socrates hopefully. The answer is stunning. Strepsiades is certainly neither sleeping nor thinking;[21] rather, metaphor has taken on body again. Wistfully imagining the *gnome aposteretris* not as a theoretical solution to his affairs, but as "a personable young women materializing in his embrace under the bedclothes,"[22] Strepsiades has found the only thing powerful enough to distract him from his discomfort: sex. Examining his own resources for a solution to his affairs, his *pragmata* (695), Strepsiades has come up with his penis. We can imagine him throwing off his covers and sitting up, comic phallus in hand,[23] as he responds to Socrates' question with "nothing at all except the penis *(peos)* in my right hand" (οὐδέν γε πλὴν ἢ τὸ πέος ἐν τῇ δεξιᾷ 734). This is a typical comic answer and gesture, or at least typical of this play. For Hubbard suggests this end to the scene may be new—the *peos* added in revision.[24] Thus, while the grounds of this joke may be the "common assumption of vulgar humour, that an adult male cannot be in bed alone and awake for long without masturbating,"[25] its inclusion here and the glee it surely arouses (even in those who theoretically disapprove of it and what it represents) enrich its significance within the intertextual dynamic of the second *Clouds*. For *peos,* or penis, used only here in the *Clouds,* is a word of great power. It returns us to the body, affording the audience "simultaneously the pleasure that was once natural in us and a powerful weapon by which to defy civilization and the adult way of perceiving the world."[26] Thus the surprised laughter, which may, finally, distance the audience from Strepsiades' gesture, still allies us to it, if for a moment. We feel an analog to the pleasure that stimulates him, and his *logos* acquires an unaccustomed power through its call on such bodily drives.[27] But the parabasis requires us to integrate this response into a larger perspective, questioning the meaning of such laughter and the comic success of such humorous gestures. Not discounting our pleasure, the audience must acknowledge that our comedy has provoked it only to put it in competition with that verbal pleasure, the *terpsis* of *logos* alone, formerly believed independent of such props as the phallus. Thus both gesture and, paradoxically, *logos* itself remind the audience of the degraded world this play, and all speech, must inhabit and of its precarious position in this world, no matter how philosophic, novel, correct, or witty it might be. For the very "success" of Strepsiades' speech models an alternative form of "verbal" power whose impact is owed not to words but to a seductive appeal to the kind of hedonistic self-interest comically summed up in the pull of the *peos.* As before, the comic vision is driven home by a pun and the attentive spectator (who, in fashioning this complex response, may reclaim a bit of *sophron sophia*) could have anticipated something like this from as far back as line 695. *Pragma,* the word used for affair above, is a common synonym for *peos,* and the play on *pragma*/affair and *pragma*/penis is a joke already used by Strepsiades at the expense of the students (197).[28] Anticipation of the blow it would deal to philosophical pretension here has simply been heightened by delay of the punch line.

The scene in its new form thus conclusively mocks the philosophic optimism that puts the drive to ponder and reason at the center of human nature. In fact, the opposite is true.[29] As such, it decisively caps the theme and dynamic which animated the first half of the play. The point put across, they are now discarded. Instead, the brief remainder of Strepsiades' instruction, his attempt to work out three "real-life" problems posed for him by Socrates, prepares for his expulsion from the Thinkery and begins to play with an important corollary to what we have seen. If not thought but desire is central to man, not language, the vehicle of thought, but action, that of the body, will be his characteristic expression.

The problems Socrates poses for Strepsiades continue his education in rhetoric, for they are legal exercises, designed to force realization of the priority of *logos* and the tongue, its instrument, over the facts of social life. They thus gratify his student's wish to learn the practical, most unjust speech, instruction in which Socrates had postponed until after the (failed) lessons about meter, rhythm, and words.[30] To solve these problems, Strepsiades is supposed to apply the methods of reasoning outlined by the clouds, and now again by Socrates, using everything he has learned; cosmological, grammatical, theoretical. If Strepsiades is ever to act the sophist, this is his chance.

Problem number one is Strepsiades' own—how to avoid paying the interest due on his debt (739–57). This concrete, personal goal at last stimulates discovery of that elusive *gnome aposteretike,* or sophistically fraudulent thought (747). Strepsiades will employ a Thessalian witch to draw down the moon from the sky. Socrates greets this solution first with bewilderment, then, when he learns that interest is paid on the new moon, with enthusiasm. This has puzzled commentators. Noting that the solution proposed parodies Socrates' scientific interests in the first part of the play,[31] they have supposed his response to be either ironic[32] or prompted by Strepsiades' adoption of science as a means to satisfaction of practical needs. Strepsiades' masterstroke, however, is more complex. Its humor and point, as in the two problems that follow, are to be found in his adaptation of traditional remedies—here a witch, later a lens, and finally suicide—to sophistic modes of thought and reasoning.[33] For through his witch, Strepsiades will, in a sense, exploit a typical sophistic argument from nature: for the solution he has in mind is nothing less than to deprive the social institution of interest payment of its natural foundation, the phases of the moon, which dictate the Attic months. Removal of the moon should make collection impossible for, as he patiently explains to Socrates, interest is payable monthly (756).[34] The witch's songs thus anticipate the rhetorical strategy Pheidippides will use in 1178ff. and 1427ff., and Strepsiades himself in 1286ff. Their ability to undermine such an important social norm as the payment of debts is a tribute to the power of this type of argument and to the power of words, for witches and wizards are sophists, the new magicians of the word in a topical disguise with appropriately sophistic trappings. Not only had spellbinding incantation become a common model for the enchanting force of sophistic rhetoric, the new magic in the city, but *logos* was frequently acknowledged to be, or to function as, a powerful *pharmakon,* while the mirror was a symbol of seduction associated with Peitho herself.[35] Thus Strepsiades is, metaphorically at least, finally a sophist, or the employer of one. He has every right to be pleased with himself, and Socrates to be encouraged.[36] Only one slight difficulty remains: it is obvious that Strepsiades' plan will never work. Not only is it improbable that he could find a witch with incantations strong enough to draw down and imprison the moon, but his entire conception is obviously much too concrete an application of sophistic technique. But the hilarious futility we sense in Strepsiades' efforts is not due solely to his continuing inability to divorce himself from the body. The epirrhema and antepirrhema have already demonstrated the Athenian indifference to supposedly regulatory heavenly phenomena, particularly the lunar calendar. It is unlikely that lack of a proper moon will suffice to deter Strepsiades' creditors from pursuing their interest. The connection between nature and social reality is not nearly as close as the sophists, and Strepsiades following their lead, would like to assume. Disappearance of the moon is simply irrelevant.

Strepsiades' solution to his second problem (758–74) is equally sophistic, equally nonsensical. When Socrates asks,

> εἴ σοι γράφοιτο πεντετάλαντός τις δίκη,
> ὅπως ἂν αὐτὴν ἀφανίσειας εἰπέ μοι.
>
> (758–59)

If some charge should be written *[graphein]* against you for five talents,
how would you remove *[aphanizein]* this, tell me.

Strepsiades' eager response—"I have discovered a most wise/sophisticated removal *(aphanisis)* of the charge" (ηὕρηκ' ἀφάνισιν τῆς δίκης σοφωτάτην 764)—and clever "solution" simply take Socrates at his word.[37] Using a magnifying glass to concentrate the sun's rays, Strepsiades will "remove" the charge itself, melting the "letters" *(grammata* 772) in the record. Thus, continuing the punning, the suit itself can be said to have been "discharged" *(diagraphein* 774). Again we see Strepsiades' prejudice for the concrete, yet Socrates' approbation is not incorrect, for, as before, Strepsiades has clearly applied central tenets of the sophistic "creed." Not only is the logic inherent in language transferred unhesitatingly to real life, but Strepsiades' confidence that alteration of the court register will be adequate to solve a lawsuit stresses the absolute precedence of *logos.*[38] Further, once again, metaphorically at least, Strepsiades does act the sophist— knowledge of celestial phenomena, here the important information that the sun is a burning rock, has led him to dissolve traditional language and traditional limits. The crude physicality of his approach should not obscure the genuine truth of its conception. As our new Pericles understands, ability to influence the wording of a charge and to manipulate it once it is recorded is central to success in court. Strepsiades has erred only in the fine points: he should seek verbal, not physical, transformation.

Strepsiades' triumph, however, is not destined to last. Encouraged by his pupil's previous, if partial, successes, Socrates gives him a tougher assignment, bidding him explain:

$$\ddot{o}\pi\omega\varsigma \ \dot{a}\pi o\sigma\tau\rho\acute{e}\psi\alpha\iota\varsigma \ \ddot{a}\nu \ \dot{a}\nu\tau\iota\delta\iota\kappa\hat{\omega}\nu \ \delta\acute{\iota}\kappa\eta\nu,$$
$$\mu\acute{e}\lambda\lambda\omega\nu \ \dot{o}\phi\lambda\acute{\eta}\sigma\epsilon\iota\nu, \ \mu\grave{\eta} \ \pi\alpha\rho\acute{o}\nu\tau\omega\nu \ \mu\alpha\rho\tau\acute{\upsilon}\rho\omega\nu.$$
(776–77)

How you would twist, rebutting *(antidikon)* the charge,
being at the point of losing, with no witnesses present.

Here is an occasion where only the tongue can prevail—*antidikon* clearly prompts for a rhetorical and sophistic strategy that shall render the presence or absence of witnesses irrelevant. It is opinion, or *doxa,* that is the issue here, about the just and the unjust, the probable and the improbable, and thus we are in the province of the *(hetton) logos.*[39] The newly confident Strepsiades can hardly wait to answer. With a fine sophistic ease, he announces that nothing could be simpler: he would simply hang himself. Socrates is enraged. This is the last straw; Strepsiades must go. Bad enough that his solution implicitly denies the powers of rhetoric, conceding that witnesses are the deciding factor in a suit and thus granting the actual situation priority over what can be said about it. Worse yet, his answer, even as it continues the theme of the physical, so clearly parodies socratic contempt for the body that the mockery somehow becomes apparent even to the character Socrates in the play. For this is Strepsiades at his most philosophic. Like a true thinker, he has changed planes, forsaking this world for the higher one. Dangling above the ground, his body would duplicate Socrates' initial perch and reproduce the position of thought, which, as we have just been reminded, must be elevated to escape the traps of *aporia* and contamination with dull earthly processes (761, following 227ff.).[40] Strepsiades has fallen prey to the habits of his teacher—captive to the charm of his idea, he has completely failed to note its consequences in the world of the body. If philosophy really is a preparation for departure from this earth, Strepsiades, in his own completely ridiculous way, has learned its lesson only too well. The picture of his suicide is the fitting end to his instruction in the Thinkery.

Up to this point in the play, the vaunted power of sophistic rhetoric has certainly not been manifest. Strepsiades' faith in it, however, remains unshaken. His expulsion from the Thinkery means ruin. At this crucial point he asks the clouds for their advice. Their response, to send his son in his place, has been seen as decisive for the rest of the play,[41] an interpretation that continues by making them moral agents responsible for the punishment of the unjust Strepsiades, and through him Socrates. The comedy, however, suggests another possibility. Perhaps here too the clouds are true to their mocking and reflective comic nature, echoing Strepsiades' words[42] as their answer reflects what had been his intentions. Strepsiades had already decided to send Pheidippides to the Thinkery, going himself only when it seemed easier than forcing his son. Now that he has failed,[43] he revives his original idea, bolstering it with his original pleas and threats: if Pheidippides will not do as he is told, he can leave home.[44]

Whatever Strepsiades' plan, however, it does not seem it will work. Certainly what he has learned in the Thinkery—the mangled bits of sophistic lore we see him deploy—profit him not at all. Pheidippides is adamant, refuses to listen, and even considers taking legal action to have his father declared incompetent. Thus pressed, Strepsiades has recourse to that alternative persuasive strategy, filial piety, which has continued to shadow the *Clouds'* comic sophistic ideal. The reciprocal respect and obligatory affection, or *philia,* of father and son bind Pheidippides to be persuaded by his father's words now, just as Strepsiades once heeded his lisping son's childish wishes.

> ἀλλ' ἴθι, βάδιζ', ἴωμεν. εἶτα τῷ πατρὶ
> πιθόμενος ἐξάμαρτε. κἀγώ τοι ποτὲ
> οἶδ' ἐξέτει σοι τραυλίσαντι πιθόμενος.
> ὃν πρῶτον ὀβολὸν ἔλαβον ἡλιαστικον,
> τούτου 'πριάμην σοι Διασίοις ἁμαξίδα.
>
> (860–64)

But come on, move, let's go. Then persuaded by/obedient to
your father, err. And I, indeed, once
I know, I was persuaded by/obedient to you, a lisping six-year-old.
The first obol I received as juror
with this I bought you a chariot for the festival of the Diasioi.

With this story, Strepsiades finally has his way. In obvious constrast with sophistic theories, his current words are effective not because of the power of skillful language—his sojourn in the Thinkery has only made him more violent and incoherent than ever—but because it is he who speaks. Thus Strepsiades' success now and that of the lisping Pheidippides earlier indirectly suggest a different model for persuasion, based neither on verbal *terpsis* nor gratification of desire. Rather, for Pheidippides then and Strepsiades now, it is an uncontrollable, extralinguistic bond that secures a receptive audience, one that is prepared to listen and be persuaded even contrary to its (perceived) self-interest. Paradoxically, it is the concession won by this extralinguistic power that paves the way for the debate of the *logoi,* which, in the person of the *hetton logos,* will demonstrate the absolute force of the new techniques of rhetoric.

7

The Debate of the *Logoi*—The Agon: Lines 889–1112

The long-delayed agon, the famous debate of the *logoi*,[1] inaugurates the last half of the *Clouds*. Although in the drama of Strepsiades and his debts we seem to be back where we started, much thematic progress has been made. In the course of Strepsiades' failure, we have learned about the sophists, their theories, their *logos*, and their students. The new approach taken in the agon, the look at sophistic rhetoric from the inside, requires that we remember what has gone before, for the debate of the *logoi*, whose position makes it the great turning point of the play, develops the theoretical implications of the preceding parts of the play to their logical if contradictory conclusions. In a clash between the "old" way—observance of traditional virtues, social custom, and the laws—and the new—skeptical determination to enjoy whatever pleasures can be obtained with impunity—the old-fashioned violence of the hand is pitted against the modern force of the tongue. The result, an apparent victory for the *hetton logos*, demonstrates sophistic rhetoric to be at once invincible and powerless. Its claim to be the most useful speech available to contemporary man is vindicated in precisely the same moment as it is exposed as only that—simply talk. For the sophists are convicted of having forgotten, or destroyed, the prerequisites for their own power, the necessary suspension of physical violence and creation of an arena for speech.[2] Not only is their *logos* a personal tool defined through its (successful) opposition to law and justice, but to exalt the power of the word and its "inevitable" achievement of the results of force (pleasure and impunity), crucial distinctions between *peitho* and *bia*—persuasion and force—have been blurred or obscured. This dissolving of old allegiances and creation of new ones creates a combustible mixture. It is ignited at contact with the sophistic/comic man, for the agon also confirms the thematically pessimistic view of human nature intimated throughout the first part of the play. Repeating in a new form the lessons of the drama and parabasis, and, of course, addressing the same audience, the *hetton logos'* appeal to Pheidippides reveals Socrates' intellectual optimism to have misled him completely about the motives and desires of his students (and men in general). Far from being potential philosophers dedicated to *logos*, these human animals conform to what we might expect of beings whose *physis* is determined by participation in the "natural" world. They are servants of the *gaster*, hedonists of the most basic sort, driven not by speech but by emotion and self-interest.[3] The result is potentially fatal, and not just for the adulterer whom the *het-*

ton logos makes his exemplar in the agon. Paradoxically, it is the complete triumph of the *hetton logos* that paves the way for the burning of the Thinkery, its home.

The debate opens in verbal violence. The characters enter exchanging insults that rapidly establish their identities and their methods. These are the two *logoi* that have been the object of Strepsiades' quest since the beginning. One is the *hetton,* who identifies himself as *logos* pure and simple (893) and claims that before a crowd (892)[4] the power of his rhetoric and novel ideas (*gnomai kainai* 896) are invincible, regardless of what is argued. The other is the *kreitton,* who proposes to annihilate the *hetton* not through the power of speech itself, but "speaking just things *(dikaia)*" (τὰ δίκαια λέγων 900). With this statement, which, if true, is fatal to the *hetton*'s power, the sophistic wrestling match is on. "But I will overthrow [you] refuting these" (ἀλλ' ἀνατρέψω ταῦτ' ἀντιλέγων 901), the *hetton logos* answers, and, not surprisingly, proves true to his word.[5] Within six lines the *kreitton* is betrayed by the same concrete and archaic assumptions we have seen with Strepsiades: "just things" *(ta dikaia)* depend on a goddess Dike, or Justice, located beside the gods (904a). The sophistically skeptical *hetton* need only cite one of the many disreputable stories about Zeus to abolish justice and throw the *kreitton* into confusion. The debate degenerates into insult,[6] and the *kreitton logos* seems at a loss. His rapid defeat and excessively early, if tacit, concession apparently vindicate the pretensions of his rival and demolish the *kreitton*'s claims to greater strength.

However, the *kreitton* has unexpected resources. When the *hetton logos* tries to capitalize upon his verbal victory, telling Pheidippides to come along and leave his rival to rave (932), the *kreitton* retorts sharply, "you will weep, if you lay a hand [on him]" (κλαύσει, τὴν χεῖρ' ἢν ἐπιβάλλῃς 933). This is as good a comic sequence as it is bad debating practice. We can imagine a long silence, for the *kreitton logos* is about to prove his strength, and it is not going to be verbal. He is not going to refute his opponent but assault him, and there is little doubt but that when push comes to shove, the *kreitton,* as his name predicts, will prevail. For the *kreitton logos* should be visualized not as feeble and superannuated, but as vigorous (if neglected) with a stature appropriate for the one who trained the heroes of Marathon and who ends his speech by promising Pheidippides a similarly cultivated body (1012ff.).[7] His physical might represents his extra-linguistic muscle: his affiliation not only with the martial and physical prowess of the Athenian past, but with the laws, the gods, and the entire social and conventional world. This *logos* is *kreitton,* not, or not simply, because he voices the traditional moral values subsumed under the name "just things," but because along with these comes the socially sanctioned violence necessary to maintain them and suppress competing *logoi* with blows if words prove unavailing.[8] Conversely, the *hetton logos,* as presented in the *Clouds,* is both dissipated and attenuated. The enormous tongue and flabby body in store for a sophistic Pheidippides probably reproduce the *hetton*'s own physique, for the power of this *logos* lies in his tongue, unsupported by anything else. He has no access to the force, emotional or physical, that sustains the conventional, social and divine. Once violence goes beyond the famous force of language, the *hetton,* who is *logos* alone, will also live up to his name, and he will be completely helpless.

The *hetton logos,* thus, is in no position to respond when the verbal process of winning Pheidippides' allegiance turns into a battle over his person. Contrary to all our expectations, it appears that debate and wordy warfare are about to degenerate into a brawl in which mastery of *logos* will be irrelevant. However, the intervention of the clouds averts the delightful comic violence our *Clouds'* "vulgar" audience would have so enjoyed. The goddesses of rhetoric renew the primacy of language and reconstruct the verbal arena, bidding the *logoi:*

> παύσασθε μάχης καὶ λοιδορίας.
> ἀλλ' ἐπίδειξαι
> σύ τε τοὺς προτέρους ἅττ' ἐδίδασκες,
> σύ τε τὴν καινὴν
> παίδευσιν, ὅπως ἂν ἀκούσας σφῷν
> ἀντιλεγόντοιν κρίνας φοιτᾷ.
>
> (934–38)

Cease from battle and abuse.
But display *(epideixai),*
both you what you taught earlier men,
and you the new
education, so that after hearing you two
refuting each other, having chosen, he [Pheidippides]
    may go to school/have intercourse.

Violence of the hand is suppressed in favor of violence of the tongue. As the clouds did earlier, the *logoi* are to make a sophistic *epideixis,* or rhetorical display. They are to speak opposite each other in a verbal battle which Pheidippides, and implicitly the comic audience invoked in 889ff., shall witness and judge.

With the suppression of physical violence, the *hetton* regains his tongue.[9] Elated, he describes his once again inevitable victory in the familiar terms of irresistible martial speech:[10]

> κᾆτ' ἐκ τούτων ὧν ἂν λέξῃ
> ῥηματίοισιν καινοῖς αὐτὸν
> καὶ διανοίαις κατατοξεύσω,
> τὸ τελευταῖον δ', ἢν ἀναγρύζῃ,
> τὸ πρόσωπον ἅπαν καὶ τὠφθαλμὼ
> κεντούμενος ὥσπερ ὑπ' ἀνθρηνῶν
> ὑπὸ τῶν γνωμῶν ἀπολεῖται.
>
> (942–48)

and then from these things of which he may speak
with novel expressions
and conceptions I will shoot him down,
and finally, if he should murmur,
in his whole face and both eyes
being goaded/stung *(kentoumenos)* just as by wasps
under the arguments he will perish.

The clouds' response to this confident assertion pushes the issues raised by the proagon even further into the background.

$$\nu\hat{\upsilon}\nu\ \delta\epsilon\acute{\iota}\xi\epsilon\tau o\nu\ \tau\grave{\omega}\ \pi\iota\sigma\acute{\upsilon}\nu\omega$$
$$\tau o\hat{\iota}\varsigma\ \pi\epsilon\rho\iota\delta\epsilon\xi\acute{\iota}o\iota\sigma\iota\nu$$
$$\lambda\acute{o}\gamma o\iota\sigma\iota\ \kappa\alpha\grave{\iota}\ \phi\rho o\nu\tau\acute{\iota}\sigma\iota\ \kappa\alpha\grave{\iota}$$
$$\gamma\nu\omega\mu o\tau\acute{\upsilon}\pi o\iota\varsigma\ \mu\epsilon\rho\acute{\iota}\mu\nu\alpha\iota\varsigma$$
$$\dot{o}\pi\acute{o}\tau\epsilon\rho o\varsigma\ \alpha\dot{\upsilon}\tau o\hat{\iota}\nu\ \dot{\alpha}\mu\epsilon\acute{\iota}-$$
$$\nu\omega\nu\ \lambda\acute{\epsilon}\gamma\omega\nu\ \phi\alpha\nu\acute{\eta}\sigma\epsilon\tau\alpha\iota.$$
$$(949\text{--}54)$$

> Now show forth, you two trusting
>   in expert
> words and thoughts and
>   opinion-striking cogitations
> which of you, speaking,
>   will appear the better.

In this clearly labeled sophistic contest the *hetton logos'* victory is assured.[11] What we have seen so far of the *kreitton logos* leaves no doubt that he will be inadequate in the war of *logoi* and subtle speculation. However, the repetition of familiar terminology and the return to a context where *logos* can have the last word should not blind us to the significance of the brief scene just witnessed. The violence of *logos* is predicated on conditions it itself is powerless to create. The verbal arena that will see its triumph is not a product of the force of speech, but must be guaranteed by a greater power.

The remainder of the agon develops the issues raised in the proagon while integrating them with the conflicting views of human nature and the goal of education that form the substance of the *logoi*'s interaction.[12] At issue is not simply the desirability of acquiring new technical skills, but, as in the earlier dispute of Strepsiades and his wife (62ff.), a vision of the appropriate life for man and how to achieve it. These aspects of the debate have been very ably discussed by Nussbaum, whose arguments have been cited frequently in previous chapters and will be central in the first part of the discussion here. Her "focus on the issue of moral education and the opposition, on this issue, between a traditional and an expert-centered conception" allows her to detail our comedy's thematically bleak view of human nature (which she calls "egoistic hedonism") and the fears such a view must arouse about the future of Athenian democracy.[13] However, her philosophical orientation and her project—to compare Aristophanes' criticism of Socrates with later ones by Plato and Aristotle—lead her to neglect both the comedy of the *Clouds* and the centrality of *logos* itself. For it is the ability to speak and even more to persuade that Strepsiades seeks for himself and his son at the Thinkery, and it is as speakers and listeners that they and others, including the audience, are investigated throughout the play and in this agon. Educational strategies (traditional habituation or abstract instruction) and presuppositions about human nature (irrational or rational, corporal or cerebral) feature as essential subtopics contributing to a larger debate about the role of *logos* in human life, its power, and the grounds for this power.

Since man's nature determines his relationship with *logos,* as well as the manner of his education and his use of what is learned, it is not surprising that, as many have observed, the debate of the *logoi* is steeped in the *nomos/physis* controversy from the start (959ff.).[14] In this controversy, the *hetton logos* will, as expected, appear as the exponent of *physis,* or nature;[15] his opponent, apparently, as that of *nomos,* or law and custom.[16] For the *kreitton logos* idealizes a way of life (and even body) formed by successful molding of resistant nature. His education consists of a series of compulsory prohibitions—not to murmur (963), not to giggle (983), not to be greedy (981ff.), not to indulge and pamper the body (965, 987ff.), not to be shameless—coupled with zealous observance of the social proprieties. His twin goals are summed up in the traditional ideals that open and close his speech: self-control and good reputation, or *sophrosyne* (962) and *eukleia* (997).[17] These are to be achieved by complete control of the individual *gaster* (981ff.), *eros* (979ff.), and voice (969ff.). But the *kreitton logos* reproduces the philosophic rejection of *gaster* without sharing its commitment to *logos.* Traditional continence is linked with silence or the disciplined sounds of collective and traditional song. Any deviation is severely punished; proper mores and the *logoi,* civic, musical, conversational, and cosmological, which sustain them, are to be enforced with blows (972).[18] As Nussbaum comments, this education is to remain "the same over time, and the same for all."[19] Novelty and the free and individual play of words, comic or philosophic, are utterly alien to it.

This nomic education subordinates the individual to the "good" of the state, making of him first and foremost a citizen able to fight and to live in harmony with others.[20] Fittingly, the clouds greet the end of the *kreitton*'s speech with praise that links him to the great city-defending ramparts.

ὦ καλλίπυργον σοφίαν
κλεινοτάτην ἐπασκῶν,
ὡς ἡδύ σου τοῖσι λόγοις
σῶφρον ἔπεστιν ἄνθος.
(1024–27)

O one practicing beautiful-towered
    wisdom most renowned,
how sweet upon your words *(logoi)*
    a chaste *(sophron)* bloom lies.

The image sums up the *kreitton*'s effect: the construction of defensive walls, interior and exterior, that mark off the space of the *polis* and keep the enemies of the social order at bay. In other words, these are the *nomoi,* the laws and customs that make up the social walls of the city and that both constitute and are maintained by the *kreitton logos.* The constrast with socratic and sophistic education is clear. As we learned during the test of Strepsiades' *physis* (478ff.), education in the Thinkery begins by tearing down the walls that hinder the natural rational quest for truth, a process visualized as stripping off the social cloak. Only elimination of conventional views and constraints—legal, social, and divine—will liberate the mind and the *logos* to be fully effective. The result should be a commitment to *logos* unsullied by distorting and worldly influences. Instead, the reverse turns out to be true. As we shall see with the *hetton logos,* it is the subjugation of the *gaster* that is discarded. Thus the first casualty of the agon is the only thing shared by the ascetic inhabitants of the Thinkery and conventional *kreitton logos:* belief that the proper life for man does not revolve around unbridled satisfaction of the desires.

However, the actual figure of the *kreitton logos* fails to argue his important brief on behalf of the traditional laws and customs in any kind of cogent or compelling way, despite the fact that, like every character except, at first, Pheidippides, he is infatuated with *logos* and anxious to speak, either ignoring or ignorant of the danger this poses. He engages in the debate because he wants to (939), and a single verbal refutation suffices to persuade him to abandon his entire position. This is not only because the *kreitton logos* has the disadvantage of fighting with his opponent's weapons: words.[21] Rather, the *kreitton logos* functions not as genuine contributor to the *nomos/physis* controversy, but as a foil for the *hetton.*[22] His role is not to provide a balanced and reasonable defense of *nomos* but rather, as he undergoes an *elenchos* of his beliefs, to provide the text of a more subtle and equally disturbing exposure of the *hetton*'s presuppositions. If, as Nussbaum says, the "aim and achievement of this negative procedure [the *elenchos* of the defender of *nomos*] will be to show Right that he himself does not really believe in the education he defends,"[23] the aim and achievement of the agon as a whole is to demonstrate to the perceptive audience the *hetton*'s incomprehension of the foundations of his own success and the extent to which this very success undermines itself. Thus, through the comedy's examination of the *kreitton logos,* we learn not what defenders of the norms were or should have been saying, but about human nature and its probable interaction with sophistic speculation (and practice).

The *hetton logos'* opposition to the traditional civic virtues and mores (however imperfectly represented in the *kreitton*) is proclaimed immediately: this *logos'* claim to fame is that he first knew how "to speak things contrary to the laws and judgements" (τοῖσιν νόμοις καὶ ταῖς δίκαις τἀναντί' ἀντιλέξαι 1040). The life he offers Pheidippides is one entirely external to the collective civic and social life, but this hardly means that under the cloak is discovered rational man. The philosophical optimism that links man's nature to "higher things" through a commitment to *logos* paralleled by renunciation of the body has been mocked from the beginning as incompatible with the Thinkery's own theories and demonstrably in conflict with the facts, or at least the comic facts of our play. Now, in the absence of Socrates, it is definitively jettisoned. There is no incompatibility between the instrumental speech proffered by the *hetton logos* and the *gaster.* On the contrary, while the *kreitton logos,* perhaps following the lead of the philosophers themselves, may paint a picture of sophistic students addicted to talk (1003, 1018, 1053), this is not what the *hetton* proposes to the worldly Pheidippides. Certainly those who study *logos* will be able to use its fantastic powers for their own advantage, nor is there to be any stigma attached to the tongue or agora (1055ff.); however, the *hetton logos* does not promise a life dedicated to the pleasures of speech.[24] Whatever the master may think, comedy and sophistic *hetton logos* agree. The cloak of social convention hides an animal little different from the others, like them ruled by "the necessities *(anagkai)* of nature" (τὰς τῆς φύσεως ἀνάγκας 1075) and devoted to hubristic satisfaction of physical appetites for food, drink, laughter, and sex. The command of *logos* simply makes this satisfaction a bit more easily achieved.[25]

The abstracted and ascetic Socrates of the first part of the play could not be more different. However, the fact that he might not recognize his *logoi* nor act as they suggest in no way obviates his comic connection to them.[26] For not only have the *Clouds'* sophists postulated such a natural man from the beginning, but our play has used the comic Strepsiades to prefigure his probable character, as well as the likely fate (and transformation) of Socrates' views and practices outside the Thinkery. In his appeal to Pheidippides, who certainly plans to be neither "professional" philosopher nor long-term student at the Thinkery, the *hetton logos* only articulates more skillfully Strepsiades' own profoundly "gastric" and instrumental view of language. The exemplary story of the adulterer demonstrates the result of combining such a speaker with the techniques of invincible persuasive skill.

Under pressure of the natural necessities *(anagkai)* man cannot help but err; at issue are only the consequences. The practical effect and unique contribution of sophistic training is liberation from all distracting and irritating constraints, internal (1078) and external (1079ff.), that detract from the pursuit of pleasure. At the moment of his inevitable transgression, the sophist differs from other men in that he need fear no punishment, human or divine; he enjoys complete impunity. The *hetton logos* closes his exposition with a concrete example of these benefits:[27]

> εἰέν. πάρειμ' ἐντεῦθεν εἰς τὰς τῆς φύσεως ἀνάγκας.
> ἥμαρτες, ἠράσθης, ἐμοίχευσάς τι, κᾆτ' ἐλήφθης.
> ἀπόλωλας· ἀδύνατος γὰρ εἶ λέγειν. ἐμοὶ δ' ὁμιλῶν
> χρῶ τῇ φύσει, σκίρτα, γέλα, νόμιζε μηδὲν αἰσχρόν.
> μοιχὸς γὰρ ἢν τύχῃς ἁλούς, τάδ' ἀντερεῖς πρὸς αὐτόν,
> ὡς οὐδὲν ἠδίκηκας· εἶτ' εἰς τὸν Δί' ἐπανενεγκεῖν,
> κἀκεῖνος ὡς ἥττων ἔρωτός ἐστι καὶ γυναικῶν·
> καίτοι σὺ θνητὸς ὢν θεοῦ πῶς μεῖζον ἂν δύναιο;
>
> (1075–82)

Very good. I proceed from here to the necessities of nature.
You erred, loved, commited some adultery, and then have been caught.
You are lost; for you are unable to speak. But following me
enjoy your nature, gambol, laugh, consider nothing shameful.
For if you should happen to be caught as an adulterer, you will argue
    back the following to him [the husband],
that you have committed no injustice; then to refer to Zeus,
that even he is weaker than love *(eros)* and women;
and yet you being mortal, how could you be more powerful
    than a god?

The *anagke* (necessity) of *eros* has compelled the adulterer to act. At the moment he confronts the offended husband, similar pressure causes him to break forth with a skillful *logos* functionally indistinguishable from the farts of the gnat, of Strepsiades, or of the clouds themselves, goddesses of rhetoric. The audience of all these sounds hears solely a product of necessity. Caught red-handed, the student of the sophists will invoke the conduct of gods in whom he does not believe to justify a restraint that he himself would not practice. He could as well fart out his fear as Strepsiades has done. The only difference is that this will succeed.

Adultery, the particular crime assigned the sophist, is carefully chosen to illustrate the full complex of characteristic sophistic attitudes and assumptions. First, and most importantly, it represents man's complete incorporation into the natural world, subject, like the other animals, to *eros,* the paradigm of the inexorable natural *anagkai.*[28] Marriage had traditionally been characteristic of the ordered human state and differentiated human sexual relations from those of animals who "couple without rules, crudely, with any other member of the species which happens to be around."[29] Adultery breaks down this order, asserting the priority of the needs of the body. In so doing it also furthers and expresses sophistic isolation. Satisfaction of private *eros* through adultery violates all social norms and represents the gratification of individual desire at the expense not only of the laws and the husband, but of the community at large. For adultery is the crime which strikes most accurately at the family and thus at the heart of man as a social being and of the city as a collection of family units; it threatens "precisely the bonds and links of society, not just a relationship between a man and wife."[30] Thus, in advertising the power of sophistic speech through a defense of adultery, the *hetton logos* presents us with the paradoxical spectacle of a *logos* which assists in dissolving the community it originally helped to found.

But adultery not only confirms the student of the *hetton logos* as the perfect sophistic man and suggests the strangely destructive nature of his speech, it gives him the perfect brief to argue. Because adulterous gods abound in myth, justification of adultery offers a unique opportunity to demonstrate sophistic freedom from traditional beliefs, while simultaneously trapping the conventional world in an open contradiction between paradigms and standards. These traits made defense of adultery a common vehicle for display and analysis (positively or negatively slanted) of the power of the sophistic word. The Nurse's famous justification of Phaedra's love for Hippolytus (Eur. *Hipp.* 433ff.) and the self-defense of Helen in the *Trojan Women* (914ff.) play on identical themes; both recall Gorgias' *Encomium* where first successful seduction and then successful defense of Helen are the ultimate symbols of rhetorical success.[31] The *hetton logos'* example thus evokes in miniature the whole controversy over the power of language, a power most visible when it is (successfully) used to defend actions abhorrent to the listener. And success is certain. Everything inside and outside the play has prepared us for this victory. We confidently expect that the novel conceptions which proved so potent in the proagon (*kainai gnomai* 901) will prove equally potent here, and they do, at least against the *kreitton logos* himself.

The occasion for the *kreitton logos'* defeat presents itself as soon as he responds to the *hetton*'s exemplary story with the indignant questions:

τί δ' ἦν ῥαφανιδωθῇ πιθόμενός σοι τέφρᾳ τε τιλθῇ;
ἕξει τινὰ γνώμην λέγειν τὸ μὴ εὐρύπρωκτος εἶναι;

(1083–84)

What then if he should be radished, persuaded by/having trusted in you, and
   plucked with ash?
Will he have some argument to claim not to be wide-assed *(euruproktos)?*

Having a radish thrust up one's ass and pubic hairs plucked out with hot ash was
one punishment for adultery.[32] Certainly it would make the punished physically
wide-assed; this much could be agreed. However, this is not the point of the
kreitton's question. He is focusing on the social/moral aspects of the situation; it
is not, or not only, the physical sensations that he finds intolerable, but the dis-
grace and humiliation inherent in public knowledge and degrading public punishment. It is here that the *hetton logos* finds his hold. Using his customary strategy,
he will dispute not the facts of the actual punishment itself but the evaluation
implied in wide-assed, *euruproktos,* an insulting term for homosexuals.[33] Thus his
retort,

ἦν δ' εὐρύπρωκτος ᾖ, τί πείσεται κακόν;

(1085)

And if he should be wide-assed *(euruproktos),* what evil *(kakon)* will he suffer?

is at once good rhetorical strategy and highly provocative. Playing on the *kreitton*'s preoccupation with reputation and *sophrosyne,* as well as his feeling that
participants in the culture of the new *logos* are already disgraceful *euruproktoi*
(909, 1022ff.), it diverts attention from the actual punishment for adultery (which,
in the painful way it makes a person wide-assed, could be considered a physical
kakon) to the wide-assed, or homosexual, condition and what we should think of
it.[34] For, if we forget about the radish and hot ash, the inner freedom of the
sophists makes it impossible that being, or being called, wide-assed could be bad,
a *kakon.* Certainly simple shame at this label is not an issue, nor a punishment or
deterrent, for the *hetton logos.* In fact, from what we have seen, pride is a more
likely response to such an ''insult.'' Moreover, once conventional beliefs are set
aside, actually being *euruproktos,* or wide-assed, might even be called good—as
a clear source of pleasure. The *hetton* proves his point ''by appealing to standard
comic assumptions, that a majority are εὐρύπρωκτοι: from which (he implies) it
follows that to be such is not a κακόν.''[35] The parabatic view of the audience,
the invocation of generic assumptions, and our (comically postulated) sophistic
theory unite to validate the view that defines man by his appetites and, as such,
inherently indifferent to chastity, moderation, and decorum (that is, to *sophrosyne*) and to normative *logos* like the *kreitton.* Once again, the vulgar *logos* linked
to satisfaction of the desires seems to triumph. If the majority are *euruproktoi,* the
kreitton logos is already the *logos* of the minority and thus really the *hetton.*[36]
Driven by his contempt for the audience, the *kreitton* concedes their collective

vice, and his consequent defeat, all too quickly. His final words play on the martial image of wordy warfare to register the full import of the long awaited, but
nevertheless astonishing, transformation the agon has worked on the status of the
logoi.

> ἡττήμεθ'. ὦ κινούμενοι,
> πρὸς τῶν θεῶν δέξασθέ μου θοἰμάτιον, ὡς
> ἐξαυτομολῶ πρὸς ὑμᾶς.
>
> (1102–4)

> We are the weaker *(hettemeth')*. O faggots,
> by the gods, receive my cloak, as
> I am deserting to you [plural].

In a hilarious use of the generically comic and obscene which mocks sophistic
techniques and attitudes and insults skillful speakers even as their power is represented,[37] the claims of rhetoric are vindicated once again. The *hetton* has swept
the field, and the wordy battle is over. It remains only for the victor to collect the
spoils.[38]

But we are as little to lament the defeat of the *kreitton logos* as to rejoice in
the victory of the *hetton.*[39] Just as the world of the *hetton logos* would be one of
contentless babble and the comedy of sex and violence, so that of the *kreitton*
would be one of oppressive silence, empty of laughter and any kind of mockery,
as well as debate. His disgust and desire to silence his opponent even before the
agon had really begun are emblematic of his general intolerance of speech and the
freedom to speak.[40] His extreme position is no more desirable than the *hetton
logos'*, yet, paradoxically enough, the *kreitton logos'* eventual defeat is owed not
only to his differences from his opponent but also to an important similarity: their
common assessment of human nature. In casting off his cloak before deserting to
his rival, the *kreitton logos* reveals their fundamental identity when "naked."
Cloak alone, symbolic expression of the social covering which masks (and re-
strains) the natural man, had set the *kreitton logos* apart and marked him as the
social being he appeared to be. For his social nature was not innate but product
of an education whose strictness suggests that the basic material was recalcitrant
and the temptations difficult to control. The very vehemence of the *kreitton's*
repudiation of pleasure concedes the *hetton's* point. As Henderson comments,
"the vices and unseemliness against which he rails are described in such lurid
detail and with such obvious longing that we must feel there is something very
attractive, not to say enjoyable, about them."[41] This attractiveness and the *kreitton logos'* own profession of an instrumental view of virtue as the best way to
achieve pleasure and avoid pain—Peleus got a wife (and a knife) for his virtue
(1061ff.); the adulterer, a radish for his vice—tacitly concede that pleasure is, in
fact, the proper goal of human life.[42] The *logoi* just differ on the fine points: how
to achieve this pleasure, perhaps the form it may take, and, most importantly,
how to talk about it.

But knowledge of comic convention suggests that the role of the audience and
their tastes in the determination of the status of the *logoi* is not quite so straight-

forward. Theoretically, the *hetton logos'* victory, won because the majority are wide-assed, should initiate a new social and civic order in which the majority would not only act, but speak, as he does. Likewise, our emblematic adulterer, if allowed to speak and carry the day with his rhetorical expertise, should create a new opinion in the husband: adultery is not a punishable offense. Writ large, this process should culminate in a society that condones adultery, this being the new majority view. However, this ideal process—the fluctuation of *kreitton* and *hetton logoi* as they move from majority to minority view, and vice versa—is duplicated in neither of the "real" worlds the debate invokes. For it is not clear that the audience, although perhaps being wide-assed, would agree individually or collectively to be called so. The concluding jokes seem to vindicate the *hetton logos* and confirm his and the parabasis' portrait of the audience and the Athenians. At the same time, however, our laughter at such standard comic *abuse* revives the claims of the *kreitton logos*. Apparently even if the majority are wide-assed *(euruproktoi),* this label retains its power as somehow shaming and comically scandalous. It provokes our (disbelieving, but pleased) laughter as it expresses and discharges our hostility against those who enjoy the power and prestige that *logos* can provide. But this very laughter suggests that the *kreitton logos* remains, in some sense, the *logos* of the majority, even if he no longer regulates their conduct. Conversely, qua *logos,* the *hetton* must remain the weaker. For although practicing what he preaches, the majority both use him to ridicule and are prepared to punish, at least with laughter, those who in action or in speech seem openly to profess his standards.[43]

The gap between speech and act—acting like the *hetton* while speaking like the *kreitton*—uncovered by the *hetton*'s last point reproduces from the other side the laments of the parabasis. There the chorus complained that the victorious *Knights* failed to influence Athenian politics; even a successful *logos* did not prompt the desired action. Here the behavior of the wide-asses is not matched by, and does not affect, their speech. Apparently, the majority, who act at the dictates of desire, fear, or self-interest, are attached to or profess particular, and perhaps contradictory, *logoi* for similar "irrational" motives: habit, affection, distrust, shame. It is in the context of this world, which resembles that proposed by the *hetton logos* in its "gastric" orientation, but with the significant difference that skillful speech does not seem to make much difference, that the other troubling aspect of this *logos'* victory should be examined.

The *hetton*'s crushing victory leaves unanswered one pressing question: the status of the adulterer. How was it possible that this man, who commanded such a supposedly invincible *logos,* ever reached the point of being "radished," and thus becoming wide-assed *(euruproktos),* whether this should be considered an evil *(kakon)* or not? For it is this surprising possibility—that the sophist might in fact pay the penalty for his adultery—that is implied and never refuted during the *kreitton logos'* defeat. The *hetton logos* proves that being wide-assed is not necessarily to be considered bad; he does not deny that such a thing could befall the adulterer at all.

The opening of the debate suggests an answer: perhaps the adulterer was never allowed to display his superior verbal power. Like the *kreitton logos* in the proagon, the irate husband may not have bothered with words. Nor if he did pause for speech, is there any guarantee that even the most technically persuasive *logos* would change his mind. Before, or even after, losing the "debate," the husband may have proceeded directly to action, to avenge himself and enforce a code of conduct he would allow to be neither violated nor questioned.[44] For this was his right; adultery and its punishment were private not public matters. Between adulterer and husband, the city did not intervene—an adulterer caught in the act could even be killed by the offended husband.[45] As a result, the adulterer's putative punishment demonstrates once again the feebleness of language outside a protected arena it itself is powerless to create. As the human community and man's escape from bestial and random violence are the gifts of speech, so, in turn, *logos,* or at least its power, is predicated on the cessation of bodily force. The mechanisms for the suppression of violence can differ—divine intervention, just kings, the laws, democratic institutions, or in our proagon, the clouds-chorus—but the necessity of a superior power, guarantor of the verbal arena, provider of listeners, remains.[46] The programmatic martial imagery associated with sophistic rhetoric since the beginning of the play has tended to obscure this fundamental point, just as the triumph of the sophist at the expense of the city has tended to obscure his dependence on it. For, of course, as the agon shows and the *hetton logos* is proud to report, the sophist is the Athenian urban man supreme: the agora, not the country outside the walls, is his natural home. His *logos,* comically pictured as his huge tongue, flourishes within the confines of democratic Athens, nourished by the city's institutions, its freedom secured by civic authority. Conversely, his body is enfeebled by urban luxury; confident of the power of the word, his followers and cohorts cannot even carry the weight of a real weapon such as a shield (988ff.).[47]

This, then, is the special aristophanic twist on the familiar choice of adultery as the representative sophistic crime. Adultery is not only emblematic of the isolation of the sophist, his stance as natural man, and his devotion to private good at the expense of the city, but this particular crime makes good on sophistic theory by exiling him from it. For the city's decision not to intervene, in a certain sense, catapults the sophist, and his *logos,* outside the walls he disdains and back into a state of nature, deprived of civic protection.[48] The hypothetical confrontation with the husband allows us to test the true efficacy of rhetoric in this natural world. The possibility of the adulterer's punishment suggests its failure. But suppression of undesired speech is not limited to the repressive representatives of conventional *nomos.* Followers of the *kreitton* and the *hetton logos* are equally poor listeners. The husband acts to silence the adulterer not only because of his affiliation with the violent and inarticulate *kreitton logos* and his emotional attachment to a certain (traditional) world, but because of a (conventionally sanctioned) liberation from social constraint that affiliates him also with our play's sophists. Set free of the democratic, civic prejudice in favor of the tongue, the husband can play the part of the natural man. His choice of the unmediated violence of the hand[49] demonstrates a natural human insensibility to speech and is prophetic for the uncertain fate of those who invoke the power of *logos* in the habitat and among the natural men the sophists themselves have postulated. The punishment of radish and hot ash masks an alternate and more alarming one, certainly identifiable as a very great evil—death.

Here we can locate the final comic irony of the agon and the *hetton logos'* victory. For the condition of this *logos'* victory is the degenerate comic audience, the modern Athenian crowd. He enters claiming them as his partisans; in the end, their tastes confirm him as the *logos* of the day.[50] Yet this is an audience of "husbands" of the *hetton*'s own creation, or at least justification. The *hetton logos* encourages Pheidippides to forget moderation and reputation and devote himself to the pleasures of the body; the "wise" (899) who make up the audience have already done so, with his approbation. The agon's final sequence shows them to be dedicated to pleasure, men to whom the requirements of *sophrosyne* are a joke.[51] The danger this poses for the primacy of speech is clear to anyone who remembers the parabasis. There a wise aristophanic *sophrosyne* appeared as fundamental for the power of the word. Its complete absence here means that in spite of his proud assumption of the simple name *logos, logos* can have little to do with the *hetton*'s success. From the perspective of our comedy, not the *hetton logos'* skill or power, but the compatibility of its content—the justification of desire— with comic man's natural inclinations is reponsible for its victory. But this is a pyrrhic victory that ultimately condemns *logos* itself to subordination. For in the double or triple use of the tongue—talking, eating, kissing—it is unlikely that the pleasures of speech alone will be able to compete with those others he proposes.[52] The conditions of the *hetton logos'* triumph are the very ones that will make it temporary.[53]

At this point it might be objected that the husband's feelings and actions are not independent of *logos*. No matter what form they take, they remain expressive of that *logos* which motivates his decisions about what to do and allows us to interpret the result. Even if, for example, the husband acts to silence the adulterer, it is on the grounds of the *(kreitton) logos* that adultery is bad that he suppresses speech. This granted, *logos* regains some significance, but not that imagined for the rhetorically skillful word by Gorgias and others, including our comic sophists. For Gorgias described an independent verbal persuasion that, uncoupled from the *eros* which had traditionally bolstered it, could impinge on the human soul from the outside and change its arrangement,[54] dominating the listener without recourse. However, Gorgias' very own examples—the *logoi* of astronomers, contestants in formal agones, and philosophers—are comically challenged in the *Clouds*.[55] Such speculative *logoi* may not be good analogs for more "realistic" ones which directly affect the listeners' interests. Instead they may foster what our play will expose as another example of philosophical/rhetorical optimism: the belief that *logos* can compel action independent of, or contrary to, desire. For while within the closed circle of words, one *logos* may, through skill, command more allegiance than another, everything in the play thus far, even the victory of the *hetton logos*, seems to suggest that it is otherwise in the world of actions. There, not words but other forces are decisive. Conversely, while concession in the context of speculation and debate may not feel risky, the next scenes shall make vividly clear that neither does it get results.[56]

By the end of the agon, our comedy, if not its story, has exposed and explored the multiple ironies and difficulties presented as inherent in the sophistic treatment of *logos*. This (comic) sophistic *logos,* divorced from many of its former partners—the democratic city, justice, and law—suffers their loss as the agon's ambiguities suggest a conclusive contradiction: natural man in the natural setting is an audience highly risky for the power of the word and deaf to the weapons of rhetoric. Preoccupied with personal satisfaction and free of all external restraint, he is liable to act (or not) as he desires, not wait to listen to someone else talk. And it is these actions, or their lack, that will occupy us for the rest of the play as the theoretical implications of the unstable and ominous triumph of the *hetton logos* take form.

The process begins right away, with Pheidippides. Nussbaum remarks that "the behavior of Pheidippides at the beginning of the play bears out the claim of Anti-Right that most men, left to themselves, choose the self-centered pursuit of pleasure."[57] As such, he is well advanced along the road to sophistry. We anticipate, now, an enthusiastic response to the *hetton logos'* plea and glad accord with Strepsiades' request that his son's tongue be honed for sophistic warfare (1107ff.).[58] This is not to be. Pheidippides, far from being convinced by the *hetton logos,* has not heard a word.[59] His total obliviousness to all the impassioned speech we have just heard is hilarious, and appropriate. For Pheidippides enacts what we have theorized about the husband: never having been *sophron,* even without instruction he feels no compulsion to attend to a *logos,* no matter how persuasive, that speaks contrary to what he conceives to be his best interests and is incompatible with his desires. His laments as he is dragged offstage duplicate his earlier objections (1112 = 103, 119). Nothing is changed. Pheidippides enters the Thinkery not because he is persuaded, but because he is compelled. Inside the play, the entire *epideixis* of the *logoi* is a failure; it might just as well never have happened.[60]

For a democracy that prides itself on its commitment to *logos* and believes its successes are founded on a priority of discussion to action, the implications of this failure are frightening. Their pertinence is underlined both by the agonistic form, which parallels debate in court and assembly, and by the fact that the audience for the *logoi* is not just Pheidippides but also, and explicitly, the assembled Athenians in the theater. This crowd is invoked in the beginning of the agon; its presence and conduct are vital to the jokes and the argument that conclude it. Further, the *logoi* themselves invoke values and embody attitudes whose clash of conservative and innovative, old and young, might seem to resolve finally into competing conceptions of the state: moderate/oligarchic and populist/democratic. Thus, the *kreitton logos'* attachment to *sophrosyne, aidos,* and reputation; his repudiation of skillful speech; his nostalgia for the good old days; and his enthusiasm for sports and music have, in the debates of the day, a certain political significance. All could identify him with those dissatisfied with contemporary politics. Thus North calls him "an oldfashioned moderate in politics"[61] while he could also be taken as figuring (moderate) oligarchs, "internationalists" who were opposed to the war and the expansion of the empire[62] or, even more dramatically, the aristocratic drop-outs, nostalgic spartanizers, who, parading Laconian fashions, devoted themselves to the upper-class, "long-haired" practices of sport and music, cultivating a programmatic *sophrosyne,* homosexuality, and *apragmosyne,* or uninvolvement in political affairs.[63] Likewise, his insulting insistence on the "ignorance" (889, 919) of the many and those who follow the *hetton logos,* while sounding paradoxical coming from the *kreitton logos,* recalls Ps. Xenophon's similar charge: that the *demos* is stupid, disorderly, and vicious, uneducated through poverty, incapable of and thus indifferent to the cultured musical and physical attainments of gentlemen (1.13).[64]

Thus the *kreitton logos* emerges as a complex of "conservative" attitudes, hostile to change, speculation, and the prominence of *logos* (with all that that implied) in contemporary society and politics. Yet this kind of social conservatism and many of its views cannot be restricted to those of oligarchic leanings. Rather they are broadly characteristic of the Athenian "generation gap," which bred what Ostwald has identified as a "tendency to find the old, regardless of the social class to which they belong, portrayed as staunch supporters of the institutions of the Athenian democracy, while the young, usually members of the upper-classes, are presented as at odds with the aims and methods of the democratic establishment and the demagogues who manipulate it." He lists as traits of this characterization: looking "on the younger generation as softies," nostalgia for Marathon and the real men of the old days, including the upper-class leaders, contempt for the present leaders as "young sexual perverts."[65] Clearly these match important points in the portrait of the *kreitton logos.* They also have a curious affinity to some of the views of the thucydidean Cleon in the Mitylenean debate. There we find Cleon praising the previously Spartan characteristic of *sophrosyne* and promoting strict adherence to even bad laws as an antidote to the Athenians' excessive trust in *logos* and fascination with the latest in rhetorical techniques.[66] His motives resemble those of the *kreitton logos.* These seeming polar opposites are one in their dislike and distrust of the modern/revolutionary affairs (*neotera pragmata* 515–16) which seem to threaten negative change (moral, social, speculative, political, artistic) at an ever-increasing tempo, and whose principle cause and manifestation they find in a novel *logos* manipulated as speculative and rhetorical tool by a limited number of sophists and their young, clever, wealthy students.[67]

Conversely, the *hetton logos'* devotion to debate, his legal ability, his indifference to traditional values and to sport, and his dedication to the agora could mark him as democratic,[68] yet this picture, too, is more complex. For the *hetton logos'* command of a powerful rhetoric, his status as a clear product of the democracy, and his emphatic rejection of *sophrosyne* do not automatically label him the contrary of an oligarchic *kreitton logos.* Rather, as Turato and Ambrosino have shown, this *logos'* views, particularly on the *nomos/physis* antithesis, are characteristic of the justification and techniques of the revolutionary aristocratic youth united in elitist political/social clubs and of young, opportunistic, power-hungry aristocrats, whose fathers supported the democracy while they themselves, perhaps feeling excluded from power, are instead ready to take advantage of it— or to change it.[69] These men represented by Alcibiades, the aristophanic Pheidippides, and platonic Callicles, frequently taken as the philosophical counterpart of the *hetton logos,*[70] have embraced democratic institutions as means to the satisfaction of the appetites and the exercise of personal power—goals to which an invincible feeling of superiority, rhetorical skill, and a disdain for all social, political, and moral constraints can contribute substantially. Thus while the philosophic Callicles is pictured as concerned with power and the comic *hetton logos,* suitably, with satisfaction of the desires, both agree in scorning self-control, equality, law, justice, and the rights of others. All are subterfuges devised by the weak many to restrain the stronger few. Adherence to them is characteristic of fools ignorant of the true laws of nature.[71] Men of such views can be considered democrats only nominally. Their ability to exploit the democracy is coupled to a total lack of allegiance to its ideology: they see no inconsistency, and certainly nothing wrong, in "pandering" to the people while simultaneously maintaining oligarchic sympathies.[72] Through speech, that most democratic of means, they captivate the *demos* to achieve traditional aristocratic goals: defending oneself, helping friends, and harming enemies.[73] It is men like these who unite in suspicion old-fashioned moderates and establishment democrats and are the object of Cleon's surprising (and dismaying) warning.

That such positions as just sketched are paradoxical and contradictory is clear in the *Clouds* and elsewhere.[74] As Ostwald points out about Callicles, "modern scholars debate whether he was a democrat, an oligarch, or an advocate of tyranny; but the question cannot be answered in these terms."[75] Our own *logoi* respond equally poorly to questions of precise political "affiliation" or "stance." The agon does not make a political "commentary" in political terms, for its focus is not institutional, but "human."[76] Its deciding argument turns not on issues of state but of sexual taste,[77] for which the Athenians in the stands, the collected citizenry, function only to provide the (comic) data. The conclusion—the dominance of individual corporal desire—which leads to the defeat of the *kreitton logos,* and as we have seen, its assimilation to the *hetton,* only manifests what has been clear all along: the centrality of desire to both the *logoi.* The *hetton logos* openly bases his appeal on satisfaction of the appetites; the *kreitton*'s eulogy of self-control is equally, if more covertly, responsive to the appetites. His speech vividly mirrors his "obsession with boys' genitals," and points out "virtuous" behavior by dreamily dwelling on its opposite.[78] In making such considerations decisive, the shape of the agon remarks the common foundation of these competing "political" *logoi* whose apparent differences have provided the "substance" of the debate. The "political" ramifications, or rather the ramifications for how we view politics, are clear.

Thus the very staging of the agon, with its personification of the *logoi,* vividly exposes the extent to which speech emerges from and must function within the constraints of human desire, on both sides of the verbal relationship. Such a spectacle mocks the whole concept of a purely verbal sophistic agon, along with its vision of an independent *logos,* emancipated from speaker and listener and operating through the power of words alone. It is equally discouraging for those who value political debate as a forum for rational decision making. Yet as we have seen before, the final significance of the *Clouds'* comedy lies not in the words (or actions) of any one of its characters, but is articulated in their interplay. Thus it is not surprising that the *Clouds'* highly human *logoi,* both of which are parodied and rejected as insufficient, do, between them, sketch complexes of attitudes and practices that at once make the democratic city possible and put it at risk. The *kreitton logos* espouses civic and martial virtues essential for the political and physical survival of the state, yet also a hostility to freedom, individual difference, innovation, and *logos* which jeopardizes precisely the values that have character- ized the greatness of Athenian democracy, and aristophanic comedy. Conversely, the *hetton*'s dedication to these values is coupled with a lack of moderation and a devotion to self-interest that imperils civic stability and social harmony and un- dermines Athens' democratic future. Whatever the precise political orientation of these *logoi* separately, together they represent a fracturing of the qualities of the ideal citizen that leads to excess and failure on both sides. In the process, as discussed in chapter 5 from a different perspective, Aristophanes' voice emerges not as identical to anything on stage but as occupying a middle ground between *kreitton* and *hetton logos,* incorporating elements of both but professing allegiance to neither. Instead, the totality of Aristophanes' *logos* implicitly constructs a dif- ferent ideal figure, our poet, whose creation, the *Clouds,* and whose educational goals prove him to be at once moderate and freedom-loving, intellectual and at- tached to his city and fellow citizens, prizing *logos* and debate, yet not mistaking them for personal weapons and, above all, devoted to the democratic ideal of productive civic discourse—of which his *Clouds* itself must be considered a re- deeming example.[79]

8

The Triumph of Practical Sophistry: Lines 1113–1302

The short scenes that follow the debate of the *logoi,* the second parabasis (1115–30), the return of Pheidippides (1131–1213), and Strepsiades' debates with the creditors (1214–1302), perform the traditional function of the iambic scenes—to play out in a variety of ways the "practical" effects of the first part of the play.[1] The plot seems to present the triumphant progress of sophistic rhetoric, yet as the speakers enact what was promised by the agon and more, the wild incongruity of it all cannot help but startle. Any residual hope that crude recourse to violence in the place of speech is characteristic only of the archaic and inarticulate *kreitton logos* is quickly shattered. The situation deteriorates ever more quickly as we witness a farcical progression from threats to specious reasoning to open violence which reveals the full dimensions our comedy assigns to the sophistic identification of *logos* as a type of force. For unlike the first part of the play, the latter "sophistic" half abounds in violence of all kinds. Vulgar comedy at its finest, it races along to link violence and fluency in new ways for the pleasure of the vulgar and the edification of the wise. Using every comic technique discussed earlier, from the concretization of metaphor to the old man beating those about him, the equation between the power of the hand and that of the tongue is read backwards to stage "sophists" who hold speech as just one option in the arsenal of weapons to effect their will. As promised by the parabasis and agon, however, the interlocutors of the sophists, the audience for *logos,* are no better. Not what they hear but what they feel seems to determine their reception of the word. Their reactions to sophistic speech range from self-interested probing of personal benefit through denial of the pertinence of argument, no matter how correct and clear. As we watch, the ground is laid for the second agon. For we are in a drama where desire rules, and those who "listen" and those who "speak" are headed for conflict.

The second parabasis (1115–30) begins the accelerating downward spiral, but lightheartedly. As the reluctant Pheidippides is escorted or dragged off stage into the Thinkery, the chorus masks his instruction (whatever form it may take) with another direct address to the audience. As in the epirrhema of the first parabasis, the clouds speak in dramatic character, yet break through the dramatic illusion to acknowledge their role as comic chorus and to continue the audience's involvement in what happens on stage. Also as in the first parabasis, the clouds extrapolate the issues of the preceding scenes to their own comic competition. Agon and

106

parabasis have shown that the character of the spectators and of the judges, their fellow citizens, makes futile any attempt to win this contest with the charms of language alone. Invocation of public good and harm is likewise irrelevant. Consequently, abandoning the rhetoric of civic duties and benefits which they invoked so prominently before (577ff.), the clouds follow the lead of the *logoi* and address the judges ad hominem. "The audience is tempted to judge according to fear and self-interest rather than by the abstract aesthetic standards discussed in the parabasis."[2] Conspicuously absent are wisdom and reputation, the values that closed the parabatic Aristophanes' appeal (560ff.). Instead the clouds try to forge a pact of mutual gratification, jokingly exhorting the judges to overlook their public function and determine the requirements of a rhetorical "justice"[3] according to the criterion just demonstrated as decisive by the *hetton logos*—private advantage. Judges and chorus should help each other, and the clouds propose to begin the bargaining, commencing:[4]

$$\tau o\grave{\upsilon}\varsigma\ \kappa\rho\iota\tau\grave{\alpha}\varsigma\ \mathring{\alpha}\ \kappa\epsilon\rho\delta\alpha\nu o\hat{\upsilon}\sigma\iota\nu,\ \mathring{\eta}\nu\ \tau\iota\ \tau\acute{o}\nu\delta\epsilon\ \tau\grave{o}\nu\ \chi o\rho\grave{o}\nu$$
$$\mathring{\omega}\phi\epsilon\lambda\hat{\omega}\sigma'\ \grave{\epsilon}\kappa\ \tau\hat{\omega}\nu\ \delta\iota\kappa\alpha\acute{\iota}\omega\nu,\ \beta o\upsilon\lambda\acute{o}\mu\epsilon\sigma\theta'\ \mathring{\upsilon}\mu\hat{\iota}\nu\ \phi\rho\acute{\alpha}\sigma\alpha\iota.$$
(1115–16)

The judges, what they will gain, if this chorus
they assist as is just, we wish to tell you.

The subsequent promises are comically familiar. Judges and audience are kin to Strepsiades and Pheidippides, exclusively interested in the pleasures and necessities of the body: food, wine, shelter, and sex (1117ff.).

But the chorus' words reveal them as attentive to the lessons of the agon in another way: they do not intend to leave things to speech alone. Initial appeals to self-interest rapidly give way to bolstering threats: failure to embrace the correct *logos*, that of this particular comic chorus, will be punished.[5] This marks another departure from the first parabasis. There the clouds attempted to guide the citizens' debate through exercise of their (natural) "voice," thunder and storm; here they are more direct. They plan to enforce their own *logoi* through extra-linguistic means. In their capacity as clouds, the chorus will destroy the fields and homes and ruin the marriages of those who fail to heed them (1121ff.). This may seem a surprising departure for the clouds, goddesses of rhetoric who are themselves appearing in a rhetorical display *(epideixis),* and who encouraged the *logoi* to do so as well. For while the violence they promise remains connected to *logos*—it serves to reinforce one at the expense of others—nevertheless, the change from the *hetton logos'* exclusive reliance on speech is clear. The completeness of the reversal is revealed in the phrasing. $\tau o\iota\alpha\acute{\upsilon}\tau\alpha\iota\varsigma\ \sigma\phi\epsilon\nu\delta\acute{o}\nu\alpha\iota\varsigma\ \pi\alpha\iota\acute{\eta}\sigma o\mu\epsilon\nu$, "we will strike *(paiein)* with such missiles" (1125), and $\chi\alpha\lambda\acute{\alpha}\zeta\alpha\iota\varsigma\ \sigma\tau\rho o\gamma\gamma\acute{\upsilon}\lambda\alpha\iota\varsigma\ \sigma\upsilon\nu\tau\rho\acute{\iota}\psi o\mu\epsilon\nu$, "we will shatter with well-rounded *(strongulos)* hail-stones" (1127), recall the martial connotations of rhetorical terminology. The image of words as projectiles was common, exploited by the sophists and used of them in Aristophanes.[6] *Paiein* was used in the first parabasis (549) for the verbal blows Aristophanes himself dealt Cleon in the *Knights. Strongulos* was a standard rhetorical term for a well-rounded, telling phrase, a term obviously derived from $\pi\alpha\acute{\iota}\epsilon\iota\nu$

στρογγύλαις σφενδόναις, "to strike with well-rounded missiles."[7] These expressions now once again describe forceful physical action.

The punning reuse of what previously functioned as a declaration of sophistic linguistic violence highlights the clouds' change in weapons, but the clouds are not, for all that, to be considered less sophistic. As the play on words makes clear, the role these rhetorical deities assign violence is a comical and logical extension of sophistic slogans that made language a form of force, assimilated it to *bia* (or physical violence), and reduced it to just one tool (if the most effective) among many, empty of moral weight or meaning. True allegiance is not to the means but to the end, personal satisfaction. Consequently, when speech appears likely to fail, nothing (certainly not inconsistency) prevents the substitution of violence and the enforcement of the action or *logos* desired. The devotees of such goddesses are not likely to be great respecters of the right of *logos* to be heard. Like their opponent, the *kreitton logos,* they prefer to dictate than to listen.

But our laughter seems to suggest that this is an overly serious reading; the second parabasis is really irreverent joking, whose humor makes, as often, the final contribution to its themes. For as the direct address and parabatic form make sure we remember, the clouds are a comic creation played by a comic chorus; our response to their threats must be bracketed by this knowledge. The joke lies precisely in their attempt to use and deny this comic identity simultaneously: as chorus they appeal to the spectators to confer victory on their play with threats of extra-verbal forces that they can claim only as characters within the fiction. Further, the lessons of the previous scenes—which have demonstrated the meaninglessness of celestial phenomena—undercut this one. Not only is the idea that the judges' weddings might be ruined funny because such intentional rain, for such a reason, is impossible outside the confines of our own *Clouds,* but there is a delightful absurdity in imagining that the clouds could do as they claim: that such threats could move from word to action. Whatever these threats may contribute to the themes of the play, they themselves are clearly empty words, and our amusement depends on this knowledge. Such pleasure confirms, in reverse, our comedy's endless play with the connection(s) of violence and speech, for here we find that such blustery thunder, without "real" force to back it, is simply laughable.

But all this is only suggested in the second parabasis, which is itself outside the dramatic action. The tension between the tenor of the parabases and agon and the apparent direction of the plot begins to mount as, the second parabasis over, the trembling Strepsiades calls on Socrates to collect what he hopes is a newly hatched sophist, ready to ward off his enemies, the creditors.

With the emergence of Pheidippides, Strepsiades' (and the audience's) fondest hopes seem to be realized. Perhaps we will finally enounter an authentic product of sophistic education and get to witness his rhetorical powers at work. Pheidippides, who now sports an intellectual pallor and is best described with the fashionable adjectives (11716ff.) and (mock) heroic terms that characterize the sophistic warrior (1154–66),[8] straightway gives dazzling proof of his newfound skills.[9] The logic that Strepsiades tried, in vain, to apply in his own lessons about legal thinking is now brilliantly executed. Combining interpretation of the wording of the law on debt (1178ff.), discussion of nature's rules and natural precedents for social forms (1183ff.), and rhetorical commonplaces (1187ff.), Pheidippides concocts an absurd interpretation of the phrase τὴν ἕνην τε καὶ νέαν (1178), "the old and new [day]" (that is, the last day of the month), that overturns the conventional meaning,[10] while simultaneously convicting Athenian officials of corruption to gratify the belly (1198ff.). Unlike his father, whose labors with words were marked by confusion and a leaden lack of skill, Pheidippides is presented as master of all the techniques the sophists have to offer.

With this new voice seems to begin a new kind of comedy. The obvious vulgarity and stupidity of Strepsiades has exposed, through a series of obscene jokes, the clash between the abstractions of the intellectual Socrates and the earthy needs and desires of the ordinary (comic) man, who in the person of Strepsiades invaded the philosophic confines of the Thinkery. As befitted its dramatic location, the criticism was theoretical, suggested through the comic *logos* rather than enacted by the characters. The figure of Pheidippides translates examination of successful sophistry and rhetoric into the "real" world outside the school. Interplay will no longer be between teacher and student, but between sophistic speaker and his audience. Socrates disappears, not to be seen again until the end of the play—if then.[11] Sophistry has a new and different representative, another comic type, familiar from earlier plays of Aristophanes and invoked in the agon: the fashionable, gilded youth who haunts the agora and has embraced the *hetton logos* and all he represents. This is no philosopher, nor does he share Socrates' concerns. Rather Pheidippides is one of the lucky few who use, abuse, and enjoy the new *logos* and its power. As such he is a member of a class as remote from most of the audience as from the dumbfounded Strepsiades. From the moment that we witness his first rhetorical sally, we are aware of how silly and how powerful he is. This is to be the promised rhetoric that will sweep everything before it. The comic portrayal of its deceptive and unrealistic cleverness in no way diminishes our expectation it will live up to its reputation, leaving all doubts to be worked out in the more prosaic world offstage.

Strepsiades' confidence, too, is restored, and he is jubilant: Pheidippides' new *logos* will participate in every negative aspect of sophistic speech—and be supremely useful. His song of rejoicing (1201–12/13), for a moment, widens the scope of the action and summons the audience to realize the civic implications of this personal drama. As Ambrosino has shown, what Strepsiades promises himself and us is that Pheidippides' skills will conclusively break apart civic equality, destroy *isonomia* and *isegorie*, equality before the law and in the assembly, and reduce his fellow citizens to the status of mute beasts (1203). Compared with the new rhetors, the ordinary Athenian will be no more able to speak than an animal, and will be equally vulnerable to exploitation. Once again, as in the agon, but from a different perspective, we see the techniques and presuppositions of sophistic rhetoric destroying the city, or at least its democratic heritage. Ambrosino has identified the result: in democratic Athens, democracy itself, erected on common possession of *logos* and common right to debate the public good, is now a sham.[12] But this is clearly irrelevant to Strepsiades. Convinced he is one of the promised few, it occurs to him neither that he cannot speak, nor that such an audience could be not only "mute", but "deaf" as well. Having already rewarded Socrates, he rushes his son off to a feast.

The audience may be less sanguine. Strepsiades' excessive and hubristic song is reminiscent of the moment in tragedy when the hero's confidence reaches its peak, and the plot twists.[13] His paratragic opening song in this scene (1154–66) has already hinted at what is to come.[14] The commentators note that as the first lines parody Sophocles' *Peleus,* the last lines (1165–66) parody Euripides' *Hecuba* 171ff., where Hecuba calls forth Polyxena to tell her of her impending sacrifice. Like Peleus, Strepsiades is father to a hero in the warfare of the day, and although he is still unaware of it, Strepsiades, like Peleus and Hecuba, has also lost his child. The difference is that he himself performed the sacrifice. As we may already suspect, sophistic education destroys filial piety and familial loyalty, leaving nothing to ensure that Pheidippides' skills will benefit his father. In trying to combine obedient son and practiced sophist, Strepsiades is guilty of trying to combine the same incompatible elements in Pheidippides that he does in his song when he rejoices in a new fangled sophistic "double-edged tongue" ($\dot{\alpha}\mu\phi\dot{\eta}\kappa\epsilon\iota$ $\gamma\lambda\dot{\omega}\tau\tau\eta$ 1160) that he calls traditionally and tragically "my bulwark, savior of the house, bane to enemies" ($\pi\rho\dot{o}\beta o\lambda o\varsigma$ $\dot{\epsilon}\mu\dot{o}\varsigma$, $\sigma\omega\tau\dot{\eta}\rho$ $\delta\dot{o}\mu o\iota\varsigma$, $\dot{\epsilon}\chi\theta\rho o\hat{\iota}\varsigma$ $\beta\lambda\dot{\alpha}\beta\eta$ 1161). Sophistic rhetoric is not something that can be readily incorporated into traditional structures. Rather it will shatter them, just as it does the traditional language and traditional notions of civic power and citizen.

The scenes with the creditors which follow the exit of Pheidippides and his father finally promise to provide the repulsion scenes that normally follow the agon. Surprisingly, however, it is Strepsiades who emerges to carry out the traditionally violent rejections of the impostors, here, ironically, the relatively just, if ridiculous, creditors. But initial impressions that Strepsiades' efforts may mark a return to the comedy of the first part of the play evaporate as the scenes progress. As he brandishes the deformed remnants of sophistic lore he has managed to retain, Strepsiades' bumbling efforts not only mock the silliness of sophistic teaching, but expose its volatile nature in conjunction with the comic/sophistic natural man. This is what Strepsiades has wanted to do from the beginning, before and after meeting Socrates. The fact that he remains a ludicrous failure does not diminish his significance. Rather, his comical actions confirm the contention of the *hetton logos* that all men err; the sophist differs only in doing so without fear. Before he entered the Thinkery and while Pheidippides was still in residence, the terrified Strepsiades had been forced to rely on unconvincing manipulation of traditional language for his defense (1137ff.). Now he has sophistic rhetoric—the "unthrowable *logos*" ($\dot{\alpha}\kappa\alpha\tau\dot{\alpha}\beta\lambda\eta\tau o\nu$ $\lambda\dot{o}\gamma o\nu$ 1229),[15] his version and his son's—at his command.

Knowledge of this complete impunity liberates Strepsiades from all lingering restraints, internal and external, and he enacts the sentiments he expressed in his joyful song moments before. His actions graphically illustrate the consequences of blurring the distinction between persuasion and violence, for the violence of these scenes is not only comic but also comically sophistic. The necessities of generic structure and Aristophanes' carefully drawn implications of sophistic theory coincide to drive what starts as a dialogue to end as violence. Meanwhile the creditors themselves, the audience for Strepsiades' "sophistic" speech, are equally comic—in their indifference to *logos*. After these scenes we can only hope that the skillful Pheidippides will salvage the situation, and that those he encounters will be more loyal and more receptive to the word.

The first creditor comes, equipped with a witness, to call upon Strepsiades to repay his debt or be taken to court. As commentators, following the scholia, have noted, he is portrayed as the typical Athenian, dedicated to his material goods and to litigation. When Strepsiades attempts to deny the existence of the loan, the creditor reminds him that he swore to pay by the gods. This is an error. Strepsiades mocks the creditor for his naive belief and declares himself ready to swear and forswear any oath required. This statement shocks the creditor but is of little practical importance. He senses no direct connection between the obligation to pay debts and the continued existence of the gods; he plans to rely not on divine support, but on the courts, to secure his money. This typical Athenian, thus, blithely ignores what had been a knockout blow to the *kreitton logos.* The great celestial discoveries that seemed so significant when they were introduced are apparently not as potent as hoped or feared. As the first parabasis intimated, the average man has only marginal interest in the gods, their existence, and their powers. Protestations of piety aside (1236), the traditional gods, who have become a joke to Strepsiades,[16] are little more to the creditor. Instead he is devoted to his stomach, his enormous *gaster.*[17] Neither the divine, nor, as we shall see, *logos,* can distract him from the juicy prospect of a lawsuit which he feels sure to win. This is an unpleasant surprise, but Strepsiades is not deterred by his disappointment. He will test the creditor's knowledge of correct speech by asking him to identify a basket.[18] The test is, of course, pro forma; Strepsiades has already decided not to pay. Nevertheless, it should determine the creditor's effectiveness in court, and, through his certain failure, have the added benefit of exposing his ignorance and thus intimidating and disheartening him (1256ff.). The creditor, however, recognizes neither his ignorance nor its consequences. Unimpressed, he simply continues to demand payment. Strepsiades' patience is at an end; he violently orders the creditor to leave.

The second creditor proves equally intransigent, even though this time Strepsiades produces much more credible arguments. Discarding discussion of the gods as ineffective, Strepsiades begins a new tack: the taking of interest is contrary to nature. His initial argument, that the supply of money should not grow over time any more than the supply of rainwater, has to be abandoned midstream; the creditor refuses to participate, stating that he neither knows anything about rain nor cares (1282). Strepsiades' second attempt begins more successfully. When he asks, "but this interest/offspring *(tokos),* what beast is it?" (τοῦτο δ' ἔσθ', ὁ τόκος, τί θηρίον; 1286),[19] the creditor comes back with an answer: like many growing things, money, too, participates in natural increase—interest represents its growth over time (1287ff.). This unexpected response is both encouraging and discouraging. On the one hand, the creditor seems to accept the pertinence of argument, and this line of argument, to the matter at hand; on the other, he proposes an acceptable natural model for the taking of interest. Strepsiades is impressed; he can answer only by proposing an alternative natural model: the increase of inanimate things like the sea. The creditor has demonstrated one problem with the argument from nature: its flexibility. It is often unclear which, if any, contradictory natural parallels are to be cited in a given situation. However, the real problem with the creditor is more fundamental. For, at first, Strepsiades' counterexample seems to be successful. The creditor readily concedes that the sea does not grow over time, even though rivers pour into it, and the form of his concession is emphatic and significant: "for it is not just *(dikaion)* that it be greater" (οὐ γὰρ δίκαιον πλεῖον' εἶναι 1292). This is clearly damning. The entire conflict has been manipulated to wrest a concession of this form from the creditor and to stage its consequences.[20] One can imagine a long pause as Strepsiades waits for the creditor to realize that he has been defeated and his demands discredited. But the creditor mysteriously fails to take this crucial final step. He does not seem to recognize that what is unjust for the sea cannot be just *(dikaion)* for man. Natural paradigms are irrelevant once again, as, in a different way, is the more familiar "equation of δίκη, righteousness and justice among men, with cosmic order and physical laws."[21] Further, participation in discussion is meaningless, and effective and ineffective reasoning equally useless; verbal concession will not be matched by behavioral change.[22] After everything is said, nothing new is done; the creditor is still resolved to collect his money.[23] Understandably furious, Strepsiades vigorously points out the proper conclusion (1292ff.)[24] and backs up his interpretation with violence. If the creditor does not leave immediately, he will be subjected to gross and painful injury.

> . . . ἄξεις; ἐπιαλῶ
> κεντῶν ὑπὸ τὸν πρωκτόν σε τὸν σειραφόρον.
> φεύγεις; ἔμελλόν σ' ἄρα κινήσειν ἐγὼ
>
> (1299–1301)

> . . . Will you pull [the chariot]? I will lay it on,
> goading *(kentein)* you, the racehorse, up the ass.
> You're fleeing? I was about to move/rape you then myself

Strepsiades' scenes with the creditors demolish cherished sophistic assumptions and expose the weakness of *logos* in the ordinary social world and among ordinary men. Language meets the fate predicted for it: it fails to gain a hearing from those deafened by self-interest, or, even more disappointingly, it fails to change the behavior of those who are, theoretically, convinced. This is due not to the stupidity of Strepsiades, for the cogency of Strepsiades' arguments makes no difference, but to the character of his interlocutors. As we watch the first creditor ignore Strepsiades' remarks and the second indulge him pointlessly, we realize that the creditors are not willing to be persuaded nor open to debate. Like the spectators of the first *Clouds,* they are indifferent to *logos.* Their intransigence underlines once again the necessity of the invisible first step in the persuasive process, for in the absence of an authentic audience willing to listen for whatever reason—self-interest, love, legal necessity, or even, we can hope, verbal pleasures—*logos* is powerless.

Strepsiades is not deterred, however, for the creditors' lack of commitment to speech is matched by his own. When words are unavailing, blows, which, unlike *logos,* operate on willing and unwilling alike, are readily substituted. This violence can be understood in terms of Strepsiades' comic character, yet it would be a mistake to see it as simply a stupid perversion of sophistic teachings. Like all his "perversions," Strepsiades' violence unveils something central through a hyperbolic and parodic rendering flesh of sophistic claims; in the structure of these scenes, his actions are alternative ways of enforcing his rhetorical points and "enslaving" his listeners. The first creditor is refused and forced to leave, ostensibly for a grammatical error that will cause his subsequent failure in court. The second creditor is driven from the stage in a way that emphatically reintegrates him with the natural world whose significance for human behavior he has just denied, for Strepsiades' final lines refer "not to a stab in one buttock, which all ages have regarded as irresistibly funny, but to the cruel practice of goading a draught-animal in the anus."[25] The physical goad (1297, 1300) replaces the verbal one of persuasion which did not work. Thus we watch a farcically violent reproduction of the tactics of Pericles, who, in the passage from Eupolis quoted in chapter 4, successfully goaded his hearers with words like a charioteer his horses.[26] While the difference must have been palpable to their various "audiences," the principle in a fantastic comic sense remains the same. As we have already learned from Strepsiades' song, those who do not command the power of sophistic rhetoric are marked by this deficiency as prey.[27] Trapped in a subordinate and bestial position, lacking the distinctively human ability to speak (which has been preempted by the possessors of the new superior *logos*), they exist to be exploited, or more crudely, screwed, deceived, fucked over, for such physical and mental violation is what Strepsiades punningly promises the second creditor (1301).[28] Thus Strepsiades acts like the rhetoricians who are buggering (his and) their audience, the Athenian public—and for the same reasons.

Imagery and theory alike make clear that this alternation between language and violence represents more than a simple contamination of sophistic notions by an inarticulate dolt. A "theoretical justification," not just freedom from fear of punishment and liberation from all social and moral constraint, encourages Strepsiades to vent his natural predilection for things physical. For Strepsiades is only making good on the clouds' own threats when he reduces the word to just one tool for working his will, and is willing to back up his *logos* with force.[29] What we see is the reversal of the equation between violence and language, which, shorn of its subtleties, has functioned since the beginning of the play as the representive sophistic claim for their *logos*. If language is equivalent to violence, violence must also be equivalent to speech. Thus, behavior imposed through physical force is as satisfactory as that induced through reasoning and persuasion, and actions required by violence seem to vindicate the inadequate reasoning which alone could not secure them. In a wild collapse of contraries, the interpenetration of speech and force, *logos* and *bia,* is complete. They are farcically and speculatively stripped of their differences and merge in a realm where persuasion and goading are equally viable alternatives, theoretically and metaphorically indistinguishable.

As we watch this hilarious scene, the familiar old man beating those present to hide his bad jokes,[30] we appreciate how appropriate Strepsiades' actions and attitudes are for the world inhabited by the second *Clouds.* Surely the audience that rejected the first *Clouds* would, in Strepsiades' position, have acted similarly—nor do we ourselves seem so very different, after a moment's reflection. For even as we appreciate Aristophanes' biting wit, our cackling at Strepsiades' antics confirms as well the rivaling pleasures of generic and hubristic violence.

9

Comic Justice: Lines 1303–1510

The clouds' song at the end of the scene with the creditors (1303–20) warns the audience that the end of the play is at hand and hints at the form it will take.[1] In the characteristic dynamic of the *Clouds,* we are about to witness the joke that will turn everything preceding on its head. Put in other terms, we will see comic justice at work, witnessing a "comedy of inversion," in which characters are entrapped by their desires and enmeshed in their own schemes.[2] This process should not be confused with moral justice, although the effects may appear similar. Comic justice, like comic triumph, functions not morally but logistically. The end remains true to the strategy we have been studying all along: the creation of a metaphoric vision which operates by taking a *logos* "seriously," or "literally," rendering it concrete, and then drawing, or rather staging, the unexpected consequences.[3] As the clouds indicate, this process is to begin with Strepsiades: this comic madman is going to find out what it is to "love" (*eran* 1303) the wrong things. Besotted (*erastheis* 1304) with the idea of denying his debts and the city's justice, he will feel the results of his desires: in the person of his son, Strepsiades, the "sophist" (1309–20), will experience what the *hetton logos* is really all about. However, the reversals will go further than that. Not just Strepsiades, but Pheidippides and Socrates too, will find themselves in the world designed by their desires and their *logoi*.[4] The triumphant progress of rhetoric will be derailed as we discover the real meaning of the denial of binding obligations, the isolation of the sophist, the assimilation of language and violence, and life in the oven of the purely natural world. The only trouble is that the consequences, while ridiculous, are not happy.[5] Nevertheless, we are not confronted with tragedy. The overly perfect and mocking symmetry of the end, coupled with delicate play with the audience's responses, continue to remind us that we are watching comic *logos,* not life, at work. The entire *Clouds* performs on a larger scale the function of the cloud chorus, mockery that reflects in appropriate (not identical) shapes the manias of its subjects—which are certainly not confined to Strepsiades but include Socrates, Pheidippides, and the Athenian public as well.

The pattern of the end begins to come clear when Strepsiades erupts from his house screaming for help (1321). After beating his unfortunate creditors, now he himself is beaten by a sophist, his own son. Apparently, Pheidippides, too, has learned the violent lesson implicit in sophistic martial imagery,[6] a lesson so highly compatible with the disposition and desires of natural man. Accomplished speaker that he is, Pheidippides has deserted language. Why, and what this means, is suggested by the comic allusion placed at the beginning of the episode. As Strepsiades recounts the quarrels about the singing of traditional poets after dinner (1355ff.) that led up to his beating, Pheidippides interrupts indignantly: his father deserved a thrashing for bidding him sing "just as if [he were] entertaining cicadas" (ὡσπερεὶ τέττιγας ἐστιῶντα 1360). His simile, and the comic reasons for its presence here, are elucidated by *Phaedrus* 258b5ff. There Socrates recounts the cicadas' history: they were once men who became so entranced by the pleasure of song that, neglectful of food and drink, they died.[7] To speak in a songful way is apparently to defer the belly and turn one's thoughts decisively to higher things. The platonic passage commends this attitude; cicadas are the appropriate Muses for a discussion of rhetoric that makes of it something very different than the *Clouds*.[8] In Pheidippides' repudiation, however, we sense once more our own sophisticated comic omen: the farting gnat. Before song became a noise that was a function of the guts; here it is rejected altogether. As far as the hedonistic Pheidippides is concerned, speech which does not further the body and express its needs and desires is a useless annoyance. The contrast with the elevated Socrates and his emaciated students, the reversal of their ambitions could not be more pointed, yet the link established from the beginning between their speculation and Pheidippides' action remains.[9]

As Strepsiades continues his story, we learn that when he did consent to sing, Pheidippides' contentious and programmatic choice was a euripidean passage about incest. Like the choice of adultery in the agon, incest here is emblematic of a whole complex of sophistic positions. Most obviously it denotes a breakdown of the familial/social order and a hegemony of the body (and hedonistic satisfaction) which render irrelevant all conventional bonds restrictive of the desires.[10] Strepsiades' incensed reaction to his son's choice provoked an immediate example of this attitude—and one that would motivate the end of the play. For as he tells the clouds: Pheidippides sang,

> κἀγὼ οὐκέτ' ἐξηνεσχόμην, ἀλλ' εὐθέως ἀράττω
> πολλοῖς κακοῖς καἰσχροῖσι. κᾆτ' ἐντεῦθεν, οἶον εἰκός,
> ἔπος πρὸς ἔπος ἠρειδόμεσθ'· εἶθ' οὗτος ἐπαναπηδᾷ,
> κᾄπειτ' ἔφλα με κᾆσπόδει κᾄπνιγε κᾆπέτριβεν.
>
> (1373–76)

and I no longer was tolerant, but straightaway smite
with many and shameful [words]. And then from there, as was fitting,
word to word we parried; then this one jumps me
and then crunched me, and kicked, and strangled, and crushed [me].

Line 1374 is homeric and martial.[11] Its use clearly recalls that other homeric line, 321, with which Strepsiades expressed his initial reaction to the voice of the clouds. That line, however, introduced the martial and self-sufficient violence of sophistic speech. This line performs the opposite task. The heroic struggle of words[12] that Strepsiades began about Euripides degenerated into a struggle of bodies, in which the sophistic Pheidippides, himself the first to forsake the power of speech, kicks and beats his father about the head and (of course) jaw (1324). Inside the hidden natural world in miniature that is the interior of the house, the rules of the city can be evaded: there was no reason to confine himself to *logos,* and Pheidippides did not do so. Since, unlike the *hetton logos,* he was stronger than his opponent, Pheidippides took the part of the *kreitton* instead, turning to violence to stifle opposing views. The irony is complete when we hear that he plunged his father back into a parody of savage and inarticulate childhood, at long last really shitting back in fear to a sophist (1386ff.).[13]

It was at this moment that we saw Strepsiades, deprived of voice and social covering, reduced to just another body, bolt from the house. Strauss believes this "flight to the public" is to find witnesses so Strepsiades can take his son to court.[14] In fact, another of Strepsiades' motives is more basic: having just spurned the city and its laws, Strepsiades now needs the community to assert the purely conventional sanctity of a father's body and protect him from the illegal force of the stronger man who is his son.[15] Surprisingly, his action precipitates another agon, in which Strepsiades will take the part of the *kreitton logos,* Pheidippides, the *hetton.* The repetition of this structure underlines both the formal sophistic/comic nature of these endless debates and the logical relationship of the first and second agon: this agon is the practical, "real-world" enactment of the consequences of the first.[16] Also like the first, it has not happened all by itself. The Athenian public seated in the comic audience has functioned like the chorus in the proagon of the earlier debate. Their collective strength and civic authority has had to suppress violence before talk could begin.[17]

Pheidippides' respect for this power is demonstrated by his change in tactics: the public world he has entered makes the time ripe for a display of sophistic rhetoric, always most useful before a crowd. Since the facts are not in doubt,[18] Pheidippides proposes to argue values. He will use the two *logoi* to persuade (*anapeithein* 1342)[19] his father that father-beating is really just (1331ff.). When Strepsiades agrees—he will listen, and implicitly be persuaded, if the right *logos* can be found (1344)[20]—the difficult first step in the persuasive process, securing the listener's complicity, is negotiated without fanfare. The logic of the play thus far, the requirements of the agonistic structure, and the precedent of the *kreitton logos'* assent combine to render Strepsiades' rather surprising agreement unremarkable. With this precondition met, the stage is set for another definitive display of rhetorical power. For like adultery, the beating of Strepsiades, father and citizen, and thus repository of the authority of the democratic city, is more than a personal or familial matter. Although our deep emotional attachment to the sanctity of parents may derive from this personal context, such violence threatens not just Strepsiades' well-being but the stability of society as a whole as a collection of families and as a hierarchical structure. Thus transgression of the traditional sanctity of the father is a test against which those who stand outside conventional civic values try themselves and their theories and, conversely, heinous behavior is measured.[21] As we saw in the first agon, the conventional world sums up those who flout its values as parricides (911). In striking his father, Pheidippides embodies the "criminal outsider."[22]

But, in spite of all this, the identification of Strepsiades with the *kreitton logos* through age, order of debate, and explicit wordplay (1346) confirms what we have suspected since the clouds' song: the sophistic Pheidippides, true possessor of "heroic spirit" (λῆμα 1350), busy with "novel and clever affairs" (καινοῖς πράγμασιν καὶ δεξιοῖς 1399), contemptuous of accepted customs (*nomoi* 1400), is sure to overcome his father. He will use by now familiar arguments: the superior rights and obligations of the knower, the mutability of law, the inflexible rules of nature, the normative practices of animals in the natural setting.[23] Roosters and other animals are not accustomed to respect their fathers (1427ff.).[24] This last argument, however, is a mistake—as we have seen, comparisons between the natural and social worlds can cut both ways. Strepsiades' retort—why not eat dung and sleep on wood too (1431)—jokes about how uncomfortable the natural world would be for the profoundly urban sophists, but is also a credible counterargument.[25] But once again Strepsiades is unlucky in his interlocutor. The sophistic Pheidippides shows himself no more committed to or convinced by *logos* than the ignorant creditors. Unprepared to change his intentions and behavior no matter what is said, he responds by denying the pertinence of this *logos,* ludicrously childishly (and ironically) appealing to the authority of Socrates to back up the denial of the power of speech inherent in his refusal to reason or concede.[26]

The limitation of speech thus once again exposed, that it can persuade only those who implicitly agree to be persuaded if the right argument can be found, will be vital at the end of the agon, but first the reverse. Appeals to reason, filial duty, affection, justice, and custom having failed, Strepsiades tries one last tack: self-interest. If Strepsiades is just in beating Pheidippides, so Pheidippides can do the same to his son—otherwise Pheidippides, too, risks a beating later (1433ff.).[27] In reply, Pheidippides advances his clinching point: if he has no son, his tears will have been in vain and his father will have the last laugh! If this argument seems astonishingly feeble, Strepsiades' response is even more unexpected. In a concession phrased for maximum irony and incongruity, he admits himself totally convinced:

> ἐμοὶ μέν, ὦνδρες ἥλικες, δοκεῖ λέγειν δίκαια,
> κἄμοιγε συγχωρεῖν δοκεῖ τούτοισι τἀπιεικῆ·
> κλάειν γὰρ ἡμᾶς εἰκός ἐστ', ἢν μὴ δίκαια δρῶμεν.
>
> (1437–39)

> To me, indeed, O men of my age, he seems to say just things,
> and for me at least it seems fitting to agree with these;
> for that we weep is appropriate, if we do not do just things.

The triumph of the sophistic *hetton logos* in the person of Pheidippides is stunning.[28] The priority of *logos* over the facts of daily life seems complete. The whole play has been motivated by Strepsiades' desire to avoid just repayment of his debts, yet now he has been persuaded that it is right not only to act justly, and to repay his son's youthful pain, but even do so at the expense of bodily harm. The startling inconsequence of the successful argument, following upon the failure of more conventional (if highly parodic) lines of sophistic reasoning, serves to make Pheidippides' sudden victory the more overwhelming, the more comical, and the more troubling. Strepsiades' views are completely reversed by what the audience laughs off as an amusing irrelevance and trivial jest.[29] This is babbling at its finest.[30] Justice is redefined[31] and the family, or at least familial hierarchy, overthrown by what is clearly a plaything of the speaker spawned by the needs of the rhetorical moment.[32]

Strepsiades' concession and the triumph of the *hetton logos* in the mouth of Pheidippides prove the sophistic slogans for their *logos:* to listen is to succumb.[33] The word seems a power equivalent to and far greater than force: for it has achieved what force, at least inside the city of Athens, could not: the (willing) enslavement of father to son. However, the very completeness of this victory proves its undoing. For if the victory of the *hetton logos* in the first agon was simply a funny setup—persuading no one except another *logos* and committing the audience to nothing more than a pleasurable laugh at an absurd and abstract event—the comedy of Strepsiades' conversion (however poetically merited by his decision to send Pheidippides to the Thinkery) is immediately diluted by rejection and dissatisfaction both on- and offstage. Offstage, disenchantment begins immediately. What is not entirely satisfying—to accept the justice of Strepsiades' beating at the hands of his son—is even less so when Strepsiades extends his conclusion to every old man, and thus, eventually, every man in the audience (1437ff.).[34] Why should everyone consent to be beaten simply because of an illogical concession on Strepsiades' part? The audience's instinctive repudiation of principle, *logos*, and agon precedes by only a moment Strepsiades' own. When, with a logical extension of his reasoning, Pheidippides turns from father to mother—it is just to beat mothers too, and he will use the *hetton logos* to prove it—Strepsiades explodes into violence himself.

Pheidippides' new proposal makes clear the full ramifications of his sophistic instruction. Most obviously, while Strepsiades may still be attached to his son, Pheidippides' affections have been transferred elsewhere, to the inhabitants of the Thinkery, whose estrangement from the community and its values he now shares.[35] But this new allegiance and Pheidippides' pride and pleasure in rhetoric and its power neither transform his nature nor translate him to a higher sphere where *logos* alone counts.[36] Instead he remains the more dangerous son of his father, in whom a greater capacity to reason and speak, coupled with freedom from convention, are explosively joined to physical violence, hedonism, and a desire to dominate. The result is that in Pheidippides' mouth *logos* indicates neither a commitment to rational thought and discourse nor the civilized preference for speech (as opposed to blows) and respect for human communality normally inherent in the choice of words. Rather, his *logos* is a tool dedicated to absolute personal gratification (but without personal application), which functions not to bring men together, but to drive them further apart. Pheidippides' preference in Euripides, coupled with the citation of *Alcestis* he is given in line 1415,[37] warned the audience of his total alienation from conventional bonds. The violent actions that result are clear comic substitutes for more shocking crimes—parricide and incest, programmatic reversals of the basics of human social order.[38] As Pheidippides acts and treats his victims in ways more bestial than human, he embodies the attitudes we already saw expressed in Strepsiades' song. We can sense the thematic aptness with which he claims the cock (a symbol of *hubris*) as his model,[39] for in such sophistic debate we seem to see *logos* itself, man's supreme achievement, the cornerstone of justice and the city, become an agent in the return to savagery.[40]

The degeneration of the word in the mouth of Pheidippides engenders and is matched by a parallel degeneration in its audience. For if Pheidippides is like the *hetton logos* and his exemplar the successful adulterer, Strepsiades renounces the part of the *kreitton*. Rather than risk capitulation to Pheidippides' latest proposal, he suddenly withdraws his agreement to listen; mother-beating is not a valid subject for debate. We are no longer in the realm of verbal skill but of emotion and self-interest.[41] In the spirit of the cuckolded husband whose violent punishment of the adulterer was the suppressed possibility of the first agon, the outraged Strepsiades responds to his son's offer to "debate" this new issue by symbolically exiling speaker and speech from the city whose most fundamental precepts they have spurned. When Pheidippides asks:

> . . . τί δ' ἦν ἔχων τὸν ἥττω
> λόγον σε νικήσω λέγων
> τὴν μητέρ' ὡς τύπτειν χρεών;
>
> (1444–46)

> . . . What if having the *hetton*
> *logos* I will defeat you, saying that
> to beat my mother is necessary?

Strepsiades screams:[42]

> τί δ' ἄλλο γ' ἤ, ταῦτ' ἦν ποῆς,
> οὐδέν σε κωλύσει σεαυτὸν ἐμβαλεῖν
> εἰς τὸ βάραθρον μετὰ Σωκράτους
> καὶ τὸν λόγον τὸν ἥττω;
>
> (1447–51)

> What else but, if you do these things,
> nothing will stop you from throwing yourself
> into the pit *(barathron)* with Socrates
> and the *hetton logos?*

Suddenly, and for the first time, we see the power of *logos* and its sophistic speakers openly reversed. The linguistic arena is shattered; the formal agon dissolves.[43] The play takes yet another new direction as the doubts of the audience seem to merge with the dramatic action and the force of language is replaced by the personal and civic violence with which Strepsiades will repress this intolerable speech. If Pheidippides continues, he might as well throw himself, Socrates, and the *hetton logos* into the *barathron,* the gully used for the bodies of those executed for crimes against the city.[44] The reflexive pronoun emphasizes Pheidippides' responsibility for his plight. The *barathron* is a fitting end for one so ignorant of the bonds and obligations that make civilized life and the power of *logos* possible. Equating language and force, Pheidippides and his *logos* will experience individual and social violence; proclaiming his independence, neither he nor his *logos* will be protected; acting the natural man, he will be acted upon by others physically and naturally.

Strepsiades' response is frequently cited as satisfying.[45] The implication of the *hetton logos* with mother-beating, the repulsive behavior of Pheidippides, and the direct involvement of the audience in the outcome ensure that character and audience react in tandem. Together with Strepsiades, however, with less excuse, the spectators discard the fundamental civic prejudice in favor of language and the processes of law and justice. Thus they experience firsthand the demoralizing and brutalizing effects of a world where legitimation of every desire and transformation of speech into an invincible aggressive weapon provoke an equally sinister reaction that suppresses *logos* and denies the possibility of persuasion. By the end of the second agon, the seeming triumph of the *hetton logos* has proved the catalyst not only of its own destruction but of the proud democratic ideology that made Persuasion a civic and political goddess.[46]

Pheidippides is, however, not the only character to suffer the comic justice of being condemned to inhabit "in reality" the world that he has chosen as most congruent with his self-interest and compatible with his desires. Strepsiades too has had such an experience. The symmetry goes beyond the fact that the agent of Strepsiades' ruin is that very sophistic attitude and *logos* which he forced upon his son—a point which the clouds' song at 1311f. makes sure we understand.[47] Rather, Strepsiades has fallen prey to his desires in a more complex way: seeking a world in which the payment of debt was irrelevant and a means through which he could avoid it, Strepsiades was all too successful. For the essence of Pheidippides' action is the denial of debt—the original debt that children owe their parents for raising them.[48] Thus, from the beginning the comedy structures the second agon to play off Pheidippides' sophistic violence against the paternal care he received, and to measure the son's technical rhetorical skills, now used against his father, against the earlier childish lisping which his father took pains to interpret.[49] This is the most grating "injustice" of all, and the one that Strepsiades ends with in 1380ff. For first Pheidippides' actions and then his *logos* return his father to a second childhood, but not one in which child repays parent's attentions. In a comically obscene image of reciprocal care, or its lack, we learn that Strepsiades, who always took Pheidippides outside to shit, himself is left within, crying and bawling his pressing need, strangled and shitting in fear of his son.

Strepsiades understands all too well what this means and his own responsibility for what has happened (1338). His shock and discomfort prompt a self-interested return to orthodoxy—where respect for parents is secured with social and divine sanctions—and stimulate a new appreciation of justice—he now wants a just return on his paternal investment.[50] The catalytic suggestion of mother-beating hastens his (re)conversion to the conventional world of the city, the laws, and the gods who will protect him. The invocation of the *barathron*, the official destination of these convicted of crimes against the city, as his son's appropriate end renews, more emphatically, Strepsiades' earlier plea to the community to defend him. Earlier it was only to stop Pheidippides' violence; now it is to destroy him, his teacher, and the sophistic *hetton logos*.

It is in the light of Strepsiades' own newly conventional values, that we should interpret the "conventionality" of the end of the play and the "morality" of the cloud chorus. In fact, true to their reflective nature, the clouds simply continue to mirror Strepsiades back to himself as they have done since the beginning. When Strepsiades charges them with orchestrating his downfall, their reply echoes Strepsiades' own changed stance and the tone of his pronouncement to his son.[51]

> αὐτὸς μὲν οὖν σαυτῷ σὺ τούτων αἴτιος,
> στρέψας σεαυτὸν εἰς πονηρὰ πράγματα.
>
> (1454–55)

Nay rather you yourself were the cause for yourself of these [misfortunes] having turned *(strepsas)* yourself to roguish affairs.

Like Pheidippides, Strepsiades is to be understood as the architect of his own ruin. The pun on his name (1455)[52] makes sure we understand this comically, not "realistically," underlining the fact that even now the clouds reflect what they confront in a comic climax shaped by the logic of verbal comedy, not "reality." Thus when Strepsiades repeats his charge, asking why the clouds did not warn, "but aroused/transported *(epairein)* a man from the country and old" (ἀλλ' ἄνδρ' ἄγροικον καὶ γέροντ' ἐπήρατε 1457), their answer

> ἡμεῖς προοῦμεν ταῦθ' ἑκάστοθ', ὅταν τινὰ
> γνῶμεν πονηρῶν ὄντ' ἐραστὴν πραγμάτων,
> ἕως ἂν αὐτὸν ἐμβάλωμεν εἰς κακόν,
> ὅπως ἂν εἰδῇ τοὺς θεοὺς δεδοικέναι.
>
> (1458–61)

We do these [things] each time, whenever we perceive someone to be a lover *(erastes)* of roguish deeds, until we throw him into evil so that he may know to fear the gods.

is a pseudo-serious repetition of the tenets of common morality[53] that speaks the language compatible with (and echoes the passion of) the new Strepsiades, even as it mirrors his regret for his previous passion for something very different. Unconventional rogues who are infatuated with delinquency, flout the (divine) rules, fail in proper respect, deny debts, will be punished by outside forces if all else fails—and its their own fault.[54] This is the kind of justice Strepsiades now needs, and what has and will befall him. But our *Clouds* insists on a comic perspective on all this "aeschylean" morality and theology[55] by interrupting the clouds' "tragic" pronouncement with an unseemly comic hiccup. Line 1458, as quoted earlier, follows the manuscripts in reading ὅταν τινὰ, a reading that, "although possible and grammatically sound," is commonly emended to ὅντιν' ἂν . The reason is "stylistic." In such a solemn moment, the comic rhythm of ὅταν τινὰ is felt to be grossly out of place—"exaggerated and for communication of the sense wholly unnecessary."[56] In fact, the intrusive rhythm is the sense, or rather the mood; its purpose is to be exaggerated and jarring, making it the last in a series of passages stressing the mocking, comic theatricality of the end of the play.[57] These passages, which frame the change in Strepsiades' fortunes, simultaneously involve the spectators in the drama theoretically, while distancing them emotionally from its tumultuous action.[58] We must maintain that larger perspective the *Clouds* has imposed: neither enjoying Strepsiades' plight too much—lest we miss the implications of his action and his kinship to the comic audience which rejected the first *Clouds*, an audience which would act as he does now—nor identifying with him and his hostility toward language, philosophers, and the abstract world of theory—lest we confirm our continuing membership in this vulgar comic audience and fail the test of our second play.

Such detachment allows us to react properly when the newly "moral" Strepsiades becomes the agent of the philosophic Socrates' appropriate destruction. Exhuming the old-fashioned rhetoric of familial affection, or *philia*, he invites his son to assist with yet another distasteful plan, this time destroying his teachers (1464–66). The paratragedy that Pheidippides' refusal provokes—"respect fatherly Zeus" ($\kappa\alpha\tau\alpha\iota\delta\acute{\epsilon}\sigma\theta\eta\tau\iota$ $\pi\alpha\tau\rho\hat{\omega}ον$ $\Delta\acute{\iota}\alpha$ 1468), intones Strepsiades—mocks the earlier paratragedy of the clouds and exposes Strepsiades' current conventional views to be as comically expedient as his former sophistic ones had been. When Zeus was inconvenient, he was discarded; now that he serves some purpose, he is revived and cultivated. Far from affirming traditional morality, Strepsiades' invocation of Zeus vindicates the sophists' theory that the gods are a convenient fiction, manufactured like the rest of the social world to meet human needs, principally the need to manipulate others.[59] Our uncertainty about exactly who or what this "fatherly" Zeus is or does[60] underlines the extent to which this god is a creation of the moment, generated by a familiar and pressing (rhetorical) need.

As Strepsiades continues, his (re)discovered traditional gods take on the role of the reflective clouds: "sanctioning" violence in the already violent and enraged Strepsiades. As he plans to proceed alone with the destruction of Socrates, a conspicuously silent Hermes[61] "advises" him to do what he has already decided—act now; don't wait or go to court; burn the Thinkery. The "charge" against Socrates repeats that already made, in vain, against the clouds (1466 = 1457). This time, however, it is bolstered by appeal to contemporary prejudice. Sophists are babbling, atheistic quacks who command a supremely powerful, bewitching, illusory—yet trivial—speech which they use to degrade and abuse their fellow citizens. This is not a surprise. The *Clouds* and the comic portrait of sophists in general have made these terms familiar.[62] Further, Strepsiades' words reflect what history has proven to be the feelings of his comic audience.[63] His individual decision here seems to prophesy that which the Athenians will take collectively later: that the proper solution to the sophistic/socratic problem is violent suppression of their *logos* and forcible removal of their persons.

Strepsiades' charge has been taken by many to be identical with Aristophanes'. The *Clouds* is felt to condone, if not actively advocate, the violence that Strepsiades displays, either because Aristophanes shared the popular prejudice, or because he felt compelled to pander to it after the failure of a first *Clouds* too sympathetic to sophistic views.[64] The parabasis alone would argue against such a simple reading. The end of the *Clouds* presents us not with a moral but with continuing mockery, for the progress of the play, as well as the construction of the end, at once reveal the truth of Strepsiades' charges and their irrelevance, the poverty of their use in his mouth. That Socrates is a pretentious quack, an atheist, and an intellectual in general is undoubtedly true from what we have seen. That he deserves to die for these crimes or that these are really the comic reasons for which the Thinkery is burned is less obvious. Play and ending have repeatedly demonstrated Strepsiades' complicity in his own ruin; responsibility can be transferred to Socrates no more accurately than to the clouds.[65] Further, shorn of contemporary antisophistic slogans, Strepsiades' accusation remains that of (sophistic) deception, the charge already made against the clouds and decisively rebutted by them. But this a familiar situation, one, in fact, which started the drama and was discussed in chapter 2. For Strepsiades' efforts to assign blame here remind us of an earlier figure accused in almost identical terms, the matchmaker who also aroused/ transported (*epairein* 42 = 1457) a self-styled countryman, while his current paratragic lamentations recall the curses of lines 41bff, which began both the narrative and thematic action of the *Clouds*. Anyone who believes the matchmaker deserved the death wished upon her there is equally free to think the same of Socrates. In fact, Strepsiades' own unruly comic *eros* betrayed him then and now. The seductive deceit practiced upon him by others was possible only because their words spoke to the passions of this lover *(erastes)* of roguish deeds (1459). He entered gladly into his compact with the *logos* that ruined him.

However, if the slogans mouthed by Strepsiades fail to capture the real reasons that Socrates and his students[66] are to die at the end of the play, this does not mean that their destruction is without logic. For like Strepsiades and Pheidippides, Socrates and his fellows deserve their end; they perish in a way comically congruent with the world they have "constructed." Their real mistake was not misleading Strepsiades, but stripping off social constraints and liberating a human nature about whose true character they were ignorant, while simultaneously preaching the virtues of rhetoric in terms calculated to oppose it to law and justice and to obscure the crucial distinction between verbal and physical violence, between *peitho* and *bia*. They are the unwitting, but appropriate, victims of their own student, who developed under their tutelage in ways never intended or suspected, for he was a vulgar man, while they believe themselves to live in an abstract world. When Strepsiades mockingly identifies the agent of the Thinkery's destruction as "that man whose cloak you have taken" (ἐκεῖνος οὕπερ θοἰμάτιον εἰλήφατε 1498), he tells the audience more than he knows. Through his sarcasm we can perceive the shape of aristophanic mockery as well: the social mores the sophists unravelled are precisely what could have protected them and their right to speak now. Instead the Thinkery is exposed to the full violence of what lies beneath the social cloak.

In deciding upon violence to suppress the speech of Pheidippides and the inhabitants of the Thinkery, Strepsiades acts in a way that brings together all the "different" attitudes toward *logos*—except possibly that of Socrates—that we have seen in the play and uncovers their basic similarity. On one hand, he remains the comic natural man and newly minted, if misstruck, sophist. His action here is consistent with the second parabasis, with his comic and "sophistic" treatment of the creditors, and with the action of his sophistic son in the second agon. Yet, as numerous critics have pointed out, he is also taking the part of the *kreitton logos,* and his words recall that *logos'* rhetoric, while mixing it with the new language of the sophists.[67] To justify his recourse to personal violence, he at once speciously invokes legal, communal force (1481ff., 1491)[68] and recycles imagery that sophistically suggests that destroying someone rhetorically (in court) and physically are equivalent. But Strepsiades' action should not be seen as "the reflex of outraged νόμος [law] striking back at its attackers and reestablishing its right to dominate and control the forces of φύσις [nature]."[69] His composite language cannot mask his contempt for the law and the courts, which would create an arena where he fears the sophists' *logos* could save them.[70] His action is clearly illegal, and this distances him from at least what the *kreitton logos* should do (although we may fear that in similar circumstances this *logos,* too, would not hesitate to evade the law). Like the adulterer and his own son, Strepsiades acts independently and his decision neither to listen nor to allow speech strikes at the heart of the democratic Athens whose forms he is invoking.[71] Not *nomos,* or law, but the natural man ensures that the sophists are physically consumed in the natural, purely physical world they created in theory, perishing at the hands of their own violent *logos* taken comic flesh. Appropriately, the blows that ruin them masquerade as speech. To the student who asks what he is doing, both Strepsiades, and, in a different way, Aristophanes ironically reply:

ὅτι ποῶ; τί δ' ἄλλο γ' ἢ
διαλεπτολογοῦμαι ταῖς δοκοῖς τῆς οἰκίας;
(1495–96)

What am I doing? What other than
I am subtly debating with the beams *(dokoi)* of the house?

The pun on *dokos,* beam, and *doxa,* opinion, cognate to *dokein,* to think or seem, mockingly assimilates Strepsiades' unwanted destruction of the roof beams to the subtleties that wrestle in sophistic debate. It intimates that what we witness are the overthrowing arguments, the *kataballontes logoi,* in deed.[72]

The Thinkery in flames thus reproduces the oven world that at first seemed the conceptual precondition for rhetoric (95ff.) and is now demonstrated to be, instead, the context of its failure and destruction.[73] This close relationship is marked by language repeated from the beginning of the play that draws attention to the theoretical perfection of the sophists' doom in the comedy of inversion.[74] For a second time we see Strepsiades as the new comic Socrates, suspended in violation of the rules of everyday life. But while earlier, in his attempts to think, Strepsiades emulated socratic indifference to the body, here the reference is more precise. In line 1503, the harsh mockery of Strepsiades' exact repetition of line 225, Socrates' second line in the play,[75] again makes the accusation of impiety and atheism that is his justification. But while we may find this charge hypocritical in Strepsiades' mouth, it rings true in a different way in the larger aristophanic context. When, in lines 1504–5, the sophists' choking screams indicate that they will enact the pun which introduced their speculation, literally becoming the human coals in the choker-oven (96) that they (parodically) supposed everyone else to be (97),[76] the remaking of the world implied in sophistic speculation acquires its final significance. In a world without gods—for the clouds simply observe impassively, as befits their sophistic role as arguments and their subsequent scientific incarnation as nonvolitional, natural phenomena[77]—the sophists' language, appropriated and used against them, is made smoke, or a fine verbal smoke screen for what is really going on.[78] The meaningless babble of the hubristic Strepsiades, with his obscene reference to the backside of the moon whose "divine honor" he claims to be defending,[79] the shrieks, torches, clubbings are the fittingly chaotic end for the theoreticians of an aggressive *logos* and a natural world, in whose noisy silence they now find themselves trapped.

It's all very funny of course. Strepsiades is acting the part of the comic boor that he has assumed all along. The topsy-turvy spectacle on stage is a recognizable parody of the revelry that typically ends comedy.[80] But, more than that, as scholia and commentators have noted, the exciting action of this new ending—the old man beating those about him, the torches, and the cries of "iou, iou"—finally provides exactly what the parabasis told us was lacking before in the verbal first *Clouds,* a lack which condemned it to failure.[81] What we see now, a satisfyingly noisy and violent "punishment" of those who commanded the power of speech, remedies this "deficiency," while creating another inversion, this time theatrical, too blatant to be missed. The realization is unavoidable: the defeat of the verbal *Clouds* is what condemns the sophists now, both thematically and dramatically. The Thinkery's complete misreading of their audience is proved not only by Strepsiades' violence but by the successful generic comedy of this new conventional ending, which he also would have enjoyed. Our very laughter shows how accurately the revised *Clouds* mirrors what experience has shown to be the nature of its audience. Like Strepsiades, we must seem vulgar and violent, deaf to the meaning and power of language and to real comic wit, complacent in the beating of those who speak contrary to our wish, followers of the *hetton logos* who prove his thesis, and more—that man is simply another animal enslaved to simple appetites and even simpler perceived self-interest, inevitably indifferent or hostile to any *logos* which does not immediately serve his desires.

The last line of the play, the curiously bald "curtain" line,[82]

ἡγεῖσθ' ἔξω· κεχόρευται γὰρ μετρίως τό γε τήμερον ἡμῖν.
(1510)

Lead the way out; for we have chorused enough at least for today.

refrains from the orderly conclusiveness of the standard comic "triumph," to leave us poised in confrontation with all we have seen and felt.[83] Yet as it returns us to the comic festival, unmasks the clouds, and completes the gradual removal of the dramatic world and substitution of the stage, this "exit" also renews our temporal, substantial, difference from the vulgar "original" audience whose tastes have shaped our *Clouds*. We are not this "first" audience, but "second" like the play we watch, and just as our play has been revised after the experience of its orginal version, so we, too, have been (re)formed by our unique experience of this new play. Thus, we can go beyond the role of passive witnesses and emotional accomplices to a series of wretched deeds which make up a comedy of equally wretched jokes (*ponera pragmata* 1455; *ponera skommata* 542) to position our reactions within the critical perspective offered by the parabasis, seeing them as but part of the logical and thematic construction of the end.

The possibility of such a perspective as well as what it promises—a potentially "new" response to our *Clouds'* recapitulated conventional comedy, evoked through the power of Aristophanes' verbal art—must rehabilitate both speech and spectators. Rejecting the role of Strepsiades, the audience can become an active participant in the production of an emblematic and metaphoric spectacle whose own *logos,* educational goals, and (postulated) achievements defy the "reality" it portrays on stage. Nor can we restrict analysis or effect to the comic stage. There is an inescapable relationship between the comedy of *logos* and the rhetorical pleasure *(terpsis)* of speech, between aristophanic and sophistic invention, between those *hettones logoi* who seek to transcend the requirements of generic and of social habituation. This does not mean that the *Clouds,* in the end, endorses the sophists and their rhetoric, nor does it retroactively drain Aristophanes' "criticisms" of merit. But it does point to the paradox that Socrates and Aristophanes have their verbal tools and respect for language in common, that those who can appreciate one will be the best audience of the other, and that even if comedian and philosopher share neither goals nor presuppositions, they are each other's best critics.

But the happier extradramatic ending we are able to construct should not blind us to its fragility. The intertextual doubleness of the *Clouds'* finale moves us beyond Strepsiades' violent suppression of *logos;* it does not leave it behind. Likewise, the mingled pleasures the end evokes, in speech and violence, puns and blows, reflect the inevitable interplay of body and mind, *gaster* and *logos* which structures and limits the word's hold on human attention and respect. To recognize this dynamic at work in ourselves and those with whom we share the democratic city is of fundamental importance. An optimistic pessimism, or pessimistic optimism about the functioning of speech and about ourselves is the best the *Clouds'* profoundly democratic lessons can leave us, its wiser audience.

Conclusion: Our Innovative, Democratic *Clouds*

The *Clouds* begins with a recognizable and no doubt familiar situation: alienation, generational conflict, debt, devotion to pleasure, and an open willingness to sacrifice public to personal good, justice and the rights of other to self-interest, truth to perjury—if only it can be done successfully and with impunity. To this probably unremarkable, if unedifying, situation lived by ordinary people are suddenly added the potent speculation and practices of the sophists. The resulting mixture is the more flavorful since the encounter is with sophistic rhetoric and theory taken in their strongest and most polemical forms. From line 94 onward, it is apparent that we are to witness a *logos* that, calling itself an invincible weapon, claims a persuasive skill equivalent to force, and a related physics and cosmology which postulate a natural, mechanical universe, inhabited by an equally natural man, best understood as just another animal. Taken together, these two branches of sophistic instruction seem to promise complete freedom from all traditional restraints, moral, civic, and divine.

The meaning of this combination for sophistic (and, finally, all) *logos* and for the comic men who learn it is the question of the *Clouds*. However, as we are warned from the moment that the chorus enters, this "question" is confronted not through debate, but through emblematic comic spectacle. The *Clouds* works not by reproducing contemporary Athens and the views of Aristophanes' originals, but by giving hyperbolic and parodic reality to what is latent and hidden. The sophists and their *logoi* are taken seriously, but in the comic mode, and this is the genius of Aristophanes' conception. The *Clouds* is not merely a comedy critical of sophists and sophistry; history records many of these now lost. Rather, if the *Clouds* is, on the one hand, the product of a tendentious and selective reading of sophistic speculation,[1] its argument is constructed through a no less selective use of the resources of comedy. Comedy itself is the medium of Aristophanes' criticism; manipulation of key assumptions of the comic genre provides his terms. His characters are comic types, portrayed in familiar ways: the otherworldly, arrogant philosopher ignorant of the conditions of his residence on earth; the reduced and parodic buffoon driven by the narrow and unpromising desires comedy postulates as defining the "ordinary," "natural" man; and the fashionable youth, who while seeming to be something new, is actually the son of his father, expressing familiar paternal vices in more extreme and sophisticated forms. The clashes between these figures motivate a drama in which standard comic techniques such as abuse of the audience, crude physical jokes, and generic imagery (for example, of farting rhetoric) stand philosophical assumptions on their heads. As we watch the *Clouds'* characteristic dynamic in which the capping joke reverses what had gone before, we are constantly reminded that (comic) man on- and offstage, as well as the comedy he enjoys, is a creature of the body, wedded to physical drives of the most basic kinds: for food, sex, evacuation, violence, and the unthinking belly laugh. Positive implications or mitigating circumstances are rigorously ignored. Sophistic and comic influence each other reciprocally and negatively. Generic assumptions color the natural man of the sophists and suggest the most reductive possible view of his motives and actions, including the act of speaking, while at the same time an imported "theoretical" structure—the (highly parodied) social and scientific speculations of the sophists—confirms the comic view and makes of man the human animal. Language, scenes, sequences, and imagery are thus endowed with a coherence that establishes them as far more than the topical, scurrilous, and simply funny jokes they could otherwise seem to be.

The picture that emerges is bleak, for if Aristophanes' usual fantasy gives words primacy over mundane reality—letting Dikaiopolis have his private peace, Peisthetairos build his airy city, and so forth—through a comic art that "has the unmistakable effect of putting language itself in the controlling position,"[2] this drama seems to proceed with the opposite rhythm. In a play that advertises comic mockery as the assumption of metaphoric shapes and could legitimately be said to examine Gorgias' well-known rhetorical principles, what Whitman calls "the priority of speech to reality,"[3] *logos,* which starts out master of the social and natural world, paradoxically and repeatedly founders on the hard facts of human existence. Although the play opens by suggesting that words can transport men up, away from the solid earth and its requirements, taking "seriously" what Peisthetairos claims for *logos* in the *Birds,* that "by words the mind is elevated and man transported,"[4] in fact, the *Clouds'* characteristic movement is down. Abstract becomes concrete verbally, thematically, and dramatically. Socrates and his *logos* are dragged to earth by a Strepsiades who is hopelessly incapable of understanding *logos,* metaphor, and speculation; however willing, he cannot leave the body far enough behind. What seems a momentary stay with Pheidippides' conversion to the pleasures of thought and discourse is revealed as illusory, and the comic audience is apparently equally lacking in perception and interest—viewing what they see on stage as "reality," demanding not verbal wit, however clever, but the simple solidities of sex and violence. In Athens outside the Thinkery, speech is enslaved to the appetites and must be construed within the limits imposed by the struggle to satisfy the desires. In this world, language—metaphor itself and metaphorically claimed as the ultimate force in the reshaping of human reality—must confront the brutally unyielding directness of the club, which mocks the sophistic *logos* whose world it destroys by archly pretending to be speech itself.

This is the more surprising since the spectacle departs, in the common aristophanic way, from popular metaphor made flesh. The drama of the *Clouds* is in one sense built on the examination of two central sophistic concepts—violent *logos* and natural man—controversial in their significance and explosive in their implications. Hostile contemporaries diagnosed their effects: to dissolve the conventional understanding of language and human society—particularly democratic Athenian society—by a fatal blurring of the mutually exclusive opposites upon which it was founded, the traditional and reassuring antitheses between man and animal, speech and force. Seen in this way, *logos,* once a central element in man's escape from the mute and ferocious isolation of the natural world, now acts, in its new sophistic guise as an aggressive tool, to return him to it. Instead of a common possession uniting the citizens in a functioning human community, this new, technically powerful rhetoric is an invincible private weapon, deployed at the expense of justice, the laws, and the city. Those who can use it are savages inside the walls, more dangerous as they are more intimate, rendered by their theoretical studies careless of every bond or constraint—familial, social, legal, moral, divine. Those who cannot are no better than beasts or slaves, always at the mercy of their more skillful fellows.

This conflict between the new *logos*[5] and the city was not chronicled solely by Aristophanes. His great triumph was to question the logic of the guiding metaphors themselves. Uncoupling violence and speech once again, he confronts them with one another in a new way, playing out a clash between a *logos* which claims to be violence, and alternatively, a violence which pretends to be speech. As the *Clouds* brilliantly shows, the excessive claims which make of *logos* a weapon are, in fact, fatal to the real power of the word. Compelled into open contest with physical force, verbal violence cannot hold its own. As the drama unfolds, it becomes increasingly clear that *logos* requires the partnership of the city (or some other authority possessed of superior strength) to protect and ensure its privileged status. Understanding the fragility of speech and cherishing (and if necessary enforcing) the difference between persuasion and force, the word and the blow, prove to be the prerequisites for creation of that arena within which language can display its power. If the word is to function as a dagger, it can do so only inside the city, in the assembly, where the use of real weapons is forbidden.[6]

In the sense, then, that the *Clouds* demonstrates the necessity of the alliance between *logos* and its former and essential partners, justice and the laws, Aristophanes' play could be said to be a conservative effort that reaffirms traditional civic values. But in the end the old patterns collapse on the wreck of the most fundamental notion of all: the distinction between man and animal. Hope that reconstruction of the language/justice/law association could help shore up this distinction—somehow exploiting man's unique possession of speech to insert a firm barrier between him and the animal world—is futile. Instead, in the *Clouds, logos,* even inside the protected confines within which it can triumph, must confront a yet more difficult adversary: its audience. The second of the key sophistic metaphors is even more corrosive than the first, for as violent *logos* is incompatible with the city and, finally, *logos'* own privileged position, so man the animal is incompatible with *logos* itself. The philosophical optimism of Socrates, who appears to believe that man's innate nature is fundamentally defined by mind and memory, cannot stand against the thematic pessimism of our *Clouds'* comedy.[7] The definition of man as the animal that speaks is an unworkable oxymoron, unable to survive his complete reintegration into the natural world. Instead, as the play progresses, the natural man postulated by comedy and liberated by sophistic instruction is revealed as a crudely physical entity, naturally indifferent to *logos*, as unlikely to transcend the body as to fly above the earth, winged only by words. Necessity and desires determine his production and reception of *logoi;* the same forces compel his actions. Voices are assimilated and characters stripped of their differences until finally there seems no escape. Speakers and listeners alike are simply bellies, defined by the lowest common denominator, corporal need. As Nussbaum says, "The *Clouds . . .* presents us with a picture of private hedonism impervious to reason and even to sympathy. These men simply do not *care* about anything but their own satisfactions when it comes to a choice. And lest we too quickly feel ourselves superior to them, the *Clouds* insists that we members of the audience are no different. We are all just *euryprōktoi* waiting passively for plea-sure." [8] In this world, the notion of a self-sufficient verbal pleasure *(terpsis)* is a foolish dream. For those who have not fled the earth, *logos* cannot help but be distorted; even the abstracted Socrates is tarred by the brush of profit seeking, albeit in passing.[9] Given all this, it is not surprising that not only metaphor, spec-ulation, theory, but even *logos* itself, are things too light for most men to grasp, or to value. Whether in the fashionable constructions of a Pheidippides or the stupidities of a Strepsiades, words count only as tools with which to conduct the struggle for survival and hegemony. And they are tools which are soon discarded, for as man is submerged in animal, his native "language" is revealed to be not verbal but physical: his allegiance given not to the tongue but to the fist.

This is the novelty of the traditionally comic second *Clouds,* a comedy forced to come to grips with the nature of its audience, men who are only apparently defined by residence in the *polis* and participation in civic institutions—including the comic festival. Comedy and sophistry concur: the grimmest joke of the new *Clouds* is that Aristophanes and the (comic) sophists apparently agree on a con-ception of man that makes them both irrelevant.[10] For comedy, too, is a doubly metaphoric *logos* and as such not exempt from the disheartening analysis that the play unleashes. As the comic Strepsiades and Pheidippides debase *logos* on stage through actions equally at home in generic humor or sophistic theory, parabases and elsewhere tell a similar story for the audience. The rejection of the first *Clouds,* which relied on the brilliance of its wit alone, has demonstrated that comic *logos,* novelty, and invention can command no more compelling interest than any other verbal creation. In their failure to appreciate the first *Clouds,* the comic audience proved itself as vulgar, violent, conventional and pledged to the appetites as any-thing in the comedy of the second. For the shape of this second play is determined by the defeat of the first. Its obscene and conventional comedy matches and mir-rors the character of its spectators, while our laughter at this debased (re)vision proves its accuracy. Onstage and off, speech is produced and consumed in the gastric economy of the belly. Blows are preferred to words; debates turn to fights; philosophers are banished or killed. Athens is filled, and nourishes itself, with raucous and vulgar rhetoric whose real purpose and content are best illustrated with the popular and derisive image of farting. The comic festivals feature equally vulgar and stupid farce. However successful, such noises can scarcely claim to have much in common with the celebrated human possession of *logos,* or with speaking and listening as rational choices. Rather, as by-products of desire and need, they are at home in the natural world now to be located in the heart of the city. Far from testifying to the power of the word, they ruinously testify to the opposite, for they function by invoking not the mind but the stomach, awakening an answering rumble in a mob avid for satisfaction.

Luckily, our second *Clouds* tempers this discouraging picture; its drama (and even "history") are not the whole story. For alongside the parodic, extreme, and emblematic figures it portrays, our comedy also models something better, fuller, and wiser: the ideal figures of the poet of the second *Clouds* and the appreciative audience he hopes to create. These are the true speakers and listeners of the *Clouds,* sketched through the very shape of the failures that we see on stage, their "off-stage" responses and virtues synthesized from the incomplete and inadequate interactions of *gaster* and *logos,* convention and novelty, freedom and repression, that make up our drama. Thus our poet rejects the roles of *hetton* and *kreitton logos* yet incorporates aspects of both to become the sophisticated lover of *logos* who is yet a civic man. He alone neither mistakes speech for a personal weapon nor discards it, but combines cleverness with a regard for the personal and public self-control, or *sophrosyne,* that founds the power of the word. Likewise, the ideal audience is equally composite: emancipated from the confining and degrading role of vulgar fools that seems its limit in the parabasis, yet not becoming abstracted and philosophical either. For the *Clouds'* multiple fractures of illusion and constant play with the audience's responses, while often acting to draw the spectators into the comedy as the crude "first" audience, also make sure we remember that this "original" audience is now only a comic fiction. We are not that vulgar audience which our *Clouds* seems to reflect, and while we recognize its kinship to ourselves, we need not duplicate its mistakes.[11] Instead, we are new spectators, shaped by experience of our new comedy. As such, we have learned to appreciate our "deformed" play for what it really is: not mistaking the conventional vulgarity of the revised *Clouds* for its totality, but instead seeing its generic excesses from the larger perspective that makes of them, and the pleasure they evoke, expressive and signifying elements of Aristophanes' amended *logos.* Such a delight in all our *Clouds'* inventions—vulgar and refined, bodily and verbal, conventional and novel—will redeem the first *Clouds'* rejection and make good on its failure, but that is not all. The knowledge and self-knowledge these wiser spectators bring from our second *Clouds* will help them assess all speech in the city. Aristophanes' true audience will greet *logos* with an alert and wary pleasure, appreciative of its power and of the grounds for this power, awake to the conflicting motives for persuasion on both sides, the intimate play of *gaster* and *logos,* appetites and mind, that informs speaking and listening alike.

It is in the training of such spectators that the *Clouds* makes its most profound "political" contribution.[12] As the play progresses, multiplying references make it obvious that the issues raised by the power or lack thereof of *logos,* and of *gaster* and the appetites, are inseparable from issues raised by democracy, with its premium placed on discussion and assent. At the same time, the confined nature of the drama emphasizes the extent to which these concerns are secondary (or nonexistent), not just to the plot, but to the characters and to people like them. Yet it is such individuals who make up the comic audience, whose attitudes toward language and actions as speakers and listeners constitute the fabric of democratic discourse(s), and in whose name democracy operates. Not its ''sympathy'' for Strepsiades, ''criticism'' of Socrates, ''denunciation'' of Pheidippides, or populist, moderate, or conservative stance make the *Clouds* profoundly political and democratic in attitude and action—although all may be true in their way[13]—but its study of and impact on our understanding of the human relationship to speech, the ordinary, social, judicial, political, speculative, and dramatic currency of the city as it is used and abused by every one of its citizens.

The second *Clouds,* thus, does reflect and sustain the public purpose and institutional optimism of the dramatic festival and its audience, the Athenian *demos* celebrating the splendor of their city and of their power in its democratic forms. Their shared laughter nurtures a public amity—that *philia* suggested by our comedy as fundamental for real persuasion—while recalling the duties of such bonds: to hear and respect the *logos* of those with whom they share their city and their lives.[14] At the same time, the challenges of the comic play, the multiple points of view it promotes in those who experience it—involved and distant, personal and civic—must also be characteristic of the participating citizen. For the tasks our *Clouds* imposes—suspension of natural sympathies and personal prejudices, postponement of (generic) expectation, interpretation and judgment of competing and ambiguous *logoi,* recognition of the pressures of necessity and desire—comically recall us to our democratic responsibilities and require the practice of skills honed in daily and in civic life: the evaluation of speeches (and speakers) to find those most true, most useful, and most just. The assumptions that motivate its comedy parallel those which must animate democracy: a confidence in the ordinary man and his ability to learn from what he sees, a belief that the mass of men in their individual choices and attitudes not only matter, but can be trusted to discover what is right. Thus the pleasures of our *Clouds* tax and extend our democratic capabilities as speakers, as listeners, and as citizens. In so doing, they perform the didactic and civic job of the poet, but at a deeply personal and individual level. And this is appropriate; for the final context of *logos,* as Gorgias and others knew well, remains the individual soul. It is there that its seduction is practiced, a seduction whose effects radiate outward to shape citizens and city.

Yet we can not write off so easily the *Clouds'* own drama. The interplay of violence, *logos,* comedy, laughter, mind, and desire that makes up its texture must leave us with similarly mingled feelings of optimism and pessimism—about ourselves, our fellow citizens, our intellectuals, our leaders, our democracy. Neither is foreign to the *Clouds;* neither is finally endorsed. The abrupt and impersonal ending, the quiet absence of that conventional revelry which might seem to conclude and order what has gone before, transfer the last word to the audience. We are left to enact our own parts, but with a little more reflection than before.[15]

Appendix: The *Clouds'* Two Versions

It is well known that our *Clouds* is a revision, the second version of a play which placed third in the comic contest of the City Dionysia in 424/3 B.C.[1] This appendix addresses two important questions: (1) how our revised *Clouds* may differ from the original play, and (2) what may have been the nature of the first *Clouds*. The significance of my positions on both these issues is alluded to here and argued for more fully in chapter 5 and the chapters that follow.

There are several types of evidence that bear on the existence of and differences between the two versions of the *Clouds*. All are ably discussed by Dover and again by Hubbard; their conclusions can only be summarized here:[2]

1. The scholia at line 1115 of our play refer to the writer's commentary on the first *Clouds* and indicate that five cola are missing at this point (the beginning of the second parabasis). This confirms revision throughout, while also suggesting that there were two independent commentaries and texts in existence, first and second *Clouds*.

2. The fact that ancient scholars identified (even if incorrectly) passages as being from *Clouds* I or *Clouds* II suggests desire to avoid confusion between two extant versions.

3. The scholia on 520 indicate that our parabasis proper, lines 518–62, differs in content and in meter from that of the first version. This is corroborated by the fact that our parabasis refers to the defeat of the first *Clouds* and records Aristophanes' reaction. Thus there is general agreement that the parabasis proper of the second *Clouds* has been completely redone.

4. The scholia on line 543 note that our *Clouds* ends with the burning of the Thinkery and the cries of the philosophers and state that this did not happen in the first version.

5. Hypothesis I (Dover) confirms the scholia by stating that the revisions included details throughout, deletion and addition of elements, change in the speaking parts (or dialogue), and inclusion of a new parabasis, debate of the *logoi* (agon), and burning of the Thinkery (end).

Citing these considerations,[3] Dover has argued persuasively for the survival into the Hellenistic period of an independent text of the first *Clouds*, which differed from our play in points throughout and in the parabasis, agon, and end. I accept these conclusions, with Hubbard's proviso that we do not know if the revisions are "entirely new, or just revised throughout (i.e., extensively reworked versions of similar elements in the original play)."[4] Nor must we assume that such a revised second *Clouds* was left unfinished, that Aristophanes intended to work on it more, but failed to do so. Even if Dover is correct in arguing that our play never was performed,[5] this does not mean that it could not be performed. Hypothesis I (Dover) merely states that the *Clouds* was revised as if the poet wished to produce it, but for some reason did not do so.[6] The issue can not really be settled by appealing to enigmatic passages, such as the treatment of the now dead Cleon as if he were still living in lines 591ff. (argued to be a carelessly overlooked relic of the first play)[7] without considering the possibility that such passages have been consciously retained for thematic or comic reasons to play a role in the work as it stands now. As Hubbard points out, the decision to retain a passage is a critical revision no less than the decision to change it.[8]

It is perhaps in response to the notion of an "unfinished" or "incompletely revised" play,[9] with attendant connotations of inferiority and the monopolization of criticism by detection of elements belonging to the first or second versions,[10] that revision on a large scale is rejected by many critics. These scholars consider only 518–62 (the parabasis proper) to be really new, and reject the scholia and the hypotheses as derived from the parabasis itself.[11] Reckford, for example, believes that "the play we have is mostly identical with the play performed in 423 B.C.," while at the same time acknowledging possible revision around the agon and perhaps "more drastic change" at the end. He bases his resistence to revision of the end on this scene's excellent integration into the play, "both in diction and in its reversal plot."[12] Reckford, of course, plans to discuss the *Clouds* at length in a later book, yet his views here illustrate how argument against revision is correlated with defense of the thematic integrity of the play we have. For Reckford surely responds to de Carli and others like him who see the end as revised for the worse, an awkward and visionless rehash of earlier imagery and terms.[13] Thus Whitman, who acknowledges the end as new, uses his feeling that it is "not very satisfactory" as evidence for incomplete revision and then wonders "how far it is justifiable to attempt an interpretation of a play which may not, as it was left, represent the poet's wishes in any very clear way."[14] Readings like this use the "fact" of revision to postpone interpretation of puzzling passages, thus slighting the comedy we have—here the effect is to overlook the subtle and highly ironic effect of the repetitive diction (see chapter 9). Yet to use the excellence, thorough integration, or thematic contribution of a particular part of the play to establish its status as original is equally tied to a particular view of what revision means. Revision is not necessarily ill-fitting, inferior, patchy, or simplifying, and original well thoughtout, integrated, superior, nor vice-versa.[15] To say that certain parts of our *Clouds* are probably new in the second version is not to dismember the play, but to open up an interesting avenue for interpretation, and one which our *Clouds* itself emphatically brings to our attention.[16]

However, even if extensive—and masterful—revision is accepted, this does not solve the problem of the nature of the first version. Here there is even less evidence: a few fragments (collected in PCG), *Wasps* 1037–59, lines 537–44 of the parabasis proper of the second *Clouds,* and the scholia.

The fragments of the first *Clouds* are insufficient to allow any real conclusions about either its content or its nature. The best that can be said is that Euripides occurred in some context and was noted for his sophisticated tragedy (392 PCG), that fragment 393 (PCG) may be a lewd description of the philosophers' withered feebleness, that some wrathful (clouds) departed (paratragically) for Parnes (394 PCG), that a conventional rite seems to have been repudiated (395 PCG), and that *kolasma* (400 PCG) suggests chastisement. This may be augmented a bit, if, following Murphy, we accept *Wasps* 1037–42 as referring to the first *Clouds.* The fact that the "chills and fevers" of line 1038 ($\tau o \hat{\iota} \varsigma$ $\dot{\eta}\pi\iota\dot{\alpha}\lambda o \hat{\iota} \varsigma$ . . . $\kappa\alpha\grave{\iota}$ $\tau o \hat{\iota} \varsigma$ $\pi\upsilon\rho\epsilon\tau o \hat{\iota}\sigma\iota\nu$) act like sycophants (1041) need not deter us, for as Murphy points out, the identification of sophists with sycophants is clear in *Birds* 1694ff. and may be suggested in *Birds* 285—Callias, who is "plucked by sycophants," was known for his generosity to sophists. Nor must we require precision in the outline of the plot; instead, these lines "are merely a description of the character of these sophist-sycophants, just as the lines that precede these describe not the plot of the *Knights* but the character of Cleon."[17] The claim of *Wasps* 1037ff. to describe the first *Clouds* is reinforced by the fact that the scholia cite *Clouds* for the word "chill" ($\dot{\eta}\pi\acute{\iota}\alpha\lambda o\varsigma$), possibly, from the form of the citation, coupled with "fever" ($\pi\upsilon\rho\epsilon\tau\acute{o}\varsigma$).[18] (Kassel and Austin print this as fragment 399 [PCG] of the first *Clouds.*) If they are accepted as referring to the first *Clouds,* they might give us a clue about that play's direction. For *Wasps* 1039, with "choked" ($\alpha\pi\acute{\epsilon}\pi\nu\iota\gamma o\nu$), recalls *Clouds* 1036, 1376, 1389, 1504, while the comically excessive "gluing together" ($\sigma\upsilon\nu\epsilon\kappa\acute{o}\lambda\lambda\omega\nu$) of legal documents in 1041 recalls *Clouds* 446, where Strepsiades hopes to be known as a gluer of lies in recognition of his success as a sophistic speaker.[19] Perhaps the first play involved some kind of legal procedings, as well as "choking" of the father, possibly, given the appearance of Euripides, for a "crime" similar to that in our version. Such a hypothesis would support Dover's suggestion that: "If the first version ended with the triumph of Pheidippides over his wretched father, it presented without irony or disguise the bleak reality which in *Knights* is overlaid by the conventional comic ending; but it presented something which the judges could not stomach, Ar. reverted in *Wasps* to convention in its crudest form, and in revising *Clouds* he gave priority to the construction of a new ending which provided the customary noise and movement and satisfied, on a superficial level, the audience's ideas of right and wrong."[20]

`All of the above is necessarily highly speculative and still does not tell us much about the nature of the first *Clouds;* here the parabasis of our play is more instructive. Chapter 5 has discussed the picture that the parabasis draws of the highly verbal and sophisticated nature of the first *Clouds,* as well as stating my view that lines 537–44 describe this first play. In this I follow Hubbard's position as given in his 1986 article and 1991 book. Without reproducing his arguments in detail, I wish to discuss this passage further, repeating his central points and adding to them where possible. The lines in question are as follows:

ὡς δὲ σώφρων ἐστὶ φύσει σκέψασθ᾽, ἥτις πρῶτα μὲν
οὐδὲν ἦλθε ῥαψαμένη σκύτινον καθειμένον
ἐρυθρὸν ἐξ ἄκρου, παχύ, τοῖς παιδίοις ἵν᾽ ᾖ γέλως·
οὐδ᾽ ἔσκωψεν τοὺς φαλακρούς, οὐδὲ κόρδαχ᾽ εἵλκυσεν·
οὐδὲ πρεσβύτης ὁ λέγων τἄπη τῇ βακτηρίᾳ
τύπτει τὸν παρόντ᾽, ἀφανίζων πονηρὰ σκώμματα·
οὐδ᾽ εἰσῆξε δᾷδας ἔχουσ᾽ οὐδ᾽ "ἰοὺ ἰού" βοᾷ·
ἀλλ᾽ αὐτῇ καὶ τοῖς ἔπεσιν πιστεύουσ᾽ ἐλήλυθεν.

(537–44)

How chaste it is by nature *(physis)*, see, it, the one who first *(prota)*
did not come stitched with leather [phallus] hanging down
red at the end, thick, for children a source of laughter;
nor mocked the bald, nor dragged on a *kordax;*
nor does an old man, the one speaking the words, with a cane
beat the bystander, hiding bad jokes;
nor did it rush in holding torches, nor cries "iou, iou";
but trusting in itself and its words it has come.

As Hubbard points out, by the time the audience arrives at these lines, they are accustomed to a temporal scheme that shifts between present and past in making claims about aristophanic comedy and its history. Thus the parabasis begins with the story of the defeat of the first *Clouds* (520–26, obviously in the past), moves in 527 to a boast about the future (including, perhaps, our present play), and returns in 528–33 to the past with a discussion of the production and reception of the *Banqueters*. With lines 534–36, the focus returns to "this comedy." Hubbard believes the reference is only to the second *Clouds*,[21] but, in fact, these lines prepare for the following association and the contrast between the two versions by linking them familially and temporally to establish a causal relationship between the experience of the first and the conduct of the second. For our comedy is like Electra in that for it, too, the "familial" bond on which it relied, this time between poet and audience, has been transgressed, eroded by irrational appetites.[22] Frightened by its original reception, what we call our second *Clouds*—that is, the second version—thus searches timidly for signs of those with whom the bond still holds, spectators who are wise enough to recognize its true worth and cherish it properly (535). (The question of why these wise spectators would want to have anything to do with the vulgar second *Clouds* is discussed in chapter 5.) Thus, when line 537 begins, we could suppose it to refer to either play, or as Hubbard proposes, to both. We do not yet know that a sharp distinction will be made between them—although later we may realize as Hubbard states that their identity lies in that nature that they share, but which has been disguised in our second version by a facade of ordinary vulgarity.[23] But, surely, to take the comedy we have been watching as *sophron* in any standard way is, by this time, rather difficult; there has already been too much vulgar farce.[24] Our laughter at this idea means the joke is on the poet himself; it is he who mistakes his product not the audience.[25] *Prota* (537) and what follows, however, turn the tables; the last laugh is on us as we begin to sort out the two very different versions of the play, first and second, and what this means. For as Hubbard has shown, following upon the temporal *protous* of line 523 which described the first audience, this reference too is temporal (not rhetorical), while μέν is *solitarium*. The aorist verbs in the relative clause which follows (537–43)—the presents are historical and sufficiently delayed to blend in without difficulty, while the perfect (544) is used of existing dramatic work, not performance[26]—confirm that at issue is the rejected and superior first version, not the product that we watch. Thus the passage makes vivid the obvious, but until the parabasis perhaps hardly considered, fact that our play is not the original *Clouds,* for that play did not include the dangling phallus,[27] mockery of baldness, the *kordax,* old men beating those present to hide bad jokes, torches, and cries of "iou." Instead these vulgar devices and the conventional generic humor which they typify act as a foil for what the first *Clouds* did rely on, itself (that is, its own clever originality) and its words (544).[28]

Hubbard's demonstration that lines 537–44 refer to the first version of the *Clouds* marks a significant advance, for interpretation has long been confused by the fact that our second version clearly, or probably, includes precisely the elements stigmatized by these lines. Hubbard lists the passages in question and points out how many of them can plausibly be considered new. They are: the end with the cries of "iou" and burning of the Thinkery (listed as new by Hypothesis I (Dover) and suggested as new in the scholia); Strepsiades' probable display of the phallus in 196ff., 653ff., and 734ff. (The analyticist critics agree this last combines motifs from two versions and Hubbard suggests not the fleas but the *peos* as new.); possible mockery of the baldness of Socrates in 146ff. and 171–73, as well as the pun in line 545 (this last almost certainly new and discussed in chapter 5); Strepsiades' probable lively dancing of 439ff. and 1201ff.; and the beating of the creditors to cover up, or reinforce, the old man Strepsiades' bad "jokes" at their expense.[29]

These passages and lines 537–44 of the parabasis become far less problematic once we accept Hubbard's view that 537–44 do not apply to our version, the second *Clouds*. In consequence, we need neither attempt to salvage Aristophanes' credibility by denying that our *Clouds* stages what it condemns,[30] nor explain the parabatic claims as humor based on blatant falsity, immediately laughable because the poet does exactly what he claims not to do.[31] Both such interpretations ignore the distinction made between the first and second versions of the *Clouds* and slight the thematic contribution of the parabasis to the play as a whole, leaving it and our passage isolated as examples of humor that requires comic discontinuity.[32] In fact, the remarkable specificity with which the drama reverses the parabasis, particularly in those passages where our comedy can reasonably be postulated to differ from the earlier version,[33] confronts us with a carefully constructed contrast between the first *Clouds* and the version we have.[34] The intertextual dynamic this creates between the play's two versions is discussed in chapter 5 and the chapters that follow; important here is that the first *Clouds* emerges as a play that rejected conventional vulgar and violent nonverbal humor in favor of sophisticated verbal wit and that this verbal and original nature was, at least for Aristophanes, both reason for its superiority and, paradoxically, grounds for its defeat, due to the stupidity of its audience.[35] Failure to accept this parabatic account of the first *Clouds* requires us to postulate reasons for its defeat *in vacuo,*[36] and overlooks the extent to which that story is substantiated by *Wasps* 1043–59. These lines, which record Aristophanes' first surviving response to his loss, outline the virtues of the original *Clouds,* the reasons for its failure, and Aristophanes' reaction in terms that anticipate our own parabasis, without, of course, its detail or thematic elaboration. Thus the poet rebukes the spectators for their shameful failure to appreciate his "most novel conceits" (καινοτάταις διανοίαις) through their own lack of understanding (*Wasps* 1044–45), even though, he swears, they never heard better comic words (ἔπη κωμῳδικὰ *Wasps* 1046–47). He insists his reputation has not suffered among the wise *(sophoi)*, although he took a spill (*Wasps* 1049–50).[37] Finally, he bids the audience "wise up" and cherish poet(s) committed to novelty and invention (καινόν τι λέγειν κἀξευρίσκειν *Wasps* 1053), fostering them and preserving their ideas. In the future such spectators, Aristophanes promises, (or, rather, comically, their cloaks) will smell of cleverness (δεξιότητος *Wasps* 1059).

Thus the parabasis of the *Wasps* and that of our *Clouds* agree: the first *Clouds'* glory was its allegiance to the latest in verbal and sophisticated cleverness, its downfall the fact that the audience was not up to such exacting intellectual standards. Further, if *Wasps* 54ff. can also be taken as indirectly responding to the first *Clouds'* defeat, the first version's "deficiencies" emerge in a way congruent with these conclusions. For Aristophanes' refusal in these lines to cater to the popular appetite for the conventionally comic, typified by (and condemned as) the despised Megarian farce, affirms his poetic standards.[38] Our poet is not going to indulge in slaves throwing sweets to the stands, the slapstick of a violent and gluttonous Heracles, or comically licentious aggression against contemporary intellectuals like Euripides (*Wasps* 57–61), thus buying favor by appeal to the mindless humor of violence, food, sex, and buffoonish attacks on representatives of the new culture. Nor is he going to return to his own successful political comedy with further attacks on Cleon (*Wasps* 62–63). Instead he offers them something in the middle—not too ambitious (*Wasps* 56), but an intelligent little story, not cleverer than they are, yet still wiser than the ordinary vulgar comedy he continues to reject (*Wasps* 64–66). This affirmation may suggest that the first *Clouds* also lacked the type of comic elements that Aristophanes condemns now, as well as perhaps bolstering the view that it was not aggressively antisophist, at least in the familiar, conventional way.[39]

Thus I accept the parabasis' description of the first *Clouds* as a witty, verbal play which rejected or diminished the role of the conventionally comic and vulgar.[40] I also believe that the second *Clouds* differed substantially from this first version and incorporated numerous vulgarities that the first lacked. I do not take this to mean, however, that our parabasis is just an apologetic tract lacking all humor, or that the first *Clouds* was neither funny nor obscene. Our parabasis abounds in jokes of all kinds—aimed at the poet, the audience, and his poetic rivals. Likewise, its very precision leaves us much latitude in imagining the first *Clouds'* resources: all types of verbal wit (including vulgar), numerous farcical situations, sudden reversals of fortune, ludicrious misunderstandings and changes of plane and tone, the success (or failure) of fantastic plans with unexpected results deriving from their verbal logic. The first *Clouds* was a comedy and could have been a farce, but of a unique, novel, and (according to Aristophanes) superior kind. Nor, conversely, do I wish to imply that our *Clouds* is somehow incomplete or botched, a sadly reduced copy of its superior original—even if the parabasis, at first sight, may seem to promote such a view. Rather, as I argue in chapter 5, our play's presentation of the defeat of the first *Clouds* and its implied negative interpretation of the obvious act of revision that the parabasis exposes—an act which could, of course, have been interpreted positively, as an improvement—is central to the second *Clouds'* particular excellence and fundamental to one of its comic projects—to educate the spectators about comedy, about *logos,* and about themselves, thus creating a newly appreciative audience. This project requires our knowledge of the differences between the first and second *Clouds,* the types of revisions that make up the second version, and the reasons for these revisions. Precisely this information is given in the parabasis. Thus the parabasis plays a central role in the *Clouds'* thematic progress while enlarging the drama of Strepsiades and sophistic *logos* to include as well the interaction of comic *logos* and its Athenian audience.

NOTES

Introduction

1. For the aspects of the City (or Great) Dionysia mentioned here, see Pickard-Cambridge 57–101.

2. Redfield 318 aptly compares theatrical production to equipping a trireme; both were liturgies, public expenses borne by selected wealthy citizens. See Pickard-Cambridge 86ff.

3. Winkler suggests that the chorus was composed of ephebes, young citizens just beginning their military training.

4. The normal number of competing comedians was five; it may have dropped to three during parts of the Peloponnesian War. See Pickard-Cambridge 83. For the parts and rites of the City Dionysia—which included public processions, sacrifice, celebration, the tragic and dithyrambic competitions, announcement of civic honors, the parading in arms of war orphans raised at public expense, and exhibition of tribute from the allies—see Pickard-Cambridge 59–70. For the regulatory role of the *demos,* see Henderson (1990) 286ff.; for the festival's promotion of social cohesion, see Longo 14, 18; Redfield 324.

5. Winkler 22. He states that ''the layout of the auditorium formed (at least ideally) a kind of map of the civic corporation with all its tensions and balances,'' exemplifying the political and social structure of democratic Athens (38ff.). But, given the fact that at the City Dionysia the audience would probably have contained an unknown number of noncitizens, foreigners, metics, boys, and perhaps women and some slaves (Pickard-Cambridge 263ff.), the notion of a purely civic assembly may be a little too restricted. For some implications of this inclusive audience in assessing the impact of the plays, see Ober and Strauss.

6. For the well-known overlap between the *demos* seated in the theater and that which, as sovereign power in Athens, made the other political, legal, and dramatic decisions, see Ehrenberg 20, 37, Henderson (1990) 275ff., Redfield 318, and Ober and Strauss 238ff.

7. I shall translate *logos* variously as word, speech, account, reasoning, or shall transliterate it, letting the context determine the exact sense.

8. See Henderson (1990) 276, 286ff. who emphasizes the *demos* as ''sponsor, spectator, and judge of agonistic performances in which the ambitious competitors make their appeals, and only the competitors are at risk.'' See also Goff 79ff. and Buxton 20ff. for the agonistic style in medicine, among other areas. For the ten judges chosen by lot from the names submitted by each tribe, five of whose votes, selected at random, determined the outcome of the comic contest, see Pickard-Cambridge 95ff. These judges were obviously intended to represent the citizens at large. In the *Clouds* the audience and the judges are addressed interchangeably. Likewise the audience could attempt to influence the judges; see Pickard-Cambridge 97.

9. This notion is parallel but not equivalent to Henderson's (1990) point that on the stage we see the ''world of the spectators in their civic roles,'' complete with *demos,* competitors for its favor, debate and invective, decision, and outcome of decision (308). Comedy, or at least the *Clouds,* requires not just that we watch a representation of the civic world but that in so doing we use and refine skills required in other democratic fora.

10. See Henderson (1990) 271ff.

11. For the weaving together of seemingly separate elements to form a complex whole as typically aristophanic, see Reckford (1987) 203.

12. The notion of *bia,* physical violence, and its contrast with *logos,* or speech, is discussed at greater length in chapter 1. I usually translate *bia* as violence or force, or leave it transliterated.

13. Those who consider the *Clouds* essentially accurate include: Nussbaum, Strauss, and Edmunds (1987). Those who see it as essentially free comic invention, aimed at an entire class of new intellectuals, include: Dover, de Carli, Gelzer, and Solomos. Schmid and Erbse believe that the *Clouds* distinguishes Socrates from the sophists and protects him from the ridicule heaped on them. Tomin feels that the joke is the misunderstanding of the historical Socrates by the stupid Strepsiades. For the "Socrates problem" and previous views, see Nussbaum 44ff., Turato (1972) 8ff. (See 74ff. for his own view that our play aimed at the real Socrates seen through the lens of Anaxgoras), Reckford (1987) 392ff., Hubbard (1991), chapter 5. (I regret that the precise page numbers in Hubbard's book became available only after the present volume was in production.) My own view—that the Socrates of the *Clouds* is a comically exaggerated version of the "real" Socrates, who brings out certain characteristics implied, if not present, in his beliefs and practices—will emerge in the chapters that follow. However, my interest is in the Socrates of the *Clouds,* the boundaries of whose characterization must be those pointed out by McLeish: "Obviously there would be no point to the joke if Socrates, Euripides and the rest retained none of their real-life characteristics. But equally obviously, once they become characters in the illusion, they move within the bounds of that illusion and not those of real life" (91). See also Ehrenberg 40. For Socrates as simultaneously one of the swarm of sophists and his own peculiar self in a chorus of intellectuals, see Dover's discussion of *Konnos* (lff.).

14. See Woodbury 108, who argues that Strepsiades, too, is often illegitimately overshadowed by Socrates. For an example of the weight of the platonic orientation, see Nussbaum, who dismisses Strepsiades' lessons as added "humorous material which is not directly pertinent" to the comic portrayal (76).

15. For a beautiful expression of the fantastic reality of the comic vision, see Whitman, especially chapter 8. For the longing for a better world, see Redfield 329ff. For fantasy and topical satire, see Moulton. For possible political positions, see the sources cited by Whitman 5ff. (whose caveats I agree with). For a democratic orientation, see Turato (1972), who also discusses previous views; following him, see Ambrosino (1986–87) and, to a lesser extent (1983); see also Henderson (1990). For the "oldfashioned moderate," see North 97ff. For a conservative position, see Ostwald, Connor, and Carter, all of whom are discussed in chapter 7. For comic discontinuity in the interests of humor, see Dover (1972) 44ff., McLeish, Fisher 129ff., and Ussher 19.

16. Critics with a philosophical, socratic orientation tend to ignore the other school. Their opponents, however, denounce them as blind to what is really going on and guilty of a hypersophisticated academic frame of mind foreign to the Athenian public. See, for example, Fisher 243ff. Such division reproduces a trend in the treatment of comedy in general, for as Henderson (1990) points out, comedy is seldom considered an organic, "persuasive mode parallel to those we call serious," but is tossed between mutually exclusive interpretative categories—serious or funny, carnival play or civic statement, art or politics—each of which isolates one part of the comic experience as expressive of the whole (273). See also Solomos 8.

17. See Moulton's analysis of *Birds* 1470ff. for the integration of elements from puns to the comic structure which illustrates, in his view, Aristophanes' "mixture of topical satire and unadulterated fantasy" (28ff.).

18. For discussion of the two versions of the *Clouds,* see chapter 5 and the Appendix.

19. Of course, the *Clouds'* real history and the reasons for its former defeat, whatever they may be and however different from the "history" given by Aristophanes, are irrecoverable. In general, scholars accept Aristophanes' explanation, but it is also possible, as Reckford (1987) points out, that the other plays were simply better (396). It seems unlikely we shall ever know. For a more detailed discussion, see the Appendix.

20. For the possibility that the second *Clouds* began as written, that is, "intended for readers," see Dover xcviii. However, in spite of the uncertainty about whether the second *Clouds* was ever produced during Aristophanes' lifetime (and the certainty that the vast majority of its audience ever since have been readers), I will continue to refer to "spectators" and "audience." This is what is built into the play; everything in Aristophanes' and in fifth-century audiences' experience and practice prepared them to respond to written comedy as a script, a guide to theatrical experience, something to be staged, even if it is read. Of course, the way in which the second *Clouds* reached the public is unknown, but see Starkie liii and note 5, Dover 270 for addenda to page xcviii. For the two independent versions of the *Clouds,* see the appendix in the present book.

21. Thus the *Clouds* eludes some of the constraints of public, festive context, single performance, and generic expectation enumerated for fifth-century drama by critics. See, for example, Longo, who uses the social political context of the dramatic competitions and the "rules of genre" to undermine the concepts of "artistic autonomy, of creative spontaneity," and other "bourgeois esthetics" by limiting the "co-ordinates within which admissible poetic trajectories will be plotted" (15ff.).

22. Of course, to reconstruct the experiences of individual spectators and the interaction of the drama with their particular beliefs and emotions is impossible. However, we can hope to trace the outlines of the experience that the play seems to attempt to privilege.

23. See Reckford (1987) for the notion of "comedy of ideas" (393). He sees a "turning point . . . in the self-awareness of Athenian comedy" occasioned by the failure of the audience to appreciate the first *Clouds* (392). Nevertheless, he believes that the "play inspires confidence about the power of the human mind and spirit (393), while acknowledging its sadness, albeit in terms of Aristophanes personally (401ff.). Nussbaum, on the other hand, feels "the play ends on a note . . . of anguish" (78–79), a picture of "private hedonism impervious to reason and even to sympathy" (95).

24. See, in particular, Turato (1972) and Ambrosino (1986–87), both of which are discussed later in this study.

25. See Goldhill (1990) for a view of tragedy as not advocating specific social or political programs but rather questioning and examining cultural and civic assumptions and ideological or speculative positions to expose their areas of conflict and contrast (114ff.).

Chapter 1

1. This is an interest that seems to have been common to playwrights and sophists alike. Thus Goldhill (1986) comments, "it is their shared response to the question of the relations of man and the city, their shared response to the problems of the language in which the discourse of those relations is formed, that link the various 'wise men' and 'teachers' who lay claim to the title of 'educator of the city' " (229). See also North 86ff.

2. Goldhill (1986) 75.

3. Kennedy 34. Cf. Democritus DK 68 B 51.

4. See Sinclair 39ff., 136ff. for the link between the new style of politics, the importance of public speaking, and the fundamental democratic principle of *isegoria,* or "equal

right of speech in the assembly'' (15). Ostwald notes that the demagogue was a ''private individual who by force of his personality and his rhetorical ability managed to persuade the people in Council and Assembly to support the measures and policies he favored'' (202). For political use of the courts, see Ostwald 208ff., 207 for Cleon.

5. Connor 116; see also Sinclair 136–37. Cf. Ostwald 201ff., Connor 108ff. for the changing terminology for political leadership after Pericles.

6. Damon, Zeno, Anaxagoras, and Protagoras are mentioned as among his familiars; see Plutarch *Pericles* 4 passim, 8.16, 36.5; Plato *Phaedrus* 270a3. Cratinus addressed Pericles as the great tongue of Greece (324 PCG; see also 326 and 327, for the pejorative flavor of this) and repeatedly satirized his power. Cf. *Cheirons, Nemesis,* and 73, 118, 258 (PCG). For the necessary role of persuasion in Pericles' power, see Sinclair 39ff.

7. See Thucydides 2.65.8. Of course, Thucydides is a biased source, exalting Pericles and Periclean Athens for his own analytic ends.

8. The Cleon of the literary record, usually written by his opponents, and the Cleon of the historical record may emerge as two rather different creatures. Certainly, it is very likely that Cleon's father did not come from the lower classes but was a wealthy manufacturer; see Ostwald 202ff., among others. However, the point here is not setting the record straight on the historical Cleon and the sources of hostility to him, be they resentment at his class, his use of the courts, his political stragegies, or his war policy (all considered by Ostwald), but investigating the complex of changed attitudes, assumptions, political practices and styles, that he came to emblematize. See Connor 168ff. and Ostwald 213ff. for the literary bias against demagogues, Ostwald 217ff. for Thucydides and Cleon in particular. Ostwald 213ff. points out that the terms of opposition to such men may, in many instances, be the flip side of their own rhetoric. See Sinclair 205ff.

9. Connor 119.

10. While the degree of qualitative change in Athenian politics after the death of Pericles is difficult to assess and to distinguish from prejudice against the new politicians, Ostwald believes that ''even after due allowance for bias in our sources is made, Athenian political life still seems to have changed enough for us to regard the death of Pericles as the dividing line between two different political styles'' (200). Sinclair, after mentioning areas of political continuity and other grounds for power, concludes that Cleon's ''early influence rested on his oratorical and political skills'' (42). However, see Connor 117ff. for Pericles' anticipation of the new forms of politics. Both Sinclair and Ostwald contrast the more traditional Nicias, himself not a member of the traditional political class. Of course, those who did not come from the traditional (noble) political class were virtually compelled to seek new routes to power (see Ostwald 203ff., Henderson [1990] 281ff.), and they certainly stayed within the democratic institutional structure.

11. For Cleon as exemplary, see Connor 139ff; for the youth of the new politicians and their new route to power, 143ff. For the rhetors' assumption of power in the assembly without the risks of office, see Sinclair 42, Henderson (1990) 282, Ostwald 202.

12. For the new rhetoric and its dramatic effects (frequently mirrored and mocked in Aristophanes), see Connor 107ff. For the new politicians' appeal to the *demos* and numerous citizens not of the wealthy upper classes, see Connor 99ff. (for terminology), Ostwald 200ff.

13. All are considered by Connor in chapter 3; Ostwald adds the effects of gathering the population inside the city, with new time for and interest (or self-interest) in political affairs (200).

14. Cleon had ''in effect severed the connection'' (Connor 150) between military exploits and social/political dominance; cf. Connor 143ff. For many laments about the qualities and qualifications of the young, new style politicians, see Connor chapter 4.

15. Connor 176. In general, see Connor 175ff. and Carter chapters 3 and 5.

16. Plutarch *Alcibiades* 10.3. For Alcibiades' mastery of the new politics, see Connor 140, who also cites this passage. Cf. Plato's similar picture of Hippocrates' motives at the beginning of the *Protagoras*.

17. For the sophists generally, see Kerferd, Guthrie; for their impact on Athenian political life, Ostwald 238ff.; for their ready availability, Capizzi.

18. Guthrie, following DK 82 A 4.3, points out that the Athenians were already *philologoi* even before Gorgias stunned them with his novel style (179 n. 3). See also DK 82 A 1.3ff., DK 82 A 35 for the effect and influence of his speech.

19. Pl. *Phdr.* 266d5ff.

20. There is no evidence that Cleon himself studied with the sophists (Connor 163ff. and Ostwald 237) but, in any case, it is clear that he was a brilliant innovator and rhetorician. See Connor 132ff.

21. See Goldhill (1986) chapter 3, Buxton 10ff. for the wide variety of ways in which speech was central to Athenian business and pleasure. For public and semipublic sophistic display, cf, the beginning of Pl. *Laches,* the setting of *Euthydemos, Protagoras,* and so forth.

22. See Th. 2.40.

23. See Th. 3.36.6: ὧν καὶ ἐς τὰ ἄλλα βιαιότατος τῶν πολιτῶν τῷ τε δήμῳ παρὰ πολὺ ἐν τῷ τότε πιθανώτατος.

24. See Th. 3.38ff. The wording of Cleon's speech leaves no doubt that it is the new sophistic speakers that he is represented as attacking. In 3.38.5, he censures the Athenians for being deceived by the newfangled rhetoric (citing the sophistic *apate*) and enslaved by the unusual; later he accuses them of attending the assembly about the city as if it were sophistic display (3.38.7).

25. It also reflects the contemporary hostility between members of the "democratic establishment" and the new, sophistically trained speakers; see Ostwald 250ff., 257 (on this passage). See also chapter 7.

26. For earlier instances, see *Iliad.* 1.304, Aeschylus *Choephori* 380ff., *Eumenides* 589 (the most similar to the sophists' use), Pindar *Nemean* 4.93–96. Cf. Louis 57ff. and Taillardat 282 for further examples.

27. See Guthrie 183 n. 1, DK 80 B 1.

28. See DK 80 A 1.55 for the title; for content, DK 80 B 8.

29. For the wrestling of sophistic *logos*, see Socrates in Pl. *Euthd.* 288a2: ἀλλὰ ἔοικεν . . . οὗτος μὲν ὁ λόγος ἐν ταὐτῷ μένειν καὶ ἔτι ὥσπερ τὸ παλαιὸν καταβαλὼν πίπτειν. Here τὸ παλαιὸν can be read as "the venerable" (LSJ παλαιός II 3 a), pointing not to age, but to the familiar character of what follows (as in Pl. *Gorgias* 499c5 and *Republic* 329a2) or it can underline the reuse of imagery formerly restricted to physical wrestling. For dramatic uses of the same imagery connected with the sophists, see Aristophanes 205.3–4 (PCG) καταπλιγήσηι, which Kassel and Austin (PCG) relate to *Kataballontes (logoi);* Eur. *Bacchae* 200ff., which Dodds ad 202 reads as a reference to Protagoras; and *Iphigenia at Aulis* 1013. For the application to the sophists themselves, see Protagoras, himself known as Logos (DK 80 A 3), called by Timon "Πρωταγόρης τ' ἐπίμεικτος ἐριζέμεναι εὖ εἰδώς (DK 80 A 1 52), where Sprague, following Untersteiner, translates ἐπίμεικτος "avid in combat" (5); it refers to verbal *agones.* Timon also called Zeno, who was credited with having invented dialectic (DK 29 A 1.25, DK 29 A 4), ἀμφοτερογλώσσου τε μέγα σθένος οὐκ ἀλαπαδνόν / Ζήνωνος πάντων ἐπιλήπτορος (DK 29 A 1.25) for his having ἐλεγκτικὴν δέ τινα καὶ δι' ἀντιλογίας εἰς ἀπορίαν κατακλείουσαν ἐξασκήσαντος ἕξιν (Plu. *Per.* 4.5; cf. Kerferd 85). Ἀμφοτερόγλωσσος surely refers to the two *logoi* (cf. *Clouds* 1108ff.) and at the same

time to ambidextrous fighters and double-edged weapons; σθένος οὐκ ἀλαπαδνόν mockingly portrays Zeno as a homeric hero (cf. *Odyssey* 18.373); κατακλείειν can be used in a military context; cf. Th. 1.109, 1.117, 4.57. For Plato's (re)use of this imagery, cf. the *Sophist*'s fifth definition of the sophist as teacher of the agonistic, militaristic, eristic art (225a1ff.; see also 222c5, 231c9, 231e1, 241c9); Pl. *Euthd.* 271c7ff., (which jokes that the brothers are expert in every kind of battle, physical and verbal) 277d1 (including *kataballein*), 288a4, 297c1, 302b5, 303a3, 305a2; and *Theaetetus* 162b1 and 169a7, where the discussion of Protagoras' views has extensive use of wrestling imagery. For Plato and "Le Dialogue combat," see Louis 57ff., particularly 60ff.

30. A comic fragment compared Miltiades with current demagogues in wrestling terms; ad esp. 361 Kock. Dk 85 B 4 may have a similar point.

31. The comparison below, which Isocrates picks up in *Antidosis* 252–53 and which clearly parallels the crimes of Pheidippides in the *Clouds,* may have been a common way of discussing rhetoric and instruction in its *techne.* Plato jokingly compares Protagoras to a boxer (*Prt.* 339e1) and Damon is described as τῶι δὲ Περικλεῖ συνῆν καθάπερ ἀθλητῆι τῶν πολιτικῶν ἀλείπτης καὶ διδάσκαλος (DK 37 A 4). Additional terms also show the overlap of the martial and rhetorical (as well as the sexual and rhetorical). κεντεῖν is closely associated with irresistible persuasion, rhetorical or sexual; cf. Eupolis 102 (PCG) and *Clouds* 450, 947, and 1300, all discussed later. τύπτειν may also have been a rhetorical term; cf. Gorgias *Encomium* 13, quoted later in the notes, and *Knights* 1379ff., where it could mean "capable of striking opinions." Finally, note the *palaistra* and the assimilation of the student of boxing to the student of rhetoric through πυκτικός, with its fashionable, intellectual suffix.

32. For politics and thus the art of speaking as fundamental to the display of traditional *arete*—to help friends and harm enemies, while doing well oneself—see also DK 82 B 19, where τὰ τῆς πόλεως πράττειν has the almost purely verbal connotations discussed below.

33. Protagoras states that the successful speaker bears a crown of glory in DK 80 B 12, a poorly attested fragment, but one whose imagery is at least thematically likely. Pericles was crowned after one funeral speech as if he were a victorious athlete (Plu. *Per.* 28.4). For platonic reuse, see *Tht.* 169b5.

34. I accept the reading in DK of πλίγμα, which is compared to Aristophanes' use of καταπλιγήσηι in 205 PCG (=DK 85 A 4), an expression which is said to be taken from the rhetors, who seem to use it to describe their contests. For the connection with wrestling, see PCG ad Ar. 205.3; LSJ likewise translates πλίγμα "crossing the legs in walking or wrestling."

35. For the ideal, see *Il.* 9.443; for its collapse, Pucci (1960) 21ff. For a possible satire along these lines, cf. Cratinus' *Cheirons.*

36. These new *erga* were performed by men ἀργόι in the traditional sense; thus the clouds are identified by Socrates as great goddesses ἀνδράσιν ἀργοῖς (*Clouds* 316). See Ambrosino (1983) 25 for this as the usual association of culture with leisure.

37. Odysseus is later called a σοφὸς παλαιστής in *Ph.* 431; cf. his role in Gorg. *Palamedes.*

38. For the tongue's supremacy, see Plato Comicus in *Zeus Kakomenos:* γλώττης ἀγαθῆς οὐκ ἔστ' ἄμεινον οὐδὲ ἕν / ἡ γλῶττα δύναμιν τοὺς λόγους ἐκτήσατο, / ἐκ τῶν λόγων δ' ἅττ' αὐτὸς ἐπιθυμεῖς ἔχεις (52 PCG). For an ironic reference to the ubiquitous nature of the tongue, see Pl. Com. 51 (PCG). Cf. also *Birds* 1694ff.

39. Cf. Buxton 126ff. and Podlecki.

40. Thus Gorgias devotes two paragraphs to the first two possibilities (*Encomium* 6–7) and seven to *logos* (8–14). The next five (15–19) discuss *eros* (which may or may not

have been present in the initial list of causes) in terms of *opsis* and the impressionable nature of the soul, a prerequisite as well for the operation of *logos*. Cf. Zeitlin 209ff. For another view of the *Encomium,* see Casertano.

41. For the *logos* as like the divine, see *Encomium* 8 and 10, Segal (1962) 120ff. The power of the divine is, however, in turn analogized to the power let loose by democratic speech; in *Encomium* 6, Gorgias speaks of the "decrees," "resolutions," and so forth of the superhuman forces with which he pairs *logos.*

42. *Encomium* 12. The text is corrupt, but the sense is clear.

43. See Pepe 275. Persuasion appears only in the sections of the *Encomium* devoted to *logos.*

44. Throughout this book I will translate *peitho* as persuasion. This usually refers to verbal persuasion, but sometimes intends the larger meaning of the Greek notion, which covers both verbal and nonverbal persuasion, as here, where the erotic persuasion involved is sexual seduction. In cases like this, I will generally include or use the word *peitho.*

45. See Buxton 45ff.

46. Thus, Gorgias once again pairs persuasion and necessity, concluding about Helen, ὁ μὲν οὖν πείσας ὡς ἀναγκάσας ἀδικεῖ, ἡ δὲ πεισθεῖσα ὡς ἀναγκασθεῖσα τῶι λόγωι μάτην ἀκούει κακῶς (*Encomium* 12). This increases the independence of *logos* while simultaneously making it more like the operation of *bia.* For as Gorgias already pointed out, δῆλον ὅτι ὁ ⟨μὲν⟩ ἁρπάσας ὡς ὑβρίσας ἠδίκησεν, ἡ δὲ ἁρπασθεῖσα ὡς ὑβρισθεῖσα ἐδυστύχησεν (*Encomium* 7).

47. See *Encomium* 13: τὰ ἄπιστα καὶ ἄδηλα φαίνεσθαι τοῖς τῆς δόξης ὄμμασιν. Following traditional practice, I have translated *doxa* "opinion" throughout.

48. See *Encomium* 11; the reliance on *doxa* means that our successes rest on an insecure foundation and accounts for their instability.

49. See *Encomium* 14. Cf. Segal (1962) 105ff. for the soul and 109ff. for *doxa.* For the mode of action of words taken as "things," see Walsh 81ff.

50. *Apate,* or deception, is a concept central to sophistic rhetoric, describing (positively or negatively) the power of speech to deceive—a power based on the man's inability to know the truth and necessary reliance on opinion, cf. *Encomium* 8 and 10; Rosenmeyer passim; Segal (1962) 112, 121, 130; Verdenius passim; de Romilly 16; Classen 222 for Protagoras and 229 for Gorgias; and for a slightly different view, Kerferd 78ff. For a history of the relationship of *apate, logos,* and *pseudos* from another perspective, see Untersteiner 108–14.

51. *Logos* functions at best only metaphorically, never able to *be* what it represents, but only to present or recall yet another *logos* to the hearer. Thus as Gorgias points out elsewhere: ὧι γὰρ μηνύομεν, ἔστι λόγος, λόγος δὲ οὐκ ἔστι τὰ ὑποκείμενα καὶ ὄντα· οὐκ ἄρα τὰ ὄντα μηνύομεν τοῖς πέλας ἀλλὰ λόγον, ὃς ἕτερός ἐστι τῶν ὑποκειμένων. καθάπερ οὖν τὸ ὁρατὸν οὐκ ἂν γένοιτο ἀκουστὸν καὶ ἀνάπαλιν, οὕτως ἐπεὶ ὑπόκειται τὸ ὂν ἐκτός, οὐκ ἂν γένοιτο λόγος ὁ ἡμέτερος· μὴ ὢν δὲ λόγος οὐκ ἂν δηλωθείη ἑτέρωι (DK 82 B 3.84ff.). See also *Encomium* 10 and cf. Verdenius 116ff., Rosenmeyer 231ff., Segal (1962) 110ff., Ambrosino (1983) 31ff.

52. Thus Gorgias claims that in following a scientific, political, or philosophical debate, we are struck by the persuasive points of the speakers as by physical blows: ἡ πειθὼ προσιοῦσα τῶι λόγωι καὶ τὴν ψυχὴν ἐτυπώσατο ὅπως ἐβούλετο (*Encomium* 13). For the "immediate, almost physical impact" of *logoi* on the soul which "aim at changing the condition of the psyche by the impingement of an outside force *(peitho),*" see Segal (1962) 105ff.

53. See *Encomium* 13. Gorgias makes his own work another example of this, when he ends with ἐβουλήθην γράψαι τὸν λόγον Ἑλένης μὲν ἐγκώμιον, ἐμὸν δὲ παίγνιον

(*Encomium* 21). The persuasive force of what he has said depends neither on his intention nor on repetition of common opinion.

54. See *Encomium* 8: δυνάστης μέγας.

55. Eur. *Hecuba* 814–19 simultaneously presents *peitho* as an overwhelming power and one in opposition to *nomos* and the orderly human community Hecuba has tried in vain to invoke.

56. Socrates' response a few lines later confirms the martial context: "Τὰ ὅπλα" μοι δοκεῖς βουληθεὶς εἰπεῖν αἰσχυνθεὶς ἀπολιπεῖν (Pl. *Phlb.* 58b4ff.). For a joke about the enslaving character of the sophistic art, see Pl. *Euthd.* 303c2.

57. Cf. Kennedy 30ff. for sophistic arguments from probability. Xenophon's phrasing recalls the collapse of the old bipartite heroic ideal into skill at speaking discussed earlier.

58. See Pl. *Grg.* 469c8ff.

59. See Segal (1962) 108–9 for Gorgias' treatment of crowds as collections of individual psyches without a separate dynamic of their own. For personal tyranny as the true end of the art of rhetoric, see the progression in the *Gorgias* as Polus and Callicles replace Gorgias as interlocutor (for example, 466b11ff.) and *Knights* passim.

60. μέγιστον ἀγαθὸν καὶ αἴτιον ἅμα μὲν ἐλευθερίας αὐτοῖς τοῖς ανθρώποις, ἅμα δὲ τοῦ ἄλλων ἄρχειν ἐν τῇ αὐτοῦ πόλει ἑκάστῳ (Pl. *Grg.* 452d5). καίτοι ἐν ταύτῃ τῇ δυνάμει δοῦλον μὲν ἕξεις τὸν ἰατρόν, δοῦλον δὲ τὸν παιδοτρίβην· ὁ δὲ χρηματιστὴς οὗτος ἄλλῳ ἀναφανήσεται χρηματιζόμενος καὶ οὐχ αὑτῷ, ἀλλὰ σοὶ τῷ δυναμένῳ λέγειν καὶ πείθειν τὰ πλήθη (*Grg.* 452e4). For a more moderate statement of the same position, see Pl. *Prt.* 318e4ff. For similar motives for Alcibiades' and Critias' association with Socrates, see X. *Mem.* I.2.14ff.

61. For pleasure, see *hedone, Encomium* 10; *terpsis, Encomium* 13. In general, pleasure is used as the translation for both. For poetry as λόγον ἔχοντα μέτρον and the implications of this for rhetoric, see *Encomium* 9; Segal (1962) 112, 122ff., 127ff.; de Romilly 4ff.; Verdenius 118; Walsh 84ff.

62. For psychic complicity, see Segal (1962) 122, who concludes that "the process [of persuasion] is not simply the conquest of a weaker subject by a stronger force, but that the persuaded is himself an accomplice to the act of persuasion, that he allows himself to be persuaded, and that persuasion is thus inseparably connected with the emotions aroused by the aesthetic process."

63. For Gorgias' poetic style and figures, see DK 82 A 1.2, DK 82 A 2, DK 82 A 4, DK 82 A 30, DK 82 A 31, DK 82 A 33. Cf. also Classen 226ff.

64. See de Romilly 20ff.

65. Aristotle notes that all convincing speech promotes a good for the audience. For the jury (which resembles the uninvolved spectators of the wrestling match and, in some sense, the assembly that enslaves the doctors, etc.) the good is the pleasure of hearing skillful speeches (Ar. *Rhetoric* 1354b–55a). The *Wasps* debases this pleasure to the ruder ones of (perceived) power and profit; cf. 548ff. See Ostwald 209ff., 220ff., 231ff., for the courts as fora where the jurors could manifest their political and social allegiances.

66. See Ar. *Rh.* 1358b for the idea that deliberative rhetoric treats the future good of the listeners. Cf. also the common aristophanic complaint about the Athenians' susceptibility to compliments. However, not the form of the compliments but the pleasure of hearing themselves praised blinds them (at least temporarily) to the other interests that should be their guide. Cf. *Acharnians* 633ff., *Knights* 1340ff.

67. This criticism is graphically summed up in the platonic image of a pastry cook speaking before children, see Pl. *Grg.* 464d5 discussed in chapter 4.

68. The final enslavement of *logos* and speakers is, of course, one of the main themes

of the *Knights*. For the platonic version, see Pl. *Grg.* 481d1ff., 513a1, 517b2, 521a2, and particularly *Tht.* 172c8. See also Henderson (1990) 276–77.

69. See Turato (1976) for rhetoric and the power of *logos,* specifically sophistic *logos,* in the *Hippolytus;* see also Goff 50ff., who notes "that persuasion can also appear in the greek sources as a form of violence" (53). For Hippolytus as representative of contemporary Athenians who shunned politics because of its new rhetorical character, see Connor 184ff.

70. The attacks continued through the end of the war, cf. *Cleophon* 405, *Sophists* 403.

71. Along the same lines may be Philonides II 2 (PCG): κρεῖττον σιωπᾶν ἐστιν ἢ λαλεῖν μάτην. Although the date is unknown, the wording makes it possible that this was a play on the sophistic claim to make the weaker *logos* the stronger *(kreitton).* For the sophistic flavor of *lalos,* cf. below.

72. For the sources, see Havelock (1957) chapters 3 and 5, Cole chapter 2 and passim; Conacher, Ostwald 281ff. For the appearance of these theories onstage as early as *Prometheus Bound,* see Havelock (1957) 52ff. For dating, see Havelock (1957) chapter 5, who shows their affinity beginning with Xenophanes; Cole, who asserts the centrality of Democritus; and the general review in Conacher 192ff., who indicates Anaxagoras as the early evolutionary thinker (196), but believes in a "common tradition on the matter which gained increasing currency during the latter half of the century" (195). See also Lovejoy and Boas 194 and chapter 7, O'Brien, Guthrie 60ff. For the democratic ideological context of this theory, with its complementary cosmological and historical speculation, see Turato (1979) 17ff. For the contrary, the mythic history of fall, see Detienne (1981) 219.

73. For these characteristics of savage man outside/before the *polis* and their civilized converses, see the sources cited in n. 72, as well as Vernant (1989) 74 for marriage, sacrifice, and agriculture as the limits that mark off the human as opposed to animal. See also Vidal-Naquet (1981a) 81ff., Turato (1979) 71ff. For such savage activities as those indulged in by dreamers, when the lower part of the soul, τὸ δὲ θηριῶδές τε καὶ ἄγριον, is liberated in sleep, see Pl. *R.* 571c5.

74. Whether the author of the fragment is Euripides or Critias, it presents a standard picture.

75. For this passage, coupled with S. *Antigone* 354ff. and A. *Prometheus,* again see Havelock (1957) chapter 3. He finds the role of languge already in A. *Pr.* 442ff. (57) and central to the idea of man's social development (80ff.). O'Brien contends that this is the first extant passage in which the life of early man is called brutish (275).

76. For language as at once the symbol and the foundation of the benefits of social cooperation, see Cole 67, who again links this to Democritus.

77. See Dierauer 32ff. with nn. 3, 4, and 5 for examples.

78. In Athens the goddess Peitho, or Persuasion, was worshipped with Aphrodite Pandemus as well as in a separate cult claimed by Isocrates (*Antidosis* 246ff.) to demonstrate the centrality of persuasion and rhetoric in political life (Buxton 33ff.). She was also named as the wife of Phoroneus (or of Argus), who was said by the Argives to have discovered fire and brought men from scattered groups into community (Pepe 63, who cites Pausanias and notes the similarity to Protagoras' account discussed later). Peitho, the goddess of marital harmony is thus situated in the family from which the *polis* sprang, the "logic being that *peitho* is a central quality in a civilized *polis*" (Buxton 36).

79. See Hesiod *Opera et Dies* 213ff., where, in a discussion of human violence, the actual contraries are *dike* and *hubris,* and 275ff., where human is contrasted with animal in terms of *dike* and *bia.* For this contrast, see later discussion.

80. The new emphasis on language may have fit well with contemporary interests, but

logos and *dike* remained tightly linked, as, indeed, they were in Hesiod, where justice (and injustice) manifest themselves most often verbally, in the judgments of kings (for example, Hes. *Op*. 225, 250, 262), in arguing true/just things, or telling lies (*Op*. 280ff.). For an example of the unjust and violent act, *Op*. 238.

81. For the opposition *peitho/bia*, see Buxton's stimulating discussion 58ff.

82. Buxton 59; I have added the translations. Buxton compares to the Lysias Isocrates' similar scheme in *Antid*. 253ff. and 294 (54).

83. See Dierauer 32 for the way in which speech began to assume the fundamental role in theories of human culture. See also Buxton 60ff.

84. The importance of this distinction was such that it was probably during this period that the nonhuman animals first became known collectively as *alogon,* in the sense of "without speech." Dierauer 33.

85. The xenophonic Socrates, in listing the benefits of the gods to men, gives a physiological explanation of human voice and language in X. *Mem*. 1.4.12. The most famous historical explanation is that of Plato's Protagoras discussed below; for others, see the sources in Guthrie 60ff. or Lovejoy and Boas.

86. For the use of animals in ethical contexts, see Dierauer 59ff.

87. See, for example, the linked passages in Hes. *Op*. 203ff. and 276ff.

88. One of the chief characteristics of precivilized, bestial existence was its disorder and randomness. See, in the passages quoted above, Eur. *Supp*. 201, DK 88 B 25.1–2, and see also the interesting comic fragment in Athenaeus 14.660–61 and the fragment of Moschion; both are quoted by Lovejoy and Boas 213ff. Cf. O'Brien 275 n. 48.

89. Protagoras wrote a book now lost, on early man; for his views, see Guthrie 63ff.; for their reworking to fit the platonic representation, see Havelock (1957) 87ff. On the social compact and Protagoras in particular, see Guthrie 135ff.

90. πολιτικὴν γὰρ τέχνην οὔπω εἶχον, ἧς μέρος πολεμική (Pl. *Prt*. 322b5).

91. See Pucci (1960) 22ff. Ambrosino (1983) notes Pl. *Prt*. 327a "pour l'équivalence entre capacité politique et usage de la langue" (58 n. 75). For Protagoras' interest in rhetoric as derivative of his "art of citizenship," see Ostwald 243.

92. For the violence felt to be inherent in other forms of government, see Buxton 59. For the much-discussed correlation between the rise of the (democratic) *polis* and of rhetoric, see, among many others, Buxton 8ff., Capizzi 171ff. and the works cited there.

93. ὁ δὲ μὴ δυνάμενος κοινωνεῖν ἢ μηθὲν δεόμενος δι' αὐτάρκειαν οὐθὲν μέρος πόλεως, ὥστε ἢ θηρίον ἢ θεός. Arist. *Politics* 1253a12. See Buxton 54ff., 59ff. for additional examples. For Aristotles' metaphysical, teleological transformation of earlier historical/anthropological theories, see Havelock (1957) 101ff.

94. Buxton 62; cf. Turato (1976) 182.

95. See Segal (1981) chapters 1 and 2 and the sources in the notes above for these definitive contraries to the civilized, adult, verbal, law-abiding citizen of a Greek *polis*.

96. See Pl. *Prt*. 327c4ff.

97. See Th. 3.82.

98. The (mis)use of speech for personal ends, and so forth, is well known in the *Iliad, Odyssey,* and *Works and Days,* to mention only a few. For *peitho* and *dolos,* see Buxton 63ff.

99. For sophists' views which could be considered prodemocratic, see Müller passim; for Protagoras in particular, Havelock (1957) 168ff. Müller also points out that the *demos,* with some justification, feared and disliked the sophists as threatening their hard-won equality at Athens (179–80). For a change in the use and perception of the sophistic social, ethical, and cosmological speculation between the period of Pericles and that after his death, see Turato (1972) 23ff. For the antidemocratic possibilities of sophistic rhetoric, Ambrosino

(1986–87), and, from another angle, Dodds 191ff. Ostwald 229ff. discusses the generation gap and the animosity of the "democratic establishment" to the wealthy young who possessed the sophistic "rhetorical and other training, wherewith political, social, and personal power could supposedly be attained and maintained through the organs of the Athenian democracy" (273). See later discussion in chapter 7.

Chapter 2

1. For the dismissal of the war as a theme, see later discussion in this chapter.

2. Throughout this book I have referred to those who possess the powerful new rhetoric Strepsiades wants as "sophists"; I have also used the expressions "intellectuals," "philosophers," and "the wise" for those who devote themselves to study, including study of *logos*, for its own sake. These groups overlap, but not totally; one of the important tasks of the comedy is to distinguish the abstracted "wise" from their self-interested products. Thus Socrates, his students, and, after his education, Pheidippides, as well as the adulterer of the agon can all be called sophists in one way or another, but only Socrates can be referred to as a philosopher. Of course, debate rages about whether or not Socrates can legitimately be classed with the "sophists," who was a sophist, and what distinguished sophists from other intellectuals and teachers. My discussion makes only an indirect contribution to this debate by studying comic "sophists." Unless obviously exempted by context, the terms "sophist," "sophistic," the name "Socrates," and so forth, should always be taken as if in quotation marks. They refer to the comic creations of Aristophanes in this play, having as much or as little concrete relationship to the historical figures and theories they mockingly evoke as can be demonstrated at any particular moment. For use of the word *sophistes*, or sophist, see Ostwald 238ff., Guthrie 27ff., Dover ad 331, and later discussion of line 94. The *Clouds* uses it only three times (331, 1111, 1309) perhaps for the first time with negative connotations (Dover ad 331). Thus line 331 lists the types of people nourished by the clouds; lines 1111 and 1309 refer to Pheidippides as becoming a sophist under the tutelage of the *hetton logos* and Socrates.

3. Comic convention generally makes the central character's plan for escaping his troubles a successful one, however outrageous, and even immoral, it may seem. Thus, Dikaiopolis concludes a private peace, the Sausage Seller triumphs and rescues his backers, and so forth. The *Clouds* is unique in not following this pattern, but of course we do not know this yet. See, among others, McLeish 64ff., 68ff.; Whitman chapter 2 and 132ff.; Fisher 39ff. For the prologue and the opening scenes as stating the themes of the play, see Fisher 24ff. For the kind of conventional plot they might have led the audience to expect, see Harriott 165ff.

4. It may be objected that this makes of the *Clouds* the spectacle of *logos* undermining *logos* and that this alone is enough to undermine, in turn, the comic criticism. As we shall see, this is an objection met by the comedy in the parabasis and end of the play. It should be noted, however, that the *Clouds'* logos takes place inside the linguistic arena established by the comic festival, a setting alluded to often and one whose conventions are built into the play's structure and assumptions. Inside this particular arena *logos*, and especially comic *logos*, is privileged. In the end, however, it is the failure of comic *logos*—that is the failure of the first *Clouds*—that lays the ground for the parallel failure of the sophists.

5. Strauss comments that Strepsiades talks to himself because his son "to whom he would like to talk is fast asleep" (12). But the problem goes deeper than that. Strepsiades' isolation has a thematic importance like that of Dikaiopolis which opens the *Acharnians*. In both plays the principal character must talk to himself because he is out of step with the

speech of the world around him. In the *Acharnians,* Dikaiopolis refuses, and is refused, participation because he accurately observes that the speech around him is bankrupt and corrupt (see Bowie). Strepsiades' case is different: he would love to have people listen to him, but his speech is powerless. In fact, dissatisfaction and isolation are characteristic of comic heroes in general, resulting from and nurturing the mad schemes that make up their comic projects. See Fisher 36ff. for Strepsiades' progressive isolation as the prologue unfolds.

6. For the "tragic coloring," see Dover ad 41; for the novelty of the prologue and its fusion of comic and tragic elements, see Harriott 7ff.

7. In keeping with the play's general suppression of the war as a motive, it is unlikely that we are intended to imagine that Strepsiades married after being forced into the city by the Periclean war strategy. For if Pheidippides is to be between eighteen and twenty (see Dover xxcii), his parents' marriage must have predated 431 by some years. This is true whether we figure from 420–417 (the probable date of the revised *Clouds*) or from 424/3, the date of the original (Dover lxxx). Further, lines 43-52 build the contrast country/city in terms of Strepsiades and his wife, never mentioning the war. γὰρ (43), ἔπειτ' (46), and ὅτ' (49) outline a progression that marks Strepsiades' rusticity in contrast to his wife's aristocratic urban connections, culminating in their very different "perfumes" when they go to bed together. Thus while we are not told at what point Strepsiades actually moved to the city, his ruinous implication in the urban world began with his wife, a connection instigated by the matchmaker. (Likewise, Pheidippides' urban nature is described by Strepsiades as a product not of the war, but of his mother and her words; see the discussion later in this chapter).

8. The normal role of *logos* in civilizing man and making him an urban being is here ironically read from another perspective.

9. For the power of langugae in the *Birds* and its pertinence to the contemporary Athenian situation, see Arrowsmith. For Peisthetairos as a sophistic rhetor and the connection between this passage and the *Clouds,* see Gelzer (1956) 79ff. and Newiger (1957) 57ff., both of whom depart from μετεωρίζειν. Gelzer (1956) sees the "up-in-the-air" quality of Socrates and his astronomical studies, the uplifting effect of the clouds, and the desire of those who arrive at Cloud-cuckoo-land for wings and flight as characterizing participants in the new culture. Newiger (1957) gives them moral implications: the sophists' ability to make "Recht Unrecht" betrays their lack of moral grounding (58).

10. *Epairein* seems to have been a contemporary technical term for the ability of skillful speech, and particularly sophistic rhetoric, to carry away its listeners. See Segal (1962) 129ff and n. 111. It is used for verbal arousal in *Birds* 1657, *Frogs* 777 and 1041, and in *Clouds* 810 and 1457, which are discussed in subsequent chapters.

11. The connection between the matchmaker and the sophistic rhetoric is reinforced by a scholiast on 42 who glosses ἐπῆρε with ἠπάτησε. For *apate* as the sophists' stock in trade, see chapter 1 and the sources cited there.

12. For these terms used to describe the power of sophistic speech, see *Encomium* 10 and 14. For sophistic rhetoric in Eur. *Hipp.,* see Turato (1976) passim, 164ff. for the nurse and the relationship to the *Encomium* and the *Clouds.* See also Goff 48ff.

13. The political implications lie just below the surface. In the Eur. *Hipp.* they are bared by Phaedra's speech at 486–89, quoted, in part, in chapter 1. Likewise, the xenophonic citation of Aspasia as Socrates' source vividly contrasts Socrates' reluctance to use speech to win friends and influence people with Pericles' reliance on words instead of action, a strategy that is contrasted with Thucydides' actions for the public good to mark Pericles' practice of public seduction (X. *Mem.* 2.6.13).

14. See Dover ad 41b.

15. For Gorgias, see chapter 1.

16. Thus in another context, Nussbaum comments, "Pheidippides, and his father with him, have an underlying respect for cleverness and verbal artifice, characteristic of the times, which makes them dangerously volatile" (69).

17. See Untersteiner 140ff.

18. Myrrhina is teasing Cinesias: (Mυ.) σισύραν οὐκ ἔχεις. / (Kι.) μὰ Δί᾽ οὐδὲ δέομαί γ᾽, ἀλλὰ βινεῖν βούλομαι. / (Mυ.) ἀμέλει, ποιήσεις τοῦτο· ταχὺ γὰρ ἔρχομαι. / (Kι.) ἄνθρωπος ἐπιτρίψει με διὰ τὰ στρώματα. / (Mυ.) ἔπαιρε σαυτόν. (Kι.) ἀλλ᾽ ἐπῆρται τοῦτό γε. (Ar. *Lys.* 933–37). See Henderson (1991) for ἔπαρσις as the technical term for "to get an erection" (112). For the highly sexual connotations of the name Myrrhina, see Detienne (1977) 63.

19. Nussbaum 67.

20. For sex as a traditional attribute of peaceful country life, see *Ach.* 271ff. In the *Peace,* peace itself is greeted as the return to the country and simultaneously as a renewal of sexual pleasure, see Henderson (1991) 64ff. In our passage this could be underlined with a pun on ἀκόρητος in line 44. The scholiasts relate this to κορεῖν (ad 44) and Starkie to κόρεις; however, it could perhaps recall κόρη as well, suggesting Strepsiades' former womanless state. Strepsiades' retrospective nostalgia says nothing about his earlier feelings. For other puns on κόρη, see Henderson (1991) 174.

21. Strepsiades' current concentration on cold cash and complaints about his wife should not label him totally anhedonic. For as we shall see, even in the abstract and uncongenial environment of the *phrontisterion,* he is characterized as exclusively prey to bodily desires. Food and sex—soup, sausage, his penis—preoccupy him during his lessons, as they do in the imagery of the lines here, where the charms of his rural existence before the advent of the matchmaker and his wife are described concretely, and above all in terms of food and drink (45, 50). This does not mean that Strepsiades is oblivious to money (259, 484) or its lack, but that this greed does not eclipse others—money is one good among the many, generally more concrete, for which he lusts. His greed and his erotic need are related (or identical) human impulses, deriving from the basic hedonistic drive to satisfy needs and desires, which in our comedy fall to their lowest common denominator, bodily pleasure.

22. Thus we may surmise that it was not, or not only, Strepsiades' *nous* that was manipulated by the speech of others, but his *peos* that compelled him to seek a wife. This comic switch, or commentary, that explains in terms of desire or *eros* what initially seems quite otherwise is also characteristic of the *Birds.* As Arrowsmith (130ff.) shows, *eros* drives every character in the play. Properly understood in the concrete comic mode, the interlopers' desire for wings is a desire for a permanent erection. "Most of those pests from Earth, arriving, panting with desire, at Cloudcuckooland, want wings or bigger wings for their *phalloi*" (137).

23. Of course, all three attributes, wealth, class, and gender, are grounds for her appeal, but the play insures concentration on her sexiness. Lines 46–55 are full of references to kissing, sex, and erotic stimulation: σεμνήν, ἐγκεκοισυρωμένην (48), μύρου, κρόκου, καταγλωττισμάτων (51), Κωλιάδος, Γενετυλλίδος (52), for which see Dover ad loc. Further, as discussed below, the final joke can be taken to have an erotic double meaning. The idea that wives were not for sexual fun, but production of heirs and management of the *oikos,* is something often ignored in aristophanic comedy, as, for example, in *Lysistrata.* There the wife Myrrhina has produced a son, but this is hardly relevant; above all she is desired sexually by her husband.

24. Thus in the *Theaetetus,* during a discussion of Socrates' philosophic functions, we learn that true midwives never make matches because they could be charged with pandering to desire instead of serving truth (*Tht.* 150a1ff.).

25. For the cult of Peitho as an attendant of Aphrodite and goddess worshipped in Athens, see Buxton chapter 2, Pepe chapter 3.

26. Buxton 31.

27. See Pepe 275 and the discussion in chapter 1.

28. Throughout the play, the traditional comic costume, with its padded stomach and buttocks, phallus, and open mouth would graphically represent the comic view of man. For the comic costume, see Stone (1981) chapter 1.

29. Ambrosino (1986–87) has recently interpreted Strepsiades' marriage as "l'immagine di un difficile 'matrimonio' tra *demos* e aristocrazia, che la *polis* democratica aveva riunti dal tempo di Clistene: quasi una personificazione della democrazia, come rapporto di tipo matrimoniale tra classi che si trovano, per così dire, nella stessa barca, pur restando irriducibilmente opposte" (100–01). In this view, the *Clouds* examines the exploitation of the *demos* via its seduction—materially, culturally, and verbally—by the higher classes to their great advantage (107ff.). Pheidippides, like Alcibiades (102ff.), becomes the product of this union: the young aristocracy nurtured and indulged by *demos* and democratic city, but ready to exploit and dominate both (105ff., 116ff.). The plot turns on the attempt of the *demos* to escape its disadvantaged political, social, and above all economic position by acquiring the power of the *hetton logos,* either personally or in the person(s) of its aristocratic leaders (117ff.), while failing to recognize the contradiction between this *logos* and democracy itself (119, 126). The play then becomes Aristophanes' warning about the conditions of the *demos,* its leaders, and the *hetton logos.* This reading, summarized here only in the barest of outlines, yields many important insights about the civic implications of the *hetton logos* that will be discussed further. However, even if we allow Strepsiades to be representative of the poorer segments of the *demos* as a whole (a debatable point, see Carter 84ff.), Ambrosino's focus on an overtly political aristophanic agenda leads her to ignore much of what actually happens on stage. Similarly, fitting the action into the form of political allegory overlooks the role of the characters' (necessarily fictive) "natures," reducing them to a set of static political clues—a process that, while perhaps valid for the *Knights,* drains of meaning the large portions of the *Clouds* that are devoted to developing these contrasting "natures." Further, Socrates loses all significance, becoming merely a vehicle for exposure to the *hetton logos,* and Strepsiades' own tenure in the *phrontisterion* becomes simply a demonstration of the inadequacy of the *demos* when confronted by the new culture. The parabasis and scenes like the repudiation of the creditors are not discussed. Thus the play is treated incompletely, with a resulting overstatment of the initial contrast between Pheidippides and Strepsiades that blurs what they turn out to have in common—for example, their violence and their greed—while at the same time ignoring the deeper contrast between these two and Socrates, as well as the parallelism of Socrates and the figure of the poet in the parabasis.

30. For *peitho*'s seat in the lips and mouth, see Buxton 190 n. 25.

31. In line 51 we learn that she smells of μύρον, κρόκος, and καταγλωττισμάτα. For the use of perfume and spices, particularly myrrh, to represent seduction and "to refer to either the clitoris or the pudenda of the woman," see Detienne (1977) chapter 3, especially 63. In *Thesmophoriazusae* 131, κατεγλωττισμένον is used of the lyric of Agathon which is arousing Mnesilochos sexually. The tongue as a tool for both sexual pleasure and speech obviously fits the dual aspect of *peitho.* See Entralgo 64ff., Nussbaum 64 for the double use of the pleasures of the tongue in the *agon.*

32. The double form of the joke in lines 53–55 is explained by Henderson (1991) as meaning both to spend too much and make love too much (171–72). For extravagance, see also Dover ad loc. The notion of weaving may also continue the portrayal of Strepsiades' wife as embodying a destructive feminine ability to manipulate signs; cf. Bergren 71.

33. Thus Strepsiades' *himation* is already threadbare even before he meets the Socrates of the play, who will strip him of it in a movement simultaneous to that of Aristophanes. One of the big questions will be what is to be found underneath. Socrates will propose one answer; Aristophanes, another.

34. Cf. Ambrosino (1986–87) 108ff. for Pheidippides' naming and education as representing class differences, pointing to upper-class exploitation of the *demos* and its power.

35. For this traditional view, see de Romilly 18, Woodbury 114–15 (with bibliography), Marzullo 99ff. It is interesting that a name formed on *hippos* later functions as a gibe against the *kreitton logos* (1070). The innovations of Pheidippides' mother remain conservative when compared with those of the sophists.

36. Points of resemblance with the debate of the *logoi* include: (1) Both are described as brawls (λοιδορία 62, 934). (2) Both take the form of speeches proposing opposed models of the ideal life and behavior. (3) Both oppose an "old" life of hardiness with a "new" one of luxury. (4) Both have the same audience. (5) In both, the representative of the simpler, more "conservative" life loses. (6) In both victory seems to be a result of more persuasive *logoi,* at least at first. (7) In both acquiescence to one speech or the other is felt to be decisive not only for the present but for the future. For the debate of the *logoi,* see chapter 7.

37. Dover comments that Megacles is not to be envisioned as "riding from country to city in a chariot, but taking part in the Panathenaic procession to the Akropolis" (ad 69). In this context, both Pheidippides' original passion for horses and the ease with which he switches to rhetoric become more comprehensible. Horses and horse racing were traditional ways to establish oneself in the public eye; however, skillful speaking was being recognized as equally or even more important. For the conjunction of horse racing and speaking in the case of Alcibiades, see the sequence in Plu. *Alc.* 10.3–11.3. For Alcibiades' subterranean presence as a model for Pheidippides, see most recently Ambrosino (1986–87) 101ff., who cites earlier bibliography and notes their common interest in horses, prodigality, maternal relationship to Megacles, association with Socrates, skill at debating, and disdain for conventional morality. See also Green 23, Turato (1972) 99ff.

38. The outcome of this short vignette may anticipate Pheidippides' behavior in the rest of the play: his "intellectualist" education (cf. Nussbaum) finally being shaped less by *logoi* than by hedonistic nature.

39. Dover ad 77.

40. See Fisher 41.

41. In the translation that follows and throughout the book I have translated *phrontis-terion* with Arrowsmith's "Thinkery," used in his 1962 translation of the *Clouds,* published under the Mentor Books imprint of New American Library.

42. See Dover ad loc. Goldberg notes that *terion* was a rare suffix for place, used to denote "official and august establishments" (255), and that *phrontisterion* would sound "solemn, pompous, and absurd" (256). This would add to the incongruity—the *phrontis-terion* on stage was surely modest—and thus would stress the novelty of what Strepsiades confronts, while at the same time, perhaps, making it more general. What we see is official, not personal. In addition, Havelock (1972) notes the prevalence of *phrontis* and its cognates and suggests parody of recognizably intellectual and socratic "jargon" (9 n. 24; see 5). The contrast in terminology and tone between lines 94–99 and the lines 91–92, as well as the φασίν of line 112, where Strepsiades resumes his description, make it clear that Strepsiades is not using his own words to describe the sophists but is to be taken as repeating what he has heard. Cf. Fisher 42 for the incongruity of this line, 54 n. 22 for another possible origin for *phrontisterion.*

43. For the meaning of σοφῶν in line 94, cf., for example, Dover ad loc., who com-

ments that *sophia* in the fifth century meant "creative skill or artistry"; *sophos*, " 'highly educated' . . . 'brilliant,' 'inventive,' 'ingenious.' " Cf. also Capizzi 167. For the double connotation of *sophos* by this period, positive, as originally, or negative, like 'overly clever,' see Guthrie 27ff. He points out that the negative slant is particularly evident in *sophistes*, especially when modified by *deinos* (32ff.). Capizzi wishes to draw a distinction between philosophers (savoir pour savoir) and sophists (savoir pour faire) (169), in which the first category would include Anaxagoras, for example, and the second Protagoras. DK 79 1, however, indicates a much wider application of the term sophist, including to Socrates; cf. Kerferd chapter 4. For the people who could be called *sophistes* in the *Clouds*, see lines 331ff. I have generally translated *sophos* with the traditional "wise," sometimes "intellectual."

44. See Segal (1975) 179. Strepsiades shares this common and comic view of the abstracted philosophers as half-dead; see his reaction in 500ff., which sums up the clash in understanding of what is essentially human.

45. The language here with its emphasis on *psyche* (and *phrontis*) has been claimed to label these ideas as distinctively socratic (cf. scholiasts ad loc. and Havelock [1972] 5 and n. 24) and retrospect can bolster this. But, as Dover points out (ad loc.), discussion of the soul was hardly confined to Socrates. The soul also has an important role to play in Gorgias as the locus of action of speech, appearing, for example, at least eight times in *Encomium* 8–14—the portion devoted to the power of *logos*. Cf. Dover for other common elements of this line (ad loc.); Fisher, who agrees with him, for bibliography (54 n. 23).

46. Thus Xenophon attempts to distinguish Socrates from the sophists by marking his unique lack of interest in the cosmos: οὐδὲ γὰρ περὶ τῆς τῶν πάντων φύσεως ἧιπερ τῶν ἄλλων οἱ πλεῖστοι διελέγετο [Sokrates] σκοπῶν, ὅπως ὁ καλούμενος ὑπὸ τῶν σοφιστῶν κόσμος ἔχει καὶ τίσιν ἀνάγκαις ἕκαστα γίγνεται τῶν οὐρανίων (DK 79 2a = X. *Mem.* 1.1.11). (See Pl. *Phaedo* 96a6 for other testimony about Socrates' early scientific interests.) Cf. Cicero *de Orator* 3.32.128, for the scientific interests of Protagoras, Prodicus, and Thrasymachus; Segal (1962) 101ff. for Gorgias' possible scientific interests. The idea that natural science, speaking, and philosophy were an incompatible mix seems modern; cf. Kerferd 38ff., who argues persuasively for the sophists' wide interests; Guthrie 41ff., who admits this interest but subordinates it to rhetorical application, as does Ostwald 240ff., 259. The restricted view is shared by Classen and Capizzi 169ff.

47. Cited by Guthrie 228, and see 226ff. for discussion of atheism. See also Kerferd chapter 13, Ostwald 274ff., Dodds chapter 6. It should be noted that in the subsequent passage "physicists," should be taken broadly, just as "sophists" was in the earlier Xenophon passage. The examples given here are Anaxagoras and Protagoras.

48. *Encomium* 13 cites the ability of the μετεωρολόγοι to change established opinions about the heavens through language.

49. Spatz observes: "Like the Sophists and Diogenes of Apollonia, Aristophanes' scholars view man as part of the natural continuum" (50). In the "real" sophistic reasoning later on in the play, this, of course, means that man is an animal who participates in and is compatible with his setting, the natural world.

50. Starkie (ad loc.) notes the pun and gives other examples. See, particularly, *Ach.* 336, 348 and Whitman, who thinks that the *anthrakes* pun there may have prompted the entire scene with the coal scuttle (71ff.). It may be that we are to hear the similarity in sound of *anthropoi* and *anthrakes* as a philosophical argument from etymology, indicating that the resources of *logos* confirm the view proposed by physics and natural science. (See Starkie ad loc.) However, etymological reasoning from the actual sound of words, independent of their meaning, does not seem to have been characteristic of sophistic speculation. Cf. Classen 230ff. and especially 235ff. for Prodicus. For a brief overview and bib-

liography which makes reasoning from the sound of words traditional and in contrast to sophistic procedures, see Woodbury 114ff. If the pun were nevertheless to seem generically philosophic, this further fusion of comedy and philosophy would underline the double nature of such a conclusion and such a being, postulated both by speculation and joking, but emphatically resident on earth and subject to its laws. See the chapters that follow.

51. Neither the sophists nor Strepsiades are responsible for this joke. The view of sophistic theory it expresses is highly parodic and never assigned to a sophist in the play. The character Strepsiades, although capable of making puns (28–29, 32–33), uses them to ridicule, and it is hardly likely that he would ridicule the very people he is urging his son to join. Dramatic logic requires that Strepsiades attempt to impress his son, whatever the effect on the audience intended by Aristophanes.

52. For the centrality and comic creativity of puns, which in some sense emblematize many of the processes of verbal and metaphoric comedy in miniature, see Whitman 260, 272ff.; Reckford (1987) 165ff.

53. For Cratinus (167 PCG) and the generic quality of the mockery here, see the scholia ad 96. For the philosophic originals, see Starkie and Dover ad loc. The scholia concluded from the common generic quality of the comedy that Aristophanes did not write the *Clouds* out of hatred such as motivated Eupolis.

54. It might be objected that such a comic reading of philosophical theory is unfair, since it operates one level above the final philosophical reduction, to matter (for example, atoms) responsive to natural laws certainly not reducible to those of desire. Our comedy does not meet, or even address this kind of intellectual or philosophical objection, for it approaches the problem from quite another angle, not confronting the merit or truth of such intellectual products, but commenting on their probable interaction with the world of matter that has become human where, our comedy asserts, even philosophers finally live and die, despite their speculative distance. For the notions of natural existence and obedience to the laws of nature have more than theoretical results and operate on more than one level themselves. And if a truly physically reductive view of man does peep through here, yet the uneasy relationship of the abstract ''scientific'' world to the ''human'' one motivated by appetite cannot be avoided: it is a short move from universe to speaking, with all that that implies about motivation and action.

55. Puns suspend the rules of signification and focus attention on the independent workings of *logos* itself, unveiling its arbitrary and ambiguous nature and demonstrating a flexibility that asserts the priority of the word over the (traditional) structures of ''reality'' it is claimed to represent (see Redfern 15). Commentators also seem to feel puns have a sexy aspect. ''The appeal, the call between different words of similar sound resembles those elective affinities between sundered souls in the old Celtic myth, or the sexual tug between bodies'' (Redfern 11; see Carson 32ff. for puns and *eros*). Likewise, puns are irresistible (see Redfern chapter 1, Culler 6). This doubly attractive nature is, in microcosm, that of *logos* which constantly tries to motivate discourse along lines suggested by the (unacknowledged and ''rationally'' illegitimate) links (conceptual and audial) between supposedly arbitrary signifiers (see Culler 11ff.), and which presents an ''overpoweringly seductive alternative to 'the world', which initially seemed the only reality'' (Culler 7). As such the pun that draws attention to the operation of comic *logos* here is an apt precursor of the sexy cloud goddesses, which in some sense represent this *logos* itself. See chapter 4.

56. For the doubling and oscillating nature of puns, see, among others, Redfern chapter 2.

57. For this as written into the comedy, see chapter 5. For another example of the use of the pun to instruct the audience about the proper perspective to take on the narrative, see Shoaf 56.

58. For this similarity, cf. Attridge's description of the pun's effect. The pun "undermines the basis on which our assumptions about the communicating efficacy of language rest . . . that for each signifier there is an inseparable signified" (140). Further, the pun and sophistic acknowledgement of the role of *apate* in their rhetoric (and in *logos* generally) are equally troublesome in their open disregard for the conventional identification of speech and reality—as Attridge remarks, the pun is "ambiguity *unashamed of itself* and this is what makes it a scandal" [emphasis original] (141).

59. In the following passage, τις may hint at the fact that the sophists will teach anyone who can afford it. Kerferd shows that this, not their fees, was grounds for the sophists' unpopularity with the traditional elite (26). Certainly the *Clouds* could illustrate some of the negative results of indiscriminate instruction based on an ability to pay (*Clouds* 226ff., 239ff.; see also Strauss 15ff.). The commerce in *logos* suggests not only its new status as one commodity among many (cf. the beginning of *Acharnians*), but also what will replace the discarded gods and their morality as the new standard—money. Thus, the *hetton logos* ridicules Peleus' virtues as without concrete reward, while Hyperbolus is the new ideal: his *poneria,* especially his rhetorical ability, has garnered many talents (*Clouds* 876, 1065ff.).

60. The close relationship between rhetoric, relativism, and agnosticism (or atheism), that is, the inaccessibility of absolute knowledge and extrahuman standards, is well known. Thus the protagorean doctrine that man is the measure of all things appeared at the beginning of *Truth* or *Overthrowing Arguments* (DK 80 B 1). See, in general, Kerferd chapter 9, Guthrie chapter 8; for Protagoras, de Carli 16; for Gorgias, the works cited in chapter 1; for the *Clouds,* Richardson 68ff., who follows the effect of the replacement of religion by science. The connection between physics and rhetoric may also be seen in DK 82 A 17, which describes a statue of Gorgias looking at an astrological globe.

61. This line hints at the connection between political preeminence and sophistic rhetoric which lies just below the surface in many passages (431ff., 1201ff., 1421ff.), and, of course, Pheidippides' attitude is going to change as he realizes the practical and political value of what Socrates has to offer. For the political implications of Strepsiades' language and Pheidippides' rebuttal in 102, see Murphy 75. See also Ambrosino (1986–87), Turato (1972) chapter 3, especially 84ff., for the connection between Socrates and the young oligarchs, whose activities Turato (1972) believes the *Clouds* is denouncing (109ff.).

62. Tomin makes line 100 (Strepsiades' claim not to know the names of the inhabitants of the *phrontisterion*) central to his argument that the *Clouds'* humor lies in seeing Socrates "refracted through the apriori preconceptions and false expectations of Strepsiades" (26). This interpretation ignores the possibility that Strepsiades is being deliberately (and humorously) evasive here. Further it is worth noting that Xenophon (X. *Mem.* 1.2.14ff.) reproduces the dynamic of the *Clouds.* Presenting the same abstemious and abstracted Socrates, indifferent to pleasure and power, he asserts that Alcibiades and Critias frequented him not out of any interest in the philosophic life, or philosophy, but because they saw: τοῖς δὲ διαλεγομένοις αὐτῷ πᾶσι χρώμενον ἐν τοῖς λόγοις ὅπως βούλοιτο. (X. *Mem.* 1.2.14–15) They believed εἰ ὁμιλησαίτην ἐκείνῳ, γενέσθαι ἂν ἱκανωτάτω λέγειν τε καὶ πράττειν (X. *Mem.* 1.2.15–16). This Socrates is thus a teacher of rhetoric, even if unintentionally, intending it to be the "higher" philosophy.

63. Acknowledgement of the influence of Protagoras begins with the scholiast who comments that he taught these *logoi*. However, the two *logoi* were not the exclusive concern of Protagoras, and sophistic practice in general could easily come to mind when confronted by the role Strepsiades assigns rhetoric. See Kerferd 84–85, de Carli 14ff.

64. I will use the Greek terminology, *hetton logos* and *kreitton logos,* rather than translating these terms. The meanings and connotations of *hetton,* weaker, and *kreitton,* stronger, are central to the discussion here and elsewhere.

65. See Newiger (1957) 135ff., Pucci (1960) 8ff., de Carli 15, Ambrosino (1983) 29ff., Classen 222ff., Guthrie 181ff.

66. Ambrosino (1983) suggests another perspective that makes the relative positions of the *logoi* stable, while their content changes. Since the *hetton* is defined as the negation of the *kreitton,* its content will change as the *kreitton* does, always becoming its opposite (38).

67. Line 112 also begins the personification of the *logoi* that will culminate in the agon. As Newiger (1957) points out, such personification, which may begin in Hes. *Theogony* 228ff., was common among Aristophanes' contemporaries (Gorg. *Encomium,* Eur. *Ph. 471* and *IA* 1013) and was often momentary and usually reserved for sophistic *logos* (140ff.). The advantages of personification are apparent when line 99 and 112 are compared. In line 99, where it is the student who speaks, the contrasted arguments serve to exhaust all possibilities and indicate his skill. In line 112, the *logoi* are emancipated from the awkward necessity of having a speaker and thus from all the extralinguistic considerations (the relationship between speaker and audience, situation, emotions of the hearers, and so forth) a speaker brings into play. Only rhetorical cogency will count. The possibility and power of such an independent *logos* is one of the issues of the play.

68. Superior to these individual *logoi,* particular accounts or arguments, remains *logos* in general, which never relinquishes its power. It is this larger *logos* that is the subject of protagorean instruction, which involves as an exercise the construction of two opposed *logoi* on any subject. Cf. DK 80 A 1. 51, DK 80 A 20, DK 80 B 6a. Once the power of *logos* in general is mastered, those who possess it are in the fortunate position of being able to make prevail any particular *logos* that appeals to them. For another view, see Kerferd 91ff.

69. Strepsiades' moral evaluation does not compromise the value-free world of the sophists, for it is his alone. He thus expresses the popular belief that things contrary to the current norms are unjust, that to justify them, therefore, requires unjust arguments, and that the *logos* using these arguments must itself be unjust. See Pucci (1960) 9; cf. de Carli 15.

70. See Newiger (1957) 135–36. The same idea, that the full power of speech is best observed in the action of the *hetton logos,* both in the sense of "unjust" and in the sense of "not generally accepted," dictated the choice of Helen as the subject of Gorgias' *Encomium.* Its converse leads to the condemnation of rhetoric through guilt by association—only a bad cause should require a good speaker; the truth can allow the facts to speak for themselves. Thus the rejection of rhetoric becomes a badge of truthfulness; see the examples cited by Turato (1976) n. 51.

71. Later, in the debate of the *logoi,* the *hetton logos* confirms this assessment of its character when it identifies itself simply as *logos* (893). See Ambrosino (1983) 32.

72. See for example the form of Strepsiades' capitulation in 1437, ἐμοὶ μέν, ὦνδρες ἥλικες, δοκεῖ λέγειν δίκαια, which is discussed in chapter 9.

73. Strepsiades' hopes and the structure of the passage combine to suppress the possibility suggested in line 99 that one could also prevail speaking just things and that this could be the source of the *kreitton logos'* strength. Strepsiades' vagueness about the *kreitton* is compatible with the protagorean formula, in which the *kreitton logos* is always bested, and is, in fact, invisible, present only as a foil for the *hetton* and the complex of actions, assumptions, and attitudes represented by its victory.

74. Newiger (1957) calls Strepsiades' request a "komischen Mißverstehen" (138). It is certainly consistent with his reasons for going to the *phrontisterion* and what has gone before. He reiterates this desire in lines 244–45, 657, in the disputed passage in 882ff. (where I take the singular *adikos logos* of 885 to be the *hetton logos,* already identified

as such several times), and, finally, in metaphorical terms at the end of the agon in 1107.

75. This definition is subsequently glossed as τὸ τὰ ὀφειλόμενα ἑκάστῳ ἀποδιδόναι δίκαιόν ἐστι (to give back to each what is owed is just) (Pl. *R.* 331e2). The *hetton logos* is, thus, the functional equivalent of the ring of Gyges proposed by Glaucon in Pl. *R.* 359b6ff. Both render the injustice of their owner invisible allowing him to act with impunity. They thus allow us to discern the true features of the essentially human, unrestrained by fear.

76. See chapter 1.

77. For this early failure as "prefiguring the final climactic downturn," see Harriott 166ff.

78. See Taillardat 337, commentators ad loc.

79. In this definition and narrowing of the comic topic, they do covertly what *Wasps* 54ff. does overtly.

80. But in fact, Strepsiades still has substantial power, even if he fears it is waning—his order to fetch the lamp and ledger is obeyed without a word (18ff.). The contrast with Pheidippides is clear, as is the reason: Pheidippides does not fear his father's force. This short passage previews the complicated relationship between language and force studied in the play. The later uses of κολάζειν (1107, 1405, 1434) describe educational beatings which reinforce the (sophistic) *logos* desired by the beater.

81. Strepsiades' political affiliations are debated. Ambrosino (1986–87) declares him an old-fashioned democrat and man of the people (100, 103, 107, 110; see also Harriott 6ff.), while Carter associates him with the quietist side of the town/country *polypragmosyne/apragmosyne* antitheses (84).

82. See Ober 43ff. for elite-elite and elite-mass communication.

83. We are reminded of this again in lines 429ff., when Strepsiades rejects any political ambitions and limits his desires to victory over his own particular creditors. This is later expanded by the clouds into the life of a legal consultant, something which was certainly not part of Strepsiades' original ambitions.

84. Contrast the situations that develop at the beginning of the *Knights* or the *Acharnians*.

85. Strepsiades is not to be imagined as a member of the lower classes, but simply as rustic. He is wealthy and classy enough to marry the niece of Megacles, to have slaves, to support the racing habits of his son (at least initially). Further, as the second agon shows, he is educated enough to know the old songs and have opinions about the new.

86. See Harriott 7 for the "realistic" tone of the prologue, clashing with the unexpectedness of Strepsiades' solution; 165ff. for the simple type of play the prologue may have suggested, 170 for the other options a typical Athenian would probably have pursued.

Chapter 3

1. Line 137 has been taken as a pointed reference to Socrates personally. See Schmid 219–20 and the commentators ad loc. For the midwifery of Socrates as derived from this passage rather than alluded to by it, see Burnyeat.

2. See Schmid 215–16.

3. The Greek reads: φωνῆς γένεσιν τὴν τοῦ ἀέρος πλῆξιν DK 60 A 1.17.

4. The Anaxagoras reads: βροντὰς σύγκρουσιν νεφῶν DK 59 A 1.9.

5. See Fisher 60.

6. For *leptos,* see Dover ad 153, who cites Eur. *Med.* 529, *Ach.* 445, *Birds* 318; see

also Antiphon 3.4.2. In the *Clouds* it is frequent: 230, 320, 359, 741, 1404, and, for the literal meaning, 177, 1018 (which must have the metaphorical one hovering in the background, however). For *stenos* used negatively of socratic questions, see Pl. *Grg.* 497c1.

7. The fade from ἄδειν, in the original question, to ἠχεῖν, in Socrates' answer, illustrates the change in status of the gnat's "song." ἄδειν is principally used for the singing of poetic song—most familiarly in the first line of the *Iliad*—although LSJ cites passages where it is used for the sound of a bow twanging or a frog croaking. Elsewhere in the *Clouds*, it is used in a parody of a tragic lament (721) and to describe the singing of song after dinner (1358, 1360). ἠχεῖν is said by LSJ to mean "sound, ring, peal." It is used of metals and the sea or, with a cognate accusative, for "sound forth," as of cymbals, laments, wails, or, in the use closest to ἄδειν, even hymns. The emphasis seems to be on the production of sound, not the conveying of meaning. The cognate ἠχή means "sound, noise" and is used "rarely of articulate speech" (LSJ). Aristophanes uses ἠχεῖν only one other time in his extant plays: *Wasps* 1489, for the creaking of the vertebrae during enthusiastic dancing. In our passage the movement is from the notion of the gnat singing to one of the mechanical production of sound.

8. Dover ad 157.

9. The *Birds* passage is: οἱ μὲν γὰρ οὖν τέττιγες ἕνα μῆν' ἢ δύο / ἐπὶ τῶν κραδῶν ἄδουσ', 'Αθηναῖοι δ' ἀεὶ / ἐπὶ τῶν δικῶν ἄδουσι πάντα τὸν βίον, (39–41). For ἄδειν and ἄδειν ὅμοιον to mean "μάτην λέγειν," see Taillardat 286, who cites this passage; Aristophanes 101 (PCG), where there is a legal context; and Eupolis 39 (PCG).

10. For cicadas as representative of wise, potent, or musical speech, cf. *Il.* 3.151; their appearances in *Phd.* 258e6ff. and 262d3ff. are discussed in chapter 9. The scholiasts sense the presence of the cicada here, commenting that production of sound makes the gnat like the musical *tettix*, but miss the joke by simply denying that this is correct (ad 158). The gnat's connection with things sophistic is reinforced by the use of λεπτός for its bowels (161), an omnipresent adjective for sophistic subtlety. See the discussion earlier in this chapter.

11. The portent of the gnat is confirmed in lines 1359–60, where Pheidippides exclaims that his father deserved to be beaten for acting as if he were entertaining *tettiges*. See chapter 9.

12. Strepsiades' analogy, the σάλπιγξ (165), which also sounds due to the passage of air from a narrow into a wider space (cf. Dover ad loc.), reintroduces the idea of purpose that Socrates' explanation suppressed. For even if such a sound is like a fart mechanically, this does not exhaust its meaning; it is clearly intentional and may have a certain informational content. Thus Strepsiades' comment here is similar to his question in 379, when he asks if Zeus could be the force compelling the clouds to knock together. In both cases his remarks uncover potential flaws in the reasoning, but ones which are never exploited.

13. Segal (1975) rightly observes that Socrates "for all his walking on air, does not have happy experiences when he ventures to explore the open tracts of the heavens" (181).

14. Note the irony that Socrates is shat upon by a lizard, a reptile that habitually crawls upon the earth, not a bird, the natural inhabitant of the sky. A similar comic revenge is apparent in the story of the mockery of Thales by his servant when that philosopher, who was looking up at the stars, forgetful of his place on earth, fell down a well (Pl. *Tht.* 174a2). For the similarity to Thales, see Pucci (1960) 30; Schmid 216, who believes it confirms Socrates as the type "natural scientist." For similarity to Anaxagoras here and throughout the play, see Turato (1972) 70 n. 137 and chapter 2 passim. Eupolis in *Flatterers* makes similar points when he identifies Protagoras: ὃς ἀλαζονεύεται μὲν ἀλιτήριος / περὶ τῶν μετεώρων, τὰ δὲ χαμᾶθεν ἐσθίει (157 PCG). He also makes the same

accusation about Socrates, but without the up and down imagery: μισῶ δὲ καὶ † Σωκράτην / τὸν πτωχὸν ἀδολέσχην, / ὃς τἆλλα μὲν πεφρόντικεν, / ὁπόθεν δὲ καταφαγεῖν ἔχοι / τούτου κατημέληκεν (Eup. 386 PCG). Kassel and Austin compare Aristophanes 691 (PCG), ὃς τἀφανῆ μεριμνᾶι, / τὰ δὲ χαμᾶθεν ἐσθίει. In fact, the charge seems to have been somewhat formulaic. The source of the Aristophanes fragment also had one of Sophocles (737 R.): μισῶ μὲν ὅστις τἀφανῆ περισκοπῶν (PCG ad Eup. 157). The difference between these two passages illuminates very clearly the comic perspective. The ridicule of the philosopher by men immersed in the immediate physical and social world is reproduced in Callicles' condemnation of Socrates (Pl. *Grg.* 484c2ff.) and acknowledged in *Tht.* 174a2ff. For the opposite perspective, see Pl. *R.* 517c5ff., *Tht.* 173c6ff.

15. See Dover (ad 156) for the student's stories as parody of a typical "orally transmitted anecdote about the wisdom, wit, or prescience of famous men" which "advertised" their virtues.

16. Eur. *Med.* 294ff. testifies to the resentment of ordinary, "stupid" people towards the *sophoi.* Those who proffer *kaina sopha,* clever novelties, incur the envy (φθόνος) and contempt of their neighbors, who consider them useless (ἀχρεῖος), not wise, and offensive for being considered better than those with a reputation for learning. This passage, which clearly overlaps the vocabulary of the *Clouds* and the opinion of the sophists it assigns ordinary men—for example, Pheidippides, at least initially, in 840ff.—was brought to my attention by Pucci. Cf. Carter chapter 6, esp. 141ff. on Anaxagoras and 146 on this passage and the attitudes it suggests. However, Carter believes that the *Clouds* presents Socrates' activities as useless, but dangerous (151), asserting that Socrates is "happy to cast his researches aside and to teach the young man [Pheidippides] the notorious sophistic technique of 'making the worse cause appear the better,' a recipe for worldly success" (152). Although this is certainly Strepsiades' motive for seeking out Socrates, this reading overstates Socrates' dramatic actions, while slighting his theoretical responsibility for what happens in the agon and after. (See later discussion.)

17. For a summary of some views about the function of laughter—release of aggression, childish pleasure and play, comic catharsis—discussed by Freud, Plato, and Aristotle, see Reckford (1987) sections 6, 32; for obscene comedy, see Henderson (1991) chapters 1, 3.

18. See Dover xxxviff. for Thales as the folkloric and comic figure of the intellectual.

19. Dover comments that "the point may be simply that Socrates' high-minded diversion of the students' interest from their empty bellies to the abstractions of geometry did not last long, and he had recourse to the crudest remedy" (ad 179). Socrates does not substitute one tactic (diversion) for another (satisfaction). Rather, the study of geometry, the abstraction of the world, is a means to satisfaction in it. This may be expressed in a mathematical sense of ʿυφαίρεσις. Socrates at once "subtracted" and stole the cloak.

20. The odd combination, in 176, of τἄλφιτ', already used in 106 as a symbol of physical livelihood, and the elevated ἐπαλαμήσατο emphasizes the high-style hocus-pocus at work to satisfy a common need.

21. The Eupolis reads: δεξάμενος δὲ Σωκράτης τὴν ἐπιδέξι᾿ ⟨ᾄδων⟩ / Στησιχόρου πρὸς τὴν λύραν, οἰνοχόην ἔκλεψεν (395 PCG).

22. See Tomin 27 for the socratic/platonic metaphor of "stripping." The passages he cites (Pl. *Charmides* 154dff., *Alcibiades* I 132a, *Tht.* 162b, 169aff.) indicate that this metaphor was frequently coupled with wrestling metaphors used of debate.

23. The *palaistra,* or wrestling school, sometimes loosely translated as "gymnasium," is the place par excellence of the cult of the body in its social form and the symbol of the old culture, which prized physical excellence. Cf. 1002ff. and 1054ff.

24. For the teacher of rhetoric compared to a trainer, see chapter 1. For Socrates'

devotion to the art of conversational, dialectical wrestling, see Pl. *Tht.* 169a5ff., especially 169c1 where Socrates states: οὕτω τις ἔρως δεινὸς ἐνδέδυκε τῆς περὶ ταῦτα γυμνασίας.

25. Dover ad 183.

26. For Strepsiades' tendency toward the "specific, concrete and physical," and his practical interest in "money, food, or sex," see Green 20. In this passage, cf. food (188), sex (196ff.), and personal advantage (203, 215ff.), all discussed below. Standard jokes include 197, 208; cf. commentators ad loc.

27. Aristophanes goes on to develop the picture of the comic audience in the parabases and elsewhere (see later discussion).

28. See Henderson (1991) 116.

29. The dynamic resembles that identified by Nussbaum in reference to the violence and indifference of democratic man toward his fellow citizens: "by making us laugh at, even sympathize with, this behavior, it [the *Clouds*] shows us (as indeed it also tells us) that we are not exempt from the play's critique" (97).

30. See Henderson (1991) 10ff. for the role of the spectator of obscene humor as vital to its successful aggression.

31. Green 22. Dover ad 206 notes the relatively commonplace nature of maps at this period.

32. Green 22.

33. For a related yet slightly different view of "educated laughter," as marking both our sense of superiority to its targets and our recognition that "it is at the same time our own potential folly that we laugh at, and in laughing, decisively reject," see Reckford (1987) 370–71. For such laughter in *Acharnians* and *Knights,* see Reckford (1987) 391.

34. See Fisher 72, Starkie ad 218, but Ambrosino (1985) imagines the *tarros* (226) on the roof (65ff.).

35. Ambrosino (1985) shows that this, not the more common "basket," is the correct translation of ταρρός (226). Thus Socrates' perch can be integrated with the parody of Diogenes of Apollonia discussed below, for as a drying rack it comically extends his theories about the damage of moisture to the intelligence (51ff.).

36. See Reckford (1967) 229, Pucci (1960) 34ff., Strepsiades' reaction in line 226, and chapter 2 for details on these common characterizations of sophists. For up-in-the-air imagery used of sophists, see Gelzer (1956), who believes it springs from the centrality of *aer* in theories of Diogenes of Apollonia who is parodied in this scene (79ff.). Pucci (1960) accepts the association of *aer* with intellectual *alazoneia,* but believes that the suspension of Socrates reflects the comic rule: "secondo la quale ogni creatore intellettuale adegua costumi ed ambiente alla propria arte" (112). Turato (1972) believes the entire scene recalls Anaxagoras (via Diogenes) as the quintessential atheist, whose theories were now used by and associated with opponents of democracy (48ff., 58ff.).

37. See Dover ad loc. and Ambrosino (1985) for the technical and philosophical vocabulary of Socrates' speech.

38. Thus in 236, ἡ φροντὶς ἕλκει τὴν ἰκμάδ' εἰς τὰ κάρδαμα, φροντίς repeats 229 while ἕλκει, ἰκμάδ', and κάρδαμα repeat 233; see Starkie ad loc. I have adapted Dover's translation of "cress" for τὰ κάρδαμα throughout.

39. Ambrosino (1985) passim, with bibliography, has worked out all the parallels in great detail; for watercress in particular, see 57ff. Contra Dover ad 230, Pucci (1960) 110ff.

40. Ambrosino (1985) 67ff., my translation. She attributes this insight to Schlegel (1983, 4ff.).

41. This philosophical rejection of the body has been implied from the beginning; see

lines 94ff. (discussed in chapter 2) and (read from the other side) Pheidippides' objections in 102ff.

42. For the paratragic tone of 223, the citation of Pindar, and poetic quality of the coinage *aerobatein* (225), cf. Dover ad loc., Rau 189. As Dover comments, Socrates is speaking to Strepsiades as a god to a mortal (ad 223). Thus, he reverses the Pindar, originally intended to show the vanity of human things, to make it indicate his more than human stature and associates himself with the immortality of what he studies.

43. Dover ad 223 notes that it "somewhat counteracts the pretentiousness" of Socrates' address.

44. For varying interpretations of Socrates' "otherworldliness," see Erbse 407ff., who surveys the equation of elevation with the forgetting of the body and mundane concerns, and Nussbaum: "If this Socrates is teaching human wisdom, he seems to believe that training of the intellect is sufficient for wisdom and all that it implies. His sphere is the air, not the gross moral earth of desire and bodily need" (70). For philosophic distance from human society as typical of philosophers, see Jaeger 153ff. who notes Anaxagoras' declaration that the heavens were his country and the platonic Socrates' assignment to philosophers of citizenship in the heavenly city in *logos,* rather than the earthly ones (Pl. *R.* 592a6). For a detailed comparison between the position of the aristophanic Socrates and the favorable picture of the philosopher presented by the *Theaetetus,* cf. Ambrosino (1985) 68 n. 81.

45. As Green observes, καταβηθ' puns on "come down and come off it" (24). Recalling what Socrates has already suffered from the lizard while similarly engaged in studying celestial phenomena, we may suspect that his encounter with Strepsiades will prove unfortunate. Cf. Strauss 16 and 315 n. 3.

46. See Strauss 325–26.

47. Strepsiades' answer to Socrates, in 248–49, is characteristically concrete. (Cf. Green passim for his typical lack of abstraction.) As Woodbury has shown, he is mystified not by the contention that the gods do not exist but by the type of payment required. He is asking: "in that case, what (coinage) do you use when you swear?" (109). As Woodbury comments, Strepsiades neither is interested in theoretical atheism nor is he ever converted to it (111). However, line 248 may have prompted the audience to think that at issue were the gods. The subsequent sudden wrenching of our attention from theology to economics emphasizes the (con)fusion of gods and money and the gods' irrelevance for even the presophistic Strepsiades. Cf. Tomin 26ff.

48. πρῶτον γὰρ (247) denies any discontinuity between Strepsiades' demand to learn to speak sophistically (i.e., learn the *logos* that does not repay), and Socrates' theological reply. (Contra Nussbaum 70.) Nor should it be taken in a purely rhetorical sense as Dover seems to suggest ad loc. See Richardson for the way in which removal of the gods (and transcendent moral law) leaves the *hetton* and *kreitton logoi* as simply two types of argument, to be chosen or rejected purely on the grounds of expediency (67ff.).

49. That Socrates intends to deny that any gods exist at all is shown by the absence of the article in line 247, although Strepsiades has just provided him with a model of its use in 246. Contrast Strepsiades' question of 1233 where he intends to ask what particular gods the creditor has in mind. (Strepsiades now believes in the god Dinos.) For Socrates' theoretical atheism and its contrast with Strepsaides' confused practicality here and elsewhere in the play, see Woodbury 108ff.

50. The expression εἰς λόγους is best understood as analogous to the similar use in line 471. εἰς would then indicate purpose. For ἐπίδειξις (269) as a rhetorical and not religious form used for displays of verbal virtuousity, see the use in 935 and Dover ad 269. What Socrates intends is the deployment of a rhetorical point, not a genuine epiphany.

51. Once they are successful as propositions, the clouds cease to be important for Socrates. His oath by breath, *chaos,* and *aer* in 627 in no way commits him to believing in these as genuine deities. (Cf. his oath by Zeus in line 331.) Rather it plays to Strepsiades and is an example of swearing by something important to one or the forces upon which one depends.

52. See Reckford (1967) 234. The intimacy of the connection between the sophists, speech, and the clouds is also suggested by *suggenesthai.* However, their contact will be mental not physical. "Intercourse" is used by Arrowsmith in his translation.

53. For the form of the prayer, see Dover ad 263–74. In my interpretation Socrates' prayer is taken as intentional manipulation of religious forms (given away, as said above, by the phrase τῷδ' εἰς ἐπίδειξιν 269) whose purpose is to persuade Strepsiades. Socrates himself is no more committed to belief in the clouds than the *hetton logos* in the traditional Olympians he introduces to manipulate the *kreitton* (902, 1045ff.). The importance of the clouds is emphasized by the fact that before Strepsiades can be exposed to them he must be initiated. (See Dover ad 254.) During the initiation, Strepsiades fears he is going to be the human victim in this weird new religion. Later in 274, Socrates encourages the clouds to receive their sacrifice (θυσίαν), and Dover comments on its absence with such an elaborate prayer. While Strepsiades' fears for his physical safety are clearly misplaced, nevertheless, in one sense, he is the sacrifice. His beliefs, way of life, and family will be transformed by his intercourse with the clouds. Contra Horn 52, who believes Socrates' prayer to be a parody unintended by the character.

54. For the details of natural science included in the invocation of the clouds, see Dover ad loc. For the clouds' double nature as "nuvole-dee" and "nuvole-acqua," see Pucci (1960) 31ff.

55. The scholiasts note that βροντησικέραυνοι anticipates the argument that the clouds are responsible for thunder. Turato (1972) 62ff. thinks they suggest Anaxagoras and his atheism.

56. Cratinus 327 (PCG) uses (καλῶν λόγων) ἀείνων to mean "glib" in the context of public oratory. The Photius passage from which the fragment is taken continues to comment that this is used to indicate cleverness in speaking. See PCG ad loc.

57. All are noted by the commentators ad loc.

58. See, for example, Köhnken and Fisher.

59. Thus Segal (1975), for example, sees it as "one of the most beautiful passages in Attic literature" (182), and Dover comments that retention of lyric alpha "is unusual in comedy, except for humorous parodic effect, which is out of the question here" (ad 275–90).

60. See for example, Dover ad 1458, Segal (1975) 193ff.

61. See Köhnken 157. See also Fisher 91ff.

62. See Fisher 102. See 100 for his analysis of the responsion.

63. See chapter 4 for the expectations of Strepsiades and the comic audience as contributing to the form of the reflective clouds.

64. Dover (ad 275–90) points out numerous similarities in sound as well as the more precise echoes: ἀρθῶμεν (276) = ἄρθητε (266), ἔλθωμεν (299) = ἔλθετε (269), to which can be added φανεραί (276–77) = φάνητ' (266). In addition, as the scholia on line 278 note, the clouds also respond to Socrates' suggestion of their whereabouts in 271, and like him identify Ocean as their father. Structurally, the clouds' ode, which in both stanzas takes the form vocative (275, 298), suggestion (276–77, 299–300), elaboration of suggestion (280–84, 301–13), also reflects Socrates' prayer which is composed of the same elements: vocative (264–65), suggestion (266), and then, after Strepsiades' interruption, another suggestion, vocative, and elaboration of suggestion (269–73).

65. Dover comments on 335ff. that Strepsiades "caricatures the language of lyric poetry by overdoing ἄν" (ad 338). This line also echoes 276 and 288, which also retain lyric alpha. Cf. Dover ad 275–90.

66. Silk 106ff.

67. See Edmunds (1987) 15ff. who agrees with Silk but finds that the bad poetry expresses the clouds' pretentious character, which resembles that of Socrates.

68. Dover ad 299; cf. ad 300 and 310 for other parallels to the conventional praise of Attica.

69. See Goldhill (1986) 67.

70. The movement from βούλομαι to χεσείω is the first indication of the equivalence of desire and necessity, a central point in the speech of the *hetton logos*.

71. See Henderson (1991) for the vulgarity of *khezein*, the low farce of excremental humor, and its popularity (187). Strepsiades' laughter at 174 confirms that what is comic is the act of shitting, not the regard for *themis*, and this is what Socrates reproves in his response. It is hard to see how Socrates could reprove as comic a religious awe that he himself had just done his best to foster and which Strepsiades simply echoes.

72. Fisher 98.

73. For the theme of diarrhea from fear, see Dover (1972) 40; Fisher 98; Henderson (1991) 189ff.

74. See Henderson (1991) 187.

75. The scholia ad 295 comment that Strepsiades knows what he is doing is wrong, but does it anyway ὑπὸ μείζονος ἀνάγκης ἐξαγόμενος εἰς τὸ παρανομεῖν.

76. The passages are linked by the repetition of the verb (κατα)χέζειν (174, 295).

77. Comedy, qua *logos*, could seem, thus, to create a world in which it is irrelevant. One solution is that of *Birds* 785ff.—to make comedy one in a series of physical desires and needs which also includes sex, food, and relief of the bowels. Comedy, whose subject is the other three, is associated with them as the fourth. Another bleaker approach is taken in our play: verbal comedy really is irrelevant; see chapter 5.

78. Henderson (1991) 187. For Aristotle's discussion of Old (as opposed to New) Comedy as characterized by the frankness of its obscenity, see Reckford (1987) 369ff.

79. Cf. Dover ad 296.

80. Strepsiades is not joking. Henderson (1991) notes that instead of aggressively exposing another, "Strepsiades' obscenities turn inward and expose their speaker" (72), creating "the familiar situation in comedy of a serious teacher questioning an ignorant buffoon who reduces everything to his own base level" (74). The base level and the self-revelatory nature of Strepsiades' obscenity are the point. Its apparent lack of motivation makes all the more effective Aristophanes' exposure of the nature of man and the implications of that nature for the philosophic enterprise and for sophistic rhetoric.

Chapter 4

1. For Aristophanes' familiarity with sophistic rhetorical theory and practice in general, see Murphy passim, Harriott chapters 2 and 3. For his use of rhetorical terminology, see Taillardat 467ff. For the sophistic flavor of the speeches of Pheidippides and the *hetton logos* with their praise of *logos*, see Murphy 92ff.; for the *Thesmophoriazusae*, see Zeitlin 208ff.; for *Frogs* 1021 as an echo of Gorgias' judgement of the *Seven against Thebes* (DK 82 B 24) and *Frogs* 961–62 as possibly gorgianic, see Segal (1962) 131, who cites the earlier literature; for *Acharnians* 633 as a reference to Gorgias in particular, see Bowie n.

22 (and note *exapatasthai* in the same line); for a direct mention of Gorgias, see *Birds* 1701ff. For violent speech in particular, see the many examples in Taillardat 282ff., 335ff., 339ff.; perhaps Aristophanes 544 (PCG); the extended passage of *Acharnians* 676ff.; *Knights* 262, 273, 847, 454ff.; and Engle chapters 2 and 3.

2. As an anonymous reader pointed out, Strepsiades' guess that the clouds are heroines ("important in village, but not in city, cults") and Socrates' answer confirm the contrast between the rural, old-fashioned, religious, and concrete orientation of Strepsiades and the urban modernity of what he confronts at the Thinkery.

3. For the trendiness of newly coined words ending in *-sis*, see Handley 129. For a commonly cited parallel, the parody of similar sophistic terminology this time ending in *-ikos*, see *Knights* 1378ff., where the sophistic rhetor Phaiax is described as: συνερτικὸς γάρ ἐστι καὶ περαντικός, / καὶ γνωμοτυπικὸς καὶ σαφὴς καὶ κρουστικός, / καταληπτικός τ' ἄριστα τοῦ θορυβητικοῦ. The overlap with *Clouds* 318 shows that it parodies established technical vocabulary incorporating words cognate to κροῦσις and κατάληψις. Cf. Taillardat 340 n. 2, Dover ad 318.

4. Dover ad loc. The martial and sophistic connotations can best be seen in another commonly cited parallel, Pl. *Tht.* 154e (see Dover, Starkie ad loc., Taillardat 340 n. 2.), where Socrates bids Theaetetus to be true to his beliefs and not simply to the requirements of his argument, commenting that if they already understood everything: συνελθόντες σοφιστικῶς εἰς μάχην τοιαύτην, ἀλλήλων τοὺς λόγους τοῖς λόγοις ἐκρούομεν. The smiting of one argument against another, independent of the speakers' real convictions, is pejoratively described as sophistic, characteristic of those who make discussion a battle and argue to defeat their opponent. The context implicitly contrasts this with philosophical reasoning together to find a truth transcending speakers and *logoi*.

5. Starkie ad loc. Its sophistic and technical connotations can be inferred from a similar coinage in *Knights* 1380 quoted in n. 3. Dover argues for " 'check' an unfavorable reaction from the audience or an argument in which an opponent trusts" (ad 318.).

6. For the military overtones, see Pl. *Grg.* 455c1ff. and *R.* 526d2ff.

7. See Ambrosino (1983) 27ff.

8. For interesting platonic reuses of this idea, see Pl. *Phdr.* 249c5ff., which rehabilitates the notion of winging by philosophic discourse.

9. See Henderson (1991) 128, and perhaps this is the joke in *Lys.* 1013. See chapter 2 and Arrowsmith 136.

10. See Taillardat 340, who cites *Il.* 5.579 and 13.147 for νύττειν. The other example of homeric parody cited by Taillardat is *Clouds* 1375 in Strepsiades' description of his argument with Pheidippides. This line is discussed in chapter 9.

11. ἀντιλογεῖν, perhaps even more precisely than the more common ἀντιλέγειν, recalls sophistic terminology and practice, because of its cognates ἀντιλογία and, particularly, ἀντιλογικός, used in 1173. For their highly technical flavor, see citations in LSJ, and note Protagoras' book *Antilogikoi [Logoi]* DK 80 B 5, apparently also called *Antilogion* a,b in DK 80 A 1.55.

12. The distribution of πείθειν and its compounds confirms that Aristophanes wishes to present the strongest possible picture of sophistic rhetoric. The sophistic figures in the play rarely describe rhetoric this moderately; they use instead the martially flavored νικᾶν and its compounds. Strepsiades, who is given to the idea of persuasion, uses πείθειν or stronger compounds six times before entering the Thinkery and four more when he persuades Pheidippides to do so. Pheidippides uses it three times during his refusal, and once when he agrees. The remaining uses are: twice by the *hetton logos* to characterize the *kreitton;* once by the chorus to Strepsiades before the second agon—where he takes the

part of the *kreitton logos*—once by Pheidippides to describe the lawmakers of the past. Pheidippides' speech in the second agon is described with ἀναπείθειν twice. Once where he ironically repeats his father's words and once by the chorus.

13. For *kapnos* as derogatory, cf. commentators ad loc. The potency of the *techne* is emphasized by the trivia upon which it is exercised, the tenuousness and ingenuity of the points made, and the speaker's lack of personal conviction. Compare the end of Gorg. *Encomium*.

14. It is particularly true of the *logos* of the *meteorologoi* that it can make the incredible and unclear appear to the eyes of opinion: τὰ ἄπιστα καὶ ἄδηλα φαίνεσθαι τοῖς τῆς δόξης ὄμμασιν ἐποίησαν Gorg. *Encomium* 13. For the invisibility of *logos*, cf. *Encomium* 8.

15. The existence of dramatic illusion in comedy has been much discussed. I agree with Bain's observations about claims that dramatic illusion was not known in ancient comedy. In chapter 1, Bain notes that dramatic illusion itself was a concept and practice familiar to the Greeks: (1) the breaking of illusion was unknown in tragedy, which had the same audience as comedy; (2) the distinction between talking about someone and pretending to be someone was known to Aristotle as the central difference between epic and tragedy; (3) the actors in Greek drama "identify themselves with the characters they are playing and speak in the person of these characters"; (4) this pretence is maintained for long periods of time, and "for such passages it is surely necessary to keep the term 'illusion' so that we can speak of the illusion being preserved" (5–11). Noting the difference between the periods when illusion was preserved and the moments when it was not is all that is required to remind the audience that something is going on theatrically, and hence to change their view of the action.

16. See Dover, who comments, "We should not infer from this that the play was composed for performance in some other theatre; the action represented occurs at some unspecified place in Attica and almost anywhere except under the shadow of the Akropolis one can point to clouds gathering over Parnes" (ad 323).

17. Thus the *Clouds* tries to promote what Muecke aptly summarizes as the appropriate response to drama in general: "It follows that drama demands a twofold reaction from the spectator, who must on the one hand be imaginatively involved in the fiction which is being presented, and on the other detached enough to allow him to 'read' or 'decode' the play according to the rules of theatrical discourse" (55). This condition is obviously enhanced by breaks in the dramatic illusion. Muecke continues: "Therefore to be effective the device [rupture of dramatic illusion] must trigger a switch, however momentary, from the involved frame of mind to the detached" (56).

18. Dover notes the rupture of dramatic illusion and comments that πλάγιαι (325) "takes account of the actual position of the chorus in the theatre" (ad 325).

19. For the εἴσοδος (326) as the entrance to the theater common to both chorus and audience, see Dearden 11–12, McLeish 39. Newiger (1957) 55 n. 6 considers these passages Aristophanes' way of drawing attention to his novel choruses.

20. For the many things that the audience and chorus shared—space, entrance, light, and theatrical experience as participants and spectators—see Padel 338ff.

21. Sifakis points out this triple identification with characters, actors, and Athenian public as characteristic of the comic choruses in general (23).

22. The introduction of noses at this point has been variously accounted for. Among other explanations are Schmid's that it refers to Diogenes and his principle of *aer* (216ff.) and Köhnken's that it refers to the clouds' tricky plan to hoist Strepsiades with his own petard (159ff.). Edmunds (1987) proposes that the clouds' noses are like Socrates' famous pug nose (16ff.). This would have the merit of making the clouds mirror Socrates, but in

a much more direct way than what we are told is their characteristic manner. Romer's suggestion about *Birds* 670–74—that the nightingale is costumed as a flute girl, with her flute as beak, making her only resemblance to a bird "illusory"—may also be pertinent. The notion of illusion created by the audience for itself, and broken by Strepsiades' "concrete" question, is interesting, but even more attractive along the same lines is Brown's suggestion, following Hipponax (88), that ῥίς refers not, or not only, to noses, but to the male genitals. The joke would be Strepsiades' reduction of the clouds first to women and then to men by "pointing out the maleness of the choreutae with a comic reference to the most obvious indicator of sex, as a result of which both the logic of the passage and the dramatic illusion are shattered" (89, contra Mastromarco). This has more than "humourous effect" (89) to recommend it. It is compatible with the ambiguities of the clouds' entrance and prepares nicely for what follows: just before learning about the clouds' "comic" function (for which, see below), we are reminded that they are, in fact, male, and necessarily, for they are a chorus. The vulgar humor and possible gestures by chorus and Strepsiades would, at the moment of the chorus' arrival onstage, indicate the distance of this play from the chaste and verbal first *Clouds*, with all the obvious ramifications for our *Clouds'* comic and rhetorical functions (on which, see chapter 5).

23. For the moral quality of clouds' shapes, see Pucci (1960) 32.

24. Strauss 18.

25. Socratic elenchus is a variant on this process, and Nussbaum, following Kierkegaard, believes the clouds mirror the reflective nature of the elenchus and its inconclusive cloudy results (76).

26. *Kairos* was discussed both by Protagoras (DK 80 A 1.52) and Gorgias (DK 82 B 13); see Kerferd 82. The rhetorician's necessary knowledge of the soul is implied by Gorg. *Encomium* and explicit in Pl. *Phdr.* 270b4ff.

27. See Ambrosino (1983) 18–19, where she also points out the contemporary understanding of the arbitrariness of language (54 n. 48). For Gorgias' disconnection of *logos* and reality as key to the power of (skillful) speech, see chapter 1.

28. See Ambrosino (1983) 20.

29. See Ambrosino (1983) 22–23.

30. See Reckford (1967) for the clouds' mockery of men's manias through "illusion and mimicry" as like the comic playwright (223), and Pucci (1960) for the clouds as spokeswomen of the poet, representing his thought (33).

31. See Dover ad 353, 355 for other passages in which these personages appear.

32. Thus in the *Peace*, Trygaius' project is a mania (*Peace* 54ff.; cf. *Plutus* 1ff.). In the *Wasps*, the play is on *philo*, and there is a list of passions that could form the subject of the play (*Wasps* 74ff.). Strepsiades' project, too, is that of an *erastes*, albeit of *ponera pragmata* (1459). Whitman defines the prototypical comic hero of the *Margites* as a "passionate madman" who foreshadows the visionary lunacy of the heroes of *poneria* (35 and chapter 2 passim). See also McLeish 67ff., although the *Clouds* does not follow the general pattern of comic resolution whereby the hero achieves his improbable satisfaction. For *eros* as a madness from the platonic perspective, see Pl. *Phdr.* 244a2ff., 265a5ff.

33. See McLeish for Aristophanes' metaphoric vision: "Aristophanes looks at one human activity (for example, politics enslaving the state) and sees another (for example, slaves bullying a foolish old master)" (158). See also, for the *Acharnians*, Edmunds (1980) 2ff., 13ff., and passim. For Aristophanes' "particularly bold and free" play with the "realizable metaphor" of drama, see Whitman 264ff.

34. See Ambrosino (1986–87) for a general statement of ancient comedy as providing to the audience "una storia paradigmatica: un racconto carico di senso, che va al di là della vicenda narrata" (107). However, she does not connect this to the ambiguities of the clouds'

entrance, instead making the message of the *Clouds* political, as first suggested by Turato (1972).

35. For the process of allusion, see Pucci (1987) 263ff. At this point it seems appropriate to recall Gorgias' insight that *logos* functions by prompting an answering—but an independent and thus quite possibly different—*logos* in the mind of the hearer. (Contra Ambrosino [1983] 21, who ignores this further complication of communication.) The difficulties of interpretation arise here, for a *logos* that may have one meaning to speaker or writer can arouse quite a different one in hearer or spectator, and this is particularly true at the metaphoric and allusive level. Thus wolves have many connotations, and even if we agree on one, for example, thievishness, this, in turn, carries different "values," negative and positive. This problem of interpretation, or, as Gorgias puts it, the difficulty of (true, unambiguous) communication, haunts all speech and signifying action, and underlines the importance of *kairos,* the attempt to gauge the listeners' souls so as to select an appropriate and inescapable *logos.* Yet even *kairos* does not seem to free us from the (comic) possibility that *logos'* site of operation, the soul of its hearer, will ultimately condition, as well as be conditioned by, what is heard—that the hearer's needs, desires, and beliefs will dictate the meaning and effect of speech rather than the other way around.

36. Reckford (1967) remarks that "to show up Strepsiades, who wants a 'cheating education' they [the clouds] have become beautiful cheaters" (225). For more detail, see Köhnken 162ff., who points out the mania attributed to Strepsiades (832, 846, 1476) in his quest for the sophistic *logos.*

37. See Pindar *Pythian* 2 for Ixion sleeping with a cloud in the form of Hera; cf. Köhnken 162ff. Likewise, a cloud forms the *eidolon* of Helen in Euripides' play (cf. Eur. *Helen* 31–35, 704–6, 1135). For these clouds as probably inspiring Aristophanes' choice for his chorus, see Dover lxviii. Reckford (1967) cites Pindar and the golden cloud of *Iliad* 14 and sees the clouds as symbols of *apate* or deception, without linking them to sophistic *apate,* instead finding comic play based on "the familiar Archaic sequence of presumption, infatuation, and retribution" (231–32).

38. See Edmunds (1987) 14ff. for the clouds as reflecting the historic Socrates.

39. See chapter 3.

40. Cf. the philosophical personification of the laws in Plato's *Crito* 50a6, the outcome of the discussion in *Prt.* 361a4, and a little differently, Diotima in *Symposium* 201d1ff., who in each case act as spokespersons for the conclusive points. For Aristophanes' strategy of personification, see Ambrosino (1986–87) 106ff.

41. For clouds figuring the necessary deception and power of language *(muthoi)* in a world of human desire and inevitable inability to know the truth, see Eur. *Hipp.* 191ff. Significantly, this is an idea voiced by the nurse, whose later speech marks her as "sophistic" (see chapter 2). As Goff comments on these lines, "because of this cloud of unknowing, we are carried away by *muthoi,* by words . . . we shall see how this line can be read to represent the experience of every character" (19).

42. See Bergren passim, Goldhill (1986) 128.

43. See Reckford (1967) 234, for the clouds as comic sirens. For the relationship between the figure of Helen and *logos,* see Zeitlin 204ff., who cites Pucci (1977) for Pandora as "emblematizing the beginning of rhetoric." The game of matching the clouds' mockery to referents could continue for a long time, given their polyvalent nature and that of *logos* in general. Ambrosino (1983) suggests that the clouds' (false) assumption of what appears to be female form mirrors "ce pouvoir, inhérent au langage, de 'rendre présent' (représenter) ce qui ne l'est pas, justement parce que le signe est autre chose que l'objet évoqué" (22).

44. See Reckford (1987) 198.

45. See chapter 5.

46. That atheism is prerequisite is underlined by the clouds' reactions: they greet Strepsiades only after the lesson debunking lightning (412) and ask what he desires only after testing his rejection of traditional gods (427ff.); see Richardson 68. Strepsiades' own total misunderstanding and substitution of new gods like Dinos is a comic deformation that indicates the likely fate of this type of argument among credulous and ordinary men. For Strepsiades' failure to adopt conceptual atheism, see Woodbury 109.

47. For the cloud chorus as not only a comic metaphor but also a term in the (parodic) sophistic argument, see Turato (1972) chapter 2. However, his connection of natural science and rhetoric is mostly concerned to document the presence of Anaxagoras which he feels is fundamental for the political message of the play—denunciation of the threat of oligarchic clubs. For a summary of views which make the chorus metaphoric, see Turato (1972) 47 n. 2.

48. For the many parallels in contemporary speculation to the following passage, see Dover ad loc.

49. For bursting with voice in our play, see 357, 960, and, as discussed in chapter 5, 583, where the thunder is the expressive omen of the clouds/chorus. For $\pi\alpha\tau\alpha\gamma\epsilon\hat{\iota}\nu$ as possibly equivalent to $\lambda\alpha\lambda\epsilon\hat{\iota}\nu$, see Taillardat 292.

50. See Dover (1972) 41.

51. $\tau\alpha\rho\acute{\alpha}\sigma\sigma\epsilon\iota\nu$, used in line 288, coupled with $\tau\grave{\eta}\nu$ $\gamma\alpha\sigma\tau\acute{\epsilon}\rho\alpha$ means "cause relaxation of the bowels" (LSJ $\tau\alpha\rho\acute{\alpha}\sigma\sigma\epsilon\iota\nu$ 4). This clearly anticipates the reduction of sophistic rhetoric to shit and farting discussed later.

52. The speaker of line 394 is unclear. As Dover notes, the manuscript tradition is divided, but the first words ($\tau\alpha\hat{\upsilon}\tau'$ $\check{\alpha}\rho\alpha$) probably indicate a change of speaker, thus Strepsiades. Dover however, continues with Socrates on the grounds that such "reasoning" is more appropriate for him (ad 394). Woodbury, however, would give it to Strepsiades as a popular etymology (112ff.). Likewise, if we think of it as a pun, then Strepsiades, who is given numerous puns tying together the comic view with the sophistic, is a convincing choice. For the possibility that *bronte* may have also been pronounced *bor(n)te*, thus resembling *porde* much more closely, see Dover (ad loc.). However Henderson (1991) points out the humor may have been in their obvious difference (195 n. 14).

53. See chapter 2 for details.

54. Plut. *Per* 6. See Pl. *Phdr.* 269e1ff., Ostwald 269ff., and Turato (1972) 50ff., 64ff., who also points out the resulting opening of religious awe to manipulation for personal, social, and political ends. Turato cites DK 88 B 25 but, as we shall see, the same process will be amply documented by the sophistic speakers in our play.

55. In the lesson about lightning, the clouds are again driven by *anagke* and their actions portrayed in the passive voice (404–5). The effect, lightning, is given a life of its own but is itself caused by impersonal forces like "rush" and "density" (406–7).

56. Of course, given the disconnection of *logos* and reality, all speech will essentially be deception, *apate*, but here again comedy translates this vulgarly. Strepsiades plans not the inevitable *apate* of all *logos* and persuasion, but the instrumental deceit of convincing lies.

57. See de Carli 13, who notes that Strepsiades' corruption precedes his sophistic education.

58. For $\pi\rho\sigma\tau\iota\lambda\hat{\alpha}\nu$ (411) as "to befoul with dung" see Henderson (1991), who notes that "references simply to *befouling someone* are uniformly vulgar, reflecting the low characters of the befouler and the befouled" (190). As is appropriate, Strepsiades' language echoes Socrates' and the previous example with $\kappa\alpha\tau\alpha\kappa\acute{\alpha}\omega$ (407, 411) and $\dot{\epsilon}\xi\alpha\acute{\iota}\phi\nu\eta\varsigma$ (387, 410). Note that both examples occur during religious festivals, evidently important to our comic hero primarily as occasions for gluttony.

59. As Newiger (1957) observes, these repetitions bring the theorizing about celestial things emphatically down to "die feste animalisch belebte Erde" (62). The repetition spans the introduction of the *dinos* and makes sure that we understand it in the proper light. In spite of Strepsiades' question of 379 and his comments of 380ff., we are not to think of *dinos* as a replacement of Zeus or the clouds any more than "physical law" implies a lawmaker.

60. See van Leeuwen ad loc.; for parody of socratic practice, Nussbaum 74, Newiger (1957) 61 n. 3, among others. Schmidt 222 detects another reference to this motto in 842.

61. See Dover ad 385, who, however, sees this as only a scientific or philosophical grouping together of things differing in scale.

62. For the obviously extremely vulgar and low connotations of defecation and the coarse, and invariably popular, humor associated with it, see Henderson (1991) 187ff.

63. See Taillardat 407ff., "La toute-puissance du demagogue-Zeus." Pericles figured as Zeus in many comedies: see, for examples, Cratinus 73, 326, *Nemesis, Cheirons,* 258 (PCG); Telecleides 18, 47, 48 (PCG).

64. The passage reads: δώσετε τὸν φόρον, ἢ βροντήσας τὴν πόλιν ὑμῶν ἀνα-τρέψω (*Wasps* 671). ἀνατρέψω also puns on the rhetorical term for refutation by turning the interlocutor's argument back against him. Cf. Ambrosino (1983) for this as a technical rhetorical term (32 and n. 73); see also *Clouds* 884, 901.

65. See Henderson (1991) 197. For Cleon's speech as a storm, see *Knights* 430, 692; as shit, *Knights* 339ff., and Engle 83ff. Cf. *Frogs* 237ff., when Dionysos' *proktos* speaks back to the croak/fart of the frogs.

66. See also *Knights* 897ff. for the effect of Cleon's shitty talk and Engle 85.

67. See Henderson (1991) 198 n. 21 and 210, where he also discusses the pathic imagery of this passage.

68. See as well *Knights* 1381, which Henderson (1991) believes levels the same insult against Phaiax, another well-known speaker (197ff., following the scholia).

69. For λαλεῖν used in context of the new rhetoric and contemporary intellectuals, cf., for example, *Knights* 1381, cited above; *Acharnians* 933; *Frogs* 91, 1491; *Peace* 653, *Clouds* 931, 1053, 1394; Eupolis 116 (PCG) quoted in chapter 1. See Henderson (1991) for τρώζειν "wound/penetrate sexually" and for the homosexual connotations here (176). The commonplace that all rhetors are pathic homosexuals is also at work here and obviously related to the idea that rhetoric is farting. For passages stating that the prerequisite for popular oratorical power was homosexuality, cf. Henderson (1991) 209ff.

70. See Eubulus 106.5 (PCG). For Callistratus, see also Eubulus 10 (PCG) and the commentary there. This riddle is quoted by Henderson (1991) 198, under the heading "farting as windiness and noise," but in the passages that he cites, the point of the jokes is frequently their application to sophistic rhetoric. For similar jokes, see Eupolis 92 (PCG) (stammering and assholes, on which, Henderson [1991] 203) and the word μεσοπέρδην, which Henderson (1991) calls "a play on the wrestling term μεσοφέρδην" (199). The play might involve invocation of the imagery of wrestling for sophistic speech, which is then analogized to farting.

71. Socrates' use of κλόνος in 387 lends a ludicrous heroic (and perhaps scientific-medical) tone to Strepsiades' stomach disorders (see Dover ad loc.). Strepsiades' answer continues the mockery: δεινὰ κέκραγεν (389) puns on the sophistic ability δεινὰ λέγειν; κράζειν is used in the *Knights* for the speech of Cleon (*Knights* 487) and the Sausage Seller (*Knights* 285, 287, 642). Further, as the fart becomes metaphorically indistinguishable from thunder, the (comic) *logos* itself reflects this process; the words for fart and thunder are the "same" (394).

72. The passage reads: βούλομαι ἀνταποπαρδεῖν / πρὸς τὰς βροντάς (293–94).

Like Strepsiades' farting and the adulterer's reasoning (1077), sophistic speech is characterized by the prefix *anti* (ἀντί), as in the code word *antilegein*. Cf. 901, 1037, 1040.

73. See *Wasps* 1305, where the satisfied Philocleon is said to be like a donkey, ἐνήλατ' ἐσκίρτα 'πεπόρδει κατεγέλα, which demonstrates that natural man cannot be successfully repressed by convention (Henderson [1991] 78ff.). As commentators have noted this recalls the *hetton logos'* injunction to Pheidippides: χρῶ τῇ φύσει, σκίρτα, γέλα, νόμιζε μηδὲν αἰσχρόν (1078) (Van Leeuwen, Dover ad loc.). Likewise, our first sight of Pheidippides farting away in his sleep (9) should alert us to his potential as a sophistic rhetor.

74. See Whitman's insightful comments, 139.

75. For the obscene use of πιέζειν to mean "hard pressed" and about to shit, see *Frogs* 3 and, on this, Henderson (1991) 188.

76. That speakers are motivated only by self-interest and desire is a commonplace of the *Knights,* and indeed of this era. Listening to debate, the skilled listener will try not to analyze what is said, but to detect why it is said. Finley 23ff. contrasts this increasing loss of faith in rational debate with the Periclean optimism.

77. This fallacy is also pointed out in DK 88 B 25.27ff., which credits the ancient inventor of religion with fostering belief in the gods through lightning and thunder.

78. See Pl. *Grg.* 463b1ff.; see also the hints in Pl. *Prt.* 313c7ff., Pl. *Phdr.* 227b6.

79. Eumaeus was speaking about beggars in Ithaca who invent illusory (ἀπατήλια *Od.* 14.127) stories of Odysseus in order to be received (and fed) by Penelope. Cf. also *Od.* 14.156ff.

80. For a very interesting discussion of *gaster,* see Pucci (1987) chapters 14–18, which discuss the *Odyssey*'s "courageous gesture" in using *gaster* to "define man's basic instincts and needs" (181). Its central role is acknowledged by Odysseus when he justifies his "epic" battle with Iris for the prize of a sausage, by citing the pressure of the stomach (*Od.* 18.52–54), in what Pucci calls "Aristophanic humor," and then associates with blame poetry (161ff. esp. 162). The mock heroics there may shadow the *Clouds* here; the overlap with the old man, Strepsiades, forced to enter the (mock) heroic sophistic battle of his day is notable. For shadows of Odysseus, see Reckford (1967) 227ff., 234.

81. See Hes. *Th.* 26, where the fact that men are *gasteres* distorts their relationship to *logos* and Pucci's (1987) discussion of this passage and the "meandering, labyrinthine ways of gain-seeking discourse, 'sweetened talk,' and adulatory and ingratiating speech" inspired by *gaster* (191ff.). For the *gaster* as productive of lies, see Arthur 102, Svenbro 50ff.

82. See DK 87 A 1.

83. ἀπατηθείς, κολακευθείς, θεραπευθείς, scholia ad *Wasps* 668, which are given as translations of the variant reading περιπεμφθείς, but are equally true of the reading in the text.

84. For an insightful discussion of the "blended imagery of politics and gluttony, suggestive enough of a greedy body politic kept complacent by obsequious demagoguery," see Whitman 92ff., who connects it with *logos* on 96ff. Cf. Taillardat 225 on this passage and 395ff. for "La politique du ventre." The extreme prevalence (dramatic, thematic, verbal) of such imagery in the *Knights* would make it easier for the audience to place our comedy in its larger imagistic context. The parabasis will recall the *Knights* explicitly and play it off against the *Clouds.* The imagery is, however, common; see *Birds* 1695ff., 1703–4 for rhetoricians associated with Gorgias called ἐγγλωττογαστόροι. (This fact was brought to my attention by Hubbard.)

85. This is a road already familiar to Paphlagon; cf. *Knights* 50ff. for Cleon's bribery of the *demos* with food, and see *Birds* 462ff. for comparison of a flattering speech to a dinner. These and other "cooking" passages are noted in Taillardat 441.

86. The passage reads: ὁτιὴ λέγειν οἷός τε κἀγὼ καὶ καρυκοποιεῖν *Knights* 343.

87. For a similar relationship between *gaster* and the production of epic poetry, see Pucci (1987) 187: "songs of *kleos* derive ultimately not only from the need of the poet but also from the narcissistic pleasure of the masters—and both bespeak the presence and effects of *gaster.*" See also 235.

88. Plato picked up this perspective in the *Gorgias.* The comic transformation of *terpsis* may peep through in line 364, where Dover has emended τερπνόν to σεμνόν in Strepsiades' description of the clouds' voice. *Terpnon* here would be doubly appropriate: it would invoke this vital gorgianic principle at the moment when the rhetorical deities appear and already be comically jarring in Strepsiades' mouth, alluding at the moment of his comic awe to the very pleasures that will undermine it. For "τερπνόν, appropriate to food (*Ach.* 881), music (*Ec.* 889), and sex (*Lys.* 553), is ill assorted with ἱερόν and τερατῶδες" (Dover ad 364).

89. As Arthur puts it, "hunger then and the belly's driving goad link men to animals and separate them from the gods" (104). See Vernant (1989) 59ff. for a history of the notion of *gaster* as "indicating the human condition in its totality," and a useful collection of passages, several of which are discussed below. See also Vernant (1981a) 51.

90. "The term *gaster* is used through a long textual tradition to represent the one who, dominated by his appetite for food, has no other horizon or mainspring than his belly" Vernant (1989) 60. For attention to *gaster* alone as characteristic of parasites, see Pucci (1987) 177ff.

91. See Vernant (1989) 60 for ancient authorities that attributed a physiological basis to this cultural synecdoche.

92. See Vernant (1981b) 73 for the violence and savagery inherent in the struggle of animals to satisfy their stomach.

93. See Detienne (1981) for this continuum, and Vernant (1989) 61 for the hesiodic role of speakers of *logos,* kings and poets, in linking human and divine and bypassing the *gaster. Gaster* could assume precise political and social meanings. Svenbro (70) has shown it characterizes those marginal elements of society that are exposed by their position to the drives of *gaster,* and, perforce, also expose the imperative nature of these drives to others through disgusting and indecorous behavior—thus behaving much like our comedy. Turato (1979) shows its association with the "cattivo selvaggio" whose devotion to his stomach (and to an anachronistic luxury) made him the antithesis of the aristocratic values of moderation and *sophrosyne* (83ff.).

94. The passage reads: διὰ γαστριμαργίαν ἀφιλόσοφον καὶ ἄμουσον πᾶν ἀποτελοῖ τὸ γένος, ἀνυπήκοον τοῦ θειοτάτου τῶν παρ' ἡμῖν (Pl. *Ti.* 73a6).

95. Xenophon writes: τοῦ δὲ μὴ δουλεύειν γαστρὶ μηδ' ὕπνῳ καὶ λαγνείᾳ οἴει τι ἄλλο αἰτιώτερον εἶναι ἢ τὸ ἕτερα ἔχειν τούτων ἡδίω (X. *Mem.* 1.6.8).

96. The Greek is: ἐγὼ δὲ νομίζω τὸ μὲν μηδενὸς δεῖσθαι θεῖον εἶναι, τὸ δ' ὡς ἐλαχίστων ἐγγυτάτω τοῦ θείου (X. *Mem.* 1.6.10).

97. The dominance of the *gaster* and its associated vices is typical of slaves (Turato [1979] 86), women (Vernant [1989] 60), beggars (Svenbro 50ff.), and, in general, the man who "vive solo a livello della *physis*" (Turato [1979] 86).

98. In reference to *Od.* 7.216, Pucci (1987) comments: "The *gaster* is portrayed as a lower *thumos,* a vital principle that forces upon men its irresistible needs; it *lives* as an *entity,* let us say as a beast, inside man and needs to be taken care of, fed, and listened to. It forces upon man forgetfulness of his griefs and makes him mindful only of eating and drinking" (174, emphasis original). In the *Odyssey* passage, the effect of the *gaster* is to deprive grief and memory of their force, to postpone *logos,* to break the link between past

and present, and hence to render irrelevant, or secondary, communication, *kleos,* and the truth.

99. For the *kreitton logos,* see chapter 7. Curiazi (1978) lists the similarities of the *kreitton logos* and Socrates/clouds in lines 414ff., but fails to understand their thematic role. Instead, she uses them as evidence of the revision of the agon to make its criticisms of contemporary intellectual trends more accessible (215ff.).

100. The *Odyssey*'s recognition of *gaster* is likewise polemical and shocking (cf. Pucci [1987] 173ff.) and is incomplete. For as Pucci points out while *"gaster* names the instinctual source of all the human activity the poem presents" (179), the poem, unable to free itself from traditional views, suppresses this potentially positive evaluation by splitting its represention of motivation and action in two and attempting to mark the dictates of the *gaster* as negative.

101. See Vernant (1981b) passim.

102. See Eur. *Cyclops* 334–38. The resemblance of this whole speech to our scene is striking. See Turato (1979) 79ff. for the implications of Polyphemos' diet, Vidal-Naquet (1981a) 86 for the savagery of the reversal of ordinary sacrifice. By comparison with the Cyclops, Strepsiades remains civilized; to the extent that he avoids cannibalism, his *gaster* is still subdued.

103. As before, the parody works at the level of diction and connotation, for shorn of its distracting comic accretions, Socrates' and Strepsiades' dialog is not per se wrong or foolish; indeed, it has philosophical and scientific dimensions and rigor. With the possible exception of Strepsiades' objection on line 379 (see notes above), Aristophanes does not attack the sophists' reasoning or expose actual shortcomings.

104. See Henderson (1991) 35ff.

105. The earlier uses of *sophos* (94) and *sophia* (361) are exclusively connected with "professional" sophists and inhabitants of the *phrontisterion.*

106. For *eikos* as a sophistic rhetorical term for the reasonable or probable, see Pucci (1960) 13.

107. The passage reads: οὐκ αὐτῇ τῇ γλώττῃ πολεμῶν, ἀλλὰ γλώττῃ καθάπερ ὅπλῳ χρώμενος—τοῦτο γὰρ ὅπλον ῥήτορος—καὶ καταπολεμῶν ἐν αὐτῇ τοὺς ἐναντίους (scholia ad 419). Likewise, Starkie (ad 419) notes: "An epic word, used in comedy only where there is an epic association. Here there is an implication that the tongue is superior to the sword." Cf. Van Leeuwen ad loc.

108. For this imagery, see chapter 1. Note here both the challenge to old aristocratic values with their obsolete physical *erga* by a new ideal that conflates action and speech and the association of *logos* and violence.

109. For lines 412ff. as enumerating the qualities of a good soldier, cf. Dover (1972) 44–45. They also recall, once again, Odysseus, first hero to make the word one of his principal weapons and to exemplify the effect of *gaster,* good and bad, on human life.

110. See Dover ad 417 and the scholia.

111. ἐπιχαλκεύειν (422) means forge on an anvil and its adjectival cognates are used of arms. Aristotle *Rh.* 1419b15 uses it in the context of rhetorical creation. The image here may be one of "honing" arguments or of forging the tongue to a weapon. Cf. 1108, 1110 and Taillardat 287.

112. For intrusion of food, literal or figurative, at awkward moments, see 262, 640, 648, 669, 675, and the repayment of Socrates at 1146. Some of these are discussed later. For Strepsiades' desire to save money, the motive of the drama, see the naming of his son, his definition of his own nature in lines 484ff., and his commendation of the sophists' intelligence, which they exemplify through their thrift, 833ff.

113. See Van Leeuwen, Starkie ad loc. For the many ancient citations of the Eupolis' passage, see PCG ad loc.

114. Note that Pericles' skill cannot escape the ambiguous nature of all (overly) persuasive speech. The magic of rhetoric operates on its hearers as a drug or incantation (κηλεῖν) driving them like animals.

115. The fragment is from *Demes*, in which Eupolis revived four famous statesmen of past Athenian greatness. For the connection between horse racing and rhetoric as ways to achieve political prominence, see the notes in chapter 2.

116. For the contrast between the clouds' offers and Strepsiades' "pettiness," see Segal (1975) 184. Cf. Schmid 219.

117. διολισθεῖν (434) is taken from the *palaistra*. It is compared by van Leeuwen and Starkie to *Knights* 491; cf. Taillardat 335ff. The pun on his name in 434 *(strepsodikesai)* and, less closely, in 450 *(strophis)* make the *logos* Strepsiades desires a reflection of his nature. For Strepsiades' name, see Marzullo passim, Dover xxv, Reckford (1967) 227ff.

118. Dover ad 445.

119. The form taken by Strepsiades' *"kleos"* is a comic consequence of his first lesson. In a world where moral evaluation is without authority, blame becomes praise, for it measures the impunity of the accomplished speaker. Cf. the *hetton logos* and Pheidippides (909, 1330). The continuum suggested here between Pericles and Strepsiades will be even more pointed at 1300ff. Cf. also 1201ff., where the antidemocratic possibilities of Eupolis' description will be exposed. Both of these passages are discussed in chapter 8.

120. See Fisher for the pnigos here, which he describes as: "a virtuoso piece of long-winded rhetoric as an example of the kind of γλῶττα he [Strepsiades] wants to master" (129).

121. For meter of 457–75, see Dover's discussion of 457–75. Fisher points out that lyric in praise of the previous speaker would be expected after the pnigos of Strepsiades' hopes (134). The abrupt switch to direct address is also "characteristic of encomiastic poetry" (Dover ad 459). Cf. also van Leeuwen and Starkie for the epic/tragic parody. This, coupled with the chorus' dance in the "high style of tragic lyric," would make a "mock heroic contrast to the small-minded hero" (Fisher 134). The different visions of Strepsiades and the chorus are mockingly fused in the ζηλωτότατος βίος (464) that Strepsiades is going to lead: the life of a wealthy rhetorical/legal consultant. Strepsiades will assume for others the same divine position the clouds hold for him (471 = 252), and for the same reason, he will furnish them with the ability to speak.

122. Strepsiades' alarmed response makes this clear: τειχομαχεῖν μοι διανοεῖ (481). Cf. Dover ad 481. Defensive walls were one of the distinguishing marks of the *polis*, frequently singled out in contexts of the contrast between the savage life outside/before and the civilized one inside/later. See Turato (1979) 71.

123. The *mechanai* are labeled as new intellectual tactics by *kainai* (480). For laws as walls, see Heraclitus' famous statement that men must fight for *nomos* as for the city walls (DK 22 B 44); for the inadequacy of city walls without the inner individual restraint necessary for community, Pl. *Prt.* 322b6ff.; for the parallel function of laws, which restrain men publicly, and religion, which works on them in private, DK 88 B 25. The image recurs for the traditional *kreitton logos* in 1024, discussed in chapter 5.

124. See Nussbaum for the loss of Strepsiades' cloak as the stripping away of "preconceptions" and "inconsistencies in his current beliefs" (74). She uses this to support her thesis that the Socrates of the *Clouds* is the historical, platonic Socrates. Cf. Tomin for platonic examples of stripping in dialogue.

125. *Physis* for Socrates was identified primarily with intellect and *psyche;* see Havel-

ock (1972), Nussbaum 70. For the sophistic optimism about the possibilities and benefits of education, see Jaeger 307ff.

126. For ὑφαρπάζειν (490) as the rhetorical strategy of "a speaker 'jumping in' to make a point before the person addressed can reply," see Dover ad 490, who cites Pl. *Euthd.* 300d.

127. For the use of the phallus in our play, see chapter 5.

128. See Green 19.

129. Socrates' response is as discouraging as the comment which elicited it. Apparently the philosophic life, devoted to the cultivation of speech, does not rely upon *logos* alone to maintain its position. Socrates is the first to exhibit an impulse that will be universal in the rest of the play, the desire to reinforce one's words with blows.

130. Numerous critics have pointed out the parodic resemblance of the *Clouds' phrontisterion*—with its mysteries (143, 824), goddesses, and initiation rites (254ff.)—to a cult. I will not add to this literature. For an outline of the problem, see Dover xli and ad 143 (where he cites parallel passages in Plato). Dover argues that the resemblance to a cult represents the exclusivity of the *phrontisterion* and the remoteness of its concerns and practices from those of everyday life. Turato (1972) 50, 53, 60ff., 101 argues for a political significance: a "religion" of atheism which would recall Anaxagoras, the limited circle familiar with his speculation (he cites Plu. *Nic.* 23), and the exclusivity of the oligarchic clubs: these are the mysteries of the young aristocrats.

Chapter 5

1. Contra Fisher 140, who believes the audience already knows that Strepsiades is incapable of learning sophistic rhetoric by this point in the play, and thus thinks he will fail.

2. See Whitman 132 for the comic heroes' possession and use of the "Unjust Discourse."

3. Clearly, I agree with Bowie about the parabasis' important role in the development of the themes around which the play is organized and its centrality in our understanding of aristophanic comedy (28). For those who hold the opposite view, see Bowie 28 n. 2. For the idea that the parabasis is a comic delaying action, see Fisher 151ff.

4. The fact that we do not have the first version of the *Clouds* is unfortunate, but not an insurmountable obstacle. We are told, for the purposes of our play, what should be considered its definitive virtues and how these contributed to its fate. For my views on the two versions of the *Clouds,* see the subsequent discussion and the Appendix.

5. For the *Hippolytus,* the only tragedy known with two versions, as similarly intertextual, see Goldhill (1986) 131ff., who shows that the full meaning of the second (our) version emerges only through comparison with the shape and defeat of the first.

6. See Dover ad 510–17.

7. It may be that we are to see a reference to rhetorical embellishment here, if χρωτίζειν (516) shares the rhetorical overtones of χρῶμα. This latter, according to LSJ, can mean style of writing or, in the plural, embellishments, or "colourable pretence" (χρῶμα IV). In the adjectival form, τὸ χρωματικός was "a form of rebuttal" (χρωματικός II.1).

8. As Sifakis has shown, the chorus assumes different "roles" in different sections of the parabasis taken in the larger sense: as comic chorus in the odes, as comic poet or comic chorus in the parabasis proper, and as its own dramatic character in the *epirrhemata* (37). Thus it would be misleading to discuss the larger parabasis in terms of the chorus'

character as clouds. Nor should the "I" of the parabasis proper, the persona of the comic poet, be taken as a soliloquy by the historical Aristophanes. It, too, is a comic creation, part and parcel of the play. For the "Aristophanes" of the *Acharnians* as "as much a literary construct as his hero," see Bowie 40ff.

9. For these as customary themes, see Sifakis 38ff.

10. Nussbaum interprets the parabasis as furthering the *Clouds'* portrayal of egocentric human nature. "Even the parabasis is in the first person, preoccupied not with public issues (as is the poet's more common practice) but with the poet's own personal grievances and merits" (94). However, this reading slights the actual content and phrasing of the parabasis and thus its clear relationship to the issues raised about *logos* in the rest of the play.

11. For the meanings of *sophrosyne* in this period, see North 85ff.

12. The interpretation of lines 537–44 is controversial; I accept Hubbard's view (presented in both his 1986 article and 1991 book) that this passage pertains only to the first version. For more complete discussion of lines 537–44, Hubbard's views, the two versions of the *Clouds,* and nature of the first *Clouds,* see the Appendix.

13. For παίειν (549) used of wordy warfare, cf. *Acharnians* 686. Starkie cites *Knights* 273, 454 as the passages referred to here (ad 549). Both of them use γαστρίζειν in a way that conflates physical and verbal force.

14. To his contemporaries this connection may not have been very surprising: "it was not for nothing that Kratinos (307) described a κομψὸς θεατής as ὑπολεπτολόγος γνωμοδιώκτης εὐριπιδαριστοφανίζων" (Dover ad 547, Cratinus is 342 PCG). As the scholia given in PCG point out, Aristophanes not only mocked but imitated and, from one perspective, was a member of the new intelligentsia, with Euripides in the dramatic vanguard, that he used in his plays. For Aristophanes' knowledge of sophistic rhetoric, see the works cited in chapter 4. For the *Acharnians'* similar linkage of the (fictional) poet of the parabasis and the action of the play, see Bowie 29ff.

15. See for example, Green 23, Spatz 53, Adkins.

16. See Dearden 113 for the failure of the first *Clouds* as due to the substitution of verbal wit for "grosser elements"; see also the Appendix.

17. See Henderson (1991) 74 for Strepsiades' taste in humor. Hubbard (1986) notes that almost all the second play's new "cheap comic devices . . . are connected with the behavior of Strepsiades" and perhaps the revision made "Strepsiades even more boorish and low-brow as a paradigm for the Athenian public" (194 n. 45). Even the favor accorded to the *Banqueters* can be worked into this negative assessment. As Fisher comments, "those who thought highly of a play in which a main character was a καταπύγων (presumably the sort of character used by the ἄνδρες φορτικοί) are not likely to give first prize to a much more sophisticated play" (154).

18. It should not be forgotten, however, that the audience(s) of the *Clouds* is as much a creation of the poet as any other character.

19. See Sifakis 60 for the general similarity of the parabasis and pnigos (lacking in the *Clouds*) to an epirrhema and pnigos of the agon in meter, use of the pnigos as "climactic conclusion to the respective parts," and agonistic function (one between characters, the other between poets). The opening of the two passages makes explicit the identity of their audiences. The parabasis begins ὦ θεώμενοι, κατερῶ πρὸς ὑμᾶς ἐλευθέρως / τἀληθῆ (518–19), while the agon starts (Κρ.) χώρει δευρί· δεῖξον σαυτὸν / τοῖσι θεαταῖς καίπερ θρασὺς ὤν. (Ητ.) ἴθ’ ὅποι χρῇζεις· πολὺ γάρ μᾶλλόν σ’ / ἐν τοῖς πολλοῖσι λέγων ἀπολῶ (889–92). But the *hetton's* response extends the implications of the agon, for he identifies the audience as the mob of Athenians at the assembly. It is there that they are called the "many" and are the condition for rhetorical success.

20. It is also a slogan and a virtue of political significance; see chapter 7.

21. For the behavior of the *kreitton* in the agon and Nussbaum's interpretation of Aristophanes' criticisms, see chapter 7.

22. See Dover ad 971 for the antiquity of the songs the boys learn and the unobjectionable, accepted nature of the "novelties" that are condemned.

23. For a somewhat related view, that Socrates and Aristophanes are alike in being misunderstood educators who have to limit their attention to a "select audience" but "Aristophanes differs from Socrates in that there is a moral dimension to his *sophia*: his comedy is not only *sophos* but also *sophron*," see Hubbard (1991) chapter 5. Because Hubbard (1991) believes that the parabasis is an act of disappointment, he also detects further similarity between the "disappointed poet . . . [and] his negative *alter ego* the ill-tempered philosopher," both are destructive, mutable, and mimetic, offering no constructive suggestions to fill the void left by their various *logoi* (chapter 5). Hubbard's reading of the parabasis as "an act of self criticism" is discussed later in this chapter.

24. For Aristophanes' comedy, which ridicules the *kreitton logos*, as itself the true "Just Speech," see Strauss 49, who, however, believes this means Aristophanes endorses Strepsiades' violence at the end. For Aristophanes' similar tactic in the agon of the *Frogs*—positioning his comedy and vision between Aeschylus and Euripides as embodying the virtues of both—see Walsh 95ff. For a different view of the agon of the *Frogs*—that in criticizing both Euripides and Aeschylus, Aristophanes presents comedy as an alternative—see Heiden, whose discussion of the *Frogs* reveals attitudes toward *logos* that overlap significantly with those in our play.

25. Reckford (1987) 397; cf. Hubbard (1986) 186ff. Reckford (1987) chapter 6 discusses this split at length in terms of fourth century analysis of comedy and the tendency of New Comedy to play to two different segments of the audience: the refined and the vulgar. This later comedy, perfected by Menander, "assumes, and builds on, a split between humor and seriousness, between higher and lower elements in human nature, and between the more refined and intelligent members of the audience, for whom Menander ultimately writes, and the numerous but insignificant remainder." (378) Reckford believes the *Clouds* is in the middle, a comedy of ideas in fifth-century form, an "old-and-new comedy" that indicates "how far Old Comedy had already traveled along the road of time." (386ff. esp. 388).

26. For Aristophanes' desire to carry his entire audience with him, see Fisher 178, Reckford (1987) 391.

27. Reckford (1987) reads the *Wasps* as Aristophanes' "healing" reaction to "this threatening split in the audience, in comedy, and even in himself" (397), a logical conclusion given his view that (excluding the parabasis proper) our *Clouds* is substantially identical with the first. However, the likelihood that the second *Clouds* was an independent and significantly revised work means our comedy, itself, could also perform this "healing." For the two versions of the *Clouds*, see the Appendix.

28. Hubbard (1986) has shown that lines 518–25 refer to "the entire audience, while the partitive genitive in v. 527 and the hypothetical condition of v. 535 seem to designate a more select group. Of course, the phrase τοῖς σοφοῖς in v. 526 is already ambiguous, being open to interpretation either as an appositive to ὑμῖν (in which case all of the audience are *sophoi*), or as an attributive adjective (in which case the general class designated by ὑμῖν is being limited here to those members who are *sophoi*)" (193 n. 43).

29. Fisher 158 points out the formal structure of these lines. I do not agree, however, with his interpretation.

30. In Pl. *Prt.* 337c2ff., Prodicus is shown distinguishing intellectual and bodily pleasure: εὐφραίνεσθαι μὲν γὰρ ἔστιν μανθάνοντά τι καὶ φρονήσεως μεταλαμβάνοντα αὐτῇ τῇ διανοίᾳ, ἥδεσθαι δὲ ἐσθίοντά τι ἢ ἄλλο ἡδὺ πάσχοντα αὐτῷ τῷ

σώματι. This seems to parallel the distinction in lines 560–62 between the types of plea-sure engendered by comedy: that of the wise and the more vulgar enjoyment of those who laugh as Strepsiades did in line 174 (ἤσθην γαλεώτῃ καταχέσαντι Σωκράτους).

31. For the progress of the beginning of the parabasis as encouraging the audience to identify with those (wise) who prefer Aristophanes, see Hubbard (1991) chapter 5.

32. I read this both as a statement about appreciation of aristophanic comedy in gen-eral, which the preceding lines have characterized as being distinguished by its novelty, and as particular encouragement to like the *Clouds,* distinguished in both versions by var-ious highly original inventions. Contra Hubbard (1991) chapter 5, who refers these lines to only the second *Clouds* and believes that Aristophanes is being ironic, since his "inven-tions" are traditional comic topoi.

33. As Muecke comments about audience address by the dramatic characters, "the audience which is drawn into the play is itself a hypothetical audience written into the play, at which the audience present in the theatre is invited to laugh, secure in its own ephem-erality" (57 n. 39). This observation is no less applicable to the *Clouds'* parabasis. For our parabasis not only addresses the spectators directly, but is set apart from the drama by structure, content, and the personae taken on by the chorus; thus it cannot help but break through the self-sufficient comic narrative, thematic and dramatic, to expose its fictionality (albeit through an equally fictional "reality" of its own).

34. Most recently Hubbard (1986) 189ff. has listed passages new in the second *Clouds* which exhibit features condemned in the parabasis. These are discussed in the Appendix and, most of them, in following chapters as well.

35. In fact, the line following the catalog of the first *Clouds'* virtues—which explicitly included refusal to mock bald men (540)—contains just such a joke. Line 545 asserts that in spite of the poet's excellence, "I will not put on (h)airs" (οὐ κομῶ; translation by Reckford [1987] 396). The pun at once mocks Aristophanes' probable baldness (for which, see Dover ad 540) and, since long hair was affected by thinkers and young aristocrats, uses the impossibility of his growing hair to assert that this new play will be neither unduly intellectual nor elitist. (See Dover ad 14 for the associations of long hair; Hubbard [1991] chapter 5, for the assertion of lowbrow revision.) This joke has been taken by Reckford ([1987] 396) and Murray (150) to prove the comic falsity of Aristophanes' claims to avoid the conventionally comic and the essential identity of the first and second versions. Yet this line itself, if conventional in humor and content, is new itself or, at least, embedded in a new parabasis, where it draws attention not to the substantial identity of the two plays but to their difference. For both sense and joke combine to provide immediate evidence that what we now watch will reverse the standards of the former play and employ exactly those traditional comic topoi that it rejected.

36. Hubbard (1986) 193. From this observation, Hubbard (1986) interprets the para-basis as Aristophanes' ambiguous apology and "self criticism," an uncomfortable recog-nition by the poet of "stylistic debasement," which he masks by "playing with his audi-ence, winking at its more perceptive members while deliberately confusing the majority" (193ff.). This reading has the merit of allowing us to accept what the parabasis is mani-festly doing: speaking about the superiority of the first *Clouds,* the ways in which it differed from the second, and why (the stupidity of the Athenian public). But it also leads Hubbard to accept the split in the audience which the parabasis seems to be trying to avoid and leaves the wise few with the difficulty discussed here: condemned to deny their merit by watching an inferior product.

37. We have no evidence that the second *Clouds* was ever performed, and the first *Clouds* seems to have been readily available along with the second. See the Appendix.

38. See chapter 2.

39. Cf. Pucci (1987) chapter 22.

40. See chapter 2 for the significant double meaning of this line and the possibility that it involved play with the phallus. In any case, the same point would have been made in line 196, which is agreed to have featured the phallus (see Hubbard [1986] 189 for references). Its inclusion there can now, with the wisdom of hindsight, be seen to make even more pointed the threatening disjunction between the world of the *phrontisterion,* with its concern for *logos* and speculation, and the world outside, dominated by the body, which in the person of Strepsiades has burst in upon them.

41. See Ambrosino (1983) 40ff. for another, more philosophical, view of the relationship between fact and discourse, and especially 41ff. for "speaking facts," which she interprets as expressing what is hidden or implicit in the *logos* itself.

42. It must be remembered that these wiser spectators exist comically, regardless of whether or not the experience assigned them matches that of any actual spectator. The second *Clouds'* persuasive strategy attempts to control responses to the parabasis and the drama, and we can trace this process. We cannot, of course, know if it was successful. It is frequently convenient to speak as if such spectators exist simply to avoid constantly stressing their merely potential nature.

43. Note εὖ φρονεῖν (562) and εὑρήμασιν (561), and see chapter 2 for the intellectual (and socratic) associations of *phrontis* and its cognates; Pl. *Tht.* 150d1, for philosophic *eurema*.

44. This is the positive side of the association of Socrates and Aristophanes discussed earlier.

45. See Sifakis 57.

46. Dover ad 563–74. For poetic vocabulary, see ὑψιμέδοντα 563, ἱππονώμαν 571.

47. Contra Segal (1975) 185, the content of the ode should not be taken as testimony about the nature of the clouds as characters, although the themes of the ode do incorporate elements of the plot. Hubbard (1991) follows Segal in believing that the clouds are associated with traditional religion in the parodos, here, and at the end. This view, that the clouds are supposed to be seen as legitimate goddesses, independent of their sophistic and comic role, pervades his assessment of the parabasis as essentially concerned with (fairly traditional) moral issues. He concludes "the breakdown of the relation between men and gods signalled by the whole syzygy is part of a broader breakdown of moral reckoning and social responsibility" (chapter 5). Fisher, on the other hand, sees a "tongue-in-cheek distortion of a conventional hymn" (161).

48. See Dover ad 563–74.

49. Scodel 335.

50. See Hubbard (1991) chapter 5 for the metrical echo of the parodos.

51. Both open with addresses to the audience that ironically refer to its intelligence and direct its attention to the legitimate grievances of the speaker(s). See Hubbard (1991) chapter 5.

52. The clouds' fulminations are again a stand-in for rhetoric. They "resemble in form the actual speeches of the Athenian lawcourts and of the assembly, and employ several common-place devices of the current fifth-century rhetoric" (Sifakis 120 n. 26). And, of course, they are addressed to the same audience; see the Introduction.

53. Given the status of thunder in the play, this may not seem too surprising, but here the comedy suppresses what we have learned about these heavenly rumblings in Strepsiades' lessons (discussed in chapter 4). For while comedy, and even verbal comedy, is not exempt from an analysis that makes of it nothing but the meaningless hot air that denotes and satisfies desire, this possible criticism is deflected by being fastened to only one type of comedy—the vulgar products of Aristophanes' rivals.

54. See Hubbard (1991) chapter 5. For the retention of this passage from the previous play, see Dover lxxx–xi and the sources cited by Hubbard. It should not be forgotten that, as Hubbard reminds us, to retain something from the first version—here mention of Cleon—is as significant as to delete it.

55. For the tanner Paphlagon as representing Cleon in the *Knights,* see Dover ad 581, *Knights* 44ff. and passim.

56. Of course, what follows traces not the Cleon of historical fact, but the comic Paphlagon/Cleon devised by Aristophanes. His prejudices and presuppositions have been described as both aristocratic (Dover ad 581, Henderson [1990] 298) and as profoundly democratic (Turato [1972], Ambrosino [1986–87]). This confusion may itself indicate the extent to which Aristophanes' point of view was not "political" per se, but comic. See the remarks of Whitman 5ff., chapter 7, and the Conclusion.

57. For the possibility that Aristophanes was the first to devote an entire drama to attacking one person, see Henderson (1990) 298.

58. Identified by the scholia; see Dover ad loc.

59. I follow Dover in taking 584–86 as referring to bad weather in general and not to lunar and solar eclipses; see ad 584 for reasons. However, even if reference is to the lunar eclipse of 10/29/425 and solar one of 3/21/424, this does not preclude taking the preceding lines as referring to the *Knights.*

60. See Hubbard (1991) chapter 5 for the similarity of the poet's role and that which the chorus claims for itself.

61. As has been noted from the scholiasts on, *Clouds* 591ff. recalls *Knights* 956. The charges of bribery and theft are ubiquitous in the *Knights.* Dover (ad loc.) notes that the stocks are also mentioned for Paphlagon in *Knights* 1048.

62. As Reckford points out, the parabasis' complaints about the victory of Cleon "despite the terrible weather portents, and as Aristophanes implies, despite everything he had shown them in the *Knights* . . . is already a rueful admission that their shared victory, and perhaps the understanding behind it, remained incomplete" (1987) 392. But he does not see the larger thematic connection to the *Clouds'* preoccupation with (failed) *logos,* discussing it only from the perspective of the historical Aristophanes and his personal difficulties with a changing audience. Henderson (1990) also accepts Aristophanes' desire for a political effect and believes that the success of the *Knights* manifested the *demos'* latent reservations about Cleon (298ff.). The historical situation is irrecoverable, but, in any case, would not detract from the thematic reading proposed.

63. For Cleon's stormy rhetoric, see chapter 4.

64. See chapter 4 for the Sausage Seller's cooking up of speech.

65. See Sifakis 57–58 for the cultic form of the odes.

66. Scodel 335 notes the contrast between ode and antode. "If Aether can be 'our father' only to clouds, Athena is 'our goddess' only to Athenians." The antode sees the divinities invoked, Apollo, Artemis, Athena, Dionysos, "from the point of view of human worshippers." This change in perspective, and thus in the "identity" of the chorus being emphasized, parallels the similar shift between the first and second stanzas of parodos. However, as Hubbard (1991) points out, Athena, who appears in the position parallel to Aether in the first stanza, is the daughter of *metis* and thus "identified with the realms of intellect and craftsmanship," but from a more "conservative" social/civic aspect (chapter 5).

67. Fisher 169.

68. Contra Newiger (1957), who believes that the epirrhema and particularly the antepirrhema show that the divine world mingles with the human (72). Hubbard (1991) believes

that it portrays the indifference to custom characteristic not just of the new intellectuals but of the new politicians, while marking the clouds as socially conservative (chapter 5).

69. The comic Athens is, of course, fictional, like every other element in the comedy. Whatever relationship to the historical city and its inhabitants that can be detected will be determined by Aristophanes' vision.

Chapter 6

1. See Jaeger, "The new *techné* is clearly the systematic expression of the principle of shaping the intellect, because it begins by instruction in the form of language, the form of oratory, and the form of thought" (314).

2. Fisher 174.

3. Starkie (ad 658) aptly cites Pl. *Euthd.* 277d1ff. which combines the metaphors of wrestling and initiation with the study of correctness of names in a way very pertinent to the *Clouds*. As Socrates mockingly puts it, the interrogation of Clinias about learning (which turns on two different meanings of the word) is the youth's initiation into the sophistic mysteries. For linguistic theory as aiming at creation of a victoriously persuasive *orthos logos,* see Classen 220ff. on Protagoras.

4. For sophists in general and Protagoras in particular, see Pl. *Cratylus* 391b4 (384b2 also mentions Prodicus). For specific passages and sophistic figures invoked in our passage, see van Leeuwen, Starkie, Dover ad loc. In general, see, among others, Guthrie 204ff., Classen (who believes the study of grammar and diction had strictly rhetorical application), Kerferd chapter 7 (who believes that it had broader philosophical significance). For reform of grammar and gender, thinkers varied in approach and in views. Guthrie points out that *orthoepeia* and correctness of names may have been different fields of study, with various thinkers taking positions corresponding to their views about knowledge and reality (205ff.).

5. For correspondence with reality, see Kerferd 73, Guthrie 219–20; for gender, Guthrie 221. These were not the only ways current of seeking precision in language. While Protagoras seems to have corrected traditional speech, Prodicus may have proceeded on the basis of meaning and popular usage (Pl. *Prt.* 341a9, Classen 232ff.).

6. See Guthrie 219ff., Classen 224ff. The effectiveness of such correct language is parodically demonstrated by Pheidippides' discussion of the due day of debts, and a mockery of the same process is seen in Strepsiades' interaction with the first creditor.

7. See Green 20–21.

8. Socrates neither knows nor cares about what everybody knows concerning Cleonymos and Ameinias. Rather, he uses these names as words, giving them as examples of the structure of a logical language where male names (or nouns) end in *-os,* female ones in *-e* or *-a,* and where male beings will have male names. For the contemporary lack of distinction between names, nouns, words in general, and even sentences, cf. Kerferd 70. Line 755 provides another example of socratic ignorance of the crucial interaction between social and natural reality—there the connection between the phases of the moon and the payment of debts, a connection meaningless in natural terms, but all-important in social ones. For another view of the relationship between comedy and what "everybody knows," see Henderson (1990) 295ff.

9. For Strepsiades' concrete orientation, see Green passim.

10. See Fisher 174ff., Henderson (1991) 74ff.

11. Nussbaum 94.

12. For the socratic (and sophistic) aspects of this scene, see, among others, Havelock

(1972) 11ff., Dover and Starkie ad loc., Schmid 220ff., Fisher 120. The essential lines of the parody are not much changed whether we believe with Dover (ad 700–706) that the advice is given by the clouds, or accept the manuscript tradition that Socrates also speaks.

13. See Fisher 180.

14. The song is not only full of philosophical language, but the final lines seem "highly poetic" (Fisher 180) and parody epic/lyric diction with γλυκύθυμος, φρῆν, ὄμμα. All these devices heighten the comic contrast between Strepsiades' hypothetical experience and his actual one.

15. See Dover (ad 702) for this bit of stage business, noted since the scholia.

16. See commentators ad loc. Dover comments about 711–15 that the "combination of symmetry and assonance to this degree is unusual, although there are comparable passages in Comedy." Thus, the exaggeration of the tragic form, as well as its contents, ensure that we will not fail to realize that what we have is comedy.

17. For "Aristophanes' " speech in Pl. *Smp.* 189c2 as platonic (re)reading of the comic movement from head to genitals and mind to desire, see Reckford (1987) section 8.

18. Nussbaum 75.

19. For *-ikos* and *-tris,* see the commentators ad loc.

20. Dover ad 729.

21. The motive for Strepsiades' prolonged silence is in obvious contrast to those of Socrates' famous withdrawals as described, for example, in Pl. *Smp.* 220c3.

22. Dover ad 729.

23. See scholia ad 734; Dover has another suggestion.

24. See Hubbard (1986) 189 n. 29.

25. Dover ad 734.

26. Henderson (1991) 37. Acknowledging that Strepsiades' words open him to ridicule for an ignorance and stupidity that would also disqualify him from appreciation of our comedy does not mean we cannot enjoy this line as a moment of true self-expression, which, for an instant, gloriously renders philosophic assumptions and Socrates equally foolish.

27. See Henderson (1991) who comments about primary obscenities: "Unlike other kinds of words that indicate sexual and excretory functions, they are incapable of nuance or multiple shades of meaning; they are simply equal-signs cutting through social barriers and pointing directly toward, and invoking in the listener, the basic emotions adhering to the organs and acts themselves" (38). Henderson, however, sees our passage as an example of the use of "primary obscenities for throw-away laughs" (39).

28. For 197 see chapter 3; for *pragma*/penis, Henderson (1991) 116.

29. *Physis* was also a common euphemism for *peos;* see Schreckenberg 58, Henderson (1991) 5. The implications of this are obvious. Cf. Spatz 52.

30. It may seem that Strepsiades' first attempt to think about his πράγματα and Socrates' first problem cover the same ground. However Strepsiades' question of 736, asking about what he should cogitate, indicates that he did not understand the goal of his first meditation to be anything so specific. That Socrates likewise was not considering Strepsiades' mundane concerns is clear in his response. In 737 he once again asks what Strepsiades wants to learn. This small misunderstanding echoes the greater one about the goal of human existence and the purpose of thinking. Cf. Starkie ad 736.

31. See Dover ad 757 for the view that this is "indiscriminate ridicule of intellectuals."

32. See Green 21 n. 19, Fisher 181.

33. The wild mixture which ensues is another case of Strepsiades' talent for combining the worst of all the worlds he lives in. This talent, already demonstrated by the outcome

of his marriage and the naming and upbringing of his son, will also evidence itself at the end of the play. For the traditional aspects of Strepsiades' solutions, see Woodbury 118ff., Green 21. An analysis restricted to their traditional aspects, however, cannot account for Socrates' approval of Strepsiades' first two solutions or for the difference between these and his last attempt, which fails.

34. In fact, it was observation of the late phase of the moon (16ff.) that prompted Strepsiades to begin his scheme. See Dover for the correlation of the Attic month and the moon, and their relationship to the payment of interest (ad 17).

35. The powerful language of spells and incantations was a paradigm in many sources for the sophistic power of words both because of the power it bestowed on its speakers and because of its ability to change human reality. Cf. Gorgias' *Encomium* 10, de Romilly chapters 1 and 2, Entralgo chapter 2. For Thessalian witches used again in the context of a discussion of rhetoric and the power of words, see Pl. *Grg.* 513a6ff. Gorgias (*Encomium* 14) compared the action of *logos* to that of a *pharmakon,* an image that became a popular positive or negative description of its powers in the hands of the sophists. Cf. Eur. *Hipp.* 478–79, for conjunction of spells and *pharmakon,* which are the nurse's current speech to Phaedra and her later one to Hippolytus; see Turato (1976) 168ff., Goff 48ff. For the platonic use of the notion of the *pharmakon* of *logos,* see de Romilly 35. For the mirror as associated with seduction and the goddess Peitho, see Buxton 45. Note that the idea of *pharmaka* recurs at 766, where Strepsiades imagines finding his remedy at the drug sellers.

36. For a different reading of Socrates' approval, see Strauss 26.

37. See Starkie ad 764 who comments that ἀφάνισιν is "a jest καθ᾽ ὁμωνυμίαν since he [Strepsiades] takes ἀφανίζειν (759) in its natural sense (='to delete')."

38. Green notes that Alcibiades is represented as "having erased the record of a charge by rubbing it off with a dampened finger" (21 n. 18). Thus, in a certain sense, Strepsiades' solution employs the most up-to-date methods.

39. For the sophistic flavor of *antidikon,* see Woodbury 122.

40. Starkie notes (ad 762) that the metaphor inherent in ἀποχάλα (762) was "developed in Plato, *Phaedo,* 81 A, where Socrates describes true philosophy as a μελέτη θανάτου, which the soul may practise by fleeing from the body and having no communication with it, but συνηθροισμένη αὐτὴ εἰς ἑαυτήν, and meditating on heaven." Thus, in one sense, Strepsiades' solution accurately reflects the philosophically approved approach to earthly problems. The mind finally decisively wins the competition between it and the body.

41. For example, see Strauss 27. It has also been taken as evidence for spotty revision on the grounds that this approach has already been tried and rejected; see Dover xcv. As will be clear, I find the clouds' and Strepsiades' exchange thematically apt.

42. (Στ.) ἀλλ᾽ ὦ Νεφέλαι, χρηστόν τι συμβουλεύσατε. / (Χο.) ἡμεῖς μέν, ὦ πρεσβῦτα, συμβουλεύομεν (793–94). The tragic rhythm (cf. Dover ad 794) of the clouds' response also reflects the paratragedy of Strepsiades' self-pity (791ff.).

43. Note that he fails as he had anticipated because he is old and forgetful, incapable of learning the fine points of the *logos:* 785ff. (esp. 790) recall 129ff.

44. As Dover ad 802 points out, 802 picks up the threat of 123.

Chapter 7

1. I have followed Dover's identification of the *logoi* as *kreitton* and *hetton,* rather than the more prejudicial *dikaios* and *adikos* (lvii).

2. See Strauss: "Socrates has no awareness of his dependence on the city . . . he

has not reflected on the context of his own doing'' (49). Strauss refers mainly to Socrates'
need for the city to replenish his group, but the principle remains the same.

3. See Nussbaum 64ff., discussed later in this chapter.

4. One of the marks of sophistic rhetoric is its power over a crowd, and this is its
natural arena. Interpreted negatively, as in Pl. *Grg.*, it comes to mean that rhetoric is
powerful only before a crowd, and thus, by extension, only over the ignorant. Cf. Eur.
Hipp. 983ff., cited by the commentators ad 892, where Hippolytus' programmatic claim of
inability to speak before a crowd debunks Theseus' (sophistic) rhetoric and denies his
charge of sophistry (953ff.). This polemic is suggested in our passage by the *kreitton*'s
insistence that the audience is made up of fools (898), presumably because of their susceptibility to the *hetton logos*.

5. Newiger (1957) comments on this line, "wir denken eher an einen Ringkampft,
der durch das 901 gebrauchte Verbum empfohlen wird" (139), and notes that the wrestling
imagery recalls the *kataballontes logoi* of Protagoras, whom he thinks the model for the
hetton logos (141ff.). As he points out, Protagoras' nickname *Logos* is reminiscent of the
hetton logos' self-identification in line 893, while the programmatic use of *antilegein* (and
the rhetorical term *anatrepein*, for which see Ambrosino [1983] 32) definitively label the
hetton logos, from the start, as the personification of sophistic—Newiger would add protagorean—rhetoric (138ff.). This is much more specific and thematically apt than the more
general invocations of violence commonly associated with agons, for which see Taillardat
335ff.

6. Note that the *kreitton logos* uses the old-fashioned verbal violence of obscene and
shaming insult (see Henderson [1991] 10ff. for this kind of obscene verbal aggression),
which the *hetton logos* relishes as tribute to his skill (cf. Strepsiades' similar attitude in
443ff.) and proof that the *kreitton* is so out of date as to be ignorant of the true location of
the power of speech. Conversely, when the *hetton* tries to insult the *kreitton* by calling him
archaic, the *kreitton* is unmoved.

7. It is, of course, impossible to prove the *kreitton*'s visible martial vigor, but it would
follow our comedy's practice of staging physically what is implicit theoretically. For the
contrast in the attitudes of the *logoi* toward physical training, see Dover lix.

8. See Nussbaum, who (following Dover lviiiff.) states, "*kreitton* suggests that the
strength of custom and convention are the backing for that Speech's position" (50 n. 15).
Strauss sees the role of force and its association with the city, but only in the context of
the end of the play, where he believes that Strepsiades' force is justified (49).

9. The *hetton* and the *kreitton logos* thus begin to recapitulate the drama of Thucydides and Pericles in their wrestling match discussed in chapter 1. One wins physically, but
before he can exploit his victory, the (unacknowledged) superior power of the crowd creates an arena in which the force of language can reverse the outcome.

10. For (sophistic) speech compared to arrows and projectiles, see Taillardat 282ff.
and Pl. *Tht.* 180a (cited by Dover ad 943). The stings of the chorus of the *Wasps,* their
rhetorical/physical *kentra* (*Wasps* 407, 420), also consist, at least in part, of contemporary
inflammatory rhetoric—words like "*demos*-hater," "tyranny," and "conspirator" (for example, 463ff.). With these the chorus plans to sting the eyes and the *proktos* of those who
oppose them (430ff.). There may also be reference to another kind of killing speech—
iambic poetry. These verses were said to sting like wasps and to have the power to kill
their victims. Cf. Elliott 3ff.

11. For the martial use of περιδεξίος meaning ambidextrous, that is, able to throw a
spear with either hand, see *Il.* 21.163. Starkie (ad 952) comments on γνωμοτύποις, "a
feature of Sophistic style (especially Prodicus and Polus) to which reference is often made
in Aristophanes." It "seems to have been a cant phrase in refined circles (*Eq.* 1379,

Thesm. 55, where it is an attribute of Agathon, who was Prodicus' pupil [Plato, *Prot.* 315 E], *Ran.* 877).'' For μερίμνα as "associated with the grubbing methods of the Sophists,'' cf. Starkie ad 101. Later, as he begins his actual refutation of the *kreitton logos,* the *hetton logos* again associates his rhetoric with violence: in 1037, he states that speaking contrary to law and custom, he will throw the opinions of his opponent into confusion (συνταρά-ξαι, which can be a military term); in 1047, he resumes the common image of a wrestling hold (Taillardat 337).

12. For an outline of their views, and the comic contrast between their claims and the likely situation in contemporary Athens, see Dover lixff.

13. Nussbaum passim; the quotations are from 50 and 94.

14. See Ostwald 260ff.; for our play 265ff.; Nussbaum 52ff., and the commentators. Indeed, this type of argument seems to have become so standard, it is hard to see how Aristophanes could have staged a convincing debate about and by sophistic *logoi* without according it pride of place. Further it will play into his comic project, as we shall see.

15. Certainly the *hetton logos'* position is no surprise. See Nussbaum 65, North 97 for his general resemblance to Thrasymachus and Callicles; the commentators, for specific points of similarity.

16. The political implications of the contrasted values of the *logoi* are discussed later in this chapter.

17. The values associated with the *kreitton logos* seem very close to those North suggests as characteristic of Antiphon's quite traditional approach to *sophrosyne* (88ff.). See also Dover ad 971 for the *kreitton* "condemning as a modern innovation something with which Ar. himself had grown up.''

18. This obviously parallels the *kreitton's* willingness to use violence earlier, a recourse to force that can be justified as benefiting the pupil; see 1409ff. The accepted violence of education in shaping the individual to the social norm is also acknowledged by Pl. *Prt.* 325c3ff., when Protagoras compares educating a child to correcting warped wood—both must be beaten into shape. A key function of this process is, of course, enforcement of a particular language and along with it a certain set of values. Thus physical violence again replaces *logos* and persuasion, a procedure not foreign to our comic sophists; see 492ff. and Pheidippides' attempt to ensure respect for Euripides in 1377ff. Cf. Nussbaum's interesting analysis of the *kreitton's* position through analogy to "The Enforcement of Morals'' by Lord Devlin (58ff.).

19. Nussbaum 54. She points out the use of plurals, indefinite singulars, and the imperfect to describe the *kreitton logos'* education.

20. See Nussbaum 55.

21. Nussbaum points out that the *kreitton logos'* "disdain for reason . . . leaves him without the ability to argue or improvise, he is ill-equipped to compete with his sophistical opponent in a contest of words. The contest that superficially presents itself as an even debate is actually conducted on the terms of Anti-Right with his chosen weapons, words, and in a place where he and not Right would feel at home: a school of philosophy and rhetoric. For Right to appear as Right Speech is for him to be immediately at a disadvantage'' (62). In fact, the *kreitton's* position is not really arguable; it is a fixed truth. Debate about the content of τὰ δίκαια, as opposed to their application, destroys their unique and compelling status. Cf. Nussbaum 58.

22. Fisher points out that the audience knows from the beginning of the agon, when he speaks first, that the *kreitton logos* will lose (196, 199). Thus the interest is not so much in what he says, as in how he is refuted.

23. Nussbaum 52.

24. Significantly, the very first point on which the *hetton* engages the *kreitton logos* is the permissibility of hot baths (1044), not of rhetoric or speculation.

25. "In the world of Anti-Right, this lack of respect in the service of personal satisfaction becomes an ideal, displacing *sōphrosynē* (cf. 1068–70)" (Nussbaum 65; cf. Dover ad 1068).

26. For Socrates' philosophical and educational responsibilities, see, among others, Nussbaum, Strauss; for his political and historical ones, Turato (1972). Nussbaum points out that Socrates remains responsible for the actions of his students, at least by the standards of the platonic Socrates, even if he never actively asserts views like those of the *hetton logos* (47).

27. The verb σκιρτᾶν in the following passage may have a special affinity with the picture of human nature out of control and thus approximating its animal counterparts. Cf. Pl. *R.* 571c6 and *Wasps* 1305.

28. See commentators ad loc. for parallel passages. For *eros* as the particular expression of natural *anagke* governing man and the other animals alike, see Schreckenberg 51ff., esp. 57.

29. Vernant (1981a) 54.

30. Goldhill (1986) 127 on the *Hippolytus*.

31. See Turato (1976) 165ff. for the similarities of these to each other and to the *hetton logos* in the *Clouds*. North compares the role of *eros* here to that which it plays in the *Encomium* and Eur. *Hipp.* 433–81; it is an "irresistible force" which "deprives man of the power of controlling his passions" (93). Thus it has obvious parallels to the irresistible force of *logos* which can have similar effects.

32. See Dover ad 1083.

33. For this as the standard rhetorical strategy when the facts were indisputable, see Murphy 96ff. This is also the approach taken by the exemplary adulterer, who, caught in the act, argues that he has done nothing unjust.

34. That being "radished" and having one's pubic hairs plucked out could be, and was intended to be, painful as well as humiliating is shown by Xenophon's remark that this was to suffer κακά τε καὶ αἰσχρά (X. *Mem.* 2.1.4–5, cited by Dover ad 1083). Xenophon's statement occurs in a discussion that considers adultery not different from heedless animal lust.

35. Dover ad 1087.

36. See de Carli 16ff.

37. See Fisher 203 for the various types of humor in this passage.

38. For military terminology, cf. Dover ad 1104.

39. See Fisher, "Aristophanes makes it clear as the debate proceeds that in fact neither Argument is any better than the other" (193 and chapter 10 passim).

40. For these characterizations of the *logoi*, see chapter 5. For the repressive nature of the *kreitton logos'* views and the incompatibility of his actions with liberty, see Nussbaum 58–62. She contrasts this with the "comic poet of the parabasis [who] has claimed the right 'to speak the truth without constraint' (*eleutheros*, 518) before the audience" (61).

41. Henderson (1991) 76. See also Fisher, "the comedy lies in the incongruity between the formality and supposed moral superiority of the speech and the pathetic situation or 'inferiority' of the speaker (198).

42. For the *kreitton's* instrumental view of virtue, as a means to bodily pleasure, see Nussbaum 56, 64. For his continuous betrayal of his real views, see Fisher chapter 10 passim. For this hedonistic calculus as the typical argument used in debating conduct and *sophrosyne* in particular, see North 96.

43. See Pl. *Prt.* 323b2 where Protagoras is made to assert that even if people are unjust, they hate those who admit to being unjust and think them mad.

44. Thus we witness "the role of irrational passions in maintaining the fabric of convention" (Nussbaum 58). But the *Clouds* will go further: not just conventional *logos* but any *logos* is subject to desire and to the desire to enforce.

45. See MacDowell (1980) 124, Dover ad 1077, and Lysias 1.5, 1.26ff., 1.34ff., 1.49ff. for the law that the husband could kill an adulterer taken in the act. In Lysias, the prosecution does not dispute the law, but apparently argues that the murdered man was not taken in the act of adultery but was entrapped, alleging that he was dragged into the house and fled to the hearth (Lys. 1.27ff.) after being summoned by the husband (Lys. 1.37).

46. That the power of speech (whether to dispense just verdicts or argue what justice may be) can be exercised only in the absence of violence is clear in Homer and Hesiod and is also a tenet of fifth-century democracy, which prized the equality and freedom of speech in Athens both as proof and foundation of the city's greatness. See chapter 1.

47. The mark of the traditional young man educated by the *kreitton* is to hate the agora and baths (991). This *logos*' preeminently civic products are visualized as resident in nature, or at least an idealized natural setting, with a body at the peak of its physical strength (1002ff.). But this world is enjoyed in a sociable way, with a companion (1006). Conversely the *hetton* praises the agora (1055) and his followers are assumed to spend all their time there (1003). This topos appears also in the *Knights*. In *Knights* 217ff., the fact that the Sausage Seller is ἀγοραῖος is one of his principal qualifications for sophistic δημαγωγικά (note fashionable ending in -*ikos*) and, later, the resurrected Demos resolves to send hunting (the peacetime equivalent of war) all the effeminate sophistic young men who haunt the agora babbling the latest intellectual buzz words (*Knights* 1369ff.). In Pl. *Phdr.* 230c6ff., Socrates also expresses his devotion to the city and his inexperience with the natural world, this time in positive terms.

48. As said above, if the adulterer were to persuade the husband that adultery was no crime, this view would become the new *kreitton logos,* privately, and perhaps eventually publicly. The city would then condone practice, not punishment. However, before this point is reached, the key issue is not verbal technique, but finding or creating an audience willing to listen and be persuaded while adultery is still a crime with the particular character described above.

49. The comic sophists, no less than the *kreitton logos,* are unattached to liberty and ready to enforce their opinions. Socrates thought of beating Strepsiades for his lack of respect (493ff.); Pheidippides will do so.

50. See Dover (ad loc.) and Stone (1980) who note that the second plural verb forms in the last speech of the *kreitton logos* (1102) address the *hetton logos* and the audience together (322).

51. As Nussbaum observes, "the concluding series of jokes about *euryprōktoi* urges us to see our leaders, our poets and ourselves as passive hedonists waiting to be stimulated" (64).

52. Again Nussbaum comments, "When Anti-Right enjoins young men to ignore *sōphrosynē* and develop the use of the tongue (1058–62), it is not only as the instrument of speech" (64).

53. For Aristophanes' equal distance from the *kreitton logos,* see chapter 5.

54. The word is *taxis, Encomium* 14. There is also the question how any *logos,* or opinion, becomes implanted in the soul if not by the kind of mechanism suggested by Gorgias. Nussbaum provides an answer taken from Plato and Aristotle which can be summed up as moral habituation and practice (87ff.). In a parodic way this is also the kind of approach suggested by the *kreitton logos.*

55. See *Encomium* 13. Cf. Reckford (1976) 233.

56. The wrestling of the *logoi* thus becomes a sport without implications, like that of the agon here. The audience is theatrically disengaged, watching from seats safe in a *kreitton*-structured world, which no argument alone will persuade them to vacate. In this context, the *hetton logos* cannot win a true victory, entailing a change in the convictions of the listeners, and contrary to rhetorical theory, the *kreitton logos* remains stronger even in "defeat." Thus we can see that Strepsiades' strange formulation at the beginning of the play is prophetic of this ordinary reaction.

57. Nussbaum 68.

58. For the mouth as a weapon to be forged, cf. scholia ad 1108, Taillardat 287. Strepsiades picks up the metaphor at 1160. Contra Woodbury, who believes it is a metaphor from schooling horses (124).

59. Gelzer (1960) notes that while the chorus designates Pheidippides as arbitrator, Strepsiades gives the final judgement (16 n. 1, 50). This break in the formal structure of the agon surely underlines Pheidippides' lack of involvement in what is happening ostensibly for his benefit.

60. The common understanding of the comic agon and its complete structure, the diallage (defined by Gelzer [1960] 47ff.), is that it resolves strife between the principal characters. More recently, Long has reviewed the agones and comments, "the paradox in the use of the agon in Aristophanes is not that he goes out of his way to introduce the agon—with or without a diallage—but that, having introduced a form eminently adapted to persuasion, he never allows the outcome of the agon to dictate the course of action in the rest of the play" (286ff.). This would concur with our interpretation. Long, however, finds the failure of the *Clouds'* agon to be Strepsiades' continuing wish that Pheidippides learn both arguments rather than only the victorious *hetton* (295).

61. North 98. For the *kreitton*'s positions, see Dover, who notes that by the *Clouds*, Marathon was deep in the past (lxiii), while the musical "innovations" the *kreitton logos* is represented as condemning were things with which Aristophanes and his contemporaries had grown up (ad 971). This chronological distance and extremely old-fashioned super-reactionary cultural stance make sure we understand the *kreitton*'s conservativism to be a parody.

62. See Carter chapter 2, 46 for our agon.

63. See Carter chapter 3, summed up on 76; cf. Ostwald 235. The militarism and rigid discipline of the *kreitton logos* may also recall a typically Spartan and oligarchic version of *sophrosyne*. For as North has shown, in Thucydides' portrait of the international scene not only is the word *sophrosyne* generally associated with Sparta and oligarchs but so is its coupling with respect for the laws, *aidos, apragmosyne,* and *hesychia,* or that leisure enjoyed by the noble youth taking his ease away from the city (102ff.). Meanwhile, the Athenians while not ceding the notion of moderation (usually called *metrios*), seem "reluctant" to use the word, and instead lay claim to restlessness, daring, and intelligence (100ff.). Later the oligarchic governments discredited such claims to *sophrosyne,* and in the fourth century the term was claimed by the democrats (116ff. and chapter 4).

64. See Ps. Xenophon *Constitution of the Athenians* 1.5 and 1.13. In 1.5, he contrasts the vice of the *demos* to the virtue of the "best," naturally least inclined to loss of control and injustice. I owe this parallel to an anonymous reader. For Cleon's reversal of this criticism, see Ostwald 258.

65. Ostwald 229, 236.

66. See Th. 3.37.3 and 38.2ff. For (the thucydidean) Cleon's embrace of "Spartan" values, see North 107ff., who believes it marks the second stage in the thucydidean picture of the deterioration of Greece; Ostwald 253ff. For the distrust of *logos* in his speech, see chapter 1.

67. Thus Ostwald finds that the "contest between Right and Wrong bears eloquent testimony to the social polarization that the new intellectualism brought about *vis-a-vis* the old, traditional values," and evidently places the *kreitton logos* on the side of the democratic "establishment" (273). See Ostwald 250ff., 273 for the "establishment mentality" and the challenges to it that emerged in the latter half of the fifth century; 257ff. for the hostility between establishment figures, including Cleon, and young sophistic speakers. In keeping with this, the *kreitton logos* is not portrayed with the openly Spartan leanings and affectations that were a badge of those disaffected with the democracy.

68. For citation of views that make the *hetton logos* a democratic figure, see Turato (1972) 95ff. and cf. Henderson (1990) n. 17, 296. For the *demos'* indifference to sport and music, see Ps. Xenophon cited in n. 64; obviously, the *hetton logos* does not share the *amathia* attributed there to the *demos*.

69. For the manipulation of socratic/sophistic views and skills for personal ends by power-hungry young, and largely aristocratic, men, see Xenophon's defense of Socrates against this charge in X. *Mem.* 1.2.12ff., Turato (1972) 29ff., 44ff., 65ff., 97ff., esp. 101ff. See also Ambrosino (1986–87) 123ff. for the antidemocratic stance and implications of the *hetton logos*. For the relationship between Alcibiades and Pheidippides, see the notes to chapter 2. That such men were of the upper class did not hinder their attacks on others of this class. Carter comments: the "politicians and lawyers, who in reality constituted a threat to the 'rich quietists', and who used the legal machinery of writs and summonses as a ladder to their own political advancement, were in fact themselves from the same cultural and financial background as those they were attacking" (125).

70. See, for example, Nussbaum 65, North 96ff., Turato (1972) Appendix.

71. See North 96ff.

72. For the junction of Critias and Alcibiades as both excessively ambitious and driven to Socrates for the same reason—desire for the power attainable through rhetorical skill— see X. *Mem.* 1.2.12ff. On Callicles, see Ostwald 244ff., who notes "the paradox of Callicles' politics suggests that he caters to the people's whims not because he believes in the principle of popular sovereignty but because he thinks that one can attain power only by manipulating the despicable rabble" (247). For a group of men in the 420s who similarly joined lack of "sympathy for the *demos* and its leaders," with exploitation of the possibilities offered by the democratic city, see Ostwald 232ff. Ostwald points out that the evidence for "oligarchic clubs" with specific revolutionary intentions is slight for this period, but that the *Knights* and *Wasps* show popular suspicion of these young men. See also Turato (1972) 106ff. A little later Alcibiades became the model of this kind of behavior; see Ostwald chapter 6.

73. For a more derogatory reading of the reasons that such men can manipulate the *demos*, see chapters 1 and 4. This picture of a purely instrumental and antidemocratic *logos* is corroborated in 1201ff., where Strepsiades' possession of the *hetton logos* (in the person of his son) leads him to abandon democratic ideals like *isonomia* for a dream of personal rule. See chapter 8.

74. I have concentrated on the *hetton logos*, but, as discussed in chapter 5, it is clear that position of the *kreitton* is equally contradictory and parodic. For the parodic "nonsense" in the *kreitton's* argument, see Dover lxiiiff., lxvi; for more philosophical difficulties, Nussbaum 58ff., who, criticizing this *logos* within the sphere of *nomos* (rather than opposing *nomos* to *physis* as does the agon), concludes, "it may be that we cannot so lightly dispense with reason, in education and in public life, if we are to preserve our *nomoi* and our heritage" (60).

75. Ostwald 246ff.; see also Turato (1972) 118 for a summary of views that make of Callicles either an extreme oligarch or fervent democrat.

76. Thus the *kreitton logos* can be referred to as *anēr* (1033) and both are comically

portrayed not abstractly but as characters with the full panoply of human faults. Cf. Fisher 193.

77. Of course, sexual conduct has political overtones, particularly in comedy, yet these are not altogether easy to trace, while the agon seems not to exploit the well-known link between homosexuality and Spartan sympathies.

78. See Dover lxivff., Henderson (1991) 217ff.

79. This would make Aristophanes close to the Periclean ideal, and, in fact, the fracturing of the (parodic) ideal citizen implicit in the comically contrasted *hetton* and *kreitton logoi* has many parallels with the similar process North has discussed for Thucydides; see 109ff. Strauss also believes that the *kreitton logos* is "justly defeated" and the "true Just Speech is the *Clouds*" because it is based on "knowledge of the nature of man" (49), however, for very different reasons and with the conclusion that Strepsiades is correct in destroying the *phrontisterion*. For the many types of polarization characteristic of Athens in the 420s, see Ostwald chapter 5.

Chapter 8

1. See Ussher 9.

2. Spatz 55.

3. In contrast to the parabasis proper, in the second parabasis the appeal to the judges to decide ἐκ τῶν δικαίων (1116) is heavily ironic and openly betrays the role of justice as a rhetorical ploy. Such an appeal is just verbal superstructure to a contest that is being waged on other grounds. In the courts, the arena to which the whole passage alludes, no one fails to urge the justice of his position—to establish it is the task of both the *kreitton* and (from another perspective) the *hetton logos*. Even Strepsiades tries this trick with his creditors in 1137ff.

4. I read ὑμῖν instead of ἡμεῖς, because, unlike Dover (ad 1116), I find the highly rhetorical flavor of this reading (cf. Dover ad loc.) outweighs any awkwardness in turning from audience to judges. Not only does this reading mark the clouds' words from the beginning as public rhetoric, but it also draws the audience more directly into the parabasis. The judges were clearly intended to represent the entire *demos* in microcosm (see the Introduction), hence alternation between them and the audience of which they are a section is not thematically or conceptually troublesome.

5. The second parabasis illustrates nicely the difficulty in drawing the line at any point in the analysis of the play—additional meanings continue to suggest themselves. Here, the possibility remains open that on the comic level the chorus is threatening another comedy.

6. See Taillardat 282ff., 469ff.

7. See Taillardat 283.

8. Note the adjectives with the trendy suffix *-ikos* in lines 1172–73. For heroic terms, see commentators ad 1158ff. and Taillardat 339.

9. Although Pheidippides emerges from the *phrontisterion* an accomplished sophist who delights in his new skills as he formerly did in horses, the reasons for his conversion are never stated. The power of the *hetton logos*, the unlimited access to pleasure that it offers, or the socratic charm that Strauss proposes (50) are among the possible explanations. (Certainly, however, the charm of socratic philosophy seems less likely than others; the rhetoric Pheidippides has learned is put to the task of procuring pleasures, of which the least potent, it appears from his behavior, is the *terpsis* of speech.) By refusing to stage Pheidippides' conversion, Aristophanes both avoids repeating what he had shown with Strepsiades (the importance of self-interest in the discovery of rhetoric and the extent to

which it duplicates the results of philosophic/linguistic zeal without committing the individual to either the values or the conduct of a philosopher) and also delays until the second agon representation of the force of language operative in "real life." But, of course, the audience is neither terribly bewildered nor surprised by Pheidippides' change of heart. By playing on conventional expectations, Aristophanes can avoid accounting for the "how" and "why" of Pheidippides' conversion, using instead our familiarity with genre to anticipate this turn of the plot. For, as an anonymous reader suggested, Pheidippides' reluctance here recalls that of Philocleon in *Wasps* 1121ff., when he does not want to prepare for the party from which he emerges completely "converted" to a new, and infinitely more pleasurable, way of life. Thus already at the end of the agon, comic convention has tipped us off: although Pheidippides thematically betrays the futility of the *logoi* by being utterly unconvinced by either of them, he will emerge an ardent sophist.

10. Pheidippides begins by assuming that the name of the day on which debts are due must refer grammatically to two days. See Starkie ad 1190. Further, the law of excluded middle renders it impossible that these should be the same day. When Strepsiades comments that this is contrary to the normal interpretation (1184), Pheidippides justifies his reasoning by appeal to the rhetorical commonplace of Solon's democratic intentions (1187). See Dover (ad loc.) and Starkie, who comments on the frequency of references to Solon and arguments from the intent of the lawgiver (ad 1186, 1187).

11. The criticism would thus work something like that in Plato's *Gorgias* where "the choice of figures and the order they appear in the *Gorgias* dramatize in an illuminating way the danger implied in rhetoric and consequences it could have. . . . Gorgias has only to acknowledge that he does not teach truth or justice; the implications and consequences of such a position are then searched through other people, less and less close to Gorgias, and considered from a wider and wider point of view. The danger is not rhetoric but the philosophy implied by the pursuit of rhetoric" (de Romilly 38–39).

12. See Ambrosino (1983) 34. She calls this passage "la féroce image d'une démocratie seulement apparente," pointing out that "dans la cité la plus démocratique du monde antique, où la parole a conquis le plus vaste champ d'action, le discours est sournoisement redevenu le privilège d'une minorité." See also Ambrosino (1986–87) 119, 124 and chapter 1.

13. See Fisher 210 ff.

14. Strepsiades' song at 1154 ff. is "largely composed of tragic phrases . . . the mixture of metrical genres is characteristic of tragic monodies" (Dover ad 1154–70). See also Rau 148ff., Fisher 210ff.

15. This is an image from wrestling (Taillardat 337 n. 1) and perhaps a reference to Protagoras' *Kataballontes (Logoi),* as well.

16. See 1240, and compare Strepsiades' earlier pleasure in the embarrassment of Socrates at 174. Strepsiades now sports the sophistic understanding of the ridiculous over his comic one.

17. As has been pointed out since the scholia, in 1237ff. Strepsiades is mocking the creditor's large belly. This visually (and comically) represents the indifference to *logos* and gastric orientation of this creditor (and the next).

18. This is the "knowledge test" which many have seen as central to the *Clouds.* As Nussbaum puts it, "Socrates, then, is an intellectualist . . . and this wisdom, which must be imparted by an expert teacher, is implied to be all that is necessary for achieving the satisfaction of one's desires. . . . The moral that he [Strepsiades] has learned from Socrates, as illustrated in the encounter with his creditors, is that the clever are justified in cheating the ignorant, that ignorance is more to be feared than vice, even that the only real vice *is* ignorance" (70). See also Strauss 36.

19. θηρίον (1286) equates the social and natural worlds through the double meaning of τόκος (Dover ad 1286). If there is not θηρίον in the natural world corresponding to interest in the human one, then the charging of interest is illegitimate. Unfortunately for Strepsiades, the joke is that due to the double meaning of τόκος there is a natural parallel.

20. Thus Dover comments that "an ordinary Athenian might not always have put the matter quite as the creditor does, but it is dramatically desirable that the creditor should be trapped into implying that his own demand for interest is ἄδικον" (ad 1292).

21. Dover ad 1292.

22. The comic contrast is the more obvious as the *kreitton logos* has just modeled the "ideal" response to successful verbal persuasion—a reversal of opinions leading to changed behavior. This proper response is also evident in Strepsiades' agreement that father-beating is just (1437), discussed in the next chapter.

23. Our play's comically expressed pessimism about the operation of *logos* in "real" life contrasts with the accepted critical understanding, both ancient and modern, of the impact of successful reasoning. Ambrosino (1983) is characteristic: "Une fois que le discours faible est devenu prédominant sur le plan rhétorique, il va aussi dominer naturellement le monde réel" (30).

24. Smyth states that εἶτα (1292) introduces "questions expressing surprise, indignation, irony, etc.; and often indicates a contrast between what a person has or has not done and what is or was to be expected of him" (599). Note that Strepsiades' formulation does not compromise the value-free universe of the sophists, even if the creditor's does. Rather Strepsiades simply shows the creditor's practices to be at variance with the processes observable in nature.

25. Dover ad 1300.

26. For successful rhetorical goading playing on *kentron* (but combined with a different image), see the *hetton logos*' boast in 947. See also the rhetorical *kentra* of the chorus at *Wasps* 431ff., discussed in the notes of chapter 7.

27. The common image of the sophist as hunter (cf. Turato [1975] 176 n. 98; Pl. *Sophist* 221d8), while obviously characterizing him as an ensnarer of others, also testifies to the demotion of the rest of humanity to prey.

28. Henderson (1991) states that *kentron* can mean *peos* (122), and notes "the threatened rape of the second creditor," additionally commenting that βινεῖν (which is functionally identical to κινεῖν) "like the English 'screw' can mean hoodwink or deceive" (152).

29. Strepsiades' actions recall Thucydides' famous description of the Corcyrean revolution (Th. 3.82.4ff.), where men were equally ready to destroy their enemies with unjust decrees and with violence.

30. See Hubbard (1986): "The old man striking an opponent with his cane in order to make up for his bad jokes (vv. 541ff.) can be none other than Strepsiades chasing off the second creditor with a κέντρον in vv. 1296–1302, after his wretchedly ignorant travesty of Socratic *sophia*" (190). See also chapter 5 and the Appendix.

Chapter 9

1. For the tantalizing ambiguity of the clouds' song, see Fisher 215–16.

2. This would be a twist on what was discussed above as the general catalyst of aristophanic plots: a mad scheme conceived by the alienated, impassioned, protagonist(s). For the "comic justice" of the end of the play and its relationship to the comedy of inversion, see Reckford (1976) 92ff., (1967) 225; Köhnken passim. Whitman identifies the

Clouds as "the dialectic kind of comedy whereby a dream defeats itself while achieving itself" (143; see 138ff.).

3. For this strategy at work, see sources cited above, Ambrosino (1986–87) 106ff. on Aristophanes' art of personification; and, on the *Acharnians,* Edmunds (1980) 2, 13.

4. Exclusive focus on Strepsiades' fate has obscured the extent to which it is structurally paralleled by those of Socrates and Pheidippides, a parallelism that should color our understanding of Strepsiades' own predicament.

5. Reckford (1967) 225–26 calls this "comic disappointment."

6. Ambrosino (1983) notes in passing that Pheidippides begins the violence "presque comme un prolongement de la violence innée du discours faible," but prefers to focus on the dominance of *logos* over the "reality of fact." (40)

7. The parallel is cited by commentators ad loc. The cicada is the proper sophistic insect of the new culture; a scholiast ad loc. calls it πολύλαλον τὸ ζῷον.

8. This discussion itself is justified by Phaedrus as one of the pleasures that make life worth living, in contrast to the servile corporal pleasures (Pl. *Phdr.* 258e1ff.).

9. Once the debate begins, Pheidippides' first speech provides another significant echo when he remarks on the sweetness of τῶν καθεστώτων νόμων ὑπερφρονεῖν δύνασθαι (1400). This recalls our first view of Socrates, who was said by Strepsiades ὑπερφρονεῖν (226) the gods. The ramifications of this celestial speculation began to be clear in Strepsiades' instruction. The final results for the ordinary man are visible now.

10. For Pheidippides' freedom from the values of the city, which predisposes him to violence, see Ambrosino (1986–87) 123, who ties this to her political argument by emphasizing the overthrow of *isonomia.* Certainly 1201ff. show *isonomia* to be irrelevant to both Strepsiades and presumably his son, but the principle of *isonomia* does not seem the basic one violated at the end.

11. See Taillardat 340. Note the use of ἀράττειν (1373) for verbal blows in contrast to line 1359, where it is clearly to be taken in a physical sense.

12. Strepsiades' choice is labeled as sophistic and appropriate by εἰκός, which occurs frequently in the end of the play. See the later discussion in this chapter.

13. For the Greek conception of "childhood as the savage time of human life," see Vidal-Naquet (1981b) 174 and the passages cited there. On the generational conflict and the reversal of roles, see Reckford (1976) 99ff.

14. Strauss 38.

15. Ambrosino (1986–87) locates here the principal irony of the *Clouds:* in its struggles against the dominant aristocracy, the *demos,* represented by Strepsiades, dispenses with the very rule of law that protects it, exalting speakers of the *hetton logos* whom it can not control and who turn against its interests (120, 124).

16. For the "parallelism of structure" as emphasizing Pheidippides as a "replica" of the *hetton logos* and his reuse of the techniques and words of that *logos,* see Dover ad 1321–44, who gives examples. See also Gelzer (1960) 18ff.

17. Gelzer (1960) notes that 1321ff., like 1437, are addressed to the audience as public (17 n. 4).

18. Note that Pheidippides is a true adherent of the *hetton logos,* willing to admit publicly to actions deemed criminal by conventional society.

19. Pheidippides' offer makes good Socrates' promise that his student's *logos* will triumph regardless of witnesses (1153) and provides the correct solution to the type of problem that Strepsiades failed to solve in 776ff. The use of *anapeithein* (1340, 1342) recalls Strepsiades' initial interaction with Pheidippides and his first description of the sophists (77, 96). The repetition makes clear the full extent of the reversal at the end, Strepsiades' responsibility for it, and the completeness of Pheidippides' transformation.

20. Strepsiades' agreement to listen (which parallels the *kreitton logos*' earlier) can perhaps be attributed to his own attendance at the Thinkery. Like that *logos,* he knows that every rule must be justifiable in debate. Cf. Nussbaum 62ff.

21. For various invocations of this topos, see Pl. *Euthd.* 298e8ff., *Euthyphro* 4a1ff. and *Grg.* 456d6ff. (quoted in chapter 1).

22. Abuse of parents was held to damage the public interest, and the full weight of the state was available against it. It was prohibited by a law attributed to Solon; the penalty was disenfranchisement; offenders were probably brought to trial through the procedure of *eisangelia,* also used for orphans. See MacDowell (1980) 92ff. For the traditional respect due to parents, see Turato (1972) 31, where he notes that beating of the father contravened one of the basic unwritten laws sustaining the city. Note that *antituptein* (1424) comically plays on the sophistic *antilegein* to suggest the equivalence of language and force for the sophistic Pheidippides.

23. For an interesting analysis of Pheidippides' arguments, see Reckford (1976) 102ff.

24. As Reckford (1976) notes, the rooster we already saw in the language lesson now comes back to haunt us (108). This comically figures the relationship between the verbal precision that Socrates was seeking, with its indifference to the conventional world of ordinary usage and desire to mirror what is observable in nature, and Pheidippides' disregard for another purely social convention, the sanctity of parents.

25. See Dover ad loc., Reckford (1976) 108. Equally to the point is Pheidippides' final phrase: καίτοι τί διαφέρουσιν / ἡμῶν ἐκεῖνοι, πλήν γ' ὅτι ψηφίσματ' οὐ γράφουσιν; (1428–29). This crucial difference of course saves the sophist and his rhetoric, but it is unclear why man in the natural state should differ from the rooster only in this.

26. Cf. Nussbaum 58ff. on this type of behavior in the *kreitton logos.*

27. For the "elliptical" form of the argument, see Dover ad 1433.

28. τὰπιεικῆ and εἰκός are terms highly characteristic of sophistic reasoning, particularly in forensic rhetoric, and indicative of something morally just, but contrary to the law (Pucci [1960] 13). What we watch is a typical reevaluation of an admitted illegal action.

29. We may wonder why this argument is so much more successful than the others. One possible explanation is that Strepsiades' capitulation is due not to the cogency of his son's *logos,* but to the fact that it is his son who speaks. Inside the family circle Strepsiades is willing to admit principles of conduct, even supported with faulty reasoning, that he denies absolutely outside it. Strepsiades cannot endure that his son lack anything to which he might have a claim even remotely just. The same force which plunged Strepsiades into debt, compelled him to enter the Thinkery, and induced him to debate in the agon, is the agent of his persuasion now: *philia* for his only child. In this debate between real people, the interlocutors' relationship turns out to be as important as—or more important than—technical skill.

30. We are prepared for this perspective on Pheidippides by the pejorative λαλῶν of 1394, which portrays as negative and trivial what Strepsiades calls *antilegein* (1339).

31. See Pucci (1960) 13 for the redefinition of justice.

32. This is the type of *gnomidion* Strepsiades aspires to in line 321, and the plaything *(paignion)* that is Gorgias' *Encomium* (*Encomium* 21). Its success is due to its use of arguments appropriate to the listener and to *kairos* rather than any conviction on the part of the speaker, who speaks only to win. Such a victory casts a new light on other similar "successes" outside the play—particularly proceeded as it is by Pheidippides' general statement of the mutability of *nomos* (1421).

33. See Pucci (1960) 13.

34. The way has been paved for this generalizing effect in lines 1391ff., sung by the clouds before Pheidippides speaks. Then, however, the danger to the old men was only

hypothetical; now the power granted to speech alone regardless of speaker, with the consequent erosion of the position of fathers implicit in this equalization of voices, makes not only the risk of being beaten for injustice, but other similar hazards, much more pressing. The young seem promised complete ascendency, since from the beginning, and in Aristophanes generally, they are the natural possessors of the *hetton logos*. Cf. 515 and *Ach.* 676ff.

35. For the sophist as alienating the young from family and normal associates, see Pl. *Prt.* 316c5. For at least Protagoras' ability to draw his students out of the city to follow him, see *Prt.* 315a3.

36. In fact, Pheidippides states his pleasure in mingling with clever and novel matters (the comically suspect *pragmata*) with ἡδύ (1399), a sensual word which recalls the *hetton logos'* description of the pleasures he can provide (1069, 1072). This is the type of pleasure Strepsiades took in the old-fashioned humor of shit we saw in line 174. For contrast of *hedone* with more intellectual delight, see also Pl. *Prt.* 337c1, quoted in chapter 5; *Phdr.* 258e1.

37. Cf. Reckford (1976) 105 for the unsettling effect of the *Alcestis*.

38. For the implicit parricide, see Reckford (1976) 109. The use of *tuptein* for rape (Henderson [1991] 172, Reckford [1976] 113 n. 20) makes even more obvious the connection of incest and mother-beating. See also Strauss 43, 40. For incest (along with cannibalism) as a mark of the animal (and savage human), see the sources cited in chapter 1.

39. For this cock as the comic stand-in for the lion, exemplar of the natural "superman" and his right to dominate others, see Turato (1972) 43ff., who compares Pl. *Grg.* 483bff. For the cock fight as emblematic of sophistic debate in a negative sense, see Taillardat 341; Pl. *Tht.* 164c4ff. where it represents the participants' desire to win at all costs and their reduction of language to a personal weapon, independent of truth; *Knights* 492ff. For the cock as symbol of *hubris*, see Demosthenes 54.9. cited by MacDowell (1980) in his discussion of the crime of *hubris* (132). If we accept the scholia that state that the two *logoi* of the agon enter fighting like cocks (ad 889), the parallelism becomes even more striking. See Reckford (1976) 107–8.

40. For the *Clouds* as documenting the civic and cultural regression to savagery, see Turato (1979) 53–54.

41. See Reckford (1976) 109–10, Pucci (1960) 13 for Strepsiades' rejection of rational argument and his decision not to listen to a *logos* which máy persuade him. For Pheidippides' error in "treating the occasion as one in which the emotions are not involved (cf. 1336) and the skill and plausibility of the argument are all that matters," see Dover ad 1440. See also Nussbaum 92, and for a similar confrontation between persuasion and deaf force, Pl. *R.* 1.327c7. In a certain sense Strepsiades' refusal to listen is less surprising than his original decision to participate. Offstage (and even in other aristophanic comedies, for example, *Ach.* 292ff.) it is much more difficult to persuade people to listen, particularly contrary to their perceived self-interest or emotional convictions, than it has been in the *Clouds*. The logic of the play begins to move closer to that governing speech in everyday Athens.

42. I agree with Reckford (1976) that "Strepsiades' violent response must somehow bowl Pheidippides over, much as characters are knocked head over heels by strong words in the Peanuts comic strip" (110 n. 16).

43. Once again form mirrors content: Strepsiades "snatches the Antipnigus from his son, and finishes it himself" (Starkie ad 1447).

44. For the *barathron*, see Dover ad 1448.

45. For the good sense of Strepsiades, see, for example, Pucci (1960) 13, Reckford (1976) 109, Strauss 43.

46. For the cult of Peitho in Athens, see Buxton 34ff.

47. This is the type of symmetry usually identified by critics. Thus Segal (1975) notes, "Strepsiades does, in fact, get what he wants, with a vengeance" (188), an observation which he embeds in a moral framework and associates with the doom of a tragic hero, rejecting the possibility that "we humans have seen in them [the clouds] only the shapes of our own ambitions" (192). Köhnken recalls Ixion and finds the entire play to be a working out of the maxim "jemanden mit seinen eigenen Waffen schlagen" (162ff., 167). See also Reckford (1967) 228.

48. This is also the continuation of the irony of the *logos* that will not repay study, and as Ambrosino (1986–87) points out, a natural extension of Pheidippides' study of the "difficile arte di non pagare i debiti" (122). Pheidippides, of course, counters his father by invoking novel debts (his own beatings as a child, 1410ff.) and educational desires (to teach his father) (1416ff.).

49. For the alternate model of persuasion this suggests, see the Conclusion.

50. Strepsiades labels Pheidippides' actions unjust and unfilial (1380ff.); he invokes custom (1420) and filial debt (1385ff.).

51. That the clouds echo Strepsiades has been parenthetically considered by Strauss 44 and Nussbaum 77 in ways different from that discussed here. For a detailed discussion of the many repetitions and parallelisms of the end, some of which are discussed here, see Köhnken 165ff., who, however, sees them more from the perspective of Strepsiades echoing the clouds.

52. The punning on Strepsiades' name which runs throughout the play (and is picked up again in line 1464) emphasizes the constancy of his nature and the extent to which it shapes his experiences, rather than the other way around. For various interpretations, see Reckford (1967) 227ff., Nussbaum 67, Dover xxv, Segal (1975) 189ff., Marzullo passim, Pucci (1960) 15ff.

53. For the chorus' statement as "fully in accord with ordinary Greek theology and ethics," see Dover ad 1458. But this does not mean that we must accept his conclusion that "the Chorus reveals itself, in solemn style, as a member of the supernatural company traditionally worshipped by the Greeks."

54. Note the repetition of ἐμβάλλειν εἰς 1448–49/50 and 1460.

55. For the aeschylean morality here, see, among others, Rau 173ff., Segal (1975) 188ff.; for the moral structure of tragedy, Newiger (1957) 67, Whitman, with reservations, 129; contra Köhnken 168. Reckford (1967) sees a parody of aeschylean tragedy in "a comic *apate,* not a tragic *ate*" (232).

56. Dover ad 1458. The other manuscript reading is ἄν τιν' οὖν, which Dover states is "not Attic." He prefers Porson's emmendation of ὄντιν' ἄν to the manuscripts' ὅταν τινά, although he concedes that this "though metrically abnormal, is possible . . . and grammatically sound; the real objection to it is stylistic. The Chorus speaks, and Strepsiades replies, solemnly. If ὅταν τινά is right, it is not only an isolated snatch of comic rhythm in a passage (1452–64) otherwise uniform in avoiding resolutions and abnormal diaeresis, but an exaggerated one and—for communication of the sense—wholly unnecessary" (ad 1458). Köhnken, on the other hand, also would not emend (164 n. 34), finding the joke "in der Diskrepanz zwischen dem Pathos der Sprach ('solemn style') und dem komisch-geringfügigen Gegenstand" (165).

57. The passages are: 1322ff., where Strepsiades calls upon his neighbors, relatives, and fellow demesmen present in the audience for help (these lines begin the proagon); 1351–52, where the chorus acknowledges its dramatic role and Strepsiades as actor (these lines begin Strepsiades' speech in the agon proper); 1391ff., where the chorus remarks on

the audience's interest in what Pheidippides will say (these lines begin Pheidippides' speech); 1437ff., where Strepsiades includes in his concession every old man present in the theater (these lines close the subject of father-beating).

58. See McLeish 80ff., Reckford (1967) 224 and particularly (1976) 102ff. for the comic "game" in Pheidippides' arguments, which carries the audience to emotional safety even as we perceive their social consequences. Reckford (1976) further points out that the familiar "comic machinery" and extremely formal structure of the agon would tend to foster detachment in the audience, reminding us that what we see is fiction (95).

59. Cf. DK 88 B 25.27ff. for this explanation of the genesis of religion, the adulterer's speech for another openly sophistic example of the manipulation of religion for persuasive purposes (1080ff.)

60. For the paratragedy and uncertainty about πατρῷος Ζέυς, see Dover ad 1468, who comments that "by the incongruity of tragic quotation, Ar. does not allow us to cease to regard Strepsiades as a comic figure."

61. For the silence of Hermes, who is actually a herm, see Dover, Starkie ad loc. Fisher comments that the language of 1476–82 cannot be taken as tragic: "a melodramatic delivery of the lines, with exaggerated gestures and emphasis on key words would indicate his [Strepsiades'] insincerity. The colloquial ἀλλὰ συγγνώμην ἔχε (1479, cf. σύγγνωθί μοι 138) would be inappropriate for genuine respect for the god and is particularly conspicuous for being followed by a mock-heroic three-word iambic trimeter" (229). The choice of the god Hermes as Strepsiades' "interlocutor" has been explained as due to his epithet στροφαῖος which echoes Strepsiades' name and nature (Marzullo 123 n. 2). The choice might also mark Strepsiades' return to the civic world: he turns from *dinos* outside Socrates' door to the herm outside his own, and from the new ψυχαγωγία of rhetoric (cf. Pl. *Phdr.* 261a7) back to the traditional one: Hermes, the leader of the dead (cf. *Od.* 24.1–14). On sophistic rhetoric and the word as the true ψυχαγωγός, see de Romilly 15, Segal (1962) 149 n. 91, Turato (1976) 171 n. 67, with further sources. For Socrates and the ψυχαγωγία of rhetoric in *Birds* 1553, see Moulton 40, Gelzer (1956) 82. For Hermes as connected with the ambiguities of persuasion and enchantment, see Kahn 136ff.; cf. Pucci (1987) 194.

62. ἐξηπάτων (1466) clearly recalls ἀπάτη, the foundation of sophistic rhetoric. For ἐπαίρειν, the equivalent of ἀπάτη in line 1457, see chapter 2. For ἀλαζών (1492) and associated terms and images frequently directed against the sophists, see Gelzer (1956) 83ff., Pucci (1960) 113ff. For ἀδολεσχία (1480) as characteristic of sophists, see Aristophanes 506 (PCG), Eupolis 386 (quoted in the notes of chapter 3) and 388 (PCG); for an ironic reuse of this charge, see Pl. *Tht.* 195b10, 195c2. For the charge of ἀσέβεια, see Pucci (1960) 114ff. For these types of charges in general, see chapters 2, 3.

63. On the contemporary antiintellectual mood at Athens, see Dodds chapter 6. Kopff feels that the destruction of the *phrontisterion* was intended to recall the burning of the Pythagoreans at Croton, another sect combining "unusual religious customs and philosophical speculation with oligarchical politics" (117). For the relationship of the *Clouds'* philosophers to Pythagoreans, see also Carter 152ff., who, however, explains the contrast between the philosophers and their students as due to Aristophanes' "unawareness" (153).

64. For the "justice" of Strepsiades' actions, see, for example, Segal (1975) 193ff., Strauss 45, Kopff. For the necessity of revising a "too favorable" earlier play, see Whitman 133ff., de Carli 25, Hubbard (1991) chapter 5, and the sources cited in the Appendix.

65. That Strepsiades is responsible for his fate has been recognized by many; the next step, that Socrates is correspondingly "blameless," at least in this regard, has been less often taken; however, see Köhnken 166ff.

66. Pheidippides' fate is unknown. Nussbaum believes that he is the student who screams from inside the Thinkery (78), but it could be that he watches passively (Strauss 52), or wanders offstage.

67. Pheidippides, from another perspective, also unites the various attitudes towards *logos* that we have seen. Most notably, his decision to use violence to suppress Strepsiades' offensive speech about Euripides does not differ significantly from the *kreitton logos'* similar violence to suppress verbal and musical innovation. For emotional reasons, both enforce (very different) *logoi* that are emblematic of the worlds they wish to inhabit and express the attitudes that will sustain these worlds. The similarity in their actions is underlined by the repetition of ἐπιτρίβειν: in line 972 this describes the beating the *kreitton logos* gave any student obscuring the old songs; in line 1376, it sums up the beating of Strepsiades for failing to acknowledge the excellence of Euripides.

68. In a sense, Socrates' fate fulfills Strepsiades' threat to Pheidippides. The crime for which he is "tried" is that of offense against the state, which carried the penalty of the βαράθρον or house razing. Cf. Dover ad 1478, 1485.

69. Henderson (1991) 77. An earlier variant on this reading is that of Strauss who finds that Strepsiades acts illegally but justly (45). The legality that Strepsiades disdains here he just invoked to protect himself from his son (1321ff.). (Cf. Dover ad loc.)

70. But, of course Socrates' *logos* did not, in fact, save him, and our play suggests one possible factor. As Socrates himself points out, he had been accused and condemned in advance, and in his absence (Pl. *Ap.* 18b1ff., 23c4ff.). At the court, the jury's fears of an omnipotent *logos* could lead to a decision not to listen at all.

71. See Ambrosino (1983), who feels that Strepsiades' action is contrary to the conventional morality he wishes to reinstate but interprets it positively: "Le monde des signes se retourne contre les spécialistes, se rallie aux parleurs ordinaires, et impose l'échange des mots sur un plan de parité, dans lequel le langage commun est le fondement de la communauté politique" (43).

72. Ambrosino (1983) notes, "Strepsiades répond aux καταβάλλοντες λόγοι par une démolition practique," but denies that the scene represents the priority of "praxis sur la pensée" (41). Cf. Starkie ad 1496 for διαλεπτολοῦμαι punning on λεπτύνειν, "to reduce to dust."

73. The replay of this imagery may be anticipated in πνιγόμενος in 1389. Strepsiades is the first "sophist" (1309–10) to be choked in this natural world.

74. For this repetition as signalling "inversion of the situation," cf. Miller 27ff. On Pheidippides' similar trick (1469 recalls 818ff.), which emphasizes his correspondence to his father's wishes, see Dover ad 1469 and Köhnken 167.

75. The repeated line is: ἀεροβατῶ καὶ περιφρονῶ τὸν ἥλιον (225 = 1503).

76. Thus the spectacle of the roof set aflame by Strepsiades, followed by the cry ἀποπνιγήσομαι (1504), recalls the sophists' idea that the heaven was a πνιγεύς (96); while the scream κατακανθήσομαι (1505) means that those within are becoming ἄνθρακες (97). de Carli notes the recall of the imagery associated with the sophists from the beginning—the cloak, the oven, the repeated lines—but finds it awkward and false, revealing only the inadequacy of the new ending which the failure of the first *Clouds* compelled Aristophanes to devise (24ff.).

77. For the clouds' lack of divinity to Socrates, see chapter 4. Cf. Edmunds (1987) who thinks that their failure to intervene derives from their relationship with Socrates and the fact that they take only verbal attitudes, never acting at all (19). Köhnken thinks it due to their exclusive concern with Strepsiades and their particular nature (168).

78. See Segal (1975) who notes how appropriately the sophists are choked by smoke,

citing Eur. *Hipp.* 954 for the "association of smoke and pretentious intellectuality" (195 and n. 32). We recall also that Strepsiades originally is made to call clouds smoke (330).

79. See Dover ad 1507 for the double meaning, scientific and obscene, of ἕδραν (1507), and see Henderson (1991) for the "wry and buffoonish coloration" here (199).

80. "The destruction of the Thinkery is in this play the counterpart of the exuberant marriage feast or the orgiastic indulgence which ends other comedies" (Segal [1975] 194). But Dover points out the ambiguous endings of *Knights* and *Acharnians,* and concludes that "when the first version of the *Clouds* was written the type of comedy which ends with unalloyed triumph and leaves no uncomfortable questions in the audience's mind was not the only type in which Ar. was interested" (xxv).

81. See scholia ad 543 and Ussher: "It [the first *Clouds*] was possibly too clever for an audience who had relished the raucousness and violence of *Knights*" (16). He feels that the new ending, the burning of the *phrontisterion,* may have been a concession to the tastes of the audience. See the Appendix for the differences between the first and second *Clouds.*

82. Dover states that the *Clouds* "shares with *Th.* a final choral utterance which is little more than the verbal equivalent of dropping the curtain (μετρίως occurs in both) but is peculiar in being entirely colourless" (ad 1510).

83. Hubbard (1991) points out the lack of the "reestablishment of order" normal in those plays which end in the hero's triumph or "feast of reconciliation"; however, he believes this leaves us "submerged in the ironic gloom of intellectual despair" (chapter 5).

Conclusion

1. As we saw with Protagoras in chapter 1, not all sources blur the difference between *peitho* and *bia* or fail to acknowledge the symbiotic relationship of *logos* and *polis.*

2. Whitman 175, speaking of the *Birds.*

3. Whitman 174, again speaking of the *Birds.*

4. ὑπὸ γὰρ λόγων ὁ νοῦς τε μετεωρίζεται / ἐπαίρεταί τ᾽ ἄνθρωπος (*Birds* 1447–48).

5. This distinction between the new and the old *logos* is one forced by the comedy. Of course, even the "old" *logos* had always been open to abuse and to use as a tool for personal gain.

6. For Socrates' mocking comparison of the tyranny worked by rhetoric to that effected by a dagger, see Pl. *Grg.* 469d1.

7. See Nussbaum 80ff. for criticism of Socrates' intellectualism and lack of concern about training the desires.

8. Nussbaum 95, emphasis original.

9. Controversy rages about whether Aristophanes really intended to portray Socrates as teaching for profit as Strepsiades states in line 98. (This question is, of course, independent of the conduct of the historical Socrates.) In general, the answer is likely to be yes, for although the motif receives little play, it is clear that Strepsiades brings Socrates a reward in 1146 when picking up Pheidippides (which could, however, be his own misconception); that in 804ff. the chorus may encourage Socrates to lick Strepsiades clean (if, in fact, they address him and not Strepsiades, as Hulley contends); and that in 876 Socrates himself seems to allude to high fees. The motives of Strepsiades are, from the first, unashamedly mercenary.

10. Whitman remarks that all comic heroes are natural men, and that "in other plays this same world of *physis* provides the motive power by which the heroic individual per-

forms his miracles.'' Heroes of comedy "do not save themselves by any particular exercise of lawful behavior, restraint of obstreperous nature, or conformity to social custom. Quite the contrary, they 'use their nature,' fulfill their 'natural necessities,' 'skip, laugh, and consider nothing shameful' except their enemies. They illustrate to the full, in fact, the liberation of *physis* from all inhibition . . . they are all gifted by nature with the Unjust Discourse and use it freely with their other talents" (132). Whitman has perceptively identified a central problem of the *Clouds*, the affinity between the concept of natural man proposed by the sophists' theories and the *hetton logos* and the comic view. However he fails to perceive its thematic importance in a play about language. Instead he is troubled by the seeming reversal of Aristophanes' normal procedure. "The question is, why did Aristophanes, in the *Clouds*, turn against what had been his authentic comic medium, expose it in a theoretical analysis and then reject it in favor of traditional morality" (132).

11. Thus the *Clouds* evades the problem identified by Redfield, namely, that "since the same 'we' is identified as problem and the solution, no concrete program emerges" (329).

12. Thus in a sense the *Clouds* doubles the comic democratic task mentioned by Redfield: "comedy weakens the control of the performers over their audience and thus increases the power of the people. In this sense it is after all a democratic art" (331). Contra Ober, who believes that theatrical "training," helped "speaker and audience to create and accept dramatic fictions regarding social status" (154).

13. In general, for these perspectives, see the preceding chapters.

14. With the exception of the "theoretical" first agon, most moments of persuasion in the *Clouds* are not compelled by rhetoric or *logos* alone. Rather, the persuasive force of the familial convinced Pheidippides to enter the Thinkery (860ff.) and prompted Strepsiades to decode and act upon his son's inarticulate wishes for food, drink, relief of his bowels (1380ff.), a toy chariot (864), and, finally, racehorses—all this despite Pheidippides' inability to string three words together without error (1402). In staging this contrasting model of successful speech, our comedy obliquely suggests that such relationships—familial, but also civic, ethnic, human—are deeply important among ordinary men to win *logos* the receptive hearing that is the precondition of its power. The parabasis refracts this through the poet's experience. There the audience is chided for failing to appreciate the poet's *logos* and thus violating their almost "familial" bond (530ff.). Like Electra, the *Clouds* was rejected by those who should love it, disinherited by their irrational appetites. Lost, it searches for signs of its proper audience and "family" (534–35). For the widespread feeling that effective communication must be based on mutual trust and respect, see, for the tragedians, Buxton chapters 4, 5; for Aristotle, Nussbaum 92ff. For the Greek view of persuasion as predicated on creation of this "familial" bond between speaker and listener, see Lupher 9ff.

15. For a similarly ambivalent effect of the double ending of Eur. *Hipp.*, see Goff chapter 5.

Appendix

1. For the victory of Cratinus' *Putine*, a response to *Knights* 526ff., and the second place of Ameipsias' *Konnos*, see Hypothesis II (Dover). Our revised *Clouds* probably dates to between 420 and 417. See Dover lxxx for the first and second versions and their dating. Bianchetti has attempted to fasten the date to the City Dionysia of 417 (238ff., passim) by considering the use of Hyperbolus. Hubbard (1991) argues for an earliest date of 419

(chapter 5). As was stated earlier, I regret the lack of precise page numbers for Hubbard's book; it was not published at the time my own went into production.

2. See Dover lxxxff., Hubbard (1986) 182ff., (1991) chapter 5 for what follows.

3. I omit Dover's argument (xcff.) about the costuming of the *logoi* as fighting cocks since it seems to me possible—and even likely—that this does refer to our agon.

4. Hubbard (1986) 183. Dover's argument has also been accepted by Bianchetti, (apparently) Fisher (20), and Fabrini, and anticipated in places by Starkie (li).

5. See Dover lxxxiff.

6. See Fabrini for the possibility that the *Clouds* could have been staged within contemporary theatrical conventions. Contra Dover lxxff.

7. See Dover lxxxi; for his list of internal inconsistencies, see xcivff.

8. Hubbard (1991) chapter 5.

9. Dover xcviii. See Hubbard (1986) 184ff. on critical reactions to the notion of an incomplete revision.

10. See Reckford (1987) 393 for a lament about the negative consequences of the question of revision.

11. See Hubbard (1986) 183ff. for citation of previous views of the degree of revision between first and second *Clouds*.

12. Reckford (1987) 394.

13. See de Carli 24ff.

14. Whitman 121; he also considers the parabasis an "ill-adjusted mingling of earlier and later passages." See Starkie lv for citations of more negative views.

15. Thus, for example, Hubbard (1991) is surely correct methodologically in disputing the claim that the presence of the *logoi* throughout the play requires that this notion be original. Integration or lack of integration is insufficient to prove that any element of the play is revised or original. As Hubbard points out, this is particularly true given the statement of Hypothesis I (Dover) that the play's revision included addition and deletion throughout (chapter 5).

16. See chapter 5.

17. Murphy 75 n. 1; see, in general, 74ff. Contra MacDowell (1971) ad 1038.

18. Scholia ad *Wasps* 1038. The scholia assume that these lines refer to the first *Clouds*, performed the year before, and record that ἠπίαλος mocks the pallor of Socrates' associates, again an issue in our play on lines 103, 1016, 1112. Alternatively, Didymos is recorded as claiming that Epiale was a *daimon* (scholion ad 1038).

19. See MacDowell (1971) ad 1041.

20. Dover xciii-iv. Other speculations about the plot of the first *Clouds* are summarized in Hubbard (1991) chapter 5.

21. See Hubbard (1991) for the atemporal quality of ἦλθ' (535) and the contrast between ἥδ' ἡ κωμῳδία (534), our play, and ταύτην τῶν ἐμῶν κωμῳδιῶν (522), the first *Clouds* (chapter 5).

22. Of course, the comparison of our comedy and Electra is facilitated by the fact that the *komodia*, like Electra, is feminine. See the notes to the Conclusion for the way in which this picture of poet and audience continues the second *Clouds'* themes.

23. See Hubbard (1991) chapter 5.

24. In fact, *sophrosyne* does not seem to be something that Aristophanes elsewhere attributes to his comedies, although he calls himself *sophron* in *Knights* 545 for having undertaken an artistic apprenticeship before staging a comedy independently. Rather, *sophrosyne*, outside our comedy, is acknowledged by the characters as "good" but somehow passive and almost stupid. (It is an attribute of Basileia in *Birds* 1537ff., along with *eunomia* and *euboulia*, but embedded in a descending comic sequence which undercuts the

traditional values by augmenting or replacing them with comic ones immediately effective and profitable.) In the current (comic) Athens, *sophrosyne* characterizes victims whose plight the comic heroes refuse to share (*Lys.* 473, 508; *Ach.* 611; *Ecl.* 767ff.; *Knights* 334), and, from this perspective, can become, parodically, even cowardly, as in *Peace* 1297. To this, compare Th. 3.82.4.

25. See chapter 5 for the way in which the parabasis proposes to redeem the *sophrosyne* of our play.

26. The aorist of τύπτειν is said by Hubbard (1991) to be extremely rare in Attic Greek, while, as he points out, βοᾷ "is very closely connected with the preceding . . . and could easily take its temporal value from the earlier verb." He also notes that the perfect can be used of an existing dramatic work not present performance, aptly comparing *Clouds* 556 (chapter 5).

27. It is not clear whether lines 538–39 mean that the actors in the first *Clouds* did not sport the phallus at all, or that they wore the tied up phallus as opposed to the dangling one. Stone (1981) 80ff. discusses these two options and provides bibliography; neither can be decisively ruled out. (However, I follow her that the reference is probably not to the circumcised phallus as suggested by Dover ad 538.) The answer will partly depend on views about the still-debated issue of whether a phallus was an invariable part of the comic costume. Stone believes that it was (98) but states that the available evidence does not allow the question to be settled finally. In any case, it is clear that rejection of the dangling or erect phallus in favor of even a coiled one could represent a comedy as less lewd and obscene than one that relied on phallic byplay and a prominent phallus (Stone [1981] 92), as the second *Clouds* almost certainly does. For, as Stone points out, the coiled phallus was minimally visible beneath the standard short chiton and not at all beneath longer garments (Stone [1981] 97ff.). It did not call attention to itself, and in the absence of phallic humor would pass unnoticed given its invariable presence and the contrast with its frequent comic prominence.

28. Hubbard (1991) points out that the parabasis' claim to reflect differences between the first and second versions is bolstered by its mention (529) of the conflict of *sophron* and *katapugon* of the *Banqueters* which parallels the contrast of the two versions of the *Clouds*, chaste and vulgar, as well as possibly presaging the new debate of the *logoi* (chapter 5).

29. See Hubbard (1986) 189ff. See also Stone (1981) 76ff.

30. Hubbard (1986) 190ff. summarizes attempts to deny that what is condemned in the parabasis appears in our second *Clouds*.

31. See Reckford (1987) 396; Fisher 155ff., Stone (1981) 75ff., Murray 150ff. This interpretation is bolstered by other instances of stylistic criticism whose humor seems to depend on using vulgar expressions while forbidding them, all cited by Murray. But Hubbard has shown some differences between the *Clouds'* assertions and these other passages; see later discussion.

32. For the parabasis as focusing the themes that animate the drama, see Bowie on the parabasis of the *Acharnians;* he cites opposing views that make of the parabasis a relic, standing apart from the drama.

33. This inverse correspondence distinguishes the *Clouds'* parabasis from other examples of "stylistic criticism." As Hubbard (1986) has shown, similar passages from other plays do not include devices present in those plays; even the words deprecated in the first lines of the *Frogs* do not appear elsewhere in the play (192ff.).

34. Since, at the very least, Strepsiades' phallus would already have been prominent before the parabasis, the contrast of the old and new *Clouds* would already be clear, even before the parabasis acknowledged it and identified its thematic significance. Of course, a

double response can be created without the kind of intertextual situation set up by the *Clouds* thematically and available to it historically. Likewise, the audience does not need exact knowledge or precise recall of the first *Clouds;* the second outlines what is essential and indicates its significance for our current play.

35. See chapter 5.

36. The most common strategy is to leave Aristophanes' general claim to novelty intact, while denying his specific assertions. Thus Reckford (1987), for example, does not accept extensive revision, but argues that the first *Clouds* was defeated because "the audience found it too talky, too intellectual, too full of ideas, with not enough knockabout action and fun'' (396); see also Ussher 16.

37. The metaphor from chariot racing is appropriate for rhetorical competition; see *Clouds* 430, Eupolis 102 (PCG), both discussed in chapter 4.

38. For the vulgarity and stupidity of Megarian humor, see Eupolis 261 (PCG), (A.) τὸ δεῖν᾽, ἀκούεις; (B.) Ἡράκλεις, τοῦτ᾽ ἔστι σοι / τὸ σκῶμμ᾽ ἀσελγὲς καὶ Μεγαρικὸν καὶ σφόδρα / ψυχρόν. † γελᾶς ὁρᾷς τὰ παιδία This combination of a joke described as *aselges*, Megarian, and insipid in connection with childish humor, recalls the conventional comedy rejected by the first *Clouds* and also in *Wasps* 57ff. Note the overlap of Heracles and *aselges* in both passages, albeit in different contexts. The invocation of Heracles here may also owe something to his connection with Megarian or vulgar comedy, as a stock figure typifying the humor of violence and food that here is pejoratively assigned this type of comedy. (Athenian comic use of the topos of Megarian humor cannot, of course, be assumed to reflect accurately its real quality.) See also Ecphantides 3 (PCG) and Reckford (1987) for the scene with the Megarian in the *Acharnians* as exemplifying the "coarse, old-style buffoonery" of "Megarian humor" (168ff.).

39. Without reference to our passage, de Carli believes that the revision of the end suggests that Ameipsias' *Konnos,* which also concerned Socrates and seems to have had a chorus of intellectuals, was more decisively—and, we might say, generically—antisophistic than the first *Clouds* and for this reason took second to the *Clouds'* third place (25). For Socrates in the *Konnos* and the overlap with the *Clouds,* see Dover lff.

40. Aristophanes' further claim that this was the reason for the first *Clouds'* failure is less verifiable, but I accept it within the context of the thematic development of our *Clouds.* We will never know the truth, particularly in the absence of the plays which placed first and second in the competition.

BIBLIOGRAPHY

The following abbreviations have been used in citations:

Dover: Dover, K. J., ed. *Aristophanes' Clouds*. Oxford: Clarendon Press, 1968.

DK: Diels, H., and W. Kranz, eds. *Die Fragmente der Vorsokratiker*. Vols. 1–3. Berlin: Weidmannsche Verlagsbuchhandlung, 1951.

PCG: Kassel, R., and C. Austin, eds. *Poetae Comici Graeci*. Vols. III.2, IV, V., VII. Berlin and New York: Walter de Gruyter, 1984.

LSJ: Liddell, G. H., R. Scott, and R. McKenzie, eds., *A Greek-English Lexicon*. Revised by H. S. Jones, Oxford: Clarendon Press, 1968.

The remainder of the works are cited by author's name and, where necessary, date of publication.

Adkins, A. W. H. "Some Nebulous Thoughts on the *Clouds* of Aristophanes." *Bulletin of the Institute of Classical Studies* 15 (1968): 146–47.

Ambrosino, D. "Nuages et sens: Autour des *Nuées* d'Aristophane." *Quaderni di Storia* 18 (1983): 3–60.

———. "Aristoph. *Nub.* 218–234 (La 'cesta' di Socrate?)." *Museum Criticum* 19–20 (1985): 51–69.

———. "Aristoph. *Nub.* 46s. (Il matrimonio di Strepsiade e la democrazia ateniese)." *Museum Criticum* 21–22 (1986–87): 95–127.

Arrowsmith, W. "Aristophanes' *Birds:* The Fantasy Politics of Eros." *Arion* n.s. 1 (1973–74): 119–67.

Arthur, M. B. "The Dream of a World Without Women." *Arethusa* 16 (1983): 97–116.

Attridge, D. "Unpacking the Portmanteau, or Who's Afraid of *Finnegans Wake?*" In Culler, 140–55.

Bain, D. *Actors and Audience: A Study of Asides and Related Conventions in Greek Drama*. Oxford: Oxford University Press, 1977.

Bergren, A. "Language and the Female in Early Greek Thought." *Arethusa* 16 (1983): 69–95.

Bianchetti, S. "L'Ostracismo di Iperbolo e la seconda Redazione dell *Nuvole* di Aristofane." *Studi Italiani di Filologia Classica* 51 (1979): 221–48.

Bowie, A. M. "The Parabasis in Aristophanes: Prolegomena, *Acharnians*." *Classical Quarterly* 32 (1982): 27–40.

Brown, C. "Noses at Aristophanes' *Clouds* 344?" *Quaderni Urbinati di Cultura Classica* n.s. 14 (1983): 87–90.

Burnyeat, M. "Socratic Midwifery, Platonic Inspiration." *Bulletin of the Institute of Classical Studies* 24 (1977): 7–16.

Buxton, R. G. A. *Persuasion in Greek Tragedy*. Cambridge: Cambridge University Press, 1982.

Capizzi, A. "La Confluence des sophistes à Athènes après la mort de Périclès et ses connexions avec les transformations de la société attique." In Cassin, 167–78.

Carson, A. *Eros the Bittersweet.* Princeton: Princeton University Press, 1986.

Carter, L. B. *The Quiet Athenian.* Oxford: Clarendon Press, 1986.

Casertano, G. "L'amour entre *logos* et *pathos.* Quelques considérations sur l'*Hélène* de Gorgias." In Cassin, 211–20.

Cassin, B., ed. *Positions de la Sophistique.* Paris: Librairie Philosophique J. Vrin, 1986.

Classen, C. J. "The Study of Language Amongst Socrates' Contemporaries." *Proceedings of the African Classical Associations* 2 (1959): 33–49.

Cole, A. T. *Democritus and the Sources of Greek Anthropology. Philological Monographs* 25, American Philological Association, 1967.

Conacher, D. J. "Prometheus as the Founder of the Arts." *Greek, Roman, and Byzantine Studies* 18 (1977): 189–206.

Connor, W. R. *The New Politicians of Fifth-Century Athens.* Princeton: Princeton University Press, 1971.

Culler, J. "The Call of the Phoneme." In Culler, 1–16.

Culler, J., ed. *On Puns.* Oxford: Basil Blackwell, 1988.

Curiazi, D. "L'Agone delle *Nuvole" Museum Criticum* 13–14 (1978): 215–18.

______. "Aristofane *Nubes* 1075–1082." *Museum Criticum* 30 (1975): 113–15.

Dearden, C. W. *The Stage of Aristophanes.* London: University of London, The Athlone Press, 1976.

de Carli, E. *Aristofane e la Sofistica.* Florence: La nuova italia, 1974.

de Romilly, J. *Magic and Rhetoric in Ancient Greece.* Cambridge: Harvard University Press, 1975.

Detienne, M. *The Gardens of Adonis.* Trans: J. Lloyd. Atlantic Highlands, N.J.: Humanities Press International, 1977.

______. "Between Beasts and Gods." In Gordon, 215–28.

Dierauer, U. *Tier und Mensch im Denken der Antike.* Amsterdam: B. R. Grüner, 1977.

Dover, K. J. *Aristophanic Comedy.* London: Batsford, 1972.

Edmunds, L. "Aristophanes' *Acharnians." Yale Classical Studies* 26 (1980): 1–36.

______. "Il Socrate aristofaneo e l'ironia practica." *Quaderni Urbinati de Cultura Classica* 55 (1987): 7–21.

Ehrenberg, V. *The People of Aristophanes.* New York: Schocken Books, 1962.

Elliott, R. C. *The Power of Satire: Magic, Ritual, Art.* Princeton: Princeton University Press, 1960.

Engle, J. M. "Playing About the Stage: Poetics, Ritual, and Demagoguery in the 'Knights' of Aristophanes." Ph.D. diss., Princeton University, 1983.

Entralgo, P. Lain. *The Therapy of the Word in Classical Antiquity.* Trans. L. J. Rather and J. M. Sharp. New Haven: Yale University Press, 1970.

Erbse, H. "Sokrates im Schatten der aristophanischen *Wolken." Hermes* 82 (1954): 385–420.

Fabrini, P. "Sulla rappresentabilità delle *Nuvole* di Aristofane." *Annali della Scuola Normale Superiore* (1975–76): 1–16.

Finley, J. H. *Three Essays on Thucydides.* Cambridge: Harvard University Press, 1967.

Fisher, R. K. *Aristophanes' Clouds: Purpose and Technique.* Amsterdam: Adolf M. Hakkert, 1984.

Gelzer, T. "Aristophanes und sein Sokrates." *Museum Helveticum* 13 (1956): 65–93.

______. *Der epirrhematische Agon bei Aristophanes: Untersuchungen zur Struktur der attischen alten Komödie.* Zetemata 23. Munich: C. H. Beck, 1960.

Goff, B. E. *The Noose of Words: Readings of Desire, Violence, and Language in Euripides' Hippolytus.* Cambridge: Cambridge University Press, 1990.

Goldberg, S. M. "A Note on Aristophanes' *Phrontisterion.*" *Classical Philology* 72 (1976): 254–56.

Goldhill, S. *Reading Greek Tragedy.* Cambridge: Cambridge University Press, 1986.

———. "The Great Dionysia and Civic Ideology." In Winkler and Zeitlin, 97–129.

Gordon, R. L. *Myth, Religion, and Society.* Cambridge: Cambridge University Press, 1981.

Green, P. "Strepsiades, Socrates and the Abuses of Intellectualism." *Greek, Roman and Byzantine Studies* 20, no. 1 (1979): 15–25.

Guthrie, W. K. C. *The Sophists.* Cambridge: Cambridge University Press, 1971.

Handley, E. W. "-sis Nouns in Aristophanes." *Eranos* 51 (1953): 129–42.

Harriott, R. M. *Aristophanes: Poet and Dramatist.* London: Croom Helm, 1986.

Havelock, E. A. *The Liberal Temper in Greek Politics.* New Haven: Yale University Press, 1957.

———. "The Socratic Self as It Is Parodied in Aristophanes' *Clouds.*" *Yale Classical Studies* 22 (1972): 1–18.

Heath, M. *Political Comedy in Aristophanes.* Hypomnemata, 87. Göttingen: Vandenhoeck & Ruprecht.

Heiden, B. "Tragedy and Comedy in the *Frogs* of Aristophanes." *Ramus* 20 (1991): 95–111.

Henderson, J. "The *Demos* and the Comic Competition." In Winkler and Zeitlin, 271–313.

———. *The Maculate Muse: Obscene Language in Aristophanes.* New York: Oxford University Press, 1991.

Horn, W. *Gebet und Gebetsparodie in den Komödien des Aristophanes.* Nuremberg, Germany: Verlag Hans Carl, 1970.

Hubbard, T. K. *The Masks of Comedy: Aristophanes and the Intertextual Parabasis.* Ithaca: Cornell University Press, 1991.

———. "Parabatic Self-Criticism and the Two Versions of Aristophanes' *Clouds.*" *Classical Antiquity* 5, no. 2 (1986): 182–97.

Hulley, K. H. "A Note on Aristophanes' *Clouds* 804–813." *Classical Journal* 69 (1974): 223–25.

Jaeger, W. *Paideia: The Ideals of Greek Culture,* Vol. 1. New York: Oxford University Press, 1974.

Jaerisch, P., ed. *Xenophon Erinnerungen an Sokrates.* Munich: Ernst Heimeran, 1972.

Kahn, L. *Hermes passé.* Paris: Librairie François Maspero, 1978.

Kennedy, G. A. *The Art of Persuasion in Greece.* Princeton: Princeton University Press, 1963.

Kerferd, G. B. *The Sophistic Movement.* Cambridge: Cambridge University Press, 1981.

Kock, T. *Comicorum Atticorum Fragmenta.* Leipzig: Teubner, 1880.

Köhnken, A. "Der Wolken-chor des Aristophanes." *Hermes* 108 (1980): 154–69.

Kopff, E. C. "*Nubes* 1493ff: Was Socrates Murdered?" *Greek, Roman, and Byzantine Studies* 18 (1977): 113–22.

Koster, W. J. W., ed. *Scholia in Aristophanem,* Vols. I.3.1–2. (in *Nubes*) II.1 (in *Vespes*). Groningen; Bouma, 1977.

Long, T. "Persuasion and the Aristophanic Agon." *Transactions and Proceedings of the American Philological Association* 103 (1972): 285–99.

Longo, O. "The Theater of the *Polis.*" In Winkler and Zeitlin, 12–19.

Louis, P. *Les Métaphores de Platon.* Paris: Les Belles Lettres, 1945.

Lovejoy, A. and G. Boas. *Primitivism and Related Ideas in Antiquity*. Baltimore: Johns Hopkins University Press, 1935; rpt. New York: Octagon Books, 1973.

Lupher, D. A. "Persuasion and Politics in Euripides." Ph.D. diss., Stanford University, 1980.

MacDowell, D. M. *Aristophanes: Wasps*. Oxford: Clarendon Press, 1971.

———. *The Law in Classical Athens*. Ithaca: Cornell University Press, 1980.

Marzullo, B. "Strepsiade." *Maia* 6 (1953): 99–124.

Mastromarco, G. "Il naso delle Nuvole (Aristofane, *Nuvole* 344)." *Quaderni Urbinati di Cultura Classica* n.s. 23, no. 2 (1986): 121–23.

McLeish, K. *The Theater of Aristophanes*. New York: Taplinger, 1980.

Miller, H. W. "Repetition of Lines in Aristophanes." *American Journal of Philology* 65 (1944): 26–36.

Moulton, C. *Aristophanic Poetry*. Hypomnemata, 68. Göttingen: Vandenhoeck & Ruprecht.

Muecke, C. "Playing with the Play: Theatrical Self-consciousness in Aristophanes." *Antichthon* 11 (1977): 52–67.

Müller, R. "Sophistique et démocratie." In Cassin, 179–94.

Murphy, C. T. "Aristophanes and the Art of Rhetoric." *Harvard Studies in Classical Philology* 49 (1938): 52–67.

Murray, R. J. "Aristophanic Protest." *Hermes* 115 (1987): 146–54.

Newiger, H-J. *Metapher und Allegorie: Studien zu Aristophanes*. Zetemata, 16. Munich: C. H. Beck, 1957.

———. ed. *Aristophanes und die alte Komödie*, Darmstadt: Wissenschaftliche Buchgesellschaft, 1975.

North, H. *Sophrosyne*. Ithaca: Cornell University Press, 1966.

Nussbaum, M. "Aristophanes and Socrates on Learning Practical Wisdom." *Yale Classical Studies* 26 (1980): 43–97.

Ober, J. *Mass and Elite in Democratic Athens*. Princeton: Princeton University Press, 1989.

Ober, J. and B. Strauss. "Drama, Political Rhetoric, and the Discourse of Athenian Democracy." In Winkler and Zeitlin, 237–70.

O'Brien, M. "Xenophanes, Aeschylus, and the Doctrine of Primeval Brutishness." *Classical Quarterly* 35, no. 2 (1985): 264–77.

Ostwald, M. *From Popular Sovereignty to the Sovereignty of Law: Law, Society, and Politics in Fifth-Century Athens*. Berkeley: University of California Press, 1986.

Padel, R. "Making Space Speak." In Winkler and Zeitlin, 336–65.

Pepe, G. M. "Studies in Peitho." Ph.D. diss., Princeton University, 1966.

Pickard-Cambridge, A. *The Dramatic Festivals of Athens*. 2nd ed. revised by J. Gould and D. M. Lewis. Oxford: Clarendon Press, 1968.

Podlecki, A. J. "The Power of the Word in Sophocles' *Philoktetes*." *Greek, Roman, and Byzantine Studies* 7 (1966): 233–50.

Poulakos, P. "Gorgias on Rhetoric." Ph.D. diss., University of Kansas (Lawrence), 1978.

Pucci, P. *Hesiod and the Language of Poetry*. Baltimore: Johns Hopkins University Press, 1977.

———. *Odysseus Polutropos*. Ithaca: Cornell University Press, 1987.

———. "Saggio sulle *Nuvole*." *Maia* 12 (1960): 3–32, 106–29.

Rau, P. *Paratragodia: Untersuchung einer komischen Form des Aristophanes*. Zetemata, 45. Munich: C. H. Beck.

Reckford, K. "Aristophanes' Ever-flowing Clouds." *Emory University Quarterly* 22 (1967): 222–35.

————. *Aristophanes' Old-and-New Comedy.* Chapel Hill: University of North Carolina Press, 1987.

————. "Father Beating in Aristophanes' *Clouds.*" In *The Conflict of Generations in Greece and Rome.* ed. S. Bertman, 89–118. Amsterdam: B. R. Grüner, 1976.

Redfern, W. *Puns.* Oxford: Basil Blackwell, 1984.

Redfield, J. "Drama and Community: Aristophanes and Some of His Rivals." In Winkler and Zeitlin, 314–35.

Romer, F. E. "When Is a Bird Not a Bird?" *Transactions and Proceedings of the American Philological Society* 113 (1983): 135–42.

Richardson, W. F. "ΔIKE in Aristophanes' *Clouds.*" In *Auckland Classical Essays Presented to E. M. Blaiklock,* ed. B. C. Harris. Auckland: Auckland University Press, 1970, 59–75.

Rosenmeyer, T. G. "Gorgias, Aeschylus, and Apate." *American Journal of Philology* 76 (1955): 225–60.

Schmid, W. "Das Sokratesbild der *Wolken.*" *Philologus* (1948): 209–28.

Schreckenberg, H. *Ananke.* Zetemata, 36. Munich: C. H. Beck.

Scodel, R. "The Ode and Antode in the Parabasis of the *Clouds.*" *Classical Philology* 82 (1987): 334–35.

Segal, C. "Aristophanes' Cloud-Chorus." In Newiger (1975), 174–97.

————. "Gorgias and the Psychology of the Logos." *Harvard Studies in Classical Philology* 66 (1962): 99–155.

————. *Tragedy and Civilization: An Interpretation of Sophocles.* Cambridge: Harvard University Press, 1981.

Shoaf, R. A. "The Play of Puns in Late Middle English Poetry: Concerning Juxtology." In Culler, 44–61.

Sifakis, G. M. *Parabasis and Animal Choruses: A Contribution to the History of Attic Comedy.* London: University of London, The Athlone Press, 1971.

Silk, M. S. "Aristophanes as a Lyric Poet." *Yale Classical Studies* 26 (1980): 99–151.

Sinclair, R. K. *Democracy and Participation in Athens.* Cambridge: Cambridge University Press, 1988.

Smyth, H. W. *Greek Grammar.* Cambridge: Harvard University Press, 1966.

Solomos, A. *The Living Aristophanes.* Ann Arbor: University of Michigan Press, 1974.

Spatz, L. *Aristophanes.* Boston: Twayne, 1978.

Sprague, R. K., ed. *The Older Sophists.* Columbia: University of South Carolina Press, 1972.

Starkie, W. J. M., ed. *Aristophanes: The Clouds.* New York: Macmillan, 1911.

Stone, L. M. "A Note on *Clouds* 1104–5." *Classical Philology* 75 (1980): 321–22.

————. *Costume in Aristophanic Poetry.* New York: Arno Press, 1981.

Strauss, L. *Socrates and Aristophanes.* Chicago: University of Chicago Press, 1966.

Svenbro, J. *La Parole et le Marbre.* Lund, 1976.

Taillardat, J. *Les images d'Aristophane: Etudes de langue et de style.* Paris: Société d'Edition Les Belles Lettres, 1965.

Todd, O. J. *Index Aristophaneus.* Cambridge: Harvard University Press, 1932.

Tomin, J. "Socratic Gymnasium in the *Clouds.*" *Symbolae Osloenses* 62 (1987): 25–32.

Turato, F. *La Crisi della Città e la Ideologia del Selvaggio nell'Atene di V Secolo a. C.* Rome: Edizioni dell'Ateneo & Bizzarri, 1979.

————. *Il Problema Storico delle Nuvole di Aristofane.* Proagones, 12 (1972). Padova: Editrice Antenore.

————. "Seduzioni della Parola e Dramma dei Segni nell'*Ippolito* di Euripide." *Bolletino dell'Instituto di Filologia Greca dell'Università di Padova* 3 (1976): 159–83.

Untersteiner, M. *The Sophists*. Trans. K. Freeman. Oxford: Basil Blackwell, 1954.

Ussher, R. G. *Aristophanes*. Greece and Rome, New Surveys in the Classics, 13. Oxford: Clarendon Press, 1979.

van Leeuwen, J. F., ed. *Aristophanis Nubes*. Leiden: Sijthoff, 1898.

Verdenius, W. J. "Gorgias' Doctrine of Deception." In *The Sophists and Their Legacy*, ed. G. B. Kerferd. *Hermes Einz.* 44 (1979): 116–28.

Vernant, J-P. "At Man's Table: Hesiod's Foundation Myth of Sacrifice." In M. Detienne and J-P. Vernant, *The Cuisine of Sacrifice among the Greeks*, 21–86. Trans. P. Wissing. Chicago: University of Chicago Press, 1989.

―――――. "The Myth of Prometheus in Hesiod." In Gordon (1981a): 43–56.

―――――. "Sacrificial and Alimentary Codes in Hesiod's Myth of Prometheus." In Gordon (1981b): 57–79.

Vidal-Naquet, P. "Land and Sacrifice in the *Odyssey*." In Gordon (1981a): 80–94.

―――――. "Recipes for Greek Adolescence." In Gordon (1981b): 163–85.

Walsh, G. B. *The Varieties of Enchantment*. Chapel Hill: University of North Carolina Press, 1984.

Whitman, C. H. *Aristophanes and the Comic Hero*. Cambridge: Harvard University Press, 1964.

Winkler, J. J. "The Ephebes' Song: *Tragoidia* and *Polis*." In Winkler and Zeitlin, 20–62.

Winkler, J. J. and F. I. Zeitlin, eds. *Nothing to Do with Dionysus?* Princeton: Princeton University Press, 1990.

Woodbury, L. "Strepsiades' Understanding: Five Notes on The *Clouds*." *Phoenix* 34, no. 2 (1980): 108–27.

Zeitlin, F. I. "Travesties of Gender and Genre in Aristophanes' *Thesmophoriazusae*." In *Reflections of Women in Antiquity*, ed. H. Foley (169–217). New York: Gordon and Breach, 1982.

INDEX OF PASSAGES

N.B.: This index includes neither passages adduced solely as examples or mentioned in passing nor passages from the *Clouds* that can be located by using the line number references in the chapter titles.

Aristotle
Politics
  1243a: 20

Aristophanes
Acharnians
  530–31: 58
  634–39: 45–46
Birds
  39ff.: 37
  1438–39: 23
  1447–49: 23
Clouds I
  PCG frgs.
  392–94: 135
  400: 135
Knights
  General: 76–78
  213–16: 61
  626–29: 58
Lysistrata
  397ff.: 37
Wasps
  54–66: 138
  620ff.: 58
  666–68: 60
  671: 58
  1037–42: 135
  1043–59: 138
PCG frg.
  691: 162

Critias
  DK 88 B 25
  1–2: 18

Eubulos
  PCG frg.
  106: 59

Eupolis
  PCG frgs.
  102: 64
  116: 17
  157: 161
  261: 205
  386: 162
  395: 39

Euripides
Cyclops
  334–38: 62
Hippolytus
  486–87: 13
Supplices
  201–4: 18

Gorgias
  DK 82 B
  8: 13
Encomium
  DK 82 B 11
  13–24, 96

Homer
Odyssey
  14.122: 60

Lysias
  2.19: 19

Plato
Gorgias
  452d5ff.: 16
Phaedrus
  258b5ff.: 115
Philebus
  58a6: 14
Protagoras
  332b: 19–20
Timaeus
  72e3ff.: 61

Plutarch
Pericles
  4: 58
  8: 12
Nicias
  23: 28

Thucydides
  3.36.6: 11

Xenophon
Memorabilia
  1.6.10: 62
  1.2.10–11: 15
  2.6.36: 23
  4.3.12: 18

Ps. Xenophon
  1.13: 103

SUBJECT INDEX

N.B.: This index only includes those persons, episodes, and concepts that would be difficult to locate by checking the appropriate line number references in the chapter titles.